D0821882

RESEARCH IN ECONOMIC ANTHROPOLOGY

Supplement 3 • 1988

PREHISTORIC ECONOMIES OF THE PACIFIC NORTHWEST COAST

RESEARCH IN ECONOMIC ANTHROPOLOGY

A Research Annual

PREHISTORIC ECONOMIES OF THE PACIFIC NORTHWEST COAST

Editor: BARRY L. ISAAC
Department of Anthropology
University of Cincinnati

SUPPLEMENT 3 • 1988

 JAI PRESS INC.

Greenwich, Connecticut   *London, England*

Copyright © 1988 by JAI PRESS INC.
55 Old Post Road, No. 2
Greenwich, Connecticut 06830

JAI PRESS LTD.
3 Henrietta Street
London WC2E 8LU
England

All rights reserved. No part of this publication may be reproduced, stored on a retrieval
system, or transmitted in any form or by any means, electronic, mechanical, photocopying,
filming, recording, or otherwise without prior permission in writing from the publisher.

ISBN: 0-89232-818-5

Manufactured in the United States of America

CONTENTS

PART III. LOWER SKEENA RIVER
AND QUEEN CHARLOTTE STRAIT

PART IV.
ARCHAEOLOGICAL OVERVIEW

LIST OF CONTRIBUTORS

Gary Coupland

Department of Anthropology
and Sociology
University of British Columbia
Vancouver

Dale R. Croes

Washington Archaeological
Research Center
Washington State University
Pullman

Leland Donald

Department of Anthropology
University of Victoria
Victoria, British Columbia

Steven Hackenberger

Department of Anthropology
Washington State University
Pullman

David R. Huelsbeck

Department of Anthropology
and Sociology
Santa Clara University
Santa Clara, California

Donald Mitchell

Department of Anthropology
University of Victoria
Victoria, British Columbia

Barbara R. Stucki

Department of Anthropology
Northwestern University
Evanston, Illinois

Gary C. Wessen   Makah Cultural and Research
                                                    Center
                                        Neah Bay, Washington

Rebecca J. Wigen   Department of Anthropology
                                        University of Victoria
                                        Victoria, British Columbia

EDITOR'S PREFACE

This volume is the third of the supplementary series that runs parallel to the R.E.A. annual volumes. Supplement 1, issued in 1980 while George Dalton was R.E.A. editor, was John Murra's dissertation, *The Economic Organization of the Inka State*. Upon assuming the editorship in 1983, I decided that the supplementary series ought to continue to be devoted to non-ethnographic (ethnohistoric and prehistoric) subjects and that each such volume ought to be thematic, covering either a particular topic or a specific geographic region. For Supplement 2, I settled on highland Mexico, a region that was familiar to me from my own research; the result was *Economic Aspects of Prehispanic Highland Mexico*, published in 1986. I selected the Northwest Coast area for the present volume because of the current interest in "complex hunter-gatherers" and "subsistence intensification." Supplement 4, which is scheduled for 1989 publication, will be jointly edited by me and Patricia McAnany, a Mayanist. That volume's working title is *Prehispanic Maya Economies of Northern Belize*.

ACKNOWLEDGMENTS

I thank all of the contributors to this volume for the alacrity with which they drafted their essays and for their good cheer in carrying out the revisions. I owe special thanks to three of them: Dale R. Croes, for encouragement and an infectious enthusiasm; and Donald Mitchell and Leland Donald, for advice on several occasions and for their agreeing on short notice to write the lengthy concluding essay. In writing the "Introduction," I was counselled by Kenneth B. Tankersley, of Indiana University, on stable isotope research on prehistoric diets; through him, Mark Schurr, also of Indiana University, shared bibliographic and other information on that topic, too. At JAI Press, Sally Johnson Whelan kept this volume moving smoothly through the production process.

INTRODUCTION

Barry L. Isaac

Fortunately, I need not present here either a general introduction to Northwest Coast prehistoric economies or a dissertation on the topic of hunter-gatherer (forager) "complexity." I am spared the first task by the kind efforts of Donald Mitchell and Leland Donald in preparing the detailed concluding essay (also see Adams 1981). I am relieved of the second undertaking by the recent appearance of *Archaic Hunters and Gatherers in the American Midwest* (Phillips & Brown 1983) and *Prehistoric Hunter-Gatherers: The Emergence of Cultural Complexity* (Price & Brown 1985). Rather than trying to summarize or supplement those rich works, I simply

Research in Economic Anthropology, Supplement 3, pages 1–16.
Copyright © 1988 by JAI Press Inc.
All rights of reproduction in any form reserved.
ISBN: 0-89232-818-5

1

admonish the reading of them—along with Mark N. Cohen's *The Food Crisis in Prehistory* (1977).

I also want to call attention to several essays on foragers in recent volumes of R.E.A.: Mark Basgall (1987) and Paul Bouey (1987) have written long essays on the emergence of acorn exploitation in native California; Leland Donald (1984) and Donald Mitchell & Leland Donald (1985) have analyzed Northwest Coast slavery, a topic long neglected; Dominique Legros (1985), in his essay on Tutchone Athapaskans of the Upper Yukon, has raised many questions about the origins of economic and political inequality; Kirk Endicott (1984) and Øyvind Sandbukt (1988) have analyzed the subsistence behavior of the Malayan Batek 'De and the Sumatran Kubu, respectively; Jean Treloggen Peterson (1984) has written about present-day economic change among the Agta foragers of Luzon; finally, Volume 10 has essays by James Savelle & Allen McCartney (1988) on Thule Eskimo diet and by Linda Ellanna (1988) and Mark Cassell (1988) on Inupiat bowhead whale hunting.

In the following, I very briefly raise three topics that bear upon the present volume's essays: (1) the relationship of economic to ecological anthropology, (2) the study of Northwest Coast diets and (3) the nature of the indigenous polity on the Northwest Coast.

ECONOMY/ECOLOGY, DIET, AND POLITY

Economy and Ecology

Because some of the studies in this volume may strike some readers as falling within "ecological" rather than "economic" anthropology, a comment is in order on the relationship between these two subdisciplines. Naturally, I shall not embark upon a review of either; for that, the reader should consult Anderson (1973), Bronitsky (1983), Cook (1973), Gross (1983), Halperin (1982, 1988), Jochim (1981), and Orlove (1980).

The dominant framework of ecological anthropology is human adaptation, i.e., the processes by which humans establish relationships with their environments. Although ethnologists (sociocultural anthropologists) often perceive this study as involving mainly (or only) cultural mechanisms, modern ecological anthropology meshes well with major aspects of physical anthropology. This coupling has produced a biocultural approach with claims to a distinctively anthropological status—as opposed to the "human ecology" approach of sociology and geography (see Micklin & Choldin 1984). The biocultural approach studies human adaptation *and* adaptability at three "levels": behavior, physiology, and genetics/demography (from Hardesty 1977:23; cf. Moran 1979:4–9).

Economic anthropology, on the other hand, is typically conceived as restricted to the cultural/behavioral dimension of the human experience, even when relationships to the nonhuman environment or to demographic factors have been explicitly recognized. In the "Introduction" to R.E.A. Volume 6 (1984), I defined "economy" and elaborated a bit upon the concept. Here, I will reiterate only the basic economic processes. By "economy" I understand the processes of *production* (extraction, transformation, elaboration), *consumption* (use, including but not restricted to final use), *distribution* (circulation; locational and appropriational movements), and *exchange* (two-way, hand-to-hand movements) of goods and services that originate, sustain, enhance, or reproduce the livelihood of individuals and groups.

A comparison of ecological and economic anthropology in terms of their respective scopes or scales of study inclines one to concede that ecological anthropology is the broader of these subfields. From the perspective of Northwest Coast studies, there was a period beginning about 1960 and lasting more than a decade during which ecological anthropology ("cultural ecology") had a near monopoly on explaining cultural systems qua systems in that area. Orlove (1980:243) characterizes the period as one in which "neofunctionalist analysis" had among its tasks "the explication of ethnographic riddles," such as the Northwest Coast potlatch (or—shudder!—India's sacred cattle). The various analytical facets of behavior or culture—kinship, religion, economy, political organization—were all shown to be "ecologically" related to the "adaptive" or "pro-survival" function of the potlatch (see, e.g., Piddocke 1965, Suttles 1960, Vayda 1961). I submit that the Northwest Coast (potlatch) studies of that period did more than anything else to excite interest in "cultural ecology" (*cum* ecological anthropology) and to make it seem an all-encompassing and self-sufficing analytical framework.

Like their Marxist successors a decade later, the early-1960s cultural ecologists sometimes gave the impression that their interests were synonymous with ethnology itself. Actually, that position is not as wild as it might seem at first blush, because ethnology is indeed the comparative study of human adaptation (and maladaptation) in its various aspects (e.g., cognitive, emotional, ideological, developmental, demographic, etc.). Why, then, do we need any other "kind" of anthropology? The most general answer is that "adaptation" is no more a theory than was the "functionalism" that preceded it, even if (indeed, especially if) elevated to the level of synonymity with the subject matter itself (see Davis 1959). Like functionalism, adaptation is both an assumption about our subject matter (human behavior or culture) and a general conceptual framework for its study. Regardless of whether the major emphasis is upon the cultural (symbolic, cognitive), the nonhuman environmental, or the human biological aspect of human adaptation, the concept of adaptation itself must be operationalized. Its mechanisms must be specified and their dynamics and statics must be explained in terms of objectified units and processes.

Broadly stated, some of the major mechanisms of human adaptation are economic, as defined above. Hardesty (1977:75) puts the matter succinctly: "economic problems are often foremost in determining an adaptive strategy. . . ." Orlove (1980:235) is a bit more expansive: "In many cases, systems of production constitute important links among population dynamics, social organization, culture, and environment." Halperin (1982, 1984, 1988) locates an "ecological paradigm" within economic anthropology and differentiates it from the "formal" and the "institutional" paradigms. Her ecological paradigm for economic anthropology "is represented by cultural ecology and cultural materialism" (Halperin 1984:246). In summary, there is fairly wide agreement that the anthropological study of human economy is one way of identifying some of the mechanisms of human adaptation.

In practice, there has been a pronounced tendency to concentrate upon economic mechanisms involved in food production and food consumption, giving the appearance that anthropologists are obsessed with counting calories and measuring energy input/output. Accompanying these interests is the necessity of calculating the numbers and densities of the people who are doing the producing and consuming; given the emphasis upon calories or energy, the interest in people (demography) is mainly a biological or energy input/output interest—no matter what the textbooks admonish in this regard.

There are good reasons why these constrictive tendencies exist, and they strike at the heart of ethnology's claim to be a science. Whatever else "science" is, it is a framework in which the units and processes of study are objectified (made "public") and operationalized (made explicit, articulated), so that observation is replicable. And, whatever else "social science" is, it is a quagmire of gooey concepts, mushy variables, slimy processes, and slippery units. As Homer Barnett (1965:213, 1983:121–122) has pointed out:

Both our classes and our names for them must be more restricted and their referents uniquely specified. . . . Our categories are too inclusive and heterogeneous to enable us to deal precisely with them, and our terms overlap and alternate. More exact specification . . . is indispensable for even the most elementary quantitative treatment of our data. . . . In order simply to count or compare instances of their occurrence it is imperative that we agree upon what constitutes a unit. Indeed, even to concern ourselves with a single instance . . . [we must] know whether in fact it is a single instance. We must know its extent and ramifications if we are to describe *it* at all.

Especially over the past decade, there has been a strong aversion in ecological/economic studies to entering that sticky swamp of sociocultural science. This skittish aversion, which we might call the La Brea Tic, has led us time and again to deal with our proper subject matter—the sociocultural dimension of the human experience—only tangentially. I have in mind, first of all, the great many studies that assess the impact of the nonhuman environment (e.g., climate, biotic communities, altitude) or of biological processes and mechanisms (e.g., metabolism, nutrition) upon the sociocultural dimension. Secondly, I refer to the popularity of studies that take the individual as the unit of analysis (see Gross 1983, Halperin 1988). In neither case is the sociocultural dimension the primary focus. We should ask whether these tendencies are good or bad. Our answer depends, I believe, on whether we have in mind the short term or the long term.

In the short term, there is nothing wrong and perhaps much to gain from the above approaches. Once we leave the sociocultural dimension aside or outside of our main focus, we often are able to agree upon the units, processes, and parameters of investigation. Such agreement gives us a superior chance of precisely defining and measuring variables in action and of assessing causality. Two points should be emphasized in this regard. First, proceeding thusly need not result in any greater extent of "reductionism" than is inherent in some aspects of *all* sciences (see Gross 1983:159–160). Second, all sciences specify causality—even if only "partially." I think causality has fallen upon hard times in ecological/economic anthropology lately. Partly as a way of turning our results back upon the sociocultural dimension through "feedback mechanisms"—or as a way of obscuring the fact that this dimension, which is our birthright, is often mere background, only scenery upon our stage—we have availed ourselves of the "feedback mechanisms" of an epigonal "systems theory." The result is that we all too often find ourselves amidst a bewildering tangle of feedback loops or lost in a conceptual fog of multiple or unassigned causality (see Carneiro 1981:54–55; cf. Salmon 1978). While all sciences seek to establish functional linkages ("systems") among the attributes and dimensions of their subject matters, all successful sciences also assign or assess priority (dependence/independence) among the interacting elements.

Turning now to the long run, we must insist upon the integral (not just lip service) inclusion of the uniquely human elements in our studies of human adaptation. Otherwise, a little bit of reductionism will indeed go a long way—clear to the extinction of our discipline. Furthermore, economic and ecological anthropology must become not merely social sciences but *cultural* sciences, as well. I believe this is the essential concern behind Barbara Bender's (1981, 1985a, 1985b) repeated attempts to raise our noses from the ground. William Marquardt (1985:67; emphasis his) has eloquently captured the point:

> Ecological explanations successfully account for a wide variety of human phenomena because humans, like other animals, are *a part of nature*. They must have food and

shelter and must reproduce themselves in order to survive as a species. However, humans are also *apart from nature* insofar as they project social relations into the environment (by means of myth, fictive kinship, rules of reciprocity, ascribed status positions, etc.) and then interact with that cognized environment. This practice sets humans apart from other animals and necessitates the constitution of anthropology as a *social* [sic!! read: *cultural*] science distinct from ecology and zoology.

Finally, our main problem is not to distinguish neatly between economic and ecological anthropology but, rather, to discern and objectify the mechanisms of human adaptation. In this volume, we are concerned with the economic mechanisms (production, consumption, distribution, exchange).

Northwest Coast Diet

The most vexing problem in the study of Northwest Coast economy, whether ethnographic or prehistoric, is the paucity of useful and reliable information on diet. No more need be said to Northwest Coast area specialists, but for the benefit of others, let me amplify: It's not simply a lack of adequate historical depth to dietary studies here, or a lack of good data on seasonal or regional variation. True, those conditions exist, but the heart of the matter is the lack of good-quality data on the more basic stuff, too: precisely what did the ordinary person usually eat and in what relative and absolute quantities?

Given that the Northwest Coast has fascinated anthropologists since the beginning of the formal discipline and that "scientific" fieldwork has been conducted in the area since early-Boas times, we may wonder why this situation exists. I can suggest three reasons. First, ethnographers have (or, at least, seemingly had) a tendency to record the things that strike them as novel and to slight other things. Most ethnographers, being drylanders and/or urbanites, have been mostly interested in fishing and hunting. By the time we learned to be more thorough in such matters, there were no more Northwest Coast Indians living under anything approaching aboriginal conditions. This brings me to the second point, namely, that even the earliest ethnographic work on the area occurred after much acculturation, disruption, and displacement of native people had already taken place. Thus, it is always possible that any particular dietary (or other) practice reflects—at least in emphasis—the Euro-American presence and not the autochthonous situation. Even at its best, the historical material on diet is sketchy (see Folan 1984). Third, the institution of "potlatch" captured anthropological interest early on, and anthropological energy went into its study instead of into pinning down the observable diet and the recoverable native knowledge about the natural environment— from which we might have established a firmer basis for inferring past dietary practices or seasonal rounds.

These data-quality problems are not unique to this culture area, of course; even our potlatch preoccupation has parallels in other ethnographic areas (e.g., the fiesta fetish in Mesoamerican ethnography, the "cattle complex" in East African studies). Rather, these problems simply are more aggravating with reference to the Northwest Coast. This area has the highest known ethnographic/historic concentration of "complex hunter-gatherers"; thus, in the modern evolutionary-ecological-economic framework of both ethnology and archaeology, the area could provide crucial insights into the processes that most interest us—if only we had higher-quality ethnographic data.

Instead, we are left to the devices of archaeology in an area with exceptionally poor preservation of organic remains, especially plant remains. As Mitchell & Donald (this volume) point out, even the "wet sites," with their superior preservation of fragile organic remains, have yielded little information on food uses of plants. Furthermore, assessing the dietary significance of faunal remains is now known to be a complicated matter, also, as Wigen & Stucki (this volume) make abundantly clear. Nutritional assessment must proceed along more than one dimension if it is to become sound.

In recent years, several promising techniques have been developed for assessing nutrition from human bone remains (see Klepinger 1984). Enthusiasm was initially high for strontium analysis, which has run into several difficulties lately. One major confounding factor is postmortem absorption of strontium from soil moisture (see Nelson et al. 1986). A second glitch occurs whenever the diet contains either molluscs (Schoeninger & Peebles 1981) or marine fish bones (Klepinger 1984:78), which concentrate strontium and thereby induce misleading dietary signatures in human bone studies.

Stable carbon isotope studies on human bone collagen have also been popular in the last several years and have seemed promising as a means of reconstructing prehistoric diets. This approach is also running into problems, though, and perhaps especially for the Northwest Coast. Schoeninger & DeNiro (1984:632) have found that the $\delta^{13}C$ values for freshwater fish, aquatic migratory birds, anadromous fish, and marine birds "have ranges that are virtually indistinguishable from those of terrestrial animals." To my mind, this conclusion—if sustained by future studies—raises large questions about the validity of the major extent $\delta^{13}C$ study on Northwest Coast prehistoric human bone (Chisholm et al. 1983). Another difficulty with the $\delta^{13}C$ studies has been spotted by H.P. Schwarcz (1986):

[T]here may be some bias introduced in the isotopic composition of collagen because bone growth does not occur at the same rate throughout the year. For example,

certain foods available at the seashore might be more conducive to bone formation
(higher levels of vitamin D?) than the foods available inland.

Sealy & van der Merwe (1986:148), toward whose study Schwarcz's re-
mark was directed, essentially agree:

> [T]he comment about the assumption of uniform bone growth throughout the year is
> well founded. Ignorance of bone formation and metabolism is proving to be one of
> the biggest limiting factors in the use we can make of stable isotope measurements
> in archaeology. This should be a major focus of future research.

This matter is a sticky wicket for the Northwest Coast, where many human
groups had different winter and summer diets (see Mitchell & Donald,
this volume), which we can assume contained different quantities of vitamin D. We can probably assume that these seasonal differences led to
greater bone growth in juveniles and higher rates of bone replacement
("turnover") in both mature and immature individuals during the season
in which *fresh* (not stored) salmon—which is chockful of both vitamin D
and calcium—was consumed. (Incidentally, in these latitudes this would
be the very season of the most intense and prolonged sunlight, which
promotes vitamin D synthesis.)

How would this affect bone chemistry and the reconstruction of prehistoric diets on the Northwest Coast? Faced with the foregoing, as well
Schoeninger & DeNiro's (1984:632) finding, reported above, that anadromous fish have basically the same $\delta^{13}C$ values as terrestrial animals—
and, by extension, as terrestrial C–3 plants—I am at a loss to explain the
exceptionally high $\delta^{13}C$ values reported by Chisholm et al. (1983). Is it
possible that very high levels of vitamin D promote ^{13}C absorption, specifically? I should add that the vitamin D content of salmon is so high
that children cannot safely eat substantial quantities of it (Lazenby &
McCormack 1985).

At the moment, nitrogen isotope analysis appears to be the most promising avenue of chemical exploration of prehistoric diet on the basis of
human bone (see, especially, Schoeninger et al. 1983: Figure 1–A vs. Figure 1–B; also, Nelson et al. 1986). This approach shares some weaknesses
with stable carbon analysis, though. In the first place,

> Although $\delta^{15}N$ values of bone collagen can be used in estimating the marine and
> terrestrial components of human diet, distinguishing between freshwater and terrestrial
> food sources by nitrogen isotope analysis may be impossible [Schoeninger et al.
> 1983:132].

Secondly, as is the case with $\delta^{13}C$, the bone collagen $\delta^{15}N$ for aquatic
migratory birds and anadromous fish "overlap the marine and freshwater
distinctions" (Schoeninger & DeNiro 1984:632).

For all of the foregoing reasons, in addition to the lack of precision at establishing "end-point values" for the relevant isotopes (see Chisholm et al. 1983:396; Hobson & Collier 1984), we should not attempt to read out "dietary signatures" in percentages directly from stable isotope studies conducted with existing technologies and techniques—as do Chisholm et al. (1983; also, see Jacobson 1986). Nevertheless, stable isotope studies, when further refined, may eventually have a huge impact upon archaeology—and, by extension of the results, upon economic-ecological-evolutionary ethnology.

The Northwest Coast Polity

The aspect of the polity that interests us here is its political economy, i.e., the extra-domestic, public-arena aspects of production, consumption, distribution, and exchange. Accordingly, we cannot avoid the thorny question of social stratification, which lies at the heart of any study of political economy. Indeed, I shall direct most of my remarks to stratification.

Early students of the Northwest Coast spoke all too casually of "chiefs" and "nobles." More recently, the whole issue of stratification has been effectively set aside or ducked through the vague and faddish usage of the term "ranked." In fact, I think the "rank society" concept was fuzzy from the outset. As proposed by Morton Fried (1967:109),

A rank society is one in which positions of valued status are somehow limited so that not all those of sufficient talent to occupy such statuses actually achieve them. Such a society may or may not be stratified. That is, a society may sharply limit its positions of prestige without affecting the access of its entire membership to the basic resources upon which life depends.

But (p. 128):

A member of an egalitarian society put down by a set of curious chances in the midst of a rank society would probably experience relatively little dislocation. He might marvel at the opulence of life, the stability of settlement, and the size of habitations, but in his social life little would strike him as really strange. The institutions which flowed from and supported the social ranking system would pervade his life but in a gentle and subtle fashion, unlikely to rouse his anxiety. . . . [T]his is a far cry from what might be expected to occur when a member of an egalitarian society is introduced into a stratified society.

In short, the second quotation (and the remainder of Fried's discussion in his chapter on rank societies) shows that Fried's initial position on stratification—"Such a society may or may not be stratified."—effectively fell by the wayside after a few tentative steps. Succinctly, a rank society is an unstratified society, indistinguishable in practice from what others call a "tribal society." I think that Fried's aversion to the word "tribe" led him to insist upon a new word—a "mere" new word, as it were— that instantly became popular because it offered relief from a lot of anthropological discomfort with existing evolutionary typologies (cf. Cordy 1981:33–47, 220–226).

The fact of the matter is that Northwest Coast polities ("societies") were not merely "ranked." They were stratified—at least, wherever slavery was practiced. So long as the topic of slavery was slighted or slavery was rationalized away as being merely part of a harmless "prestige" game, and so long as we could believe that slaves were few in numbers, we could think of Northwest Coast polities as being internally differentiated mainly by a graded series of prestige positions. Thanks largely to the 10-year research efforts of Leland Donald and Donald Mitchell, we now know that some of the northern polities had slave proportions of 20–30 percent. Compared with the rest of the population, slaves did not simply occupy a lower "rank" or simply enjoy lowered "prestige"; rather, slaves on the Northwest Coast occupied a *social class* with different access to resources and different labor requirements—in a nutshell, different life-chances— than nonslaves (see Donald 1983, 1984; Mitchell 1984, 1985; Mitchell & Donald 1985; cf. Ruyle 1973).

Were there "chiefs" and "chiefdoms" on the Northwest Coast? Although political structure doubtless exhibited considerable regional variation, I have seen nothing to date in either the ethnographic or the archaeological literature to convince me that there were ever "chiefdoms"— in any meaningful, analytical usage of that term—on the Northwest Coast (cf. Carneiro 1981:48ff). I agree wholeheartedly with Richard Kurz, Jr. (1987:35), who includes several of these polities in his "tribal" sample:

> Although the societies of this culture area are famous for their hereditary crests and other insignia and ceremonies, and although they appear to have some hereditary positions that have some politico-economic powers, the hereditary insignia and positions appear always to occur within single descent groupings (lineages or ramages). In other words, these societies appear to *lack the salient features of chiefdoms, namely, a centralized political-economic office that exercises its function throughout a polity that includes not only the officeholder's own descent group but other such groupings as well.* [emphasis added]

We have the word, also, of the old hands. Frederica de Laguna (1983:71–72) writes of the Tlingit:

> The Tlingit are not (and never were) a single political unit or tribe. . . . The real unit of Tlingit society is the exogamous, matrilineal descent group, the clan. . . . It is the clan that owns the most important natural resources and wealth; the tribe owns nothing. And it is in the clan that political legal authority is vested. . . .

Philip Drucker (1983:87–88; his emphasis) writes:

> Southern Kwakiutl aggregations called 'tribes' and the historic 'confederacy' were socioceremonial entities, leaving the local group as the *only* political unit. . . . The local group was considered to be the kinship unit. . . . Ownership of economic resource sites was vested in [the] local group. . . . Ownership of socioceremonial 'privileges' was vested in [the] local group. . . . Each local group was autonomous in decisions of war and peace.

Leland Donald (1983:109) writes:

> Nowhere on the Northwest Coast was there regular political unification above the local community level and even the Nuu-chah-nulth-aht [Nootka] federation was no exception to this. . . . Federations were . . . summer versions of the winter village community, whose building blocks were local groups rather than the descent groups of the winter village communities.

The best case to date for the existence of a chiefdom on the Northwest Coast has been made by Kenneth Tollefson (1987) for the Puget Sound Indians. It is problematical, though, because the political development of which he writes might have emerged partly in response to "the intrusion of both raiding northern Indians and white traders" (p.128–129). In passing, let me put on record here Tollefson's other interesting studies of village organization and political economy (Tollefson 1977, 1982, 1985).

In their redistributive behavior, the leaders of Northwest Coast polities were quite like the "big-men" described for (other) tribal societies, and very different from the chiefs of political chiefdoms (see Carneiro 1981; cf. Ferguson 1983). Because I have discussed this matter at considerable length in the "Introduction" to R.E.A. Volume 10 (1988), I will be brief here. In a nutshell, the reasonably thorough and wide redistribution of the wherewithall that comes his way is the hallmark of a big-man, not of a chief. A chief is to a great extent insulated from general redistributive demands because he is sustained by political office, a permanent structural position with certain inherent powers. A chief can *compel* a following; he does not have to entice one. A big-man, in contrast, does not occupy a political office; he is literally a self-made man who attracts a following through his political skill and, above all else, his generosity.

Robert Carneiro (1981:63) points out that "the concept of redistribution became attached to that of chiefdom" as the result of accident and error; in neither Polynesia nor Africa is the notion of the "redistributive chiefdom" sustained upon close scrutiny. Most of the stuffs that flow toward the chief through taxation ("tribute") do not get widely redistributed; rather, the chief distributes this wherewithall narrowly and selectively to maintain and reinforce the power of his office and his ability to maintain himself in that position. As Carneiro (1981:61) puts it:

> By the selective distribution of food, goods, booty, women, and the like the chief
> rewards those who have rendered him service. Thus he builds up a core of officials,
> warriors, henchmen, retainers, and the like who will be personally loyal to him and
> through whom he can issue orders and have them obeyed. In short, it is through the
> shrewd and self-interested disbursement of taxes that the administrative machinery
> of the chiefdom . . . is built up . . . [T]he chief . . . is no longer a redistributor. He
> is an appropriator and a concentrator.

A chief can be "an appropriator and a concentrator," whereas a big-man cannot, because the political unit that a chief heads is not primarily a kinship unit. True, political relations in a chiefdom are often softened by a metaphor of kinship and by the marriage of some commoner women to some royal men. Nevertheless, the political unit ("chiefdom") over which a chief rules is not composed primarily of his close consanguineal kin, nor are most of his subjects linked to one another throughout the polity by close—or even, any—kinship ties. In short, a chiefdom constitutes itself *territorially;* not kinship but the exercised power (coercive force) of chiefly office knits into a single political unit the inhabitants of a particular region. In contrast, where political scope is defined and confined largely by consanguinty, steady coercion is not possible—and we do not find chiefs (cf. White 1959:309–311; Carneiro 1981:63–67).

Getting back to the Northwest Coast, Mitchell & Donald (this volume) tell us that "a prevailing ethic of generosity left little room for any independent household to hoard what it had produced. Those in control . . . were . . . motivated to share their exceptional bounty." Again: "The ideological basis of Northwest Coast economic activity . . . involved interplay of two dominant themes: personal aggrandizement and generosity." After all, what is the Northwest Coast famous for among social scientists? Give-aways, "potlatches," feasts.

I will not enter into the question of how we might recognize a chiefdom versus a tribe archaeologically. This issue will already be familiar to archaeologists (see Peebles & Kus 1977, Creamer & Haas 1985; cf. Ames 1985) and will bore ethnologists.

One other issue deserves brief mention: Were there "nobles" on the Northwest Coast? I am not convinced that the term is useful here. Clearly, leadership of the kin-group polities or subdivisions of them was widely hereditary, in the sense that group leaders were always chosen from particular "families." But did these families constitute a "nobility," with all the connotations of that term, when the offices and perquisites they enjoyed were confined to small polities inhabited mostly by their consanguines? Before leaving the topic, let me point to the lengthy essay by Ruyle (1973); I think his essay raised a lot of key issues without clarifying any of them, but the discussion published with the essay makes it still worth consulting.

REFERENCES

Adams, John W. (1981) "Recent Ethnology of the Northwest Coast." *Annual Review of Anthropology* 10:361–392.

Ames, Kenneth M. (1985) "Hierarchies, Stress, and Logistical Strategies among Hunter-Gatherers in Northwestern North America." Pp. 155–180 in T.D. Price & J.A. Brown (eds.) *Prehistoric Hunter-Gatherers: The Emergence of Cultural Complexity*. Orlando: Academic Press.

Anderson, James N. (1973) "Ecological Anthropology and Anthropological Ecology." Pp. 179–239 in J.J. Honigmann (ed.) *Handbook of Social and Cultural Anthropology*. Chicago: Rand McNally and Co.

Barnett, Homer G. (1965) "Laws of Socio-Cultural Change." *International Journal of Comparative Sociology* 6:207–230.

—— (1983) *Qualitative Science*. New York: Vantage Press.

Basgall, Mark E. (1987) "Resource Intensification among Hunter-Gatherers: Acorn Economies in Prehistoric California." *Research in Economic Anthropology* 9:21–52.

Bender, Barbara (1981) "Gatherer-Hunter Intensification." Pp. 149–157 in J.A. Sheridan & G.N. Bailey (eds.) *Economic Archaeology*. Oxford: British Archaeological Reports, International Series, 96.

—— (1985a) "Prehistoric Developments in the American Midcontinent and in Brittany, Northwest France." Pp. 21–57 in T.D. Price & J.A. Brown (eds.) *Prehistoric Hunter-Gatherers: The Emergence of Cultural Complexity*. Orlando: Academic Press.

—— (1985b) "Emergent Tribal Formations in the American Midcontinent." *American Antiquity* 50:52–62.

Bouey, Paul D. (1987) "The Intensification of Hunter-Gatherer Economies in the Southern North Coast Ranges of California." *Research in Economic Anthropology* 9:53–101.

Bronitsky, Gordon, ed. (1983) *Ecological Models in Economic Prehistory*. Tempe: Arizona State University, Anthropological Research Papers, No. 29.

Carneiro, Robert L. (1981) "The Chiefdom: Precursor of the State." Pp. 37–79 in G.D. Jones & R.R. Kautz (eds.) *The Transition to Statehood in the New World*. Cambridge, ENG: Cambridge University Press.

Cassell, Mark S. (1988) " 'Farmers of the Northern Ice': Relations of Production in the Traditional North Alaskan Inupiat Whale Hunt." *Research in Economic Anthropology* 10: in press.

Chisholm, B.S., D.E. Nelson, and H.P. Schwarcz (1983) "Marine and Terrestrial Protein in Prehistoric Diets on the British Columbia Coast." *Current Anthropology* 24: 396–398.

Cohen, Mark N. (1977) *The Food Crisis in Prehistory: Overpopulation and the Origins of Agriculture*. New Haven: Yale University Press.

Cook, Scott (1973) "Economic Anthropology: Problems in Theory, Method, and Analysis." Pp. 795–860 in J.J. Honigmann (ed.) *Handbook of Social and Cultural Anthropology*. Chicago: Rand McNally & Co.

Cordy, Ross H. (1981) *A Study of Prehistoric Social Change: The Development of Complex Societies in the Hawaiian Islands*. New York: Academic Press.

Creamer, Winifred, and Jonathan Haas (1985) "Tribe versus Chiefdom in Lower Central America." *American Antiquity* 50:738–754.

Davis, Kingsley (1959) "The Myth of Functional Analysis As a Special Method in Sociology and Anthropology." *American Sociological Review* 24:757–772.

de Laguna, Frederica (1983) "Aboriginal Tlingit Sociopolitical Organization in Native North America." Pp. 71–85 in E. Tooker (ed.) *The Development of Political Organization in*

Native North America. Washington, DC: American Ethnological Society, 1979 Proceedings.

Donald, Leland (1983) "Was Nuu-chah-nulth-aht (Nootka) Society Based on Slave Labor?" Pp. 108–119 19 in E. Tooker (ed.) *The Development of Political Organization in Native North America.* Washington, DC: American Ethnological Society, 1979 Proceedings.

——— (1984) "The Slave Trade on the Northwest Coast of North America." *Research in Economic Anthropology* 6:121–158.

Drucker, Philip (1983) "Ecology and Political Organization on the Northwest Coast of America." Pp. 86–96 in E. Tooker (ed.) *The Development of Political Organization in Native North America.* Washington, DC: American Ethnological Society, 1979 Proceedings.

Ellanna, Linda J. (1988) "Demography and Social Organization as Factors in Subsistence Production in Four Eskimo Communities." *Research in Economic Anthropology* 10: in press.

Endicott, Kirk (1984) "The Economy of the Batek of Malaysia: Annual and Historical Perspectives." *Research in Economic Anthropology* 6:29–52.

Ferguson, Brian (1983) "Warfare and Redistributive Exchange on the Northwest Coast." Pp. 133–147 in E. Tooker (ed.) *The Development of Political Organization in Native North America.* Washington, DC: American Ethnological Society, 1979 Proceedings.

Folan, William J. (1984) "On the Diet of Early Northwest Coast Peoples." *Current Anthropology* 25:123–124.

Fried, Morton H. (1967) *The Evolution of Political Society.* New York: Random House.

Gross, Daniel (1983) "The Ecological Perspective in Economic Anthropology." Pp. 155–181 in S. Ortiz (ed.) *Economic Anthropology: Topics and Theories.* Lanham, MD: University Press of America (Society for Economic Anthropology, Monograph 1).

Halperin, Rhoda H. (1982) "New and Old in Economic Anthropology." *American Anthropologist* 84:339–349.

——— (1984) "Polanyi, Marx, and the Institutional Paradigm in Economic Anthropology." *Research in Economic Anthropology* 6:245–272.

——— (1988) *Economies Across Cultures.* London: Macmillan.

Hardesty, Donald L. (1977) *Ecological Anthropology.* New York: John Wiley & Sons.

Hobson, Keith A., and Stephen Collier (1984) "Marine and Terrestrial Protein in Australian Aboriginal Diets." *Current Anthropology* 25:238–240.

Jacobson, L. (1986) "On Isotope Analysis and Seasonal Mobility." *Current Anthropology* 27:518–519.

Jochim, Michael A. (1981) *Strategies for Survival: Cultural Behavior in an Ecological Context.* New York: Academic Press.

Klepinger, Linda L. (1984) "Nutritional Assessment from Bone." *Annual Review of Anthropology* 13:75–96.

Kurz, Richard B., Jr. (1987) "Contributions of Women to Subsistence in Tribal Societies." *Research in Economic Anthropology* 8:31–59.

Lazenby, Richard A., and Peter McCormack (1985) "Salmon and Malnutrition on the Northwest Coast." *Current Anthropology* 26:379–384.

Legros, Dominique (1985) "Wealth, Poverty, and Slavery among 19th-Century Tutchone Athapaskans." *Research in Economic Anthropology* 7:37–64.

Marquardt, William H. (1985) "Complexity and Scale in the Study of Fisher-Gatherer-Hunters: An Example from the Eastern United States." Pp. 59–98 in T.D. Price & J.A. Brown (eds.) *Prehistoric Hunter-Gatherers: The Emergence of Cultural Complexity.* Orlando: Academic Press.

Micklin, Michael, and Harvey M. Choldin, eds. (1984) *Sociological Human Ecology.* Boulder, CO: Westview Press.

Mitchell, Donald (1984) "Predatory Warfare, Social Status, and the North Pacific Slave Trade." *Ethnology* 23:29–48.

——— (1985) "A Demographic Profile of Northwest Coast Slavery." Pp. 227–236 in M. Thompson, M.T. Garcia & F.J. Kense (eds.) *Status, Structure and Stratification: Current Archaeological Reconstructions.* Calgary: Proceedings of the 16th Annual Conference of the Archaeological Association of the University of Calgary.

Mitchell, Donald, and Leland Donald (1985) "Some Economic Aspects of Tlingit, Haida, and Tsimshian Slavery." *Research in Economic Anthropology* 7:19–35.

Moran, Emilio (1979) *Human Adaptability.* North Scituate, MA: Duxbury Press.

Nelson, B.K., M.J. DeNiro, M.J. Schoeninger, and D.J. De Paolo (1986) "Effects of Diagenesis on Strontium, Carbon, Nitrogen and Oxygen Concentration and Isotopic Composition of Bone." *Geochimica et Cosmochimica Acta* 50:1941–1949.

Orlove, Benjamin S. (1980) "Ecological Anthropology." *Annual Review of Anthropology* 9:235–273.

Peebles, Christopher S., and Susan M. Kus (1977) "Some Archaeological Correlates of Ranked Societies." *American Antiquity* 42:421–448.

Peterson, Jean Treloggen (1984) "Cash, Consumerism, and Savings: Economic Change among the Agta Foragers of Luzon, Philippines." *Research in Economic Anthropology* 6:53–73.

Phillips, J.L., and J.A. Brown, eds. (1983) *Archaic Hunters and Gatherers in the American Midwest.* New York: Academic Press.

Piddocke, Stuart (1965) "The Potlatch System of the Southern Kwakiutl: A New Perspective." *Southwestern Journal of Anthropology* 21:244–264.

Price, T.D., and J.A. Brown, eds. *Prehistoric Hunter-Gatherers: The Emergence of Cultural Complexity.* Orlando: Academic Press.

Ruyle, Eugene E. (1973) "Slavery, Surplus, and Stratification on the Northwest Coast: The Ethnoenergetics of an Incipient Stratification System." *Current Anthropology* 14:603–617, 624–631.

Salmon, Merilee (1978) "What Can Systems Theory Do for Archaeology?" *American Antiquity* 43:174–183.

Sandbukt, Øyvind (1988) "Resource Constraints and Relations of Appropriation among Tropical Forest Foragers: The Case of the Sumatran Kubu." *Research in Economic Anthropology* 10: in press.

Savelle, James M., and Allen P. McCartney (1988) "Geographical and Temporal Variation in Thule Eskimo Subsistence Economies: A Model." *Research in Economic Anthropology* 10: in press.

Schoeninger, M.J., and C.S. Peebles (1981) "Effect of Mollusc Eating on Human Bone Strontium Levels." *Journal of Archaeological Science* 8:391–397.

Schoeninger, M.J., and M.J. DeNiro (1984) "Nitrogen and Carbon Isotopic Composition of Bone Collagen from Marine and Terrestrial Animals." *Geochimica et Cosmochimica Acta* 48:625–639.

Schoeninger, M.J., M.J. DeNiro, and H. Tauber (1983) "Stable Nitrogen Isotope Ratios of Bone Collagen Reflect Marine and Terrestrial Components of Prehistoric Human Diet." *Science* 220:1381–1383.

Schwarcz, H.P. (1986) "*Comment on* Sealy & van der Merwe's 'Isotope Assessment and the Seasonal-Mobility Hypothesis. . .' " *Current Anthropology* 27:146–147.

Sealy, Judith C., and Nikolaas J. van der Merwe (1986) "Isotopic Assessment and the Seasonal-Mobility Hypothesis in the Southwestern Cape of South Africa." *Current Anthropology* 27:135–144, 147–150.

Suttles, Wayne (1960) "Affinal Ties, Subsistence, and Prestige among the Coast Salish." *American Anthropologist* 62:296–305.

Tollefson, Kenneth D. (1977) "A Structural Change in Tlingit Potlatching." *Western Canadian Journal of Anthropology* 7:16–27.

———— (1982) "Northwest Coast Village Adaptations: A Case Study." *Canadian Journal of Anthropology* 3:19–30.

———— (1985) "Potlatch and Stratification among the Tlingit." Abhandlungen der Volkerkundlichen Arbeitsgemeinschaft, Heft 42. (Nortorf, West Germany)

———— (1987) "The Snoqualmie: A Puget Sound Chiefdom." *Ethnology* 26:121–136.

Vayda, Andrew P. (1961) "A Re-examination of Northwest Coast Economic Systems." *Transactions of the New York Academy of Science (Ser. 2)* 23:618–624.

White, Leslie A. (1959) *The Evolution of Culture*. New York: McGraw-Hill Book Co.

PART I

HOKO RIVER ARCHAEOLOGICAL COMPLEX

HOKO RIVER ARCHAEOLOGICAL COMPLEX:

MODELING PREHISTORIC NORTHWEST COAST ECONOMIC EVOLUTION

Dale R. Croes and Steven Hackenberger

INTRODUCTION

Hoko River Archaeological Complex

The Hoko River site complex is located about 30 km from the northwest tip of the Olympic Peninsula, along the Strait of Juan de Fuca (Figure 1). The complex consists of two temporally distinct areas of prehistoric occupation: (1) an upriver waterlogged (wet) and adjoining (dry) campsite area (45CA213) dating from 3000 to 2200 BP, and (2) a rivermouth site within a large rockshelter (45CA21), occupied from about 900 to 100 BP.

Research in Economic Anthropology, Supplement 3, pages 19–85.
Copyright © 1988 by JAI Press Inc.
All rights of reproduction in any form reserved.
ISBN: 0-89232-818-5

Figure 1. Location of the Hoko River Site Complex

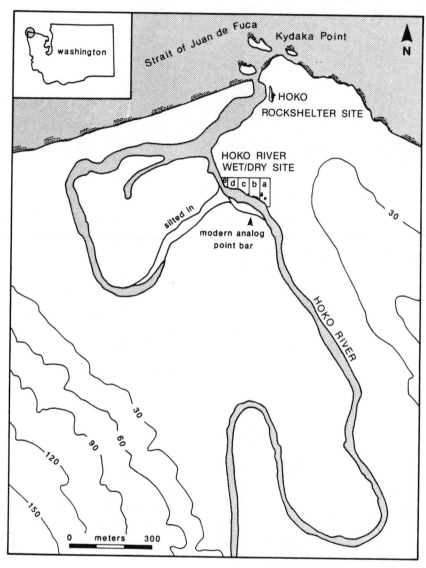

Excavations of the upriver "wet/dry" site (45CA213) began in 1973 (Croes 1976, Croes & Blinman 1980, Howes 1982, Stucki 1983, Gross 1986). Water-saturated silt/sand deposits exposed along the edge of the Hoko River contain over 25 layers of well-preserved organic vegetal mats that encase discarded perishable artifacts, including basketry, cordage, fishing hooks, hafted microlith "fish" knives, woodworking tools, and carved-wood art as well as animal bone and rare shellfish remains (Croes & Blinman 1980, Flenniken 1981). A predominance of flatfish, roundfish, and rockfish remains have been recovered from the wet site in association with over 300 wooden offshore-fishing hooks, indicative of the fisheries focus at this early site (Croes & Blinman 1980, Hoff 1980, Stucki 1983).

The cut bank above the wet deposits represents a cross section of an ancient point bar, upon which the original fishing camps were established (Figure 1; Stucki 1983). These dry campsite deposits can be stratigraphically traced to corresponding wet layers of organic material below the river high-tide line. The dry deposits lack any preserved organic debris, but they include campsite floors and contain numerous features, such as slab-lined "hearths," concentrations of fire-cracked rock debris, and vein quartz microlith manufacturing areas (Flenniken 1981; Howes 1982; Gross 1984, 1986). Spatial patterns of these remains suggest distinct activity areas, possibly including part of a dwelling (Howes 1982, Gross 1986). Because of poor preservation, the dry site yielded only stone artifacts, including thick, ground-slate points, bifacially-flaked contracting-stem points, and quartz crystal microblades.

The rivermouth rockshelter site (45CA21), investigated since 1979, contains over 3.5 vertical meters of relatively undisturbed shell midden. Over 1,300 distinct layers have been recorded, representing several types of depositional features associated with occupations from the historic period back to about 900 BP. Eight major chronological "states" have been defined to describe the formation of site deposits. These states are recognized on the basis of event-step analyses of the more than 1,300 stratigraphic features and layers (Stucki 1983, 1984, 1985) or "depositional periods" (Wigen & Stucki, this volume). Deposits inside the rockshelter contain living surfaces, including hearths and refuse areas. An extensive refuse area with abundant shell and bone remains occurs in areas extending from the back of the rockshelter to the beach below its mouth. Bone tools, especially numerous varieties of bone points, are frequent in this site, while stone and shell artifacts are less common (Croes 1985). High frequencies of fishbone indicate a primary use of salmon, followed by round-fish/rockfish and only limited amounts of halibut/flatfish (Wigen 1985; Wigen & Stucki, this volume).

The earlier wet/dry site seems to have served most consistently as a spring and summer halibut/flatfish and Pacific cod/roundfish camp (Croes & Blinman 1980). We infer that the rockshelter site was used most consistently as a fall-winter and/or spring station, from which salmon, roundfish, and a variety of other resources were taken.

Regional Archaeological Phases

The Hoko River wet/dry site (3000-2000 BP) produces artifacts technologically identified with the Locarno Beach Cultural Type (Howes 1982, Mitchell 1982, Gross 1984; Figure 2). These assemblages include thick, faceted ground-slate points, quartz crystal microblades, bifacially-flaked contracting-stem projectile points, microlithic technology, formed whetstones, chipped schist "knives," and slab-lined "hearths" (Mitchell 1971; Howes 1982; Gross 1984, 1986). On the basis of the lithic artifact assemblage and other data, Mitchell (1982) has designated the Hoko wet/dry site occupations as a westerly extension of Locarno Beach (Figure 3). This period of southern Northwest Coast prehistory has been considered a formative era of the classic Northwest Coast ethnographic pattern and is believed to reflect "a more specific adaptation to the coastal environment than did earlier types" (Mitchell 1971:70). The wood and fiber artifacts represent over 90 percent of the total number of discrete artifacts recovered from Hoko and provide a new perspective on this formative period (Croes 1976, 1977, 1980a-c; Croes & Blinman 1980). For example, we have recovered over 300 bentwood and composite wooden offshore fishing hooks, along with cordage leaders and line floats (Hoff 1980, Croes 1980c). The sophistication of this equipment indicates an early specialization in offshore fisheries.

In contrast, the Hoko Rockshelter bone tool assemblage (dating about 900–100 BP) is technologically similar to contemporaneous Gulf of Georgia Culture Type assemblages and differs sharply from the earlier stone and bone assemblage recovered at the Hoko wet/dry site (Mitchell 1971, Gross 1984, Croes 1985). In fact, the appearance of the Gulf of Georgia type bone tool assemblage represents a dramatic shift throughout the southern coast toward an emphasis on bone technologies for forming artifacts (Carlson 1983). The small bone bipoint appears to be one of the most important parts of the assemblages from this time period (Carlson 1983). Over 60 percent of the bone artifacts recovered from the Hoko Rockshelter are of this variety, and this high a percentage is typical of assemblages from other Gulf of Georgia type sites (Mitchell 1971:47). Earlier phases show less than 5 percent bone point artifacts.

At the nearby Ozette Village wet site (45CA24), the bone tool assemblage (dating to about 250 BP) contains varieties of small, bone bipoints identical to those found at the Hoko Rockshelter site (McKenzie 1974), but at the Ozette wet site their associated wooden components are preserved. Most

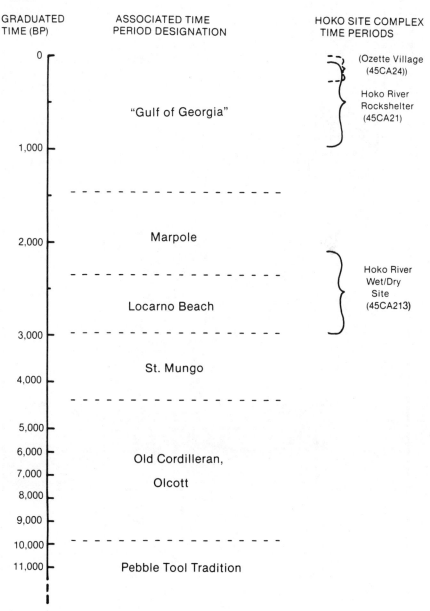

Figure 2. Cultural Phase/Type Sequence on the Southern Northwest Coast

GRADUATED TIME (BP)

ASSOCIATED TIME PERIOD DESIGNATION

HOKO SITE COMPLEX TIME PERIODS

0

(Ozette Village (45CA24))

Hoko River Rockshelter (45CA21)

"Gulf of Georgia"

1,000

2,000

Marpole

Hoko River Wet/Dry Site (45CA213)

Locarno Beach

3,000

St. Mungo

4,000

5,000

6,000

7,000

Old Cordilleran,

Olcott

8,000

9,000

10,000

11,000

Pebble Tool Tradition

Figure 3. Distribution of Locarno Beach Culture Type Sites (after Mitchell 1982, Ham 1982)

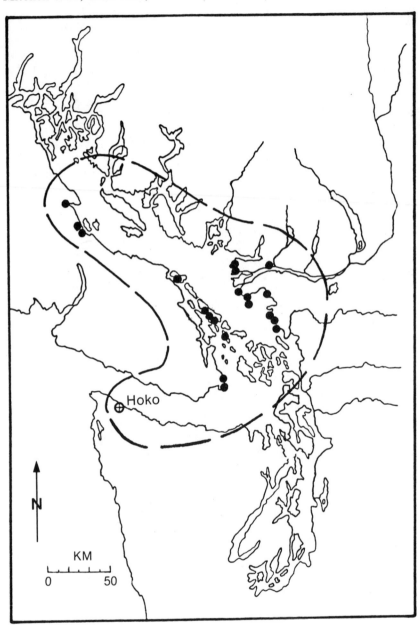

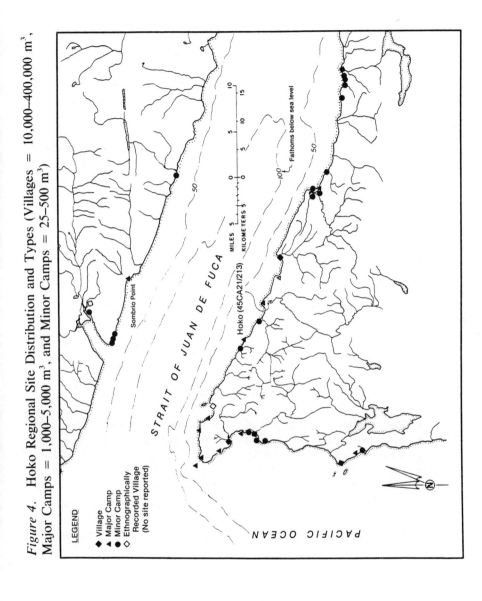

Figure 4. Hoko Regional Site Distribution and Types (Villages = 10,000–400,000 m³, Major Camps = 1,000–5,000 m³, and Minor Camps = 25–500 m³)

of the Ozette bone points have been identified as fishhook barbs or harpoon points.

Local Archaeological Site Data

Thirty-six prehistoric habitation sites have been recorded within the study locale (Figure 4). These shell-midden sites have been located during systematic coastal surveys and/or through ethnohistoric accounts. Using site records delineating the areal extent and depth of these shell middens, we estimated the volume (in m^3) of each site. The resulting estimates fall within three categories, which we label by type of habitation: (1) village (n = 7), (2) major camp (n = 11), (3) minor camp (n = 18). The villages have shell middens that are extensive and deep (10,000–400,000m³). Major resource camps have 1,000–5,000m³ of shell midden, while minor resource camps have 25–500m³.

Three winter villages are evenly spaced at about 25 km apart on the southern Strait of Juan de Fuca, with three major camps located in between, while an additional three winter villages are spaced 3–8 km apart on the outer Pacific Coast and are associated with seven interspersed major camps. Minor resource camps occur in the immediate vicinity of villages and major camps. Within this regional context the two Hoko sites represent major camps associated with winter villages at Neah Bay and/or Clallam Bay.

REGIONAL MODELING OF CULTURAL EVOLUTION

Some Synthetic Propositions

We shall examine six propositions that represent our synthesis of current hypotheses about the nature and rate of economic changes thought to be crucial to the development of Northwest Coast societies. At the outset, we should note that we do not discount Fladmark's (1975) argument for the possible importance of the early (5000 BP) stabilization of anadromous fish populations (if, in fact, this did occur), but we do not agree that this phenomenon represents a necessary and/or sufficient cause of economic changes on the Northwest Coast. For each proposition it is possible to cite works presenting related ideas, although not always stated as hypotheses by the original authors:

1. Population growth and regional population circumscription occurred by 4000–3000 BP and depleted resource bases (Schalk 1977; Ames 1979, 1981; Matson 1983).
2. Resource depletion (lowered economic efficiency) required the intensification of resource use in late spring, summer, and fall, and

the storage of greater amounts of resources for use in winter and early spring (Schalk 1977, Matson 1983).

3. Intensified resource use and increased storage permitted higher human population carrying capacities (continued population growth) and increased the sedentism of social groupings (Schalk 1977, Ames 1981, Matson 1983).

4. Maintenance of higher population levels depended primarily on the use of anadromous fish resources (Fladmark 1975, Schalk 1977).

5. Efficient use of anadromous fish required centralized authority (social ranking) for the organization of labor and/or the redistribution of resources (Suttles 1968, Fladmark 1975, Schalk 1977, Ames 1981).

6. Resource depletion required resource management, and resource ownership facilitated such management while creating differential access to resources and the accumulation and expenditure of wealth to retain rights to manage the use of resource areas (Matson 1983, Richardson 1982, Easton n.d.).

An Exponential Model of Population Growth

We need a general model to project population growth in order to evaluate the postulate that human population growth was one primary causal factor in the development of Northwest Coast economies and societies—and, specifically, that population growth resulted in resource depletion and intensified forms of resource utilization. Figure 5, which is based on computer simulation, depicts the kind of exponential population growth resulting from the lowest viable initial population size and annual rate of human population growth. Starting at 9000 BP with a population of only 50 for the entire Olympic Peninsula and a fixed annual net growth of only 0.1 percent (Hassan 1978, 1981), the population would be 7,500 ($0.3/km^2$) by 4000 BP, 24,000 ($0.94/km^2$) by 3000 BP, and possibly 70,000 ($2.7/km^2$) by 2000 BP. The model predicts a doubled population of 175,000 (about $7/km^2$) by 1000 BP and a greatly increased population of 300,000 ($12/km^2$) by 500 BP. Of course, the exponential population model will accelerate population growth, and this kind of unchecked growth cannot occur for long. The exponential growth must eventually slow down and reach a cultural/biological plateau or "carrying capacity." To estimate when this would most likely occur in this coastal area, we explored historic population records for the early contact period. For the period just before white settlement (approximately 1840–1860), Kroeber (1939) estimated native population density to be 0.30-$0.75/km^2$ of coastal lands; his estimate is probably low with respect to the pre-European Contact period, since his calculations follow dates of major smallpox epidemics, estimated to have lowered populations by as much as 50 percent or more. From less specific 1803–1805 estimates provided for this region by Jewitt (1815:39–41), we

Figure 5. Exponential Population Growth Starting with 50 People and Assuming a Net Growth of 0.1%

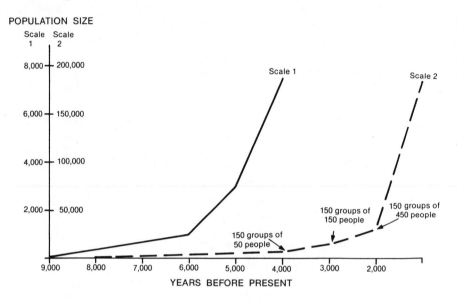

predict at least 1.5 persons/km², which also may be low, due to possibly earlier smallpox epidemics and other factors (Jim Haggarty, personal communication). Our main conclusion is that we would conservatively expect exponential population growth in this region to begin reaching an ethnohistoric carrying capacity at 4000–3000 BP. Therefore, we project this time period to be especially sensitive to initial population growth limits and regard it as one to carefully explore in our modeling of cultural and economic evolution in this region.

Assuming territories of at least 160 km² for each social grouping (thought of as winter settlements), our modeling projects as many as 150 groups of 50 (or 7,500 people) in the Olympic Peninsula by 4000 BP (after a process of population growth and social fission), as many as 150 groups of 150 (or 22,500 people) by 3000 BP (as the outcome of social fission of increased numbers of families), and by 2000 BP, 150 groups of 450 (or 67,500 people). Thus, we can readily perceive the potential for rapid increases in population size and for circumscribed populations at 4000–3000 BP. (However, it could also be argued that, on the basis of an initial population size as low as 100 people at 9000 BP, such population increases and circumscription could have occurred as early as 5000 BP.)

Nash (1983b:19) suggested that logistic growth curves for the Northwest Coast populations may have developed for regions with coastal ranges and narrow coastal plains. Our conclusion is that, if many local populations could have grown to even 50 people each by 4000 BP, then, due to the exponential nature of population growth, local populations could have tripled in the next 1,000 years. What we must next demonstrate, however, is the preferred local population levels and the point in local population growth at which circumscribed populations would begin depleting specific resources.

Decision Models of Seasonal Resource Intensification and Depletion

In our approach it is particularly important to incorporate models of economic decision making to assist in understanding (1) how population growth accelerates and (2) how local population growth might begin to deplete resources and lower economic efficiency, causing cultural controls on population growth or shifts in economic decision making practices.

Our two models (presented below) predicting patterns of subsistence, settlement, and population for the Hoko River region are based on a mixed-goal economic decision model initially developed by Jochim (1976) and expanded here with the flexibility of computer simulation techniques. We rely on two major organizational principles, as described by Jochim (1976:10): (1) "The problems requiring solutions or choices can be conveniently formulated as systems," and (2) "These problems can best be approached in the context of [evolutionary] human ecology."

Jochim's (1976:10) and our basic assumptions concerning human decision making are, in his words:

1. Economic behavior is the result of conscious choices.
2. These choices are deliberative rather than opportunistic.
3. The deliberation is rational, based on preferences among consequences.
4. The probabilities of the outcomes of choices are uncertain and must be estimated.
5. The choices seek to satisfy predetermined aspiration levels, not to maximize any specific measures.
6. The choices will allow or prefer mixed-strategy economic solutions.
7. A desire to limit effort underlies all economic decisions.

The three problem areas analyzed with our economic decision models are:

- proportional seasonal resource-use;
- regional human population maintenance and seasonal aggregation; and
- seasonal site placement.

Jochim presents two major social goals guiding the decision making process in predicting outcomes for these problem areas and supports the choice of these goals with ethnographic evidence. These two goals are (a) to attain a secure food and nonfood income, and (b) to realize low-cost maintenance of human population aggregations (Jochim 1976:25). Goal attainment is estimated through equations evaluating resource characteristics and uses of faunal and floral resources known to be important to hunter-gatherer-fishers on the basis of ethnographic and archaeological data (Jochim 1976:23ff). The values used to judge attainment are derived by delineating key attributes of each important resource in terms of (1) edible weight [W], (2) proportional nonfood (artifact) yield [N], (3) food energy (calories) [C], (4) resource density [D], (5) common aggregation size [A], and (6) resource mobility (range) [M].

When we add caloric estimates, Jochim's equation for obtaining a secure food income means that a resource becomes of greater proportional significance in the diet, the greater its edible weight, caloric value, nonfood yield, and density, and the lower its mobility or range. The secure-income equation is: WNCD/M. For establishing a population aggregation at minimum cost, a resource becomes more important in the diet, the larger its yield and aggregation and the less mobile its behavior. The low-cost equation is: WNCA/M.

These two major social goals (secure income and low-cost aggregation) parallel concepts of optimal foraging theory, if we recognize the separate probabilities of (1) food pursuit versus (2) food capture. The most important feature of the decision model is that the two goals are attained in the programming by (a) separately evaluating the obtainable value of each resource in terms of each goal and then (b) averaging these values for each resource to best satisfy both goals (Jochim 1976:25–27). This type of decision making process is opposed to assuming a single, undifferentiated goal, such as caloric maximization. To solve for these goals and predict the proportionate use of each resource, we identify resource attributes and record these values in appropriately structured computer equations.

The tool used to build and operationalize the predictive models is DYNAMO II (DYNAmic MOdels) simulation programming (Pugh 1976, Richardson & Pugh 1981). This computer software compiles and executes continuous simulation models and is particularly applicable to modeling changes in economic behavior on the basis of the decision model originally developed by Jochim (1976). The simplicity and flexibility of our program allows us to conceptually test the effects of changes in both decision structures and resource values (Figure 6; see also Croes & Hackenberger 1985).

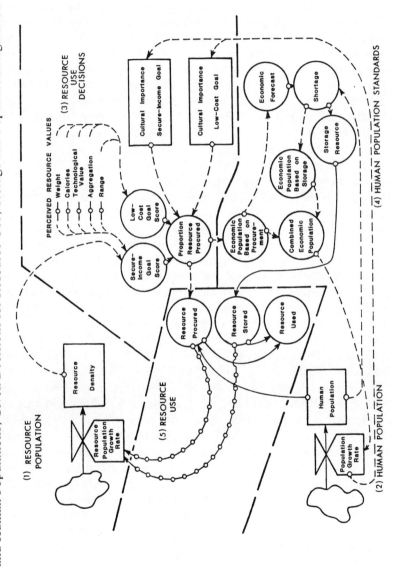

Figure 6. Generalized DYNAMO Flow Chart for Simulation of Relationships Between Resources and Human Populations, Given Decisions for Resource Use, Storage and Population Regulation

31

MODELING THE HOKO REGIONAL ECOSYSTEMS

Paleoenvironmental Reconstruction

After 13,000 BP, climatic amelioration on the outer Olympic Peninsula was rapid, with high precipitation levels (Heusser 1973; Huesser et al. 1980). Forest vegetation in the newly deglaciated subalpines consisted of lodgepole pine. However, precipitation reached a minimum and summer temperature a maximum by 8000 BP. From then until about 3000 BP, Douglas fir was abundant, although Sitka spruce dominated. Cooler, moisturer conditions returned by 3000 BP, and from then to date a western hemlock and western red cedar assemblage has been dominant.

Alpine glaciation and planktonic assemblages from deep-sea cores indicate that temperature changes have been frequent since 3000 BP but not of sufficient magnitude (about 1°C change in mean summer, surface ocean temperature) to affect coastal vegetation (Griggs et al. 1970; Moore 1973; Stucki 1983, 1985). The consequences of these ocean temperature changes on marine resources remain to be evaluated.

Postglacial marine inundation was 32–34m above present mean sea level on western Vancouver Island, 200 km north of the Hoko River Site (Clague et al. 1980; Stucki 1983, 1985). After 4500 BP, sea level curves show gradual emergence due to tectonic uplift at about 1mm/year (Ando & Balazs 1979; Hicks 1978; Stucki 1983, 1985). Geoarchaeological and geological research (Park Snavely, personal communication; Blinman 1980; Stucki 1983, 1985) also indicates tectonic uplift in the Hoko vicinity over at least the last 3,000 years. This uplift was gradual, causing minimal alteration to vegetation and animal communities. Our site-specific studies of macroflora (primarily evergreen cones and seeds), pollen (Ecklund-Johnson 1980, 1984; Blinman & Peterson 1980), and fauna (Huelsbeck 1980, Friedman 1980, Fisken 1980, Gross 1980, Croes & Blinman 1980) corroborate these conclusions. The uplift raised the overall river valley floodplain and the Hoko River wet/dry and Hoko Rockshelter sites to approximately 3m and 10m above sea level, respectively; however, the river continued to downcut the floodplain. Therefore, the uplift probably had minimal effect on the local environment (Stucki 1983). The river mouth would be more affected by ocean currents and resulting spit formation. The intertidal zone may have decreased in area with the uplift, due to gradual erosion and the formation of a steeper beach area. However, the gradual rate of uplift would not have precipitated sudden changes in available intertidal food resources.

Thus, the general Hoko River environment from 3000 BP to Euro-American contact (about 150 years ago) is proposed to be similar to the

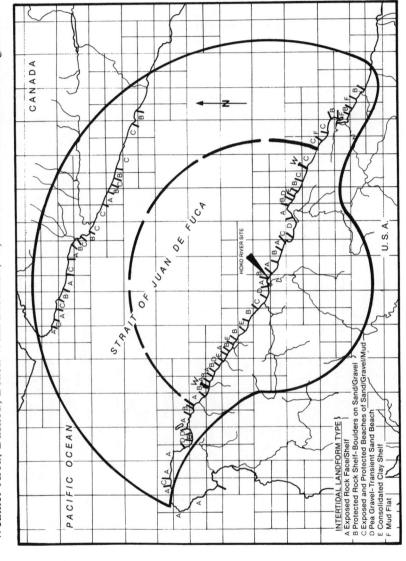

Figure 7. Regional 4 × 4km Grid System to Control for Spatial Resource Distributions, with Regional Catchment Outlined by a 1-Day Travel Distance via Canoe and Overland (Bad-Weather Area, Dashed; Beach-Walk Distance, W) and Intertidal Landforms Designated

INTERTIDAL LANDFORM TYPE
A Exposed Rock Face/Shelf
B Protected Rock Shelf-Boulders on Sand/Gravel
C Exposed and Protected Beaches of Sand/Gravel/Mud
D Pea Gravel-Transient Sand Beach
E Consolidated Clay Shelf
F Mud Flat

HOKO RIVER SITE

PACIFIC OCEAN

STRAIT OF JUAN DE FUCA

CANADA

U.S.A.

33

Figure 8. Terrestrial and Offshore Eco-Units Important for Characterizing Spacial Resource Availability

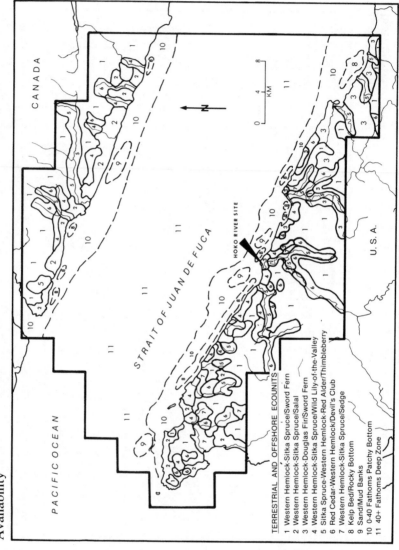

TERRESTRIAL AND OFFSHORE ECOUNITS

1 Western Hemlock-Sitka Spruce/Sword Fern
2 Western Hemlock-Sitka Spruce/Salal
3 Western Hemlock-Douglas Fir/Sword Fern
4 Western Hemlock-Sitka Spruce/Wild Lily-of-the-Valley
5 Sitka Spruce-Western Hemlock-Red Alder/Thimbleberry
6 Red Cedar-Western Hemlock/Devil's Club
7 Western Hemlock-Sitka Spruce/Sedge
8 Kelp Bed/Rocky Bottom
9 Sand/Mud Banks
10 0-40 Fathoms Patchy Bottom
11 40+ Fathoms Deep Zone

34

protohistoric environment. We therefore propose that resources were generally or potentially available in similar configurations over the last 3,000 years.

To provide systematic spatial control of resource information and to improve our estimates of resource availability, the Hoko study region has been mapped with a 4 × 4 km and 2 × 2 km grid (Figure 7; see also Bigley n.d.). We designate three general areas of landform classification: (1) intertidal (Figure 7), (2) terrestrial, and (3) offshore (Figure 8). Within these areas, we define ecounits (ecological units) and estimate resource availability by season.

Delimiting an Economic Region

The abundance of offshore-fishing equipment and offshore fish remains at the Hoko River sites demonstrates these people's ability to travel in open waters by at least 3000 BP (Croes & Blinman 1980). Therefore, we are confident that the economic region incorporates an area easily navigated by canoe, including the open strait, estuaries, and rivers. Ethnographic accounts of canoe travel are used to estimate the average distance that could be traveled in a day's time (Swan 1869, Thompson & Freeman 1930). Such accounts were obtained for each season, allowing a good-weather (spring-summer-fall) estimate of 4.5 km/hr and a poor-weather (winter) estimate of 2.7 km/hr. An estimate of 2–3 km/hr is calculated for beach and overland foot travel, along predominately steep grades and in mostly heavy forest with very dense undergrowth. Using these travel rates, Figure 7 shows an economic area for the Hoko vicinity in which we delimit a single day's trip (12 hrs) from the river mouth vicinity and back, with at least 2 hours for resource procurement. The proposed economic region is 1,720 km². This catchment area centers at Hoko River, simply because that is the area of our research interest; we are aware that Hoko River may have been peripheral to the empirically-defined economic region. In future modeling we plan to use the regional grid to control for possible territorial limits imposed by culturally defined territories and their possible shifts through time.

Seasonal Resource Attributes

Major resources in the Hoko River vicinity include fish, sea mammals, land mammals, mollusca, birds, and plants. Faunal analyses indicate that the primary food resources were: blacktail deer, Roosevelt elk, northern fur seal, northern and California sea lions, harbor seal, gray whale, waterfowl, barnacles, bivalve shellfish (e.g., mussels, clams), salmon, roundfish (e.g., lingcod, greenling/sculpin, Pacific cod), rockfish, and hal-

Table 1. "Constant" Resource Attributes

Species	Cal/kg (raw)[a]	Edible Weight[b] (kg)	Proportional (%) Nonfood Value[c]	Annual Harvesting Efficiency (%)[d]
Blacktail Deer (Odocoileus hemionus columbianus)	2140	105.0	1.10	25
Roosevelt Elk (Cervus canadensis roosevelti)	1800	198.0	1.08	20
Harbor Seal (Phoca vitulina richardsi)	1512	84.0	1.03	15
Northern Fur Seal (Callorhinus wisimus)	1518	92.0	1.03	100
Sea Lions (Eumetopias jubatus and Zalophus californianus)	1517	320.0	1.03	15
Gray Whale (Eschrichtius robustus)	840	15,583.0	1.03	100
Roundfish/Rockfish/ Sculpin/Perch[e]	884	1.0	1.00	20
Salmon	2170	3.6	1.00	65
Halibut/Flatfish	900	6.5	1.00	60
Waterfowl[f]	2300	1.2	1.05	25
Clams[g] } shellfish	800 } 875	0.035 } 0.03	1.001 } 1.001	20 } 15
Mussel[h]	950	0.025	1.005	12
Barnacles[i]	900	0.002	1.00	40

36

[a]See Field et al. (1973a:3, 1973b:5) on deer and elk, respectively; Osborn (1977:191) on harbor seals, Northern fur seals, sea lions, and gray whale; Watt & Merril (1975) on waterfowl, roundfish, halibut, shellfish, and barnacles; and Watt & Merril (1975) and Osborn (1977) on salmon.

[b]Edible weight is derived from: Proctor et al. (1980:A-91,221) for deer and elk; Angell & Balcomb (1982:108) for harbor seals, Everitt et al. (1979:33-35) and Gustafson (1968:49-51) for fur seal and sea lions, Osborn (1977:118) for whale; M. Pederson, personal communications (1980) for roundfish; Osborn (1977) and Hunn (1981) for salmon; discussions with informants and size of vertebrate remains for halibut; average weights for several waterfowl; Bigley (n.d.) for clams; Bigley (n.d.). Wessen (1982), and Miller (1983) for mussels; and Bigley (n.d.) for barnacles.

[c]Nonfood value is calculated as a factor that increases edible weight value by a percentage proportion (see text). Deer and elk provide skins/hides, tallow, antler, and usable bones; see Singh (1956:83,92), Swan (1869:17,20), and Gunther (1936:117). Harbor seal skins were used as floats and the bladders as oil-storage containers (Swan 1869:30, Gibbs 1877:175, Gunther 1936:117). Fur seal skins were used for blankets (Gunther 1936:116) and possibly as oil containers (Gibbs 1877:175). Sea lion stomachs were dried as oil containers; hides were stripped and used as ropes, and intestines as bowstrings (Gunther 1936:115). Gray whale bones were used for artifact manufacture (clubs, bark beaters); sinew for ropes, cords, and bowstrings (Swan 1869:22); and intestines/stomachs for oil containers (Swan 1869:22). Waterfowl feathers were used in fletching, down and skins in weaving, and bones as drinking tubes and tube beads (Croes 1977). Mussel shells were occasionally used to make blades and other artifacts (Wessen 1982, Miller 1983, Waterman 1920:32-33), but since very few mussels are used as nonfood shells in comparison to numbers collected, they are given a very low nonfood value (1.005). Clams were even less frequently used for making artifacts (Wessen 1982, Miller 1983), so they are given an even lower proportional nonfood value (1.001). Roundfish, salmon, halibut/flatfish, and barnacles, which have no known nonfood use, are given a 1.0 proportional nonfood value.

[d]Annual Harvesting Efficiency is the percentage of animal population within the catchment region that can be harvested annually without depleting the annual size of the population. Personal communications: R. Johnson, Washington Department of Game (1981), for deer and elk; B. DeLong, Marine Mammal Laboratory, NOAA, Seattle (1983), for harbor seal, fur seal, sea lions, and gray whale; M. Pederson, Department of Fisheries, University of Washington, Seattle (1983), for roundfish; E. Salo, Fisheries Research Institute, University of Washington, Seattle (1983), for salmon; D. Caughran, International Halibut Commission, Seattle (1983), for halibut; T. Wahl (1983) for waterfowl; V. Gallucci, Center for Quantitative Sciences, University of Washington, Seattle (1983), for clams; R. Baine, Department of Zoology, University of Washington, Seattle, for mussels and barnacles.

[e]"Roundfish" includes various codfish, rockfish, greenlings, sculpins, and surf perches that frequent patchy, rocky bottom and/or kelp beds.

[f]"Waterfowl" includes ducks, scoters, murres, grebes, gulls, loons, swans, geese, albatross, and shearwater.

[g]"Clams" include butter (Saxidomus giganteus), littleneck (Protothaca staminea), horse (Tresus sp.), razor (Siliqua patula), and cockle (Clinocardium nuttalli).

[h]"Mussels" include both California mussels (M. californianus) and edible mussels (M. edulis).

[i]"Barnacles" include the horse (Balanus cariosus) and the gooseneck (Pollicipes polynerus) barnacles.

37

Table 2. Seasonally Variable Resource Attributes

Species[a]	Density (No./km²)[b]	Seasonal Aggregation (Individuals in spring/summer/fall/winter)[c]	Search Unit (No./km²)[d]	Data Sources (Personal Communications)[e]
Blacktail Deer	1.44	2/2/3/2	6/6/4/6	L. Parsons (p.c.1981), R. Johnson (p.c. 1983)
Roosevelt Elk	.24	12/9/14/14	14/16/12/12	R. Johnson (p.c. 1983)
Harbor Seal	.1	2/4/3/2	30/30/20/20	
Northern Fur Seal	.1/.001/.01/.1	4/1/1/2	10/200/200/50	B. Delong (p.c. 1983)
Sea Lions	.26/.001/.01/.1	5/2/5/5	25/900/200/100	
Gray Whale	.002/.001/.001/.0015	2/1/1/1	600	M. Pederson (p.c. 1983)
Roundfish	1000	100	3	B. Wood (p.c. 1979), E. Salo (p.c. 1983)
Salmon	4/6/25/10	10/20/2000/200	75/50/2/75	
Halibut (flatfish)	75	100/290/100/100	4/2/20/250	M. Pedersen (p.c. 1978), D. McCaughran (p.c. 1983)
Waterfowl	20/40/45/25	30	3	T. Wahl (p.c. 1983)
Clams	1021/1276/1021/766	2000	.5	
Mussels	618/772/618/463	2000	.5	
Barnacles	898/1123/898/674	4000	.5	
Shellfish (clams and mussels combined)	1038/2047/1638/1228	2000	.5	

[a]Latin names and other details are specified in Table 1.

[b]Density (D) in the catchment is derived from: L.D. Parsons, Personal Communications (p.c. 1981), Colson (1953), R. Johnson (p.c. 1983) for deer, and Proctor et al. (1980:A-91,221) for deer and elk; Everitt et al. (1979:63,22-23,29-30) for harbor seals, sea lions and gray whales; Scammons (1874:154), B. Delong (p.c. 1983), Singh (1956:21) and Swan (1869:30) for fur seal; B. Wood (p.c. 1979) and E. Salo (p.c. 1983) for salmon; M. Pedersen (p.c. 1978), D. McCaughran (p.c. 1983), and Cross et al. (1978) for halibut; Wahl et al. (1981) for waterfowl. Bigley (n.d.) provides the summer density for clams, mussels, and barnacles; since fall and spring weather and tides would restrict human access, 80 percent of the summer figure is used; still further limitations in winter bring it down to 60 percent.

[c]Seasonal Aggregation (A) is the common group size estimated according to average manner in which animals aggregate as units. It is derived from: R. Johnson (p.c. 1983) for deer; Harper (1971:5) for elk; Everitt et al. (1979) for harbor seal, sea lions, and gray whales; Marine Mammal Biological Laboratory (1971) for fur seals; M. Pederson (p.c. 1983) for roundfish; E. Salo (p.c. 1983) for salmon; D. Caughran (p.c. 1983) for halibut; T. Wahl (p.c. 1983) for waterfowl; Bigley (n.d.) for clams, mussels, and barnacles.

[d]Search Unit (Mobility/Range) (M) is defined as the size (in km²) of area necessary (once the collector is in the resource habitat) to find and capture the resource. It is derived from: R. Johnson (p.c. 1983) for deer; Proctor et al. (1980,2:221) for elk; Croes and Hackenberger (1985:Appendix 1) for harbor seal, fur seal, sea lions, gray whales; M. Pederson (p.c. 1983) for roundfish; E. Salo (p.c. 1983) for salmon; D. McCaughran (p.c. 1983) and Bell (1981) for halibut; T. Wahl (p.c. 1983) for waterfowl; Croes and Hackenberger (1985:Appendix 1) for clams, mussels, and barnacles, which are given a very low range of .5 because they are not mobile.

[e]Affiliations of persons who provided advice for resource values through personal communications: L. Parsons, Big Game Program Manager, Washington Department of Game (1981); R. Johnson, Big Game Program Manager, Washington Department of Game (1983); B. DeLong, Marine Mammal Laboratory, NOAA, Seattle (1983); M. Pederson, Department of Fisheries, University of Washington, Seattle (1983); B. Wood, Fish Biologist, Washington Department of Fisheries, Olympia (1979); E. Salo, Fisheries Research Institute, University of Washington, Seattle (1983); D. McCaughran, International Halibut Commission, Seattle (1983); and T. Wahl, NOAA, Seattle (1983).

ibut/flatfish. Together these resources probably account for at least 75 percent of the annual diet at Hoko. Plant foods may account for most of the remaining 25 percent of the annual diet as has been projected by preliminary modeling, which will be refined with future fieldwork (see also Ecklund-Johnson 1984). This study seeks to estimate the relative importance of the above-listed faunal resources in the total diet and their pattern of use during the year. The resource attributes identified as most significant in terms of the goals set by many ethnographic fishers-hunters-gatherers (see Jochim 1976) include:

1. *Edible Weight* (W): the kilogram weight (average) for total edible parts.
2. *Resource Density* (D): a seasonal value estimating the number of individuals per km^2 in the entire catchment area. The Hoko catchment area covers 1,720 km^2, of which 900 km^2 is offshore and 820 km^2 is terrestrial. The model values are for the entire 1,720 km^2 catchment; therefore, a density of 1,000 for roundfish means 1,000 × 1,720, or an estimated 1,720,000 in catchment area.
3. *Common Aggregation Size* (A): group sizes estimated according to average manner in which animals congregate as units; e.g., habitat groupings (barnacles, shellfish), mating groups, pods, flocks, rafts, schools, etc.
4. *Mobility/Range* (M): resource mobility or range defined as the size (in km^2) of average area necessary to find and catch the resource.
5. *Nonfood Yields* (N): the proportion (percentage) of the animal's total carcass weight contributed as nonfood resources, e.g., 1.1 means that 10 percent additional animal weight is provided as nonfood material resources, and 1.0 means 0 percent (nothing) additional.
6. *Calories/Food Energy* (C): a value for total food (raw) energy per kilogram, including all edible parts.
7. *Harvesting Efficiency* (HAREFF): an estimate of the percent of the local animal population that can be harvested without progressively depleting it.

Our next step involved the calculation of these seven values for the major resources (Tables 1 and 2). We estimated some of these values from data presented as part of ecological studies. Other estimates were given by regional experts or were derived from Hoko Project-sponsored biological fieldwork. Fortunately, a marine ecosystem research program has been conducted in this region of the Strait of Juan de Fuca by the Environmental Protection Agency and administered by the National Oceanic and Atmospheric Administration (NOAA). Several resulting reports record the seasonal distributions, abundance, and behavioral characteristics of sea mammals, marine birds, fish, intertidal resources, and other important marine fauna (Cross et al. 1978; Everitt et al. 1979, 1980; Wahl et al. 1981; Manuwal et al. 1979; Nyblade 1979; Simenstad et al. 1980). Many of these studies were conducted specifically in the Hoko River study area.

Table 1 presents data for four generally constant resource attributes (caloric content, edible weight, nonfood value, and harvesting efficiency) for the significant animal species found in the Hoko River vicinity. Table 2 presents values for three seasonally variable attributes (density, aggregation, and search unit [range]) for the catchment area. The categories of caloric content and search unit (Hassan 1981) are additions to Jochim's (1976) original model. Some species' values remain constant, while others vary according to patterns of migration and social behavior. Actual value assignments derived for each resource are discussed in the notes to Tables 1 and 2.

MODEL 1: MICROECONOMICS OF SEASONAL DECISION MAKING

Model 1 does not consider year-to-year decision making and so precludes the examination of long-term storage practices. This model probably applies best to the earliest economies postulated for the Strait region, prior to 4000 or 5000 BP. Before then, Northwest Coast economies probably were not as heavily dependent on storage (e.g., Old Cordilleran and St. Mungo cultural phases; see Matson 1981). Model 1 also provides insight into decisions regarding resource procurement and population maintenance within each season and therefore is important for defining an economic context in which storage practices developed.

Model 1 represents patterns of seasonal resource use, population levels, and settlement, as well as a means to examine the sensitivity of the modeling by adjusting both resource values and the decision making rules. Examining adjusted resource values is important since (1) natural changes can be expected through time and space, and (2) the process allows us to test for the possible effects of erroneous estimates in model predictions. By modifying rules for decision making, we also examine the effects of changing the prescribed economic goals: secure income and low-cost human population aggregation. Therefore, Model 1 allows us to assess the effects of both resource configuration changes (environment) and economic goal shifts (decision making), providing alternative outcomes to compare with changing archaeological patterns observed from the early periods (10,000–4000 BP) into the transition stages, generally considered Locarno Beach, Marpole, and Gulf of Georgia cultural types (Mitchell 1971, Matson 1981).

Seasonal Resource Use

Computer program runs of Model 1 produce a predicted proportional use of key resources by season for the Hoko region, reflecting a pre-storage and possibly early coastal economy (Figure 9). The four seasons reflect three major economic time period divisions, with spring appearing as a transitional period (Table 3). The spring season includes an emphasis on roundfish, halibut/flatfish, and elk, but a decline from winter in the use of roundfish, elk/deer, and shellfish. Fur seal and sea lions receive only a relatively limited use in spring, as they move in routes adjacent to the Hoko region in their migration north. Halibut/flatfish begin to become important resources as summer approaches. In fall, salmon procurement in the region's four main rivers dominates over all other resource use. In winter, the greatest procurement emphasis is on roundfish, followed by elk/deer and shellfish. Proportional dependence on shellfish and presumably other intertidal resources is the greatest in winter/spring (Figure 9). This pattern is important to note because the importance of shellfish as

Figure 9. Seasonal Proportional Resource Use and Population Levels as Simulated in Model 1 Computer Program Pre-storage Predictions

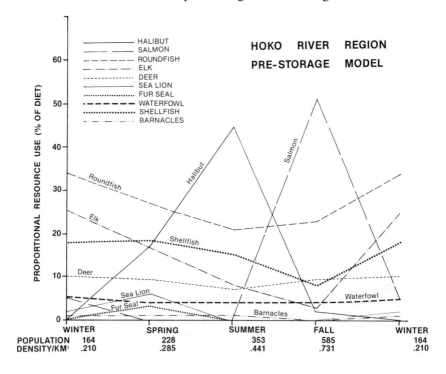

Table 3.   Hoko River Vicinity, Predicted Ranked Order of Resource
           Procurement, by Season

Winter		Spring	
Model 1	Model 2	Model 1	Model 2
Roundfish	Deer/Elk	Roundfish	Halibut
Elk	Roundfish	Shellfish	Deer/Elk
Shellfish	Shellfish	Halibut	Roundfish
Deer	Salmon	Elk	Shellfish

Summer		Fall	
Model 1	Model 2	Model 1	Model 2
Halibut	Halibut	Salmon	Salmon
Roundfish	Deer/Elk	Roundfish	Deer/Elk
Shellfish	Roundfish	Deer	Roundfish
Elk/Deer	Shellfish	Shellfish	Shellfish

a resource is predicted to be a critical determiner in human population
regulation (below).

Seasonal Population

Based on Jochim's (1976) model and Douglas' (1966) notions of carrying
capacity and critical resource limiters, we predict supportable human
population levels by season (see population values below X-axis, Figure
9). These population estimates account for a mixed-goal resource selectivity and offer an alternative to carrying capacity models based on total
biomass available for human use (see, e.g., Casteel 1972), which often
greatly overpredict population levels. In our models, as in Jochim's, population size is determined by proportional resource uses, densities, and
harvesting efficiencies.

The seasonal carrying capacity of the Hoko study area and the size of
seasonal coresident populations are defined by the cultural choices of proportional resource use and by spatial arrangement of these resources. The
carrying capacity is limited to the minimum figure supportable by the various resources when used in their chosen proportions (Jochim 1976:71ff).
This culturally defined carrying capacity is equivalent to our contemporary
notions of standards of living. For this estimate, it is necessary to calculate
the biomass and harvest efficiency of the resources. Given each resource's
proportional dietary contribution and an estimate of a human's seasonal
caloric need, the supportable human population can be calculated. Since

the estimated levels of proportional use for each resource are aspired to, the lowest population figure for any one type of resource represents the maximum desirable population without storage (see Figure 9). The formula used for each resource per season is:

$$\frac{W \times D \times C \times (1{,}720/\text{km}^2 \text{ of region}) \times (\text{percent harvest})}{(\text{percentage of diet}/182{,}500 \text{ calories per person per season})}$$

Of particular significance is the result that the desired pre-storage winter population size in the Hoko region is determined by proportional shellfish use. Based on values presented in Table 2 and a harvesting efficiency of 15 percent, winter population should be about 164 people (0.21/km²). Spring and summer population levels are also determined by shellfish use and should approximate 228 people (0.29/km²) and 353 persons (0.44/km²), respectively. Though fall populations are likewise determined by shellfish use and should approximate 585 people (0.73/km²), salmon desirability reduces the fall importance of shellfish and alleviates seasonal population regulation based on shellfish availability. Therefore, high fall regional population densities might be expected.

Overall, however, low pre-storage human population densities (<0.3/km²) are expected, limited by the available resources in the critical winter season. Such low densities correspond to population levels estimated for nonstorage subsistence economies generally (Hassan 1978) and follow our predictions for population densities on the southern Northwest Coast prior to 4000 BP. Contrary to common characterizations of the Pacific Northwest, our resource surveys and model predictions indicate that (1) low shellfish biomass and (2) its economically desirable attributes (high density and high aggregation) potentially act together to limit the population densities of pre-storage human groups.

A correspondence of predicted seasonal population sizes with those actually in our study region 3000–2500 BP (the Hoko wet/dry site 45CA213) depends on rates of regional population growth and resource distributions throughout the entire area of the Strait of Juan de Fuca and the Olympic Peninsula. If areas surrounding our restricted study region contain similar patterns and levels of resource availability, then the likelihood of seasonally large population increases in the Hoko region would be reduced. If pre-storage populations were socially constrained to particular territories (circumscribed), then regional population levels would be regulated throughout each season at the lowest seasonal population level, around 164 people (0.2/km² of land). This population size approximates the limit at which population circumscription is estimated just before 4000 BP, according to our model of exponential population growth (Figure 5); it is also consistent with population sizes expected for the Old Cordilleran/St. Mungo time periods (Matson 1981).

Seasonal Settlement Locations and Sizes

In our modeling, resource distributions are believed to be a major determinant of site location. Therefore, we consider predicted seasonal resource use in relationship to the regional distribution of the various resources in order to predict settlement types and locations. The distributions of seasonal resources are summarized according to associated ecounit or landform types as illustrated in Figures 5 and 6.

The desire to be close to resources provides a rationale for a gravity model of settlement locations. The results of model equations predict which habitation sites would be located closest to the least mobile, most aggregated, and densest resource, relative to the dietary proportion in which it is desired. Using the equation noted in Table 4, the relative value of

Table 4. Relative Distance Score (*R*) from Base Camp to the Center of Distribution of Each Resource (based on Jochim 1976)[a]

Resource	Winter		Spring		Summer		Fall	
	Score	Rank	Score	Rank	Score	Rank	Score	Rank
Deer	4.4	4	5.4	5	7.1	5	20.5	4
Elk	21.0	5	27.2	7	43.5	6	175.1	7
Fur Seal	83.3	—	19.3	6	570.1	—	3170.0	—
Sea Lion	170.0	—	46.1	—	2500.0	—	2440.0	—
Roundfish	0.3	1	0.3	1	0.4	1	0.3	1
Salmon	33.4	6	88.5	—	90.0	—	30.8	5
Halibut	175.0	—	3.5	4	3.8	4	31.4	6
Waterfowl	2.0	3	3.0	3	2.1	3	2.0	3
Shellfish	0.6	2	0.6	2	0.8	2	1.7	2
Barnacle	0.7	2	0.7	2	0.6	2	1.1	2

[a]*Gravity Model Equation* based on first settlement placement goal:

$R^2 = w\,c\,n\,a\,h\,/\,p$

Where *R* is the distance between two bodies and *p* is the dietary proportion.

w = edible weight
c = calories
n = indexed nonfood value
a = aggregation
h = harvesting efficiency

locating habitations close to each resource can be calculated on a seasonal basis. The lower the reported value, the closer to a resource we would expect people to locate.

In each season, the model predicts that habitation sites would occur nearest to the same three resources: roundfish, shellfish, and waterfowl (ranked 1st, 2nd, and 3rd in Table 4). Therefore, where these resources best co-occur, we could expect to find year-round habitation sites. However, shellfish may not be used in some months due to (a) seasonal low tides in evening hours, (b) the possible overexploitation of shellfish beds near habitation sites, and/or (c) the occurrence of toxic red tide. Consequently, late-fall/winter/early-spring habitation sites are expected to be located close to roundfish and shellfish resources, while late-spring/summer settlements are expected to be located near roundfish and flatfish resource areas. In late fall, winter, and early spring, temporary campsites would be established for hunting elk and deer, reflecting a more terrestrial orientation in the pre-storage period. In early fall, temporary campsites would be expected on upper courses of rivers with salmon runs (ranked 5th in Table 4) and deer population (ranked 4th in Table 4). Due to the predicted effectiveness of exploiting salmon and deer over territorial distances of several kilometers, a series of camps rather than major habitation sites would be expected on rivers with fall salmon runs. Once a storage economy based on salmon developed—with the need to procure, process for storage, and transport resources to a main settlement—then major seasonal villages would be expected. Interestingly, camp locations near deer resources are ranked by the simulation higher than salmon in the pre-storage context.

Given the overlapping distribution of important winter resources (Figure 10), we expect late-fall/winter/early-spring habitations to occur in three principal areas: Physt, Clallam Bay, and Neah Bay. Assuming a total pre-storage human population in winter of about 160 people, then about 50 people might be located in each of these villages. (Interestingly enough, these are the 3 ethnographic winter village locations.) Second, given the overlapping distribution of spring/summer resources (roundfish and flatfish), we expect the populations to be dispersed along the Strait among 4–8 major resource camps (Figure 10). If a year-round regional population size of 160 is maintained, then about 25 people would settle at each location in the spring and summer. If people move into the study area from adjacent regions, however, each of the six locations might have about 50 people, since the total possible spring and summer populations are 228 and 345, respectively. Third, in fall as many as 50–150 people or, more likely, their assigned task specialists (as few as 10–50), might take deer and salmon at separate minor camps along 4–5 productive rivers and streams (Figure 10).

Figure 10. Summary of Spatial Availability of Winter, Spring/Summer, and Fall Resources Used in Predicting Prehistoric Settlement Patterns

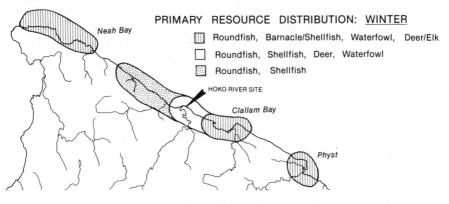

PRIMARY RESOURCE DISTRIBUTION: <u>WINTER</u>

Roundfish, Barnacle/Shellfish, Waterfowl, Deer/Elk

Roundfish, Shellfish, Deer, Waterfowl

Roundfish, Shellfish

HOKO RIVER SITE

Neah Bay

Clallam Bay

Physt

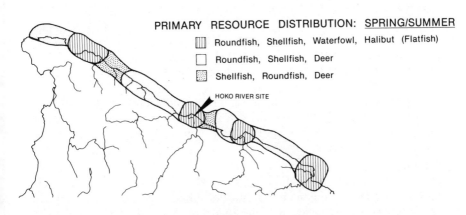

PRIMARY RESOURCE DISTRIBUTION: <u>SPRING/SUMMER</u>

Roundfish, Shellfish, Waterfowl, Halibut (Flatfish)

Roundfish, Shellfish, Deer

Shellfish, Roundfish, Deer

HOKO RIVER SITE

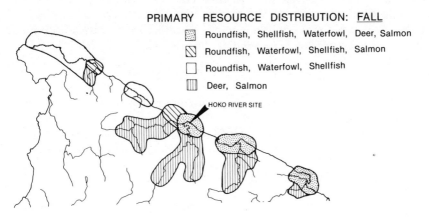

PRIMARY RESOURCE DISTRIBUTION: <u>FALL</u>

Roundfish, Shellfish, Waterfowl, Deer, Salmon

Roundfish, Waterfowl, Shellfish, Salmon

Roundfish, Waterfowl, Shellfish

Deer, Salmon

HOKO RIVER SITE

Sensitivity of Resource Value Changes

By adjusting the model's resource values from hypothetical minimums to maximums, we examine the potential importance of natural resource fluctuations in terms of the effects on (1) their proportional use, (2) human population size, and (3) settlement location in the Hoko River region. The structure of our computer programming easily allows an analysis of the range of variability possible and is not restricted to the specific expected value.

During our five years of model building, we have conducted sensitivity analyses to judge the effects of changing our resource values over extended ranges and evaluating the results obtained with Model 1. For example, early on we were able to state that the aggregation of sea lions was the most important variable affecting the overall proportional use of spring resources. That is, relatively slight changes in the high values for sea lion aggregation produced large increases in the use of these species and lowered the relative dependence on other resources such as shellfish. This finding was altered, however, when we found that sea lions had limited use at the sites and that their use was dependent on hunting trips across the Strait of Juan de Fuca to the single haul-out area at Sombrio Point on Vancouver Island (see Figure 4).

As examples of sensitivity analysis through modeling, we present tests involving changes in the densities of three resources in winter—deer, mussel, and roundfish (Figure 11, A-C). Our analyses indicate that the relative range of possible changes in resource density values for each season has the greatest impact on winter resource procurement and, thus, also on supportable population sizes. However, given the commonly expressed ideas regarding the importance of salmon productivity for human population size, we also examine the effects of changing fall salmon density on proportional resource use and human population maintenance (Figure 11, D). We summarize important points resulting from each sensitivity analysis in reference to corresponding illustrations.

Winter Deer Density from .01 to 2/km² (Figure 11, A):

- Changes have little effect on population or proportional use of other resources.
- Therefore, deer density is of minor concern, either in terms of accuracy or possible effects on economic changes, in our study area.

Winter Mussel Density from 1 to 2,000/km² (Figure 11, B):

- Changes have limited effect on proportional procurement (5–14 percent) of mussel, and no other resource's proportional use is significantly affected.

- However, human population increases dramatically (a 60 percent increase when mussel density increases from predicted 500 to 1,000/km^2).
- Similar trends can be expected by increasing dependence on shellfish, which can be overexploited, thus causing local population stress.

Winter Roundfish Density from 1 to 2,000/km^2 (Figure 11, C):

- Increased population growth is much less dramatic compared to the rapid increase predicted by adjusting mussel densities.
- If the density of roundfish is doubled from our estimate of 1,000 to 2,000/km^2, only about 20 more people would be supported under the desired mix of resource use.
- This limited effect on human population levels is the consequence of a relatively small decrease in proportional shellfish use.
- Most of the proportional increase in roundfish use is made up through a decreased reliance on deer.

To summarize the above three winter season sensitivity tests, we note that deer and roundfish resources become less important for population maintenance as their densities vary, whereas shellfish densities have a major impact, which is particularly important if these latter resources are stressed through overexploitation. Further, from our economic goal assumptions, shellfish procurement insures users a secure income, whereas deer and roundfish are relatively more important as sources of low-cost population aggregation. This difference in goal orientation is further explored by adjusting decision-making emphases below.

Fall Salmon Density from 0.1 to 40/km^2, with corresponding increase in aggregation from 1 to 4,000/km^2 of river course (Figure 11, D):

- Even with a 50 percent reduction in our original estimate of salmon density (10/km^2), proportional use drops only about 10 percent, and the supportable fall population remains over twice that of winter.

Therefore, significant changes in salmon density and aggregation have only slight effects on their proportional use and on human populations in a pre-storage economy, as may be archaeologically reflected in salmon use and human population for periods prior to 3000 BP (the St. Mungo and Old Cordilleran time periods).

Sensitivity of Economic Goal Changes

As a related example of sensitivity analysis, we change the relative importance of the two proposed economic goals and examine the sensitivity

Figure 11. Proportional Use of Winter Resources, with Adjusted Range in Density of Deer (A), Mussel (B), and Roundfish (C); and Proportional Use of Fall Resources, with Adjusted Range in Density and Aggregation of Salmon (D)

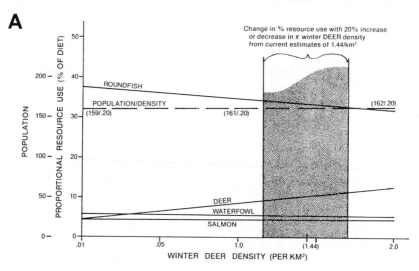

A

Change in % resource use with 20% increase or decrease in *x* winter DEER density from current estimates of 1.44/km²

ROUNDFISH

POPULATION/DENSITY
(159/.20)   (161/.20)   (162/.20)

DEER
WATERFOWL
SALMON

WINTER DEER DENSITY (PER KM²)

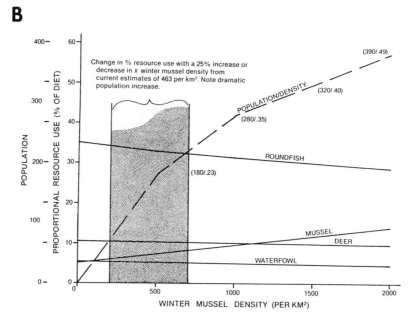

B

Change in % resource use with a 25% increase or decrease in *x* winter mussel density from current estimates of 463 per km². Note dramatic population increase.

(390/.49)

POPULATION/DENSITY
(320/.40)
(280/.35)

ROUNDFISH

(180/.23)

MUSSEL
DEER
WATERFOWL

WINTER MUSSEL DENSITY (PER KM²)

50

Figure 11. continued

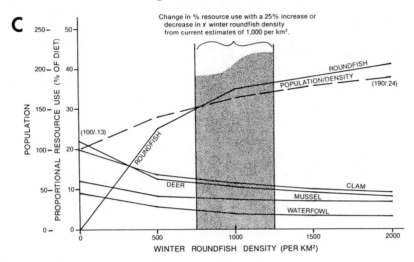

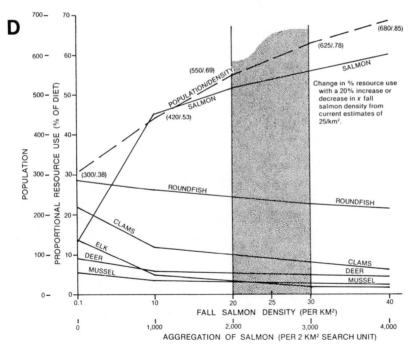

of a pre-storage economy to changes in decision making. Whereas Jochim (1976) predicted equal balance (50/50) between the goals of attaining a secure income and low-cost aggregation of population, we propose that people may give greater or lesser cultural weight to these economic decisions. We simulate this change by increasing the relative importance of achieving low-cost population aggregation (with a numerical weighting factor) from 0.1 to 2 times the importance of gaining a secure income. The results are summarized on a seasonal basis, in terms of their effects on proportional resource use and population size:

Winter (Figure 12):

- Doubling the importance of low-cost aggregation results in a dramatic increase in elk proportional use (from almost 0 to 35 percent).
- Roundfish use decreases significantly (from about 60 to 20 percent).

Figure 12. Proportional Resource Use and Population in Winter, with Assumed Change in the Importance of Achieving a Low-Cost Population Aggregation. (Note that the X-Axis Starts with the Low-Cost Goal Being One-Tenth as Important as a Secure Income and Ends with Low-Cost Being Twice as Important.)

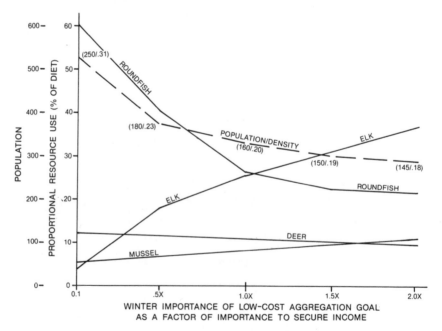

- Simultaneously, aspired winter population levels decrease almost by half (42 percent), from 250 to 145 people, if lower-cost but less secure procurement strategies are employed.
- The population decrease is due to the associated increase in the desired proportional use of mussel (up to 8.5 percent of winter diet).

The dramatic increase in elk use and lower population maintenance probably reflect the economic goal emphasis observed in the earlier (before 3000 BP) time periods (St. Mungo and Old Cordilleran). At these times, a lower cost for winter population aggregation may have been valued much more than in the following time periods, when winter secure income (e.g., roundfish) may have increased in importance because of resource stress created by human population growth and territorial circumscription.

Spring:

- Increasing importance of low-cost aggregation noticeably increases the proportional use of elk (from 0 to 20 percent) and to some degree the use of fur seal (from 1 to 4 percent) and sea lion (from 1 to 8 percent), but decreases the use of roundfish (from 50 to 20 percent).
- Population levels drop from 350 to 200 people, again because of an increase in desired proportional use of mussel.

Summer:

- Increased importance of low-cost population aggregation results in greater proportional use of halibut/flatfish (from 30 to 50 percent).
- Elk use also increases (from 1 to 10 percent) and this effect lessens a still greater potential emphasis on halibut.
- Population levels decrease from 410 to 340 people, again due to increase in desired mussel use.

Fall:

- Salmon and elk use increases, as mussel and roundfish use decreases.
- As mussel use decreases in favor of salmon, population increases from 400 to 800 people.

Fall is the only season in which increased low-cost aggregation results in higher population levels. This particular test is significant in projecting the future effects of storage practices as they increasingly focus on fall riverine salmon resources.

From the above decision-making sensitivity tests, we conclude that economic goal changes produce noteworthy shifts in proportional resource use for each season. These latter changes are especially significant in winter and spring, when greater economic diversity is predicted. At least over short periods, as much as twice the winter/spring population might be maintained if achieving low-cost population aggregation is made one-tenth as important as pursuing a secure income. In contrast, low-cost aggregation would be more important than secure income in fall, when the use of salmon increases sufficiently to decrease mussel desirability and thus increases (doubles) aspired fall population levels. Clearly, then, socioeconomic goals can set standards that determine supportable populations, given limits of resource availability. These standards may regulate winter population sizes at lower naturally-supportable sizes or may encourage larger winter populations (supported at greater costs) that may cause stress on some local resources through overexploitation. Low-cost standards may also increase fall use of salmon and increase population levels.

As we will discuss later, in our evaluation of coast-wide economic changes, findings for winter resource use have implications for explanations of economic changes observed in the archaeological record between 5000 and 3000 BP (the Old Cordilleran and St. Mungo cultural time periods). The common pattern observed is decreased use of land mammals and increased use of shellfish, fisheries, and sea mammals. In our modeling, changes in shellfish or land mammal densities have little effect on proportional resource use, but changes in economic goal orientation definitely do have such an effect. Lowering aspirations for low-cost population aggregation and increasing the goal of maintaining a secure income would result in increased use of roundfish and halibut/flatfish and decreased emphasis on elk. Such a goal change, in conjunction with a stabilizing and circumscribed human population density at about this time (4000–5000 BP), would be expected to initiate changes leading into the formative period of classic southern Northwest Coast cultural development (Locarno Beach cultural time period and beyond).

Findings for fall resource use have implications for explaining economic changes observed in the archaeological record somewhere between 3000 and 1000 BP (Locarno Beach, Marpole, and Gulf of Georgia cultural types). Increased use of salmon and fall salmon storage, postulated during this time period, may be initiated by aspirations for low-cost aggregations, given means of sustaining a secure income with winter resources.

MODEL 2: PROPORTIONAL RESOURCE USE, SETTLEMENT, AND POPULATION WITH STORAGE TECHNOLOGY

The storage model (Model 2) is constructed with relatively simple programming modifications of Model 1 (Croes & Hackenberger 1985: Appendix 3). In Model 2, seasonal cycles have been programmed to occur through a sequence of several years. This model allows the exploration of resource population trends that would be affected by intensified human use (e.g., possible resource depletion). Model 2 requires accurate estimates of the net productivity rates of resources, which are programmed to offset the effects of harvesting rates practiced by human populations. By modeling long-term trends in resources and human population levels, we can also propose ideas of how people may perceive long-term (periods up to 100 years) resource trends and forecast their own storage needs.

Like Model 1, Model 2 estimates proportional resource use, population maintenance, and site placement. In addition, Model 2 predicts proportional resource procurement for both immediate use and storage for use in subsequent seasons. Model 2 accounts for levels of stored resources in determining aspired population levels. Figure 6 presents a general flowchart depicting the relationships between variables used to simulate economic decision making, resource populations, human resource use, and human population maintenance. The outcome of this modeling provides a set of assumptions regarding the adaptive advantage of storage practices for increasing human populations along the southern Northwest Coast.

Proportional Resource Procurement

The estimated proportion of resource calories procured in summer and fall for use in winter and spring is graphically illustrated in Figure 13. Shaded areas represent possible changes in proportional procurement represented in a computer run for over 50 years. In winter and spring, when shellfish populations are most susceptible to overexploitation (given desired levels of use), shellfish densities can be depleted in the Hoko region to levels where their use would have to be greatly reduced. In our model, a population of 160 people (using stored resources) could overexploit shellfish within 40 years by using 15–20 percent of the available shellfish population each year, if the shellfish population has a net reproductivity of 15–20 percent (witness the 25-year cycle with 330 persons, Figure 14). Therefore, winter and spring shellfish procurement can vary between 20 and 0 percent of resource procurement.

Halibut and salmon procurement intensified with storage, as enlarging human populations increased harvesting pressure on other resources, especially deer/elk, roundfish, and shellfish, decreasing their relative availability. In Model 1, halibut made up 50 percent of summer procurement for immediate consumption, and salmon made up 55 percent of procurement for fall consumption. With storage and increased human population levels, summer/fall proportional procurement emphases would increase to 80 and 100 percent for halibut and salmon, respectively. Table 3 shows the ranked order of resource procurement for each season. (Note that we

Figure 13. Proportional Resource Procurement by Season as Predicted with Model 2 Storage Programming. (Shaded Areas Illustrate Range of Variation over 50 or More Years; Absolute Resource Quantities Are Estimated for a Population of 160.)

HOKO RIVER REGION STORAGE MODEL

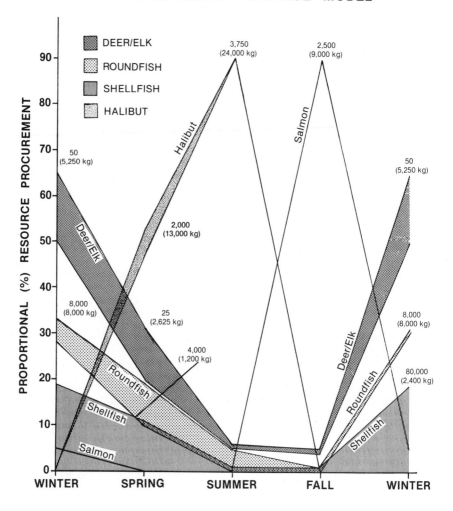

are discussing procurement, not consumption, as we add a storage emphasis.)

In Model 2, roundfish can be overharvested to a degree, as well. Therefore, deer and elk make up the greatest amount of fresh resources procured in winter and spring. If the low-cost population aggregation goal were weighted more important than secure income prior to local population

Figure 14. Projected 25-Year Shellfish Depletion Cycle with a Simulated Storage Economy and the Resulting Regional Human Population of 330 Individuals (0.2 Persons/km^2)

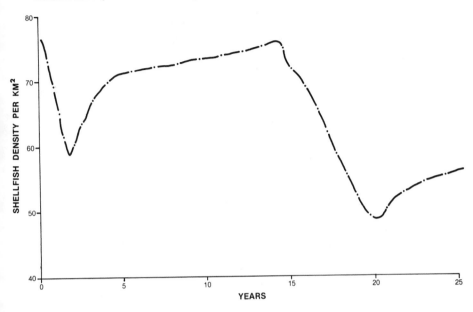

circumscription, then deer and elk, not shellfish, might have been more sensitive to depletion (a situation potentially common in the Old Cordilleran/St. Mungo time periods). These earlier circumstances possibly encouraged population budding-off or migration in addition to intensified population controls.

If sea mammal densities and aggregations had been higher within the Straits in spring, as they are on the outer coast, then procurement of these resources might have been significantly increased when stored resources were available. Coincidentally, these observations on resource procurement fit with the idea that, when stored resources (highly secure income) are available, resource procurement can focus on less certain (greater search effort and risk) but lower-cost resources (greater capture yields). This pattern can explain the eventual focus on large sea mammals (whale, fur seal, and sea lion) developed through the historic period among the West Coast Makah/Nootkan, whose territories are closest to sea mammal migration routes along the outer coast.

In summary, we predict from storage modeling that (1) population circumscription would require greater use of locally sensitive shellfish, deer/elk, and roundfish resources, which would become increasingly overexploited; (2) halibut and salmon procurement become intensified for both use in their respective seasons and storage for use in winter and early spring; and (3) with increased security of subsistence through storage, sea mammal hunting, which entails higher risk but greater yield, would be emphasized along the west coast migration routes. These trends may be common to the evolution of late prehistoric and ethnohistoric Northwest Coast resource-use patterns.

Population Maintenance

We propose several ways of measuring storage needs for population maintenance. These formulations focus on principles for forecasting the need for stored resources on the basis of remembered information about past resource availability and previous population levels. Out of several possibilities, we chose three forecasting alternatives. Each alternative compares an aspired human population level with the lowest population level for winter or spring (without storage) remembered on the basis of past resource availability.

Although several cultural variables can be used in modeling human memory, we have chosen to simulate memory with an equation that retains the lowest estimate for human population (as calculated in Model 1) while the program progresses on a year-to-year basis (Croes & Hackenberger 1985: Appendices 2 and 3). Each of our three alternatives, however, is developed by assuming a different means for judging aspired population levels. The alternatives are defined as follows:

1. Lowest remembered population, with past winter or spring pro-curement compared to the current year's winter and spring pro-curement.
2. Lowest remembered population, with past winter or spring pro-curement compared to current population levels supported with storage.
3. Lowest remembered population, with past winter or spring pro-curement compared to highest procurement population in summer and fall.

All three forecasting procedures result in storage of resources in suf-ficient amounts to support 800–900 people (maximum of 1 person/km^2 of land). In each alternative, a very low winter and spring population level is remembered on the basis of a year or more of overexploitation of shell-fish. Subsequently, an increasing amount of resource storage is imple-mented when shellfish densities are reduced through overuse in winter and spring. Storage of resources procured in summer and fall increases through time at a pace consistent with human population increases.

Human population can increase from 250 ($0.3/km^2$) to 800–900 people ($1/km^2$) in as little as 100 years, given a short-term growth rate of 4 percent per year. This rate is equivalent to 5 groups of 50 people in the Hoko region increasing to 5 groups of up to 180. This growth rate is possible with a 7.5 percent annual birth rate (30 percent of fertile women having children each season) and a 3.5 percent annual death rate sustained for the 100-year period. With a net annual growth of only 0.1 percent, this magnitude of population increase might take up to 1,000 years. We suggest that this may have occurred between 4000 and 3000 BP—the St. Mungo time period (Matson 1981).

The theoretical upper limit of human population with storage is controlled by the availability of spring/summer halibut and flatfish and the degree to which the use of this resource lowers the need to use shellfish and to store fall river salmon for winter and early spring. Without spring/ summer flatfish storage, fall salmon availability would determine the maximum population level—given that shellfish use still directly limits the number of people in winter and spring supportable on the basis of fresh resources. With depletion of shellfish (due to higher human population levels with storage), their proportional use declines to the point at which halibut and salmon are more critical limiters of summer and fall populations. These resource-rich seasons are ones in which stored resources would not be greatly used, assuming complete use or spoilage of the previous year's provisions.

Absolute Resource Procurement Estimates for Storage-based Populations

With an estimated storage-based upper limit of 900 people in the Hoko region, our models predict that up to 30,000 halibut (190,000 kg) are procured for use in summer, and 25,000 salmon (90,000 kg) are procured for use in fall. Up to 25,000 halibut and 20,000 salmon are stored. Some 4,000 roundfish are also taken for consumption in summer and 2,000 for storage, although roundfish would also be taken fresh in winter and spring. These figures indicate relatively greater use of salmon than those given for 160 people because, with increased human population, more salmon must be procured and stored for spring use. However, similar levels of halibut and salmon procurement are indicated at our highest predicted population size. A greater emphasis on halibut than salmon is the result of earlier and greater availability of halibut and the greater need for stored resources in winter. Obviously, a "wise" procedure would be to "bank" (literally) on summer flatfish resources for winter and adjust fall salmon fishing needs according to the amount of flatfish processed through the summer.

At these levels of procurement, up to 50 percent of the regional halibut population and 70 percent of the riverine salmon population would be procured. Therefore, to predict theoretical limits of population growth based on storage, we must justify our high levels of harvesting efficiency for salmon and halibut or explore lower harvesting levels in the model to test for effects on proportional resource use and human population maintenance.

Although estimates of harvesting efficiency for these resources are important in predicting human population growth above 800–900 people, one must also carefully assess yearly fluctuations in all resource populations, especially halibut and salmon. These upper human population figures indicate the use of about 200 fish/person for an entire year, or about 1,000 kg/person—an average catch of about 4–5 fish/fisherperson/day throughout the summer and fall. In winter, each person would also use 2,666 shellfish (about $9m^2$ of mussels/person/winter) or about 80 kg of shellfish meat.

Settlement

With increased proportional procurement of deer/elk, halibut, salmon, and roundfish, the pull of these resources is increased, but the ranked ordering of each resource is similar to results for Model 1 (see Table 4). Therefore, general geographic settlement patterns would remain similar, although size of settlement populations would increase (see Figure 10).

ARCHAEOLOGICAL EVALUATION OF THE HOKO RIVER REGION MODELS

Testing of our economic decision models and their implications for economic and social change in the Hoko River region presently is the main focus of the Hoko research program (see Wigen & Stucki, this volume). Here, we offer the initial stage of our model testing, reflecting the preliminary implications of evaluating the broad regional economic patterns and change on the Northwest Coast. Additional objectives are to identify the types of archaeological data needed to test economic decision models and to suggest ways to improve collection of such data.

Using the Hoko complex data alone, we cannot expect an exact fit between the sites' data and our predictions for regional patterns. We also are aware of the many problems in estimating resource food values from faunal remains (Klein & Cruz-Uribe 1984, Grayson 1984). For these reasons, we cannot yet statistically test the degree of fit between model predictions and archaeological data. However, the nature of our evaluation requires use of these estimates, and ongoing developments in archaeological faunal analysis will allow their future refinements. By exploring general patterns of the Hoko site data, we do in fact demonstrate the validity (usefulness) of our modeling for interpreting the archaeological record and can recommend data recovery procedures for future and continued site specific investigations.

Using available site survey data, we first test site location and population size estimates. We also examine predicted proportional resource use by analyzing categories of resource remains recovered at the two Hoko River sites representing over a 3,000-year span. Finally, we discuss how our data relate to similar time periods represented at other sites along the southern Northwest Coast.

Overview of Regional Site Location and Estimated Population Size

Assuming $10m^2$ of site extent/person (Miller 1983), we can estimate population sizes at the six winter villages identified in our overall region (Figure 4). The estimated areas of these village sites provide population predictions of 200–800 people/winter village, a number consistent with overall ethnohistoric population projections. The ten major resource camps have areas reflecting population estimates of 15–75 people/camp, whereas the 14 minor camps would be occupied by as few as five people (Figure 4).

If contemporaneous, the known and located winter villages in the overall region may represent a total regional population size of 1,200–4,000 and a density of about $1.5–3.3/km^2$ of land. The lower estimates are consistent with model predictions for population density in the Hoko catchment area, and the upper limits are similar to the ethnohistoric estimates discussed earlier. Only about 150–750 people would be represented by the surface dimensions of all recorded major and minor campsites. This discrepancy may indicate that (1) many camp sites remain undiscovered, (2) "winter" villages have fewer persons/m^2 of surface compared to camps, or (3) as much as one-fourth to two-thirds of the population remains in the "winter" village year-round, as indicated for protohistoric "winter" villages along the West Coast (James Haggarty, personal communication).

The estimated lower limit of population density for the region ($1.5/km^2$) nears the ethnohistoric population estimate (Jewitt 1815:39) as well as the population density predicted by our Model 2 ($1/km^2$). Therefore, the first level of regional site data analysis appears to correspond with the conservative projections.

3000–2200 BP: Proportional Resource Use, Hoko River Wet/Dry Site

The Hoko wet/dry site faunal remains reveal a distinct and seasonal economic emphasis on offshore fishing, dependent upon a well-developed technology for hook-and-line procurement of flatfish and roundfish (Figure 15); over 200 composite (flatfish/halibut) and 100 bentwood (roundfish/ Pacific cod) fishhooks have been recovered (see Hoff 1980). The general site analysis provides information consistent with our postulates regarding proportional resource procurement predicted with our storage Model 2. At Hoko River—and, we suggest, in many other coastal sites of this Locarno Beach time period and style—use of riverine salmon, though seasonally important, may have been less emphasized in initial *storage-based* economies. Perhaps this emphasis on riverine salmon developed later, after an intensification of offshore fisheries, as storage practices continued to expand, possibly because of the overexploitation of winter resources (primarily shellfish) and/or further population increases.

Figure 15. Frequency of Identified Fish Bones Recovered from the Hoko River Site. (Note the High Emphasis on Offshore Flatfishes and Round-fishes.)

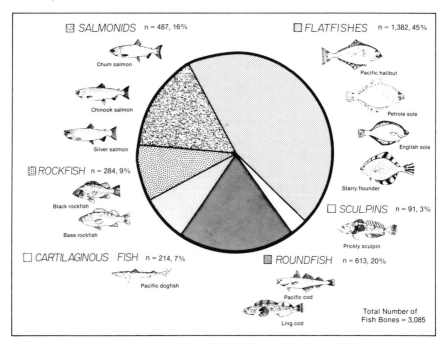

At the Hoko River wet site, approximately 13m^3 have been excavated directly from 28 well-separated and preserved vegetal mat strata (dating 3000–2200 BP; see Stucki 1983). Combined, these strata have thus far yielded 3,322 identifiable and analyzed fish, waterfowl, and land/sea mammal faunal elements; shellfish are rarely preserved in these water-logged deposits, though occasional shellfish samples demonstrate that a wide range of species were collected (Tucker 1984). Using meat-weight estimates per element, Table 5 presents estimates of proportional resource use from the nine best-represented layers (each containing 9 percent or more of the faunal elements recovered). These vegetal mats contain cultural refuse discarded along sequential shores of fishing camps located upon a depositional river point-bar (Stucki 1983).

Land mammals (9 percent), sea mammals (5 percent), and waterfowl (6 percent) constitute 20 percent of resource use by meat-weight. This general use of nonfisheries resources best fits spring/summer, whether for Model 1 or 2. Since the larger mammal elements are infrequent and waterfowl are expected to be consistently used in all seasons, less significance can be given to these data.

In terms of fisheries, halibut/flatfish overwhelmingly constituted the highest percentage of resource use, averaging 53 percent, followed by roundfish (15 percent) and salmon (15 percent). Since flatfish and roundfish (averaging 68 percent of use) are pursued offshore and the salmon may also be caught offshore, we can expect that the procurement emphasis is not riverine. Halibut and Pacific cod may be obtained in similar offshore areas (soft bottom areas or banks) using the two distinct hook types, composites for halibut and bentwood for Pacific cod (Hoff 1980).

Assuming a spring through fall occupation at the wet site, the pre-storage model (Model 1) predicts an average of about 19 percent use of salmon, 25 percent use of roundfish, and 23 percent use of flatfish. These predicted proportions differ from observed values for these fish (15/15/53 percent; Table 5); halibut/flatfish occur in greater proportions than expected. This discrepancy may be due to the site occupation's having typically begun or increased in size in late spring or early summer, when halibut use is expected to be high (approximately 18–46 percent use), possibly in combination with offshore salmon (as opposed to fall riverine salmon).

The storage model (Model 2) predicts a fishmeat weight ratio of 0.375 salmon to 0.05 roundfish to 1 flatfish, based on resource procurement. Therefore, wet site data for estimated fishmeat weight ratio (0.28:0.28:1) differ from those predicted. Roundfish occur in higher percentages than predicted by Model 2, whereas salmon occur in lower than expected percentages. Considering the storage assumption of Model 2, we would expect that storage was practiced at Hoko and that camp occupations began in

Table 5. Percentage of Resource Use by Wet Site Level Estimated from Meat-Weight, Using MNI for Mammals and Element Counts for Fish and Waterfowl

Estimated Time Period	Level	Roundfish	Salmon	Halibut & Flatfish	Deer & Elk	Sea Mammal	Waterfowl
2,200 BP	9 C	30	4	52	16	0	14
	8 AE	13	19	67	0	0	0
	7 AN	19	18	27	13	19	4
	6 AO	22	15	24	30	0	8
	5 AP	5	37	52	0	0	6
	4 AV	12	8	70	0	0	8
	3 AX	1	1	48	24	24	2
	2 AZ	16	9	63	0	4	8
3,000 BP	1 AZZ	11	22	59	0	0	7
	X̄	15	15	53	9	5	6

early spring, with a subsequently greater reliance on sun-drying spring/summer halibut for winter use.

Several taphonomic expectations, such as possible differential disposal of roundfish, flatfish, and salmon remains, must be examined. If fish are being thoroughly processed for drying and storage, then considerable skeletal elements may be removed from the site in dried fish, and fish used during site occupation would result in more of their skeletal elements being discarded on location. Examination of types of elements reveals more flatfish (28 percent) than salmon (12 percent) cranial bones being deposited in comparison to their postcranial remains. Many flatfish appear to have been brought to the site and processed for drying, the heads being possibly consumed and discarded into the river and backbone sections dried, whereas salmon brought to the site may have been typically eaten fresh and all their remains discarded. This procedure may be expected to result in conserving the majority of the flatfish meat for storage but consuming fresh ocean-caught salmon, which are fatty and poor for drying.

Comparing predictions of Models 1 and 2 with wet deposit faunal remains suggests that halibut storage was emphasized, with an opportunistic emphasis on "low-cost" roundfish and offshore salmon for fresh consumption. Seasonal site occupation generally began by mid-spring. Examination of the "dry" onshore campsite areas reveals post mold and smudge fire features in proposed drying rack areas, with fish processing tools in the immediate vicinity—additionally supporting the perceived emphasis on drying flatfish (Gross 1986).

3000–2200 BP: Wet/Dry Site Population Estimates

Using an analogy to an existing river point-bar straight across the river (Figure 1), believed to approximate the original point-bar on which the Hoko fishing camp was situated (Stucki 1983), we estimate that up to 100m^2 of shoreline vegetal mat layer may form along the prehistoric camp per depositional period. Presently excavated vegetal mat volumes may represent a sample as small as 1 percent of the original area. Therefore, we increase wet sample values by a factor of about 100 in order to estimate absolute amounts of prehistoric discarding of faunal remains. From the rough projections, up to 1,394,800,000 calories may be expected from faunal remains discarded along the prehistoric point-bar camp. As many as eight people could be supported for 500 years of successive 6-month (double) seasons on the caloric equivalent estimated for recovered remains (@ 182,500 calories/person/3-month season).

If remains were discarded uniformly across dry living area deposit (75 percent of the point-bar) as well as wet vegetal layers (25 percent of the point-bar), then an occupation of up to 24 people may be represented.

Larger occupation sizes can be predicted, since much thicker, though much less well preserved, midden deposits have been found to be accumulated in the onshore campsite areas (Gross 1984, 1986). Unfortunately, no bone or shell was preserved in these non-waterlogged, "dry" middens.

A living surface up to $2,640m^2$ may have existed for the actual point-bar camp. At $10m^2$ of open site area per person, this area would allow a population as large as 265. However, based on Model 1, we can predict aggregations of *at least* 25 people in each resource campsite during the spring/summer, and from Model 2, we would expect as many as 75 persons as a task grouping at a storage processing camp such as Hoko. Since 2200–3000 BP ago may have been the formative period for a storage-based economy, possibly as many as 50 persons occupied the early camp.

3000–2200 BP: Settlement Patterns

Based on Models 1 and 2, the settlement model would indicate a use of the Hoko vicinity as a spring/summer offshore-fishing camp and a fall riverine salmon-fishing camp (Figure 10). The first aspect of this model appears to be supported at the wet site. Suggestions for the lack of fall emphasis include: (1) the fall base camp was located elsewhere at this time or (2) the emphasis in these early storage-based economies was primarily on offshore fishing and only secondarily on riverine salmon. We support the second explanation as part of a hypothetical evolutionary sequence, as reflected from evaluation of the later, downriver rockshelter.

900–100 BP: Proportional Resource Use, Hoko Rockshelter Site

The Hoko Rockshelter shell midden, in sharp contrast to the earlier Hoko River wet/dry site, has abundant preservation of vertebrate fauna (over 70,000 analyzed) and invertebrate fauna (over 500,000 elements tabulated). We shall first examine the absolute estimate of approximately 800 years of resource use, as revealed through a highly complex series of strata composing up to 3.3m thickness of shell midden deposit (Stucki 1985). Since shellfish are well-represented, and since our modeling indicates it is a highly significant resource in evolutionary trends in economic decision making, we discuss shellfish distribution first and then address the overall distribution of other fauna.

Shellfish

Since our modeling projects this resource as a population limiter and also as being sensitive to overexploitation, we have begun to carefully examine the pattern of its use in the site. Our first data set consists of the

estimated meat-weight from a 1 × 1m test unit excavated in arbitrary 10-
and 5-cm levels to a depth of 265cm (Miller 1983). We also have examined
the standardized estimated mussel meat-weight versus that of other major
shellfish taxa (Miller 1983:121–125). A second data set is 61 column samples (20cm × 10cm × the natural thickness of strata excavated in 61
trench profile locations; see Tucker 1984), providing natural stratigraphic
level distributions of shellfish. From both data sets, the estimated mussel
meat-weight averages about 67–68 percent of the total meat-weight of all
rockshelter shellfish species. Clams contribute 12–24 percent and barnacles
4–7 percent of the estimated meat-weight.

These estimates correspond to predictions of a least-cost resource use
model formulated specifically to shellfish distributions at the Hoko River
mouth (Miller 1983). The predicted and observed proportions translate
into a ratio of about 5–10g of mussel meat/3g clam/1g barnacle meat.

Model 1 programs, with separate variables of mussel, clam, and barnacle
(as well as other resources), estimate a meat ratio of 1g mussel/3g clam/
0.5g barnacle. The difference between our expectations and Miller's (1983)
predictions and corresponding archaeological estimates stems from our
larger modeling estimate for the *regional* density of clams compared to
the lower clam densities known for the immediate Hoko River mouth locale. However, in two test unit levels and seven column samples, the
estimated meat-weight of clams, snails, and/or barnacle exceeds the estimated meat-weight of mussel. Although column samples indicate that
the extreme of this variation occurs in the upper portion of rockshelter
layers, the column samples and test unit levels combined suggest that
relatively high barnacle, clam, and snail concentrations occur in a series
of layers defined as stratigraphic State No. 5 (Stucki 1985; ''Depositional
Period 5'' in Wigen & Stucki, this volume). As stratigraphically defined,
this state or period contains the thickest and most extensive shell layer
in the rockshelter (Stucki 1985). In the two test unit levels where the meat-
weight estimate for mussels is less than that for other shellfish species,
this reversal appears to be related to an increased absolute number of
clam, barnacle, and snail, combined with mid-range values for absolute
mussel meat-weight estimates. Since barnacle and snail occur in protected
rockshelf ecounits with mussels (Figure 7), the reduced frequency of mussels suggests that they were less available.

Substantial support of a mussel depletion hypothesis for stratigraphic
State 5 has been made through studies of mussel age ranges at harvest
(Hurst 1986). When mussel overexploitation occurs and use of other species increases, the age of the average mussel harvested should also decrease. The 1985 excavation of the rockshelter deep-interior provided excellent whole, uncrushed shell specimens for studying age and size at
harvest. The dominant species *(M. californicus)* exhibited its lowest age

and size averages in stratigraphic State 5, indicating heavy harvesting and overexploitation. A decrease in shell size with a corresponding decrease in age begins in the early stages of State 5 and terminates with a dramatic decrease in age at the end of this state, averaging 3.0 years at harvest compared with a site mean of 6.7 years (Hurst 1986). In fact, throughout the top four states so far tested (of eight total), *M. californicus* age remains low, averaging less than 7.0 years. This figure, combined with the fact that this species typically reaches a *minimum* of 7–20 years and may potentially reach 50–100 years in age (Suchanek 1981:147), indicates a consistent human pressure on this species and an ongoing potential for periodic overuse and/or natural destruction (e.g., by disease and storm damage), causing drastically reduced availability.

To some degree, shellfish data can also be used to project percentage proportional use at the site. Taking rockshelter living floor space as about 50m^2, Miller (1983) estimates that groups of 5–8 people may have inhabited the interior (versus the entire outer area) at any one time. If we (a) use an estimate of 7 people, (b) take the calculated mean of 246,375 calories of shellfishmeat/m^3 of rockshelter deposit (600m^3 total), (c) assume 900 calories/kg of shellfish meat and a need of 182,500 calories/person/season ($\times$ 2 seasons), and (d) also estimate at least 800 years of seasonal rockshelter use—then shellfish averages 7 percent of total caloric intake during each two-season occupation period.

This estimate is approximate for several reasons. Most important among these, excluding sampling bias, are the possibilities that (1) the shelter was not occupied every year, (2) it was occupied for more than two seasons each year, (3) shellfish processing represented in the rockshelter fed more people than those who occupied the rockshelter, (4) the rate of shellfish accumulation was discontinuous or variable, and (5) not all the shellfish processing occurred at the shelter. In the first case, if the deposits represent as few as 400 years of double-season use, then shellfish would amount to about 14 percent of the seasonal diet. In the second and third cases, if as many as three seasons of use per year are represented, or if 2–3 times more people were fed by the seven shellfish processors, then shellfish use might represent as little as 2–5 percent of these people's diets. However, if all of the first three possibilities apply, then shellfish use would still contribute 2–14 percent of the seasonal diet. If alternative (4) or (5) obtained, then in some periods shellfish may have made up as little as 1 percent or as much as 30 percent of the diet. These possible extremes are suggested by observed ranges for shellfish meat-weight/m^3 in column samples (Table 6). This variation is relevant in testing our predictions concerning long-term and cyclic overexploitation of shellfish.

Despite the numerous calculations and the series of assumptions leading to our averaged estimate of 2–14 percent shellfish in the diet, we conclude

Table 6. Mean Meat-Weight (g)/10cm³ from Column Samples,
by Depositional State[a]

Depositional State	Number of Samples	Mean Meat-Weight (g)/10cm³		
		Mussel	Barnacle	Clams
8	10	120	10	24
7	1	61	0	0
6	21	182	40	68
5	8	444	26	262
4	5	183	27	64
3	10	333	3	45
2	3	70	0	60
1	3	87	17	64
Overall	N = 61	219	22	81

[a]"Depositional States" (Stucki 1985) or "Depositional Periods" (Wigen & Stucki, this volume) are major stratigraphic deposits indicative of heavy rockshelter use periods.

that the Model 1 prediction of a consistent seasonal use of about 10–18 percent use of shellfish throughout the year is slightly high for the Rockshelter. More importantly, however, we interpret the range of shellfish meat/m³ in different states within the Rockshelter as evidence supporting the considerable fluctuation in shellfish procurement predicted by Model 2 (Table 6). The fall through winter variation in Model 2 resource procurement consisted of a range of 0–20 percent shellfish use because of overexploitation of local shellfish populations. Besides the shellfish variability noted in the rockshelter, the *M. californicus* and *M. edulis* mussel data reveal a consistent fall/early-winter season of harvest in eight out of nine areas sampled in the four upper states within the Rockshelter deep-interior (Hurst 1986). This variability and the seasonality data best reflect a Model 2 fall/winter prediction.

Fish

Using the calories/m³ for each major fish resource, derived from element counts (NISP)—and again assuming the above conditions regarding the nature and length of rockshelter occupations—we have calculated the following estimates for seasonal proportional resource use: roundfish, 12–46 percent; salmon, 9–68 percent; halibut, 2–7 percent (Table 7). Since sizable excavation samples mainly have been derived from upper stratigraphic States (4–8), the more meaningful proportional resource use averages are calculated from these States as follows: roundfish, 19 percent; salmon, 59 percent; and halibut, 5 percent (Table 7).

These fish use proportions place the main site use emphasis on fall/

Table 7. Percentage of Resource Use by State, Derived from Rockshelter Faunal Remains Estimated in Calories/m^3

Depositional State[a]	Shellfish[b]	Roundfish[c]	Salmon[c]	Halibut & Flatfish[c]	Waterfowl[c]	Fur & Harbor Seal[d]	Deer & Elk[d]	Sea Lion[d]
8	3	12	68	4	4	3	2	4
7	1	15	65	3	2	6	4	3
6	2	19	58	5	5	5	3	3
5	5	26	50	7	3	4	4	2
4	3	23	56	4	7	3	4	0
X̄ 4-8[e]	(3)	(19)	(59)	(5)	(4)	(4)	(3)	(2)
3	7	16	39	7	4	7	6	13
2	1	42	36	5	5	3	7	0
1	6	46	9	2	2	0	11	24
X̄ 1-8	(4)	(25)	(48)	(5)	(4)	(4)	(5)	(6)

a "Depositional States" (Stucki 1985) or "Depositional Periods" (Wigen & Stucki, this volume) are major stratigraphic deposits indicative of heavy rockshelter use periods.
b Shellfish data are based on mean meat-weight/10cm^3 in 61 column samples (Table 6).
c Fish and waterfowl caloric estimates are based on element counts/m^3 (Wigen & Stucki, this volume).
d Land and sea mammal caloric estimates are based on MNI/m^3 (Wigen & Stucki, this volume).
e States 4-8 have a larger proportional sample (m^3) represented for site excavation area; therefore, they are used as the best representative sample.

70

early winter, with calculations ranging somewhere between Model 1 and 2. The average roundfish use (19 percent) is below Model 1 year-round estimates, but "fits" a late fall/early winter Model 2 prediction. The salmon estimate of as much as 68 percent and average of 59 percent is higher than expected from Model 1 in fall (52 percent) but lower than expected for Model 2 fall (92 percent), but fits well in a late fall/early winter estimation (50–60 percent). Halibut remains suggest they were processed and dried (possibly in earlier spring/summer seasons) and brought to the site in a preserved form for consumption, resulting in mostly post-cranial remains discarded at the site (Wigen 1985:14). This pattern is just the opposite from wet site remains, where flatfish cranial remains dominate, indicating drying for storage and probably consumption of heads fresh (page 65 above). If we assume that one element equals one fish entering the rockshelter deposits, halibut use is estimated to average only five percent—also fitting Model 1 and 2 predictions for early fall and late winter.

Waterfowl

Predictions for use of this resource average 4 percent, which is about as expected in most Model 1 or 2 seasons. This figure is also close to the average of 6 percent use calculated for the 2200 to 3000 BP period at the Hoko River Wet/Dry site (Table 5).

Sea and Land Mammals

Wigen (1985) interprets the significant presence of fur seal yearlings in the rockshelter as evidence for winter through spring use of the shelter. Fur seal MNI/m^3 represents an average of four percent use in the seasonal diet, with a range of 3–6 percent (Table 7). Though by bone elements (NISP) Wigen & Stucki (this volume) predict a probable increase in use of this species, our calories/m^3 percentage estimates, based on MNI, reflect a consistent dietary proportion through time. This figure relates best to the regional Model 1 prediction of 4 percent in spring. . Sea lion is expected to constitute 6 percent of the diet in winter/spring and the MNI/m^3 follows these estimates (Table 7).

Deer/elk combined comprise 5 percent of the seasonal diet based on average MNI/m^3. This estimate is less than the predicted lowest-use season (fall) in Model 1 (15 percent) but equal to the lowest use seasons (summer/fall) in Model 2 (5–6 percent). If the Model 2 fall/winter use estimates (30–40 percent) are applied, then the prediction greatly exceeds the 5 percent estimates for the rockshelter. Therefore, an early-fall Model 2 estimate may apply best.

Proportional Resource Use by Stratigraphic States (or Depositional Periods)

Proportional resource-use estimates are calculated by depositional states in Table 7. The figures are given for each state independently of an estimated time period and site population creating the layer formations. (Radiocarbon dates currently are being processed.) This type of estimate for proportional resource use therefore differs from the above absolute estimates given on the basis of several assumptions regarding the nature and length of rockshelter occupations.

Since States 1 through 3 have a relatively small sample, most attention is again given to upper States 4 through 8. States 4–8 combined represent a shift to relatively high salmon use with decreasing use of roundfish. Whereas proportional use of seal, sea lion, and shellfish fluctuate between states, general trends can be seen in the increased use of salmon and decreased proportional use of roundfish (Figure 16), as well as a less patterned decrease in deer/elk use (Table 7). Proportional use of salmon and roundfish, if fish elements are accurate indicators of resource use (see caution in Wigen & Stucki, this volume), may be used to infer gradually increasing reliance on salmon, possibly taken from the river and by trolling in offshore open waters, and decreasing importance of nearshore fishing for roundfish. Though fur seal and harbor seal gradually increase in proportional use to State 7, they do not appear to reflect (by MNI) a rapid increase in dietary proportion. By element count (NISP), though, they do seem to increase dramatically (Wigen & Stucki, this volume). Waterfowl remain consistent at about 4 percent use. Model 2 anticipates the fluctuation in proportional use of shellfish. State 5, in particular, reflects variable shellfish use and potentially a marked period of increased exploitive pressure on California mussels (Hurst 1986).

The general pattern suggests increasing fall/winter occupation through time in order to best procure fall salmon entering the river at this location, and/or increased salmon trolling in all seasons. The projected increase in fur seal use from the site, based on element counts (NISP; see Wigen & Stucki, this volume) may indicate a progressive increase in stored resources (Model 2), allowing an increased focus on less certain (i.e., greater search effort and risk) but lower-cost resources with greater yield.

900–100 BP: Rockshelter Population Estimates

Since the food resources analyzed from the Hoko Rockshelter provide an average estimate of 8,309,496 calories/m^3 of rockshelter shellmidden deposit, we project 4,985,697,600 calories procured over 800 years, or an average of 6,232,122/year. If we assume one main season of occupation

Figure 16. Proportional Salmon Calories to Roundfish Calories, Using Estimates from Fish Elements

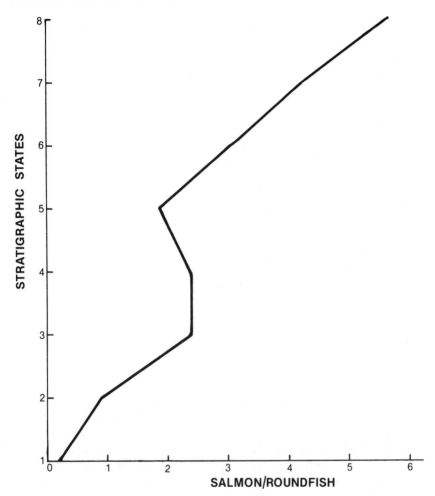

and 183,500 calories/person/season, then an average of 34 persons would be supported during an average season at the rockshelter. This estimate may be low, especially since not all food resources are measured (e.g., plant foods). However, this figure falls within the 15–75 people projected for major campsite types, based on their surface area (Figure 4). Using $10m^2$ of site extent per person (Miller 1983), the $342m^2$ of overall Hoko Rockshelter surface area also projects a population of 34 persons for the site.

900–100 BP: Settlement Pattern

Models 1 and 2 predict a use of the Hoko vicinity as both a spring/ summer offshore-halibut fishing camp and a fall riverine-salmon fishing camp (Figure 10). In contrast to the much earlier and separate Hoko River Wet/Dry site, the rockshelter supports the second aspect of modeling. Suggestions for the lack of a spring/summer emphasis include: (1) that camp may have been located elsewhere at this time or (2) the emphasis in the later storage-based economies was mainly on riverine salmon and only secondarily on sea mammals and offshore fishing. We support the second explanation as part of a hypothetical evolutionary sequence.

Summary of Hoko River Site Complex Data and Model Evaluations

In the Hoko River wet site, faunal data suggest the initial development of a Model 2 type resource storage pattern by 3000–2200 BP, with a particular focus on offshore halibut and roundfish and a much more variable use of salmon (which could also be derived mostly offshore). The later rockshelter shellmidden deposits provide preliminary data reflecting considerable fluctuations in the relative use of mussel and clam/barnacle/snail. This fluctuating distribution of a faunal category probably reflects cycles of shellfish overexploitation (especially of mussel, as indicated by low age at harvest). Shellfish are predicted to be critical as a human population limiter and thereby likely to be instrumental in an initial and early emphasis on storage practices. The rockshelter faunal distributions also may reflect a steady temporal increase in salmon fishing and fur seal hunting, with a correspondingly decreasing use of roundfish. As projected by our modeling, fall/winter salmon procurement will steadily increase in emphasis as storage becomes more important in maintaining human populations, and sea mammal hunting will correspondingly increase as storage activities expand. This increased emphasis on salmon probably would include offshore fishing by trolling and jigging, and offshore hunting for fur seal. This expanded emphasis may be reflected by the dramatically increased numbers of bone bipoints (60 percent of the artifacts versus 5 percent in earlier periods), representing components of offshore fishing equipment (especially trolling, jigging, and set-hook barbs) as well as harpoon points for hunting (Croes 1985).

CONCLUSION

We will now proceed through a set of hypotheses developed from our research and relate these statements to research in other regions of the Coast. We suggest a revised and general chronological explanation of economic and social evolution along the southern Northwest Coast.

1.   In modeling hypothetical prehistoric trends for this region, and probably for the entire coast, we postulate exponential population growth and eventual circumscription as significant factors affecting overall subsistence and settlement practices. From original occupation of this region until approximately 5000–4000 BP, populations probably remained small, hunting-gathering groups dispersing over the entire region. An initial exponential population growth, which may best be illustrated as a sigmoidal (S-shaped) curve, would have an initial *lag,* or slow growth, period after the first hunter-gatherer populations moved into this area. These groups would reflect the sparsely documented Pebble-Tool Tradition (Borden 1975, 1979; Figure 17, A).

2.   As these populations increased, the exponential population growth would have accelerated into a *log* phase, representing a rapid population growth and occupation (Figure 17, B). As increasing group sizes, relative to territory, caused carrying capacity pressures, subgroups moved over additional territories through migration and/or budding off. These smaller populations (characterized as people of the Olcott [Carlson 1983] or Old Cordilleran tradition [Matson 1981, 1983]) probably pursued economic

Figure 17.   Proposed Model of Exponential Population Growth with Northwest Coast Cultural "Phases/Types" Representing Stabilized Economic Plateaus or Stages Separated by Periods of Relatively Rapid Exponential Population Growth

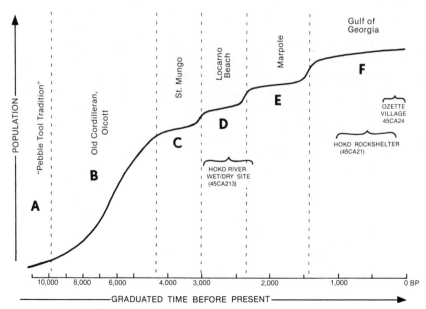

goals stressing a lower-cost population maintenance and less secure income, involving a relatively high (fall/winter/spring) proportional use of land mammals (elk and deer) and limited emphasis on winter fisheries, shellfish, and/or storage of summer or fall resources.

3.   As small groups expanded and regional circumscription occurred, population growth would begin to *plateau* and stabilize (Figure 17, C). A more conservative emphasis on achieving a secure income is expected to have occurred, characterized by intensified use of regional roundfish and halibut/flatfish fisheries and shellfish resources (but not necessarily by heavy reliance or emphasis on storage). This period is predicted to have occurred most likely 4000–3000 BP and archaeologically is best manifested in the St. Mungo period (Matson 1981, 1983). During this period, territorial circumscription led to intensified shellfish use, as observed in the development of greater accumulations of shellmidden site deposits. However, this increasingly desired (because of its secure income characteristics) resource is predictably sensitive to overuse. Therefore, problems of over-exploitation of shellfish territories could be expected toward the end of this time period.

4.   As populations continued to grow (even at very low net rates) and/ or shellfish resources were depleted, the emphasis on storage technologies involving late spring, summer, and fall resources would be adopted by some groups as an alternative to strict population controls. Given this new emphasis on storage, we would predict the formative period of ethnographic Southern Northwest Coast cultural evolution, the Locarno Beach Cultural Type (Mitchell 1971; Carlson 1983; Matson 1981, 1983). This period would include another rapid, exponential population growth leading into an economic stabilization reflected in Locarno "style" (Figure 17, D). During this formative period, intensified resource use and storage probably involved several major (mixed-goal) resources available in late spring and summer, and we expect that offshore flatfish/halibut and some roundfish were of greater importance than salmon to the *storage economy*. We would expect that the spring/summer flatfish received initial regionwide emphasis as a stored food because: (a) in many ways it is an easier and more consistent fishery to maintain when compared to upriver salmon fisheries (which require building and maintaining traps and moving the catch to the village); (b) initially it may have been more practical to "bank" on a spring/summer resource for winter with a secondary, as-necessary, emphasis on fall salmon; (c) sun drying in spring/summer was more dependable and, because of ultraviolet production of concentrated vitamin D, offshore fish become more nutritional for fall/winter use than if they were smoke-dried (Krantz 1981:409). Besides the obvious specialization in this spring/summer offshore fisheries at the Hoko River site, there appears to be an increased emphasis at other Locarno Beach sites in this

off- (or near-) shore (flatfish, roundfish, rockfish) fishery, not observed earlier or later (Stiefel 1985:196–198).

Given the potential need to intensify the use of several major types of coastal resources during this transitional period, and given the innovations in both equipment and storage technologies, we doubt that any special characteristics of using anadromous (or nonanadromous) fish populations in themselves required the development of a centralized authority to govern food production (Schalk 1977), such as often is needed for advanced forms of agricultural production. Like Matson (1981, 1983), we predict that conditions of resource depletion, combined with rapid growth of extended-family social units, promoted ownership of circumscribed resource territories. Thus, differential access to resources arose as the specific consequence of the need to manage resources, not people. Differential access to resources and extended-family maintenance of resource ownership and management resulted in the differential accumulation of wealth and social ranking. Whereas we dismiss arguments made for the significance of centralized authority as the result of organized labor to procure salmon (especially since salmon might have been a later economic storage focus, as in Marpole time periods), we leave open the possibility that social ranking, territory ownership, and the ritualized distribution of resources (i.e., ethnographic potlatching) were also adaptations to fluctuations in year-to-year availability of resources (Suttles 1968). These adaptations would have potentially taken early root or "matured" in the early Locarno Beach transition period in this region, since resource fluctuation is a phenomenon that would exaggerate the constant factors in shellfish resource depletion, affecting populations at this predicted threshold of rapid growth.

It is difficult to test archaeologically for the initiation of social ranking, territory ownership, and means of resource distribution, but some suggestion of social rank can be derived from clothing recovered from the Hoko River wet site. Specifically, the conical basketry hats from this site have different forms that may prefigure later ethnographic trends. A distinctive knob-top (n = 4) construction is recorded in contrast to a rounded or flat top form (n = 3). Ethnographically and at the late Ozette Village site (Figure 17, F), the higher-ranking owner of family territory and property wore a knob-top hat and commoners wore the flat-top forms. This pattern may be reflected in this similar contrast in hats seen 2,500–3,000 years earlier, in the transition period.

In this regard, recent work on the upper Skeena River, British Columbia, has revealed the 3,000-year-old Paul Mason village site (GdTc 16) with a series of preserved housepits. In comparing size, shape, and consistency of these housepits with those from later village sites in the area, Coupland (n.d.:20) has concluded that "their homogeneity in size and structure supports the model of an egalitarian social organization. If hereditary chiefs or high-ranking individuals existed at the Paul Mason site, their status was not reflected in their dwellings." Therefore, we conclude from available data that this period reflects some features of later social systems, but in a formative, initial sense only, not revealing the degree of hierarchy of later periods.

5.   Though we have an archaeological hiatus in the Hoko region during the next southern Northwest Coast cultural time period, the Marpole (2400–1400 BP), we can predict the economic evolution necessary to create the patterns recorded for this era (Mitchell 1971; Carlson 1983; Burley 1980; Matson 1981, 1983). As resource storage becomes increasingly part of the solution to economic and population pressures and resource fluctuations, a logical extension of the practice would be an increased emphasis on summer/fall resources, expanding overall storage production. At this time, a growing emphasis on riverine salmon resources and storage thereof is expected and, along with this, a locational shift of archaeological shell midden sites into riverine and estuarine areas. This type of settlement and site distribution along riverways (for instance, up the Fraser Delta) is characteristic of Marpole sites (Burley 1983). Such a rapid change would not require a major shift of peoples from upriver interior areas onto the coast (Burley 1983). Instead, *in situ* accelerated population pressure and mixing of interior-coastal ideas and techniques might act to expand production. As suggested by Mitchell (1971:52), the Marpole may well have developed a focus on riverine salmon fisheries never again equalled. This shift is predicted to be part of the solution to maintaining a desired standard of living while population pressures continued. We would expect another small but rapid population increase and a new adaptive economic plateau, representing the Marpole Phase (Figure 17, E).

6.   In the final period, the Gulf of Georgia Cultural Type/Phase, we would predict further intensification of offshore fisheries, including offshore salmon procurement. This intensification would be stimulated by increased emphasis on low-cost population aggregation (particularly in fall/winter), assuming that suitably secure income (stored resources) were well established. A coastwide emphasis on bone technologies and particularly on bone points becomes prevalent (averaging over 60 percent of the collections, whereas in early periods—especially Marpole and Locarno Beach—they contributed less than 5 percent of the artifacts [Mitchell 1971:47]). This trend in bone technology is well-documented in the Hoko Rockshelter shellmidden (Croes 1985). Observing the bone points in their complete form at the contemporary and waterlogged Ozette Village site (45CA24) makes clear that many such "points" are in fact fishhook barbs associated with a variety of offshore, jigging, and trolling hooks (Croes 1985). Most likely, the increased frequency of bone points at many places

is related to the increased use of salmon trolling and jigging equipment (as well as herring rakes) to intensify the procurement of anadromous fish in nearshore waters prior to their entry into rivers in summer and fall. These increased economic foci would contribute additional anadromous fauna to the dense middens of this late time period, as noted in the Hoko Rockshelter (Figure 17, F). Also, an outer-coast emphasis on sea mammals is postulated during the last 900 years, as seen in the fur seal emphasis in later middens at Hoko (Wigen 1985; Wigen & Stucki, this volume), and the sea lion and whale emphasis at Ozette and other West Coast sites. Increased occurrence of harpoon points during this time period also corresponds with an emphasized sea mammal pursuit. This pattern would create another rise in population and a new economic plateau, which stabilized until the historic period (Figure 17, F).

From this research, the well-documented *CULTURAL PHASES (TYPES)*—Pebble Tool, Old Cordilleran, St. Mungo, Locarno Beach, Marpole, and Gulf of Georgia—appear to be better termed *ECONOMIC STAGES (OR PLATEAUS)* that are underlain by (a) early exponential population growth, (b) eventual territorial circumscription (about 4,000 BP), and (c) critical resource stresses. Thus, the regionwide horizontal trends seen in these economic stages or plateaus may reflect a widespread pattern and resulting shift in subsistence solutions, not cultural style or population shifts.

Our computer-based economic decision making modeling provides a tool to simulate and better explore factors contributing to cultural evolution along the Northwest Coast. Our results support Nash's (1983a:5) proposal that "the seesaw battle of discontinuity vs. continuity may be resolved in the process of conducting work in other paradigms, such as the ecological paradigm, where the 'discontinuity' might be understood as more of an adaptive change. . . ." We contend that the major assemblage changes observed archaeologically along the southern Northwest Coast are most probably linked to shifts in subsistence adaptation.

Similar trends may be common in other maritime areas around the world, especially as coastal groups became circumscribed and dependent on resources of a limited territory, and specifically on shellfish. We suggest the examination of our predictive modeling results in other areas of the Northwest Coast, as well as in coastal hunter-fisher-gatherer sites elsewhere. The overuse of shellfish resources, followed by an increased emphasis on stored and/or other foods, may prove to be an important factor in other emerging complex maritime cultures, as is proposed here on the Northwest Coast of North America.

ACKNOWLEDGMENTS

The Hoko River Project research is cosponsored by the Makah Tribal Nation and has been made possible through the support of the M.J. Murdock Charitable Trust, the National Endowment for the Humanities, the Washington State Office of Archaeology & Historic Preservation, the Caughey Foundation, and Crown Zellerbach Corporation. Numerous project researchers, Makah community members, field personnel, and students have contributed to data recovery, analysis, and synthesis. Special editorial assistance was provided by Barry L. Isaac. Though this research owes its existence to these and many previous researchers, the results and conclusions remain the responsibility of the authors.

REFERENCES

Ames, Kenneth M. (1979) "Stable and Resiliant Systems Along the Skeena River: The Gitskan/Carrier Boundary." Pp. 219–239 in R. Inglis & G. MacDonald (eds.) *Skeena River Prehistory*. Ottawa: Archaeological Survey of Canada, Mercury Series 87.

——— (1981) "The Evolution of Social Ranking on the Northwest Coast of North America." *American Antiquity* 46:789–805.

Ando, M., and E. Balazs (1979) "Geodetic Evidence for Aseismic Subduction of the Juan de Fuca Plate." *Journal of Geophysical Research* 84:3023–3028.

Angell, Tony, and Kenneth C. Balcomb III (1982) *Marine Birds and Mammals of Puget Sound*. Seattle: University of Washington Press.

Bell, F. Heward (1981) *The Pacific Halibut, The Resource and the Fishery*. Anchorage: Alaska Northwest Publishing Company.

Bigley, D. (n.d.) "Hoko River Region Environmental Reconstruction Report." Manuscript on file, Hoko River Archaeological Project, Pullman, WA, 1980.

Blinman, Eric (1980) "Stratigraphy and Depositional Environment." Pp. 64–88 in Dale R. Croes & Eric Blinman (eds.) *Hoko River: A 2,500 Year Old Fishing Camp on the Northwest Coast of North America*. Pullman, WA: Washington State University, Laboratory of Anthropology, Reports of Investigations No. 58.

Blinman, Eric, and Kenneth L. Petersen (1980) "Pollen Analysis of an Organic Mat Sequence." Pp. 101–104 in Dale R. Croes & Eric Blinman (eds.) *Hoko River: A 2,500 Year Old Fishing Camp on the Northwest Coast of North America*. Pullman, WA: Washington State University, Laboratory of Anthropology, Reports of Investigations No. 58.

Borden, Charles E. (1975) *Origins and Development of Early Northwest Coast Culture to About 3,000 B.C.* Ottawa: Archaeological Survey of Canada, Mercury Series Paper 45.

——— (1979) "Peopling and Early Cultures of the Pacific Northwest." *Science* 203:963–971.

Burley, David V. (1980) "Marpole: Anthropological Reconstructions of a Prehistoric Northwest Coast Culture Type." Burnaby, BC: Simon Fraser University, Department of Archaeology Publication No. 8.

——— (1983) "Cultural Complexity and Evolution in the Development of Coastal Adaptations Among the Micmac and Coast Salish." Pp. 157–172 in Ronald J. Nash (ed.) *The Evolution of Maritime Cultures on the Northeast and Northwest Coasts of America*. Burnaby, BC: Simon Fraser University, Department of Archaeology, Publication No. 11.

Carlson, Roy L., ed. (1983) *Indian Art Traditions of the Northwest Coast*. Burnaby, BC: Archaeology Press.

Casteel, R.W. (1972) "Two Static Maximum Population Density Models for Hunter-Gatherers: A First Approximation." *World Archaeology* 4:19–40.

Clague, J.J., J.E. Armstrong, and W.H. Mathews (1980) "Advance of Late Wisconsin Cordillera Ice Sheet in Southern British Columbia Since 22,000 years B.P." *Quaternary Research* 13:322–326.

Colson, Elizabeth (1953) *The Makah Indians; a Study of an Indian Tribe in Modern American Society*. Minneapolis: University of Minnesota Press.

Coupland, Gary (n.d.) "Household Variability and Status Differentiation at Kitselas Canyon." Paper presented before the Canadian Archaeological Association Conference, University of Manitoba, 1985.

Croes, Dale R. (1976) "An Early "Wet" Site at the Mouth of the Hoko River, the Hoko River Site (45CA213)." Pp. 201–232 in Dale R. Croes (ed.) *The Excavation of Water-saturated Archaeological Sites Wet Sites on the Northwest Coast of North America*. Ottawa: National Museum of Man, Mercury Series Number 50.

—— (1977) *Basketry from the Ozette Village Archaeological Site: A Technological, Functional and Comparative Study*. Ph.D. dissertation, Washington State University.

—— (1980a) "Cordage from the Ozette Village Archaeological Site: A Technological, Functional and Comparative Study." Pullman, WA: Washington State University, Laboratory of Archaeology and History, Project Report No. 9.

—— (1980b) "Basketry Artifacts." Pp. 188–222 in Dale R. Croes & Eric Blinman (eds.) *Hoko River: A 2,500 Year Old Fishing Camp on the Northwest Coast of North America*. Pullman, WA: Washington State University, Laboratory of Anthropology, Reports of Investigation No. 58.

—— (1980c) "Cordage." Pp. 236–256 in Dale R. Croes & Eric Blinman (eds.) *Hoko River: A 2,500 Year Old Fishing Camp on the Northwest Coast of North America*. Pullman, WA: Washington State University, Laboratory of Anthropology, Reports of Investigations No. 58.

—— (1985) "Hoko Rockshelter Bone Artifact Distribution." Attachment B in *Interim Annual Report, Hoko River Archaeological Project, Phase XIV*. Washington, DC: National Endowment for the Humanities.

—— (n.d.) "Lachane Basketry and Cordage: A Definitive and Comparative Study." Ms. on file, Archaeological Survey of Canada, National Museum of Man, Ottawa, 1975.

Croes, Dale R., and Eric Blinman, eds. (1980) *Hoko River: A 2,500 Year Old Fishing Camp on the Northwest Coast of North America*. Pullman, WA: Washington State University, Laboratory of Anthropology, Reports of Investigations No. 58.

Croes, Dale R., and Steven Hackenberger (1985) "Prehistoric Ecosystems and Economics: Regional Computer Models for the Northwest Coast of North America." Attachment E in *Interim Annual Report, Hoko River Archaeological Project, Phase XIV*. Washington, DC: National Endowment for the Humanities.

Croes, Dale R., and Fekri Hassan (n.d.) "The Dynamics of Northwest Coast Adaptation Systems as Derived From Ethnographic and Wet Site Archaeological Data; a Time Perspective." Paper presented at the Conference on Current Research in Anthropology, Washington, DC, 1977.

Cross, J.N., K.L. Fresh, B.S. Miller, C.A. Simenstad, S.N. Steinfort, and J.C. Fegley (1978) "Nearshore Fish and Macroinvertebrate Assemblages along the Strait of Juan de Fuca, Including Food Habits of the Common Nearshore Fish." Washington, DC: U.S. Department of Commerce, National Oceanic and Atmospheric Administration Technical Memorandum ERL MESA-32.

Douglas, Mary (1966) "Population Control: Primitive Groups." *British Journal of Sociology* 17:263–273.

Easton, Norm (n.d.) "Straits Salish Reef-netting and Social Structure: A Test Case in Economic Anthropology." Paper presented before the Northwest Anthropological Conference, Simon Fraser University, 1982.

Ecklund-Johnson, Debra (1980) "Macroflora Analysis." Pp. 91–101 in Dale R. Croes & Eric Blinman (eds.) *Hoko River: A 2,500 Year Old Fishing Camp on the Northwest Coast of North America*. Pullman, WA: Washington State University, Laboratory of Anthropology, Reports of Investigations No. 58.

——— (1984) "Analysis of Macroflora from the Hoko River Rockshelter, Olympic Peninsula, Washington." Attachment F in *Interim Annual Report, Hoko River Archaeological Project, Phases XIII and XIV*. Washington, DC: National Endowment for the Humanities.

Everitt, R.D., C.H. Fiscus, and R.L. DeLong (1979) "Marine Mammals of Northern Puget Sound and the Strait of Juan de Fuca: A Report on Investigations November 1, (1977)-October 31, (1978)." Washington, DC: U.S. Department of Commerce, National Oceanic and Atmospheric Administration Technical Report, ERL MESA-41.

——— (1980) "Northern Puget Sound Marine Mammals." Washington, DC: Interagency Energy/Environment R & D Program Report, EPA-600/7-80–139.

Field, R.A., F.C. Smith, and W.G. Hepworth (1973a) *The Mule Deer Carcass*. Laramie: University of Wyoming, Agricultural Experiment Station, Bulletin 589.

——— (1973b) *The Elk Carcass*. Laramie: University of Wyoming, Agricultural Experiment Station, Bulletin 594.

Fisken, Marian (1980) "Analysis of Whale Bone." Pp. 114–117 in Dale R. Croes & Eric Blinman (eds.) *Hoko River: A 2,500 Year Old Fishing Camp on the Northwest Coast of North America*. Pullman, WA: Washington State University, Laboratory of Anthropology, Reports of Investigations No. 58.

Fladmark, Knut R. (1975) *A Paleoecological Model for Northwest Coast Prehistory*. Ottawa: National Museum of Man, Mercury Series No. 51.

Flenniken, J.J. (1981) *Replicative Systems Analysis: A Model Applied to the Vein Quartz Artifacts from the Hoko River Site*. Pullman, WA: Washington State University, Laboratory of Anthropology, Reports of Investigation No. 59.

Friedman, Edward (1980) "Analysis of the Bird and Mammal Bone." Pp. 111–114 in Dale R. Croes & Eric Blinman (eds.) *Hoko River: A 2,500 Year Old Fishing Camp on the Northwest Coast of North America*. Pullman, WA: Washington State University, Laboratory of Anthropology, Reports of Investigations No. 58.

Gibbs, George (1877) *Tribes of Western Washington and Northwest Oregon*. Washington, DC: Smithsonian Institution, Contributions to North American Ethnology 1:157–241.

Grayson, Donald K. (1984) *Quantitative Zooarchaeology*. New York: Academic Press.

Griggs, G.B., L.D. Kuln, J.R. Duncan, and G.A. Fowler (1970) "Holocene Faunal Stratigraphy and Paleoclimatic Implications of Deep-sea Sediments in Cascadia Basin." *Paleogeography, Paleoclimatology, Paleoecology* 7:5–12.

Gross, B. Timothy (1980) "Analysis of Mollusk Remains." Pp. 117–124 in Dale R. Croes & Eric Blinman (eds.) *Hoko River: A 2,500 Year Old Fishing Camp on the Northwest Coast of North America*. Pullman, WA: Washington State University, Laboratory of Anthropology, Reports of Investigations No. 58.

Gross, Lorraine (1984) "Determination of the Nature of Short Term Changes in the Site Functions at a Fishing Camp (45CA213) on the Hoko River, Washington." Attachment H in *Interim Annual Report, Hoko River Archaeological Project, Phase XIII and XIV*. Washington, DC: National Endowment for the Humanities.

——— (1986) *Determination of the Nature of Short Term Changes in Site Function at a Fishing Camp on the Hoko River, Washington*. Master's thesis, Washington State University.

Gunther, Erna (1936) "A Preliminary Report on the Zoological Knowledge of the Makah." Pp. 105–118 in Robert H. Lowie (ed.) *Essays in Anthropology Presented to A.L. Kroeber*. Berkeley: University of California Press.

Gustafson, Carl E. (1968) "Prehistoric Use of Fur Seals: Evidence From the Olympic Coast of Washington." *Science* 161:49–51.

Ham, Leonard C. (1982) *Seasonality of Shell Midden Layers and Subsistence Activities at the Crescent Beach Site (DgRr1)*. Ph.D. dissertation, University of British Columbia.

Harper, James A. (1971) *Ecology of Roosevelt Elk*. Portland: Oregon State Game Commission.

Hassan, Fekri A. (1978) "Demographic Archaeology." Pp. 49–103 in Michael B. Schiffer (ed.) *Advances in Archaeological Method and Theory, Vol. 1*. New York: Academic Press.

——— (1981) *Demographic Archaeology*. New York: Academic Press.

Heusser, C.J. (1973) "Environmental Sequence Following the Fraser Advance of the Juan de Fuca Lobe, Washington." *Quarternary Research* 3:284–306.

Heusser, C.J., L.E. Heusser, and S.S. Street (1980) "Quarternary Temperatures and Precipitation for the North-west Coast of North America." *Nature* 286:702–704.

Hicks, S.D. (1978) "An Average Geopotential Sea Level Series for the United States." *Journal of Geophysical Research* 83:1377–1379.

Hoff, Ricky (1980) "Fishhooks." Pp. 160–188 in Dale R. Croes & Eric Blinman (eds.) *Hoko River: A 2,500 Year Old Fishing Camp on the Northwest Coast of North America*. Pullman, WA: Washington State University, Laboratory of Anthropology, Reports of Investigations No. 58.

Howes, Donald W. (1982) *Spatial Analysis at a Northwest Coast Fishing Camp: The Hoko River Site*. Master's thesis, Washington State University.

Huelsbeck, David R. (1980) "Analysis of Fish Remains." Pp. 104–111 in Dale R. Croes & Eric Blinman (eds.) *Hoko River: A 2,500 Year Old Fishing Camp on the Northwest Coast of North America*. Pullman, WA: Washington State University, Laboratory of Anthropology, Reports of Investigations No. 58.

Hunn, Eugene S. (1981) "On the Relative Contribution of Men and Women to Subsistence among Hunter-Gatherers of the Columbia Plateau: A Comparison with *Ethnographic Atlas* Summaries." *Journal of Ethnobiology* 1 (1):124–134.

Hurst, Gwen (1986) "Shell Middens: Seasonality and Exploitation." Attachment C in *Final Annual Report, Hoko River Archaeological Project, Phase XIV*. Washington, DC: National Endowment for the Humanities.

Jewitt, John R. (1815) *A Narrative of the Adventures and Sufferings of John R. Jewitt, Only Survivor of the Crew of the Boston, During Captivity of Nearly Three Years Among the Savages of Nootka Sound: with an Account of the Manners, Mode of Living, and Religious Opinions of the Natives*. Middletown, MA: Loomis and Richards.

Jochim, Michael (1976) *Hunter-Gatherer Subsistence and Settlement*. New York: Academic Press.

Klein, R.G., and K. Cruz-Uribe (1984) *The Analysis of Animal Bones from Archaeological Sites*. Chicago: University of Chicago Press.

Krantz, Grover S. (1981) *The Process of Human Evolution*. Cambridge, MA: Schenkman Publishing Company.

Kroeber, A.L. (1939) *Cultural and Natural Areas of Native North America*. Berkeley: University of California Publications in American Archaeology and Ethnology, 38.

Manuwal, D.A., T.R. Wahl, and S.M. Speich (1979) "The Seasonal Distribution and Abundance of Marine Bird Populations in the Strait of Juan de Fuca and Northern Puget Sound in 1978." Washington, DC: U.S. Department of Commerce, National Oceanic and Atmospheric Administration Technical Memorandum ERL MESA-44.

Marine Mammal Biological Laboratory (1971) *Pelagic Fur Seal Investigations, 1970–1971.* Seattle: National Marine Fisheries Service, U.S. Department of Commerce.

Matson, R.G. (1981) "Prehistoric Subsistence Patterns in the Fraser Delta: The Evidence from the Glenrose Cannery Site." Pp. 64–85 in K.R. Fladmark (ed.) *Fragments of the Past.* Vancouver: *B.C. Studies* 48: Special Issue.

—— (1983) "Intensification and the Development of Cultural Complexity: The Northwest Versus the Northeast Coast." Pp. 125–148 in Ronald J. Nash (ed.) *The Evolution of Maritime Cultures on the Northeast and Northwest Coasts of America.* Burnaby, BC: Simon Fraser University, Department of Archaeology, Publication No. 11.

McKenzie, Kathleen H. (1974) *Ozette Prehistory—Prelude.* Master's thesis, University of Calgary.

Miller, David Glen (1983) "The Hoko River Rockshelter: Intertidal Resources." Attachment L in *Interim Annual Report, Hoko River Archaeological Project, Phases XIII and XIV.* Washington, DC: National Endowment for the Humanities.

Mitchell, Donald H. (1971) "Archaeology of the Gulf of Georgia Area, A Natural Region and Its Cultural Types." *Syesis* 4: Supplement 1.

—— (1982) *The Gulf of Georgia Sequence.* Weston, CT: Pictures of Record, Inc.

Moore, T.C., Jr. (1973) "Late Pleistocene-Holocene Oceanographic Changes in the Northeastern Pacific Ocean." *Quaternary Research* 3:99–109.

Nash, Ronald J., ed. (1983a) *The Evolution of Maritime Cultures on the Northeast and the Northwest Coast of America.* Burnaby, BC: Simon Fraser University, Department of Archaeology, Publication No. 11.

—— (1983b) "The Progress and Process of Theory Building: The Northeast and Northwest Coast." Pp. 1–25 in Ronald J. Nash (ed.) *The Evolution of Maritime Cultures on the Northeast and Northwest Coasts of America.* Burnaby, BC: Simon Fraser University, Department of Archaeology, Publication No. 11.

Nyblade, C.F. (1979) "The Strait of Juan de Fuca Intertidal and Subtidal Benthos." Washington, DC: U.S. Environmental Protection Agency, Report for the Interagency Energy/ Environment Research and Development Program.

Osborn, Alan J. (1977) *Aboriginal Exploitation of Marine Food Resources.* Ph.D. dissertation, University of New Mexico.

Proctor, Charles M., John C. Garcia, David V. Galvin, Gary B. Lewis, Lincoln C. Loehr, and Alison M. Massa (1980) "An Ecological Characterization of the Pacific Northwest Coastal Region." Portland, OR: Department of Interior, U.S. Fish and Wildlife Service, Biological Services Program, FWS/OBS-79/11 to 79/15.

Pugh, Alexander L. III (1976) *DYNAMO II User's Manual.* Cambridge: MIT Press.

Richardson, Allan (1982) "The Control of Productive Resources on the Northwest Coast of North America." Pp. 93–112 in N.M. Williams and E.S. Hunn (eds.) *Resource Managers: North American and Australian Hunter Gatherers.* Boulder, CO: Westview Press.

Richardson, George P. and Alexander L. Pugh III (1981) *Introduction to System Dynamics Modeling with Dynamo.* Cambridge, MA: MIT Press.

Scammons, C.M. (1874) *The Marine Mammals of the Northwest Coast of North America Together with an Account of the American Whale Fishery.* San Francisco: John H. Carmany.

Schalk, Randall F. (1977) "The Structure of an Anadromous Fish Resource." Pp. 207–239 in Lewis R. Binford (ed.) *For Theory Building in Archaeology.* New York: Academic Press.

Simenstad, C.A., W.J. Kinney, and B.S. Miller (1980) "Epibenthic Zooplankton Assemblages at Selected Sites Along the Strait of Juan de Fuca." Washington, DC: U.S. Department of Commerce, National Oceanic and Atmospheric Administration Technical Memorandum ERL MESA-46.

Singh, Ram Raj Prasad (1956) *Aboriginal Economic System of the Olympic Peninsula Indians, Western Washington*. Sacramento, CA: Sacramento Anthropology Society, Paper No. 4.

Stiefel, Sheryl K. (1985) *The Subsistence Economy of the Locarno Beach Culture (3,300– 2,400 BP)*. Master's thesis, University of British Columbia.

Stucki, Barbara R. (1983) *Fluvial Processes and the Formation of the Hoko River Archaeological Site (45CA213), Olympic Peninsula, Washington*. Master's thesis, Washington State University.

——— (1985) "Geoarchaeology Investigations at the Hoko River Rockshelter (45CA21)." Attachment A in *Interim Annual Report, Hoko River Archaeological Project, Phase XIV*. Washington, DC: National Endowment for the Humanities.

——— (n.d.) "Evaluating activities at a Northwest Coast shell midden site using renewal processes." Paper presented before the Society for American Archaeology, Portland, OR, 1984.

Suchanek, Thomas H. (1981) "The Role of Disturbance in the Evolution of Life History Strategies in the Intertidal Mussels *Mytilus edulis* and *Mytilus californianus*." *Oecologia* 50:143–152.

Suttles, Wayne (1968) "Coping with Abundance: Subsistence on the Northwest Coast." Pp. 56–68 in Richard B. Lee & Irven DeVore (eds.) *Man the Hunter*. Chicago: Aldine.

Swan, J. (1869) *The Indians of Cape Flattery, with Notes by George Gibbs*. Washington, DC: Smithsonian Contributions to Knowledge 16.

Thompson, W.F., and Norman L. Freeman (1930) "History of the Pacific Halibut Fishery." Vancouver: Report of the International Fisheries Commission, No. 5.

Tucker, Todd R. (1984) "A Shell Deposit in a Northwest Coast 'Wet' Site: Hoko River (45CA213)." Attachment I in *Interim Annual Report, Hoko River Archaeological Project, Phases XIII and XIV*. Washington, DC: National Endowment for the Humanities.

Wahl, T.R., S.M. Speich, D.A. Manuwal, K.V. Hirsch, and C. Miller (1981) "Marine Bird Populations of the Strait of Juan de Fuca, Strait of Georgia and Adjacent Waters in 1978 and 1979." Washington, DC: U.S. Environmental Protection Agency, Report for the Interagency Energy/Environment Research and Development Program.

Waterman, T.T. (1920) *The Whaling Equipment of the Makah Indians*. Seattle: University of Washington Press.

Watt, Bernice K., and Annabel L. Merril (1975) *Handbook of the Nutritional Contents of Foods*. New York: Dover Publications.

Wessen, Gary C. (1982) *Shellmiddens as Cultural Deposits: A Case Study from Ozette*. Ph.D. dissertation, Washington State University.

Wigen, Rebecca J. (1985) "Basic Vertebrate Fauna Analysis, Hoko River Rockshelter Site." Attachment C in *Interim Annual Report, Hoko River Archaeological Project, Phase XIV*. Washington, DC: National Endowment for the Humanities.

TAPHONOMY AND STRATIGRAPHY IN THE INTERPRETATION OF ECONOMIC PATTERNS AT HOKO RIVER ROCKSHELTER

Rebecca J. Wigen and Barbara R. Stucki

INTRODUCTION

This essay examines some of the factors affecting the analysis of faunal remains in the study of a prehistoric subsistence economy. In this case study, we determine the extent to which vertical changes in faunal remains recovered from deeply stratified shell midden deposits at the Hoko River Rockshelter site (45CA21) can be attributed to changing economic conditions.

The record of economic activities at a site is often incomplete. Many studies have shown that taphonomic agents—including flowing water, gravity, weather, and carnivores—that act on bones during site formation are important determinants of the observed composition of faunal assem-

Research in Economic Anthropology, Supplement 3, pages 87–146.
Copyright © 1988 by JAI Press Inc.
All rights of reproduction in any form reserved.
ISBN: 0-89232-818-5

blages (Ascher 1968; Krause & Thorne 1971; Schiffer 1976, 1983; Behrensmeyer & Hill 1980; Fuchs et al. 1977; Woods & Johnson 1978). Taphonomic processes alter the record of past activities by differentially
disturbing or removing bones and other remains.

The association of the original faunal specimens may also be altered by
pedoturbation or other disturbance processes (Woods & Johnson 1978).
Transformation of the archaeological record can occur at any time during
the history of the deposit—during deposition (burial transforms), after
burial (diagenetic transforms), or during excavation (exposure/sampling
transforms) and analysis (systematics/typology transforms) (Gifford
1981:387).

The character of site use through time—including the duration of occupation, the size of the settlement, and the range of activities conducted
at the site—also influences what is discarded and, thusly, what becomes
part of the archaeological record (Binford 1977, 1981; Yellen 1977a,b).
For example, researchers studying contemporary hunter-gatherer communities have observed that, as the duration of site occupation increases
or as more people occupy the site area, more time is invested in establishing
and maintaining refuse disposal areas. The floors of houses at the nearby
Ozette site were regularly swept (Samuels 1983). Refuse discarded in areas
adjacent to rivers or near the shoreline is more likely to be removed from
the archaeological record. Such variations in bone disposal patterns, along
with different butchering techniques, can influence the structure of the
faunal assemblage (Brain 1981). In addition, subsistence strategies that
incorporate seasonal migration will result in sites that contain only a portion of the total economic resources utilized by a group over the year.

Differential deposition or loss of bones can skew an assessment of the
diet and procurement strategy employed by a group of people. It is therefore important to identify the effects of natural and cultural site formation
processes and to isolate changes in the archaeological record resulting
from variations in economic activities.

Our approach combines two sets of data. First, we examine site stratigraphy and sediments for evidence of changing site use that might have
altered the range of site activities or bone disposal patterns. Second, we
evaluate the degree to which taphonomic processes have affected the in-
tegrity of the faunal assemblage. We are then in a position to assess
changing economic strategies represented in the deposits of the Hoko
Rockshelter.

THE CASE STUDY: HOKO RIVER ROCKSHELTER SITE

The Hoko River Rockshelter (45CA21) is located at the mouth of the Hoko
River, about 30 km from the northwest tip of the Olympic Peninsula,

Washington. The present-day climate in this region is maritime, with cool temperatures, prolonged cloudy periods, and high humidity. Annual and diurnal temperatures range between 32°F (0°C, winter) and 66°F (19°C, summer). Mean annual precipitation is 210.44 cm, most of which falls between October and March (Franklin & Dyrness 1973, Philips & Donaldson 1972). Vegetation is dominated by coniferous forest.

Hoko River Rockshelter is the largest natural shelter habitation site so far discovered along the Northwest Coast. In five seasons of field work, 43 1×1 meter units have been excavated, to a maximum depth of 3.3m (Figure 1). Twenty-five of these units are located on the interior of the shelter. The two radiocarbon dates obtained from hearth deposits collected

Figure 1. Distribution of Excavated Units

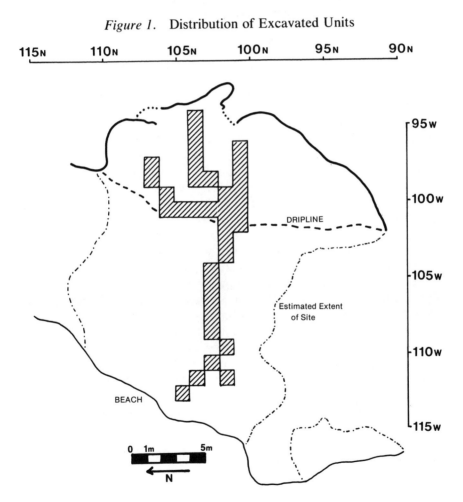

2.5m below surface, near the base of the cultural deposits, indicate that the site was occupied during the 800 years previous to contact with Europeans. The rockshelter remains totally undisturbed by vandalism.

Sediments in the rockshelter contain a high proportion of shell, and thus we can characterize this site as a "shell midden." A diversity of fish, bird, and land and sea mammal remains were recovered (Table 1 and Appendix A) in addition to abundant shellfish. Most of the fishbones represent locally available rocky-bottom fish, although salmon represents 18 percent of the total fish remains and flatfish, including halibut, make up about 4 percent. Sea mammal species account for 60 percent of the mammal bones; of these, 50 percent are northern fur seal. Harbor seal, whale, sea lion, coast deer, and elk each contribute 3–5 percent of the total mammal remains. Diving birds (ducks, murres, auklets, grebes, loons, and cormorants) comprise the majority of the bird bone.

A total of 1,657 artifacts have been found. The most commonly recovered artifacts are small, thin bone points, probably used as fishhook barbs or as parts of composite harpoons (Croes 1985). Ground mussel shell knives, chipped-stone points, hammerstones, stone net sinkers, ground-slate tools, abraders, and anvil stones were also recovered. The variety of artifacts and faunal remains in the rockshelter attests to the intensity and diversity of activity that took place there.

Sediments in the rockshelter consist primarily of the remains of human activity. These layers contain various proportions of charcoal, ash, shell, bone, gravel, sand, and humus (Figure 2). Noncultural deposits of sand from weathered bedrock occur in the lower 70 cm of the site, where they interdigitate with layers of humus, charcoal, and shell. Bedrock consists of silty sandstone. Small concentrations of granule- to cobble-sized gravel from rooffall occur infrequently throughout the sequence of deposits, especially in areas near the dripline. The surface of the site is also covered by a thin layer of rooffall that collected after the site was abandoned.

The shelter is finely stratified, with a high degree of resolution of individual layers. To date, 1,342 small, discrete layers have been recorded from 48m of trench profiles (Table 2). Most layers have well-defined, abrupt boundaries. They range 1–17 cm in thickness and extend in length from a few centimeters to over 8 meters. Many of these deposits appear to be the result of a specific event, such as the single use of a hearth. Among these deposits are 337 features, including well-defined hearths, pits, and the outlines of stakes and small posts.

The high resolution of the strata indicates that the archaeological remains were protected from extensive erosion or turbation. A few of the layers have been disturbed by rodent burrowing, but these burrows are uncommon and are usually identifiable by their distinctive shape and the friability of their contents. The process of colluviation that was responsible for the

Table 1. Faunal Remains Recovered, Showing Common and Scientific Names, Number of Identified Specimens (NISP), and Minimum Number of Individuals (MNI)[a]

Fishes	NISP	MNI
Dogfish *Squalus acanthias*	976	39
Skate *Raja* sp.	60	7
Ratfish *Hydrolagus colliei*	209	51
Sturgeon *Acipenser* sp.	5	1
Pacific Herring *Clupea harengus*	372	27
Northern Anchovy *Engraulis mordax*	45	13
Salmon *Oncorhynchus* sp.	9,777	142
Trout *Salmo* sp.	12	4
Steelhead *Salmo gairdneri*	5	3
Eulachon *Thaleichthys pacificus*	9	2
Pacific Cod *Gadus macrocephalus*	324	19
Hake *Merluccius productus*	293	12
Surfperch Embiotocidae	1,161	41
Wolfeel & Prickleback *Anarrhichthys ocellatus*, Stichaidae	312	11
Rockfish *Sebastes* sp.	5,092	138
Sablefish *Anoplopoma fimbria*	71	6
Greenling Hexagrammidae	15,817	458
Lingcod *Ophiodon elongatus*	2,212	48
Buffalo Sculpin *Enophrys bison*	130	12
Red Irish Lord *Hemilepidotus hemilepidotus*	4,610	124
Staghorn Sculpin *Leptocottus armatus*	24	5
Great Sculpin *Myoxocephalus polyacanthocephalus*	12	4
Cabezon *Scorpaenichthys marmoratus*	763	27
Sculpins Cottidae	57	15
Arrowtooth Flounder *Atheresthes stomias*	174	9
Petrale Sole *Eopsetta jordani*	96	13
Halibut *Hippoglossus stenolepis*	716	17
Rock Sole *Lepidopsetta bilineata*	48	7
Starry Flounder *Platichthys stellatus*	134	10
Sand Sole *Psettichthys melanostictus*	8	2
Sanddab *Citharichthys sordidus*	2	1
Rex Sole *Glyptocephalus zachirus*	1	1
English Sole *Parophrys vetulus*	16	4
Curlfin Sole *Pleuronichthys decurrens*	4	3
Flatfish Pleuronectiformes	996	30
SITE TOTAL	44,543	1,306
Mammals		
Squirrel *Tamiasciurus* sp.	4	3
Beaver *Castor canadensis*	25	6
Small Rodents Rodentia	16	5
Rabbit Leporidae	21	7
Whale Cetacea (excluding Delphinidae)	86	4
Porpoise Delphinidae	226	10
Dog *Canis familiaris*	90	6
Wolf? *Canis lupus*	2	1

Table 1. Continued

Mammals (cont'd)	NISP	MNI
Black Bear *Ursus americanus*	1	1
Raccoon *Procyon lotor*	26	7
Marten *Martes americana*	1	1
Mink *Mustela vison*	1	1
River Otter *Lutra canadensis*	27	6
Sea Otter *Enhydra lutris*	37	8
Skunk *Mephitis mephitis*	17	6
Cougar? *Felis concolor*	1	1
Northern Fur Seal *Callorhinus ursinus*	2,333	37
Northern Sea Lion *Eumetopias jubata*	39	11
Elephant Seal? *Mirounga angustirostris*	2	1
Elk *Cervus canadensis*	149	9
Coast Deer *Odocoileus hemionus*	158	11
SITE TOTAL	3,368	155

Birds		
Common Loon *Gavia immer*	77	11
Small Loon *Gavia arctica, G. stellata*	42	10
Red-neck Grebe *Podiceps grisegena*	4	3
Western Grebe *Aechmophorus occidentalis*	31	8
Small Grebe *Podiceps auritus, P. nigricollis, Podilymbus podiceps*	117	20
Albatross *Diomedea* sp.	73	10
Shearwater *Puffinus* sp.	198	14
Fulmar *Fulmarus glacialis*	26	4
Cormorant *Phalacrocorax* sp.	133	9
Great Blue Heron *Ardea herodias*	8	2
Swan *Cygnus* sp.	11	5
Small Goose Anserini	2	2
Medium Goose Anserini	26	4
Large Goose Anserini	15	5
Dabbling Ducks *Anas* sp.	14	5
Mallard *Anas platyrhynchos*	5	2
Gadwall *Anas strepera*	3	1
Wigeon *Anas americana*	1	1
Diving Ducks *Aythya* sp.	44	8
Goldeneyes *Bucephala* sp.	44	7
Common Goldeneye *Bucephala clangula*	5	4
Barrow's Goldeneye *Bucephala islandica*	8	3
Bufflehead *Bucephala albeola*	14	5
Oldsquaw *Clangula hyemalis*	13	5
Scoters *Melanitta* sp.	240	24
Merganser *Mergus* sp.	3	3
Small Duck Anatinae	28	6
Medium Duck Anatinae	220	17
Large Duck Anatinae	121	12
General Duck Anatinae	85	12
Hawks Accipitridae	7	4

Table 1. Continued

Birds (cont'd)	NISP	MNI
Sharp-shinned Hawk *Accipiter striatus*	2	1
Bald Eagle *Haliaeetus leucocephalus*	112	10
Falcon Falconidae	1	1
Sandhill Crane *Grus canadensis*	2	1
Sandpipers Scolopacidae	3	2
Small Gull *Larus* sp.	42	7
Medium Gull *Larus* sp.	103	13
Large Gull *Larus* sp.	143	17
Black-legged Kittiwake *Rissa tridactyla*	1	1
Common Murre *Uria aalge*	378	27
Pigeon Guillemot *Cepphus columba*	1	1
Marbled Murrelet *Brachyramphus marmoratus*	26	7
Rhinoceros Auklet *Cerorhinca monocerata*	4	2
Tufted Puffin *Fratercula cirrhata*	5	3
Songbirds Passeriformes	59	11
Raven *Corvus corax*	2	1
Northwestern Crow *Corvus caurinus*	2	2
Pelican? *Pelecanus* sp.	2	1
SITE TOTAL	2,506	334

[a]Fish common and scientific names after Hart 1973. Mammal common and scientific names after Cowan and Guiguet 1978. Bird common and scientific names after Godfrey 1986.

deposition of silty sand at the base of the rockshelter may also have washed cultural remains downslope in the early period of shelter occupation. However, most cultural deposits of this period are not mixed with silty sand, suggesting that the effect of this process on the archaeological material was limited. The midden deposits of Hoko Rockshelter should, thus, provide a detailed record of prehistoric economy and other activities.

EXAMINATION OF THE SEDIMENTS

The rockshelter provides a protected area for conducting different tasks. Its fixed space would also have constrained the number and types of activities that could have taken place within its boundaries. Therefore, to examine the way in which prehistoric people utilized the rockshelter, we had to consider both the remains of activities and changes in the size and shape of the space available for use. The site is bounded to the north and west by the Hoko River. The rock cliff limits the location of activities to the east, and a steep slope and dense forest are found to the south. The

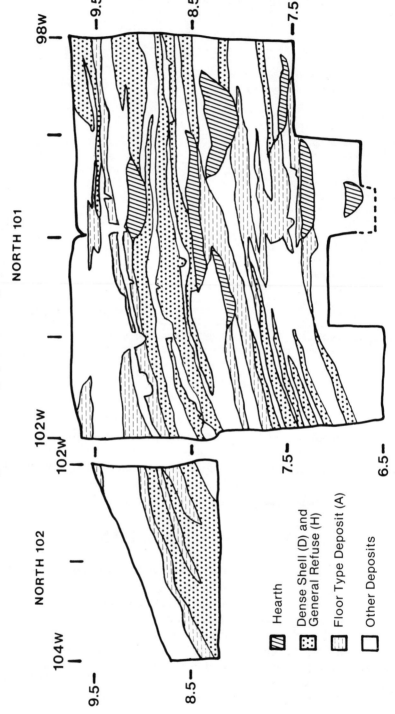

Figure 2. Stratigraphic Drawing of Wall Profile

NORTH 101

NORTH 102

Hearth

Dense Shell (D) and General Refuse (H)

Floor Type Deposit (A)

Other Deposits

94

Table 2. Layer Types in the Hoko Rockshelter Shell Midden

Layer Types	Description	Primary Constituent	Other Major Constituent	Frequency
A1	humus floor	humus	(none)	292
A2	shell & floor	humus	shell (≤20%)	35
A3	hearth & floor	humus	charcoal & ash	78
A4	pebble & floor	humus	pebbles (≤20%)	18
A5	sand & floor	humus	sand	6
B1	true hearth	charcoal & ash	sand	326
B2	gravel & hearth	granule/cobble	charcoal	23
C1	weathered bedrock	silty sand	gravel	57
C2	rooffall	gravel	silty sand	17
C3	silt & humus	silty sand	humus	12
D	shell refuse	shell	(none)	97
E1	shell & humus	shell	humus	32
E2	humus & shell	humus	shell (>20%)	45
F	hearth refuse	(variable mix of charcoal, ash, and humus)		137
G	shell & sand	(variable mix of shell and sand)		7
H	general refuse	(not applicable) mixed		207
I	humus & sand	(generally equal mix of humus and sand)		8
J	humus & pebbles	(variable mix of humus and pebbles)		26
K	shell & hearth refuse	shell	charcoal & ash	3
			Total Layers =	1,426

interior of the rockshelter, between the dripline and back wall, extends over approximately 107m². Archaeological deposits outside the shelter cover 150m², extending downslope to a small terrace that terminates at the edge of the beach.

The size of the area within the dripline, the roof height, and the floor slope are important factors in determining the amount of livable space through time within the shelter. The original base of the rockshelter sloped to the northwest. Gradual infilling reduced the steepness of this slope and provided an increasingly large and more level area for habitation. However, as the shelter filled with refuse, the amount of headroom decreased concomitantly. Eventually, the back of the shelter became too narrow for occupation (Figure 3).

As the shelter configuration changed, the number of people occupying its interior may have varied. With moderate infilling of the shelter, the number of people occupying it could have increased. During later occu-

Figure 3.   Cross Section of Site, Showing Pitch of Roof and Distribution of Activity Zones

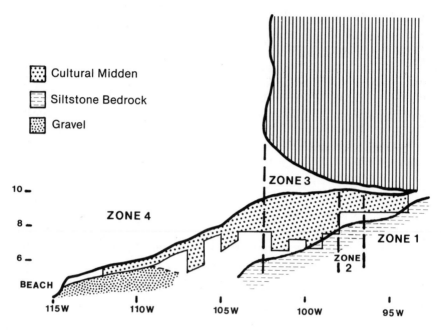

pation, though, there was less headroom, restricting the number of people. Based on the present configuration of shelter, there is about 50m² of livable space. Miller (1983) estimates that a maximum of 5–8 people could have occupied the present shelter interior. His estimate is based on early reports of house floor space (Swan 1869, 1971) and contemporary studies of house size and population estimation (LeBlanc 1971, Narroll 1962, Weissner 1974).

Through time, the inhabitants of the shelter may have modified the types of activities they conducted there to adapt to the change in shelter shape. Thus, variations in the faunal record could have arisen as a result of changing site use, rather than solely from alterations in subsistence strategy. To test this hypothesis, we first examined the sequence of deposits for major differences in the types of sediments deposited through time. We found that, except for the high frequency of noncultural deposits near the base of the shelter, in general the site appears to contain a uniform assemblage of layers containing organic midden refuse from human activity. On the interior of the rockshelter, 27 percent (n = 188) of the layers consist predominately of humus; 42 percent (n = 293) contain high proportions of ash and charcoal; 28 percent (n = 195) are composed of shell, bone, and gravel refuse; and 3 percent (n = 22) of the layers consist of rooffall.

Secondly, we checked for changes in the distribution of different deposits that might reflect alterations in discard locations or in spatial organization. Four activity zones have been identified from the location of remains on the surface of the site (Figure 3). The exterior has deposits containing high concentrations of whole debris, especially shell and bone. The distribution of large mammal bones indicates that activities involving large remains were probably conducted in this area (Stucki & Wigen n.d.). The central activity zone is characterized by high shell fragmentation, hearth remains, and low concentrations of debris. Sterile talus and colluvium are deposited in the southern and northern ends of this portion of the site. The intermediate zone, occurring between refuse dumps to the back and swept living floors in the central area, is characterized by the greatest diversity in constituent sizes and types (Miller 1983). The deep interior of the shelter has concentrated whole shell and bone refuse areas.

Stratigraphic profiles show that these four activity zones remained in essentially the same locations throughout the history of the site. The back and exterior of the rockshelter are areas of concentrated shell and bone refuse. The central activity zone contains a high proportion of hearths and what appear to be more frequently cleaned "living floors" (Figure 2). The only observable shift is the location of the "living floor" deposits. As the shelter filled, the locations of floors gradually extended westward. Pits, stakes, and well-defined hearths remained clustered in the central portion of the site, however.

A third analysis of changing site use was based on an examination of prehistoric activities reflected in site sediments. Broad categories of activities can be identified from the composition and configuration of deposits containing only a few types of remains. For example, layers of dense shell and bone probably reflect the remains of different resources concentrated in secondary refuse dumps (Schiffer 1972). Hearths, pits, and stakes were used to store or process different resources.

"Living floors" consist primarily of humus, with low quantities of other refuse, especially of large, bulky items, such as shell or gravel. "Living floors" are so designated because they appear to reflect housekeeping activities, such as sweeping, that keep the area clear of refuse (Yellen 1977a). These deposits do not cover the entire interior of the rockshelter. Instead, they are usually found adjacent to hearths and pits in the central activity zone.

However, most layers in the rockshelter contain a heterogenous assemblage of humus and many other remains. Establishing a one-to-one functional association between these deposits and specific activities is difficult, though, because of three factors characteristic of human behavior. First, activities are often conducted in several stages occurring in different areas (Schiffer 1972). Therefore, debris from one activity can be scattered in more than one deposit, and refuse deposits may accumulate the remains of different activities. Second, housekeeping activities, trampling, scavenging by dogs, and re-excavation of deposits during the construction of pits can lead to unintentional relocation and mixing of refuse from different activities (Kent n.d., Gifford-Gonzales et al. 1985). Third, activity-specific deposits, such as hearths, can be used for a variety of functions. They may also be subject to reuse. It is likely that remains from only the most recent use of the hearth are preserved in the archaeological record.

Given the problems of defining specific activities from sediments, we chose instead to examine broad changes in the character of site use. If the way in which the site was used remained constant for 800 years, then the relative proportion of different types of layers should also be constant through time. Alternatively, variations in the number of secondary refuse, "living floors," or of other types of deposits through time may indicate changes in the type or intensity of tasks performed at the site.

Layer types were classified by evaluating (1) the degree of diversity of remains and (2) the consistent association of specific constituents within a layer. For example, high concentration of a few types of remains, such as shell or charcoal, may be the product of a specific activity or depositional process. The composition and constituent concentrations of each deposit were visually estimated in the field. These estimates were checked for bias through an analysis of column samples from selected units (Stucki n.d.).

Many layers in the rockshelter contain only one constituent in high concentration (greater than 70 percent of the layer). These layers will often have a specific secondary constituent that consistently associates with the primary layer element (Table 2). The most common layers in this category are humus-rich "living floors" (Types A1–A5 in Table 2). The primary constituent in these deposits is humus, with less than 20 percent of shell (A2), charcoal and/or ash (A3), pebbles (A4), or sand (A5). Variations in secondary constituents may reflect the different activities that took place on "living floor" surfaces. Other layers with a high concentration of a specific constituent include hearth deposits (B1, B2), noncultural deposits with silty sand or rooffall (C1, C2), and shell refuse (D).

Most of the remaining layers consist of two predominant constituents that occur in proportions ranging from 30 to 70 percent. Included in these are layers of mixed shell and humus (E1, E2), mixed humus and silty sand from weathered bedrock (C3), charcoal and ash mixed with humus as hearth refuse (F), shell and beach sand (G), humus and beach sand (I), humus and pebbles (excluding rooffall) (J), and shell mixed with hearth refuse (K). Deposits of Types G, I, and K are uncommon and usually occur as feature fill or in association with features. Layer Type H contains a high diversity of constituents, each occurring in low concentration. We have therefore designated this type of deposit as "general refuse."

Shifts in activities conducted at the rockshelter through time should be reflected in statistically significant variations in the relative frequency of different types of deposits. To examine variation, the number of "living floors," hearth remains, refuse, and noncultural deposits was calculated per 5-cm level per excavation unit. Analysis was limited to units excavated in the central activity zone, because this area shows the greatest diversity of deposits. Results for three units are presented in Figure 4. The histograms clearly show that there have been variations in the frequency with which layers of different types were deposited through time.

Changes in the character of deposition observed in these units were traced over the entire site. Eight distinct depositional periods were identified in the central activity zone. The chi-square statistic was used to assess whether or not frequencies of different layer types observed in the depositional periods differ significantly from those that would be expected if site use had remained constant for 800 years.

We excavated unequal proportions of the eight depositional periods, or DPs (see Table 3). Therefore, to compare the frequency of layer types between periods, we calculated the density per period of each type of deposit. The density of layers per cubic meter is very low for most types of deposits. Because chi-square is unstable when computed from a table with such small cell sizes, we grouped layer types into five categories: "living floor" deposits (A1–A5 in Table 2), hearth remains (B1, B2, F), shell refuse (D, E1, E2, G, K), other refuse (H, I, J), and rooffall (C2, C3). In addition, layer density was calculated per each $3m^3$, so that the minimal expected size of most cells is sufficiently large (greater than 5) to assure a stable chi-square. Results of the chi-square analysis are shown in Table 4. A high value of chi-square indicates that the frequencies of different layer types are not homogeneous with respect to the eight depositional periods. Apparent variations in the number of layer types observed in the excavation units thus reflect statistically significant alterations in patterns of deposition over the last 800 years. For example, during DP–5 the intensity or frequency of resource processing, especially of shellfish, appears to have increased, as reflected in the abundance of thick, dense shell deposits and a high density of other refuse (H, I, J) deposits throughout the site. Alternatively, less effort may have been expended during DP–5 in maintaining refuse areas, suggesting a shift to more short-term, activity-specific use of the site. In contrast, in DP–2, DP–4, and DP–6,

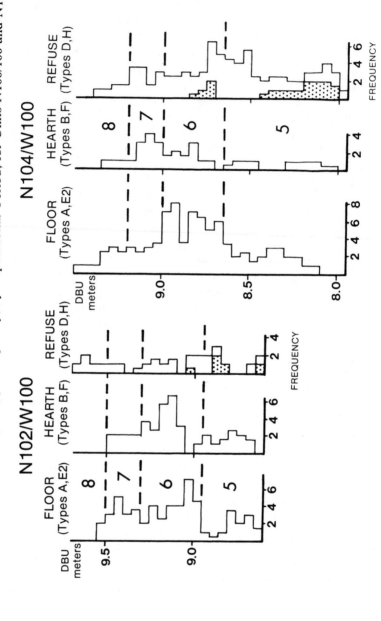

Figure 4a. Vertical Changes in Layer Type Frequency, by Depositional Period, for Units N100/100 and N102/100*

*DBU Meters = Depth Below Unit Datum, in Meters. Dotted areas represent rooffall.

Figure 4b. Vertical Changes in Layer Type Frequency, by Depositional Period, for Unit N104/100*

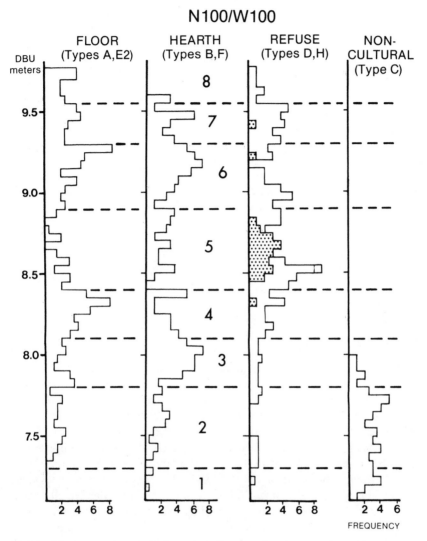

N100/W100

*DBU Meters = Depth Below Unit Datum, in Meters. Dotted areas represent rooffall.

Table 3.   Volume (in Cubic Meters) Excavated, by Depositional Period, Showing Quantities of Excavated Material in Which Fish, Bird, and Mammal Remains Were Identified

Depositional Period	Taxa			Stratigraphy[a]
	Fish	*Bird*	*Mammal*	
8	7.35	7.55	7.65	1.60
7	1.10	1.20	1.20	3.60
6	2.70	3.40	3.85	6.40
5	2.00	2.30	3.00	6.25
4	1.40	1.25	1.65	2.15
3	0.70	0.70	0.70	1.35
2	0.95	0.95	0.95	1.50
1	0.80	0.80	0.80	1.45
Totals (m³)	17.00	18.15	19.80	25.30

[a]Cubic meters in which stratigraphy was examined in defining Depositional Periods.

the central activity zone is characterized by abundant "living floors" and features. During these periods, shellfish remains were primarily deposited in refuse areas outside or to the back of the shelter.

We must be cautious in our interpretations of these results, because chi-square was calculated using layer frequencies that were not corrected for the volume of each layer. Under these circumstances, a small collection of shells ranks equally with a thick shell layer. This is especially a problem with refuse deposits that are quite variable in size and thickness in the central activity area. Thus, in DP–5, which consists primarily of unusually thick and extensive shell deposits, the observed frequencies of these deposits are not significantly different from the expected frequencies. Layer frequency, therefore, may not account for the full range of variability in depositional patterns. However, the high value of chi-square supports the hypothesis that site use varied during the 800 years of occupancy.

The stratigraphic sequence in the rockshelter was examined for evidence of changing site use that might influence interpretations of vertical changes in the faunal record. We found considerable consistency in the general use of the site reflected in the sediments. Remains of a wide range of activities are found in diverse types of deposits, even in the earliest site occupation. The spatial distributions of the four main activity zones also remains almost unchanged, in spite of alterations in the configuration of the rockshelter through time. However, we conclude from the high value of chi-square that there is considerable variation in the intensity or frequency of specific activities in the eight depositional periods. This is reflected in the statistically significant variation in types of layers deposited through time.

Table 4. Chi Square Analysis of Hoko Rockshelter Layer Types and Depositional Periods (DPs)

DPs	Observed versus Expected[a]	Floor (A)	Hearth (B,F)	Rooffall (C2,C3)	Shell Refuse (D,E)	Other Refuse (G,H,I,J)	Total
8	o.f. (DP)	10	4	3	3	6	
	o.d./m³	18.75	7.50	5.63	5.63	11.25	
	e.d./m³	12.14	21.83	2.38	5.36	7.05	48.76
7	o.f. (DP)	35	41	1	14	20	
	o.d./m³	29.17	34.17	0.83	11.67	16.67	
	e.d./m³	23.04	41.42	4.51	10.16	13.38	92.91
6	o.f. (DP)	67	89	2	19	34	
	o.d./m³	31.41	41.72	0.94	8.91	15.94	
	e.d./m³	24.63	44.29	4.82	10.87	14.30	98.91
5	o.f. (DP)	28	45	2	22	26	
	o.d./m³	13.44	21.60	0.96	10.56	12.48	
	e.d./m³	14.70	26.44	2.88	6.48	8.54	59.04
4	o.f. (DP)	28	47	5	15	20	
	o.d./m³	39.07	65.58	6.98	20.93	27.91	
	e.d./m³	39.96	71.86	7.82	17.63	23.20	160.47
3	o.f. (DP)	8	31	2	4	2	
	o.d./m³	17.78	68.89	4.44	8.89	4.44	
	e.d./m³	26.01	46.77	5.09	11.47	15.10	104.44
2	o.f. (DP)	10	22	4	4	3	
	o.d./m³	20.00	44.00	8.00	8.00	6.00	
	e.d./m³	21.42	38.51	4.19	9.45	12.44	86.00
1	o.f. (DP)	2	14	3	1	3	
	o.d./m³	4.14	28.97	6.21	2.07	6.21	
	e.d./m³	11.85	21.31	2.32	5.23	6.88	47.59

χ^2 = 86.88, df = 28, p 0.001

[a]o.f. (DP) = observed frequency in the Depositional Period; o.d./m³ = observed density per cubic meter; e.d./m³ = expected density per cubic meter.

EXAMINATION OF THE FAUNAL ASSEMBLAGE

Fauna was identified from part or all of 40 excavation units. These units were chosen subjectively to cover as many different areas of the site as possible. Relatively few bird and mammal bones were recovered as compared with fishbones. In order to improve the sample, bird and mammal bones were identified from a larger number of excavation units than were the fishbones. Bird bone was identified from 18.15m³ of deposit, mammal bone from 19.80m³, and fishbone from 17.00m³ (Table 3). The units were excavated in 5-cm arbitrary levels and waterscreened through ¼-inch hardware cloth. Large bones were recovered *in situ*. The preservation of bone was excellent throughout the site deposit.

Identifications were done mostly by Wigen, assisted by Ray DePuydt, who identified a portion of the mammal and bird bones. The reference collections used were Wigen's personal collection and those of the Archaeological Division of the British Columbia Provincial Museum, Washington State University, and University of Victoria. The identified specimens were recorded on computer load sheets using the system created for the Ozette site by Paul Gleeson in 1977/78 (see "Ozette Faunal Computer File" in Heulsbeck 1983), modified somewhat for the situation at Hoko. Unidentifiable specimens were counted and all specimens recovered were weighed.

The faunal remains were quantified according to the number of specimens and the minimum number of individuals (MNI) measure. We calculated the MNI by determining the most frequently occurring element (anatomical part, e.g., femur), sorted by age and side, in each depositional period (DP). In some cases, the MNI for fish was calculated by determining the average number of vertebrae for a species and dividing that number into the total number of fish vertebrae present in the depositional period. A potential problem in calculating MNI exists where there are general categories, such as large duck, as well as specific categories, such as *Anas platyrhynchos*. Some bones from the same individual might well be in both categories and raise the MNI improperly. In the case of ducks, for instance, we have combined all of the remains that would be in the large-duck category, whether identified to the species level or not, and calculated the MNI from this larger group.

Both MNI and the number of identified specimens (NISP) are difficult to interpret (Grayson 1979, 1984; Klein & Cruz-Uribe 1984). The NISP is affected by the presence of whole animals as well as differential preservation and breakage of bones. The MNI tends to overrepresent species with low NISPs, and often the actual numbers of MNIs per species are so low that they are statistically meaningless. The number of bones recovered from Hoko River Rockshelter is sufficient to ameliorate both these problems. In several cases, to create more substantial numbers for analysis, the MNIs for separate species have been combined, even though it was possible to identify the elements more precisely. For example, all flatfish species are combined to produce one flatfish category.

As a result of the excavation strategy and the differential depth of the various depositional periods below surface, we excavated unequal proportions of the eight main depositional periods. DP–1, which consists of the lowest deposits, is represented in only three units. DP–2 is found in four of the excavation units, and DP–3, in five units. All the deposits from these three deepest periods were excavated in the southern portion of the site, from N100–101/W98–106 (Figure 1). The upper DPs, 5 through 8, are well-represented throughout the site, in both the interior and exterior, in 21–25 excavation units.

The 8 DPs range 10–70 cm in thickness, which can also vary within a period in different portions of the site. The combined effects of variations in spatial distribution and in thickness resulted in depositional periods of greatly differing volume. The largest periods, 5 and 6, each represent about 25 percent of the excavated volume of the site. The remaining 50 percent of the excavation was distributed in DPs 1 through 3 (4 percent each), DP–4 (about 10 percent), DP–7 (about 15 percent), and DP–8 (7 percent). Table 3 shows the volume excavated from each depositional period.

The variable volume of the depositional periods precluded the direct comparison of their quantities of bone, which would have been useful for looking at differences in intensity of occupation. Therefore, we calculated the NISP and MNI density per cubic meter for each depositional period (Appendix A). An assumption that necessarily accompanies these density figures is that the rate of deposition in each period is the same throughout the deposit. In fact, we both feel that some change in rate almost certainly took place. For example, the discarding of high amounts of bulky shell at certain times would speed up the rate of deposition. Dating of the depositional period boundaries will help control this problem and is in progress.

TAPHONOMIC FACTORS

The bone assemblage readily shows several patterns that have economic implications. The proportion of salmon compared to other fishes increases through time (Appendix A, Table A–2). There is a sudden increase in the density of fur seal NISP and MNI in DP–5 (Appendix A, Table A–4). Finally, there is an increase in the density of all bones, which peaks in DP–6 and then declines in DP–7 and DP–8. Before final interpretation of the trends noted here, we must consider the taphonomic factors that might influence them. Our aim is to be as certain as possible that our interpretation of the faunal assemblage can sort cultural from noncultural variables.

A wide variety of processes destroy bone deposited in sites (Gifford 1981). No accepted method has yet been developed to determine exactly how much bone has been destroyed at a particular site, however. Of special importance is whether bone has been *differentially* destroyed. In our case, we must try to determine if bones in the depositional periods have been affected differentially by weathering and decay. We were particularly concerned that there might have been a progressively greater destruction of bones in the older depositional periods that would make comparisons among periods misleading.

At the Hoko Rockshelter the main agents that affect bone are people and dogs, plus natural decay forces. People affect the elements present through their butchering practices. Some bones of an individual animal might not be brought to the site; this is the "schlepp" effect. Particular elements may be broken either to extract marrow or to produce raw material for tools. Dogs affect the bone specimens present by gnawing, and they thusly affect certain elements more severely than others. Dogs can also influence where bones are deposited by carrying them into "den" areas to be chewed. Weathering and decay are complex factors that affect various elements in different fashions. Elements from different animals will probably be affected differently due to structural variations.

Taphonomic Processes Affecting Fish Specimens

Vertebrae of fish are probably more durable than the majority of cranial bones. Many fish cranial bones are thin and flattened, while vertebrae tend to be denser and round. Certainly in many shell middens, vertebrae are recovered in higher numbers than are cranial bones, despite the fact that most fish have 2–3 times as many cranial bones as vertebrae. If, then, vertebrae are more durable than cranial bones, one method of looking for greater destruction of bone in the older depositional periods is to examine the ratio of vertebrae to cranial bones in each period to see if there is any change.

Table 5 shows the percentage of vertebrae in the total NISP of various fishes. We chose to examine these fishes because they are found in high numbers in the site and their bones are structurally different from each other. If more cranial bones than vertebrae are destroyed, then the percentage of vertebrae should rise in the older periods. Salmon and flatfish elements show this pattern in Table 5, suggesting greater loss of cranial bones in the lower levels and supporting the idea that cranial bones are more fragile than vertebrae. Calculation of the Spearman rank correlation coefficient for salmon and flatfish yielded a rho of .96 for salmon and .71 for flatfish—significant at the .01 and .05 levels, respectively.

Red Irish lord and rockfish show a reversal of the above pattern, however; their cranial bones are recovered in higher percentages in the lower levels. Calculation of the correlation coefficient for them yielded a rho of − .67 for red Irish lord and − .80 for rockfish—significant at the .05 and .01 levels, respectively. An explanation for these different patterns might be found in the different skeletal structure of these fishes. Subjectively, we think that salmon cranial bones are particularly fragile, that flatfish

Table 5. Proportion (Percentage) of Vertebrae to the total NISP (Number of Identified Species) of Several Species of Fish, by Depositional Period

Depositional Period	Salmon with Broken Vertebrae	Salmon without Broken Vertebrae	Red Irish Lord	Flatfish	Greenling	Rockfish	Halibut
8	66.8	33.1	32.1	55.2	38.2	29.4	89.5
7	68.2	54.5	25.4	46.0	35.3	27.8	77.8
6	66.8	51.2	20.8	57.8	28.6	22.6	86.1
5	64.5	46.0	22.3	52.2	24.6	23.3	85.8
4	73.0	52.2	24.1	63.1	27.0	22.6	78.0
3	75.0	56.6	18.5	64.5	31.8	25.8	100.0
2	77.4	58.7	24.3	55.5	33.1	20.2	85.7
1	81.8	33.3	19.8	71.4	24.2	19.6	100.0

107

crania are more durable, and that the crania of rockfish, red Irish lord, and greenling are the toughest of these fishes' bones. (We are unable to make any judgement about the relative durability of their respective vertebrae.) In view of these subjective estimates, the high percentage of red Irish lord and greenling cranial bones may indicate that they are more durable than the cranial bones of salmon and flatfish. At any rate, bones from different fish taxa appear to be affected unequally by decay. This realization implies potential difficulty in comparing the salmon NISP directly to the NISP of such fishes as greenling, rockfish, and red Irish lord.

Returning to consideration of the possibility of progressively greater destruction of bone in the lower depositional periods, it appears to be confirmed. The apparently more fragile parts of the fishes—cranial bones in the salmon and vertebrae in red Irish lord, greenling, and rockfish— are found in progressively lower percentages in the older depositional periods. This will have to be taken into account when comparing the fish proportions between periods.

Salmon vertebrae can be examined in another way, as well. They have a very distinct surface texture on the body of the vertebrae. Therefore, fragments of salmon vertebrae are easily identified, which is not the case for most other fishes. This ease of identification has two consequences. One is to raise the NISP of the salmon relative to other fish whose broken vertebrae are less identifiable. Secondly, the identifiability of fragmented salmon vertebrae can be used to examine breakage of bones from the older to more recent periods. Hypothetically, if bone in the older depositional periods is more affected by decay, there should be more broken salmon vertebrae. The pattern is not perfect, but higher numbers of broken vertebrae are found in the older periods, supporting the hypothesis of greater deterioration (Table 5).

Halibut bones present a problem in the rockshelter deposits. The number of vertebrae present ranges between 100 percent and 77.8 percent of the total halibut NISP, the highest proportion of any of the fishes (Table 5). Vertebrae are about 32 percent of the total identifiable elements in a halibut skeleton. The high percentage of halibut vertebrae in the rockshelter deposits indicates either extensive destruction of the cranial bones or very few cranial bones brought into the rockshelter. Halibut are large fish whose cranial bones are easy to find; therefore, poor recovery by the excavators is not a problem. The structure of the bones, both cranial and vertebral, suggests that they are less durable than those of other fishes such as rockfish or greenling. Again, unfortunately, there are no empirical data to support this. Nevertheless, the cranial bones might have decayed more than the vertebrae. The smaller flatfish are similar to halibut in structure, and we would expect their vertebrae-to-NISP ratio to be similar to that for halibut. The flatfish ratio is very different, however, ranging from 71.4

percent to 46.0 percent. Therefore, we suggest that the low number of halibut cranial bones is not due to their greater rate of decay but to some other factor. The very large size of halibut compared to other fish suggests that they may have been butchered differently. Swan (1869:23) records that the Makah smoked halibut for later consumption, doing the initial butchering on the beach. Quite possibly the rockshelter halibut were butchered on the beach and the heads were discarded there. If only smoked halibut was eaten in the rockshelter, no cranial bones would be present, either. However, as the rockshelter seems to have been inhabited over several seasons, both fresh halibut and smoked halibut may have been eaten. Therefore, the high percentage of vertebrae to cranial bones in the rockshelter could indicate either consumption of smoked halibut or initial butchering of the halibut outside the rockshelter.

Taphonomic Processes Affecting Mammal Specimens

Elements in mammal skeletons also have different levels of durability. Brain (1981), Binford & Bertram (1977), and Binford (1981) have provided information on the survivability of different ungulate elements. They examined the patterns of bone destruction produced by humans, nonhuman predators, and scavengers. Brain (1981:21) determined for goat and bovid bones that the "survival of a part is related *directly* to the specific gravity of that part, but *inversely* to the fusion time expressed in months." The pattern Brain found probably holds for deer and elk.

Sea mammal bones are structurally quite different from those of ungulates, however, and undoubtedly will show a different destruction pattern. To date, no studies have been done to determine the durability of different seal elements. Intuitively, we feel that some patterns should be similar. The proximal ends of seal humeri and femurs are filled with cancellous bone. These ends tend to be prime candidates for chewing by animals such as dogs. Vertebral bodies are also likely candidates. The most durable elements are probably teeth, mandibles, distal humeri, distal tibias, and the tarsals and carpals.

Examination of the fur seal elements indicates that complete animals were brought into the rockshelter. All parts of the skeleton are represented (Appendix B, Table B–1), although not equally. The most obvious pattern is an overrepresentation of forelimb elements—scapula, humerus, radius, ulna, carpals, and metacarpals—which constitute 17 percent of the fur seal NISP. In contrast, hindlimb elements (pelvis, femur, tibia, fibula, tarsals, and metatarsals) constitute 10 percent. These figures include all identifiable specimens of the elements and may indicate only that forelimb bones can be identified from smaller pieces than can hindlimb bones. Counting only whole elements, we find 60 complete forelimb elements (humerus, radius, ulna) and only 24 complete hindlimb elements (femur, tibia, fibula).

Interpretation of the above patterns could imply either differential deposition or differential preservation. It possibly results from a butchering pattern that emphasizes bringing forelimbs into the rockshelter more frequently than hindlimbs. This interpretation would not conflict with the indications of whole animals being deposited but would simply imply that sometimes only the front legs were brought into the shelter. In seals, the forelimb bones (and presumably the musculature) are larger than the hindlimb bones. Therefore, if only part of a seal were to be used by the hunter, it might well be the meatier forelimb.

A second possible explanation would involve some factor causing differential preservation. Possibly the forelimb bones survive better than the hindlimb bones. Comparisons of the percentage of fragmentary to whole specimens for each element reveal the percentages to be similar, 24–26 percent whole bones, with only two exceptions. The number of whole tibias is low, only 16 percent, and the number of complete ulnas is high, 38 percent of the total. Considering these figures to be measures of rates of breakage, there doesn't seem to be greater breakage of any bone except the tibia. Therefore, the suggestion that hindlimb bones might be underrepresented due to greater breakage of elements is not supported.

We are left with the conclusion that the overrepresentation of fur seal forelimbs reflects a butchering pattern rather than a preservation problem. When assessing the importance of fur seal in the diet, we must remember that whole animals were not always used. Partial use would reduce the amount of meat that seals contributed to the diet.

Although the sample is not very large, the distribution of parts of fur seal elements shows some patterns (Appendix B, Table B–1). Whole and broken shafts of the femur, humerus, radius, and ulna are more frequently recovered than is either end. The proximal ends of the radius, ulna, and tibia are found in higher numbers than the distal ends. The proximal ends of the radius and ulna are recovered only slightly more commonly than the distal ends, but the difference between the incidence of the proximal and distal ends of the tibia is very marked. A total of 15 proximal tibia articulations but only two distal articulations were recovered. The tibia shaft is recovered in lower quantity than the proximal end, unlike the case of the other long bones. Brain's (1981:139) data indicate that the distal tibia of ungulates is one of the more durable bones, while the proximal tibia is less durable. The ungulate pattern does not seem to apply to the seal tibia, and the different pattern of tibia breakage may well reflect the different structure of seals and ungulates.

The shafts of the seal long bones occur in quite high numbers; for several elements they are the most frequently recovered part (Appendix B, Table

B–1). This situation points out another contrast in structure between ungulate and sea mammal limb bones: ungulate bones are essentially tubes filled with marrow, while seal bones are filled with cancellous bone. Seal long bones would be more difficult to crack open for this reason and perhaps were not a source of marrow. However, since dogs appear to preferentially chew areas of bone with large amounts of cancellous tissue, seal bones may have been preferred by dogs over deer or elk long bones. Certainly, many of the seal humeri recovered have been chewed by dogs. In addition, the long bones of the small (harbor and fur) seals at Hoko were probably not good raw materials for tools, because of the cancellous interior, the very curved surfaces, and shortness. Therefore, they would have remained in the site deposits rather than being broken up during tool manufacturing.

The sample of deer and elk bones from Hoko Rockshelter is fairly small; NISPs are 165 and 149, respectively. The elements recovered represent all areas of the skeleton for both species, implying that whole animals were brought to the rockshelter at least some of the time (Appendix B, Table B–2). The distribution of elements for both is very similar; thus, even though elk are much larger than deer, we will discuss them together. Unlike the case of fur seals, no whole limb bones of deer or elk were recovered. Quite possibly the shafts of the limb bones were broken in order to remove the marrow. Brain (1981:139) offers some general information on the durability (high, medium, low survivability of elements) of bovid bones broken as the result of carnivore activity. A simple comparison of the deer and elk elements recovered from Hoko Rockshelter reveals that 74 percent of the bones are those with a high survivability rating. This result suggests that a high level of destruction of deer and elk bones has taken place, possibly from dogs chewing on them.

The deer and elk elements present show an underrepresentation of hindlimb bones, particularly the femur. Only two femur fragments were recovered, both elk. The metapodials were recovered in quite high numbers. These long, straight bones were frequently used as raw material for tools. Accordingly, metapodials may have been specifically collected even if the whole animal was not brought to the site, raising their numbers compared to other elements. Another factor that may account for the high number of metapodials is that the articular surfaces and shafts are easy to identify, even when broken into fragments.

To check for an overall pattern of greater destruction of deer and elk elements in the lower depositional periods, we examined the percentage of identified bone in each period. There was not a significant correlation of the overall rank orders of the 8 DPs. When we examined the correlation by level in three excavation units (N100/W96, N100/W100, and N100/W102), though, we found that two units, N100/W96 and N100/W102, showed significant, positive rank correlations at the .01 and .05 levels, respectively. In at least some units, then, a higher amount of unidentifiable bone appears in the lower levels, suggesting greater breakage of bone in the earlier periods.

Taphonomic Processes Affecting Bird Specimens

As in the case of fishbones, no studies of the durability of different bird elements have been done. Intuitively, we suspect that the bird cranial elements, sternum, and synsacrum are quite fragile, although parts of these elements may be reasonably durable. We cannot make any predictions of relative durability of limb bones. The strength of bones varies among species of birds. The loons and grebes have particularly dense bones, an adaptation for diving. These species' bones would presumably survive better than those of most birds. There may be other, less obvious variations in preservation between species, as well.

Differences in the distribution of elements among species could result from varying processing patterns or different levels of bone durability. There is also the problem of the degree of identifiability of elements in different species. For example, although foot phalanges of loons and grebes are quite distinctive and will be identified, many other birds' phalanges are not distinctive and will only rarely be identified. Therefore, when element distributions are examined, the lack of foot phalanges is the result of identification difficulties, not necessarily a taphonomic result. With these problems in mind, we decided to compare large taxonomic groups and in general to concentrate on the long bones.

The taxa examined (grebes, loons, Alcidae, and Anatidae) showed two general patterns (Appendix B, Table B–3). In the Anatidae and Alcidae, the body elements were found in the highest percentage (Table 6), followed by wing elements. This pattern approximates the natural ratio found in a complete skeleton; the body elements would constitute 64 percent, the wing and leg long bones would each constitute 14.5 percent, and the cranium, 0.7 percent. Leg elements are most common for the loons at Hoko Rockshelter. The grebes are different again, with wing and body elements being most frequent. In the grebes and loons the percentages of limb and body elements are similar, unlike the percentages among duck and murre elements, which show a distribution very similar to the natural one. Apparently, either the body elements of the loons and grebes are underrepresented or the limb elements are overrepresented. Because the limb bones of grebes and loons are denser than those of most other birds, this pattern may reflect a higher survival rate of limb elements than body elements in contrast to the pattern for other birds. We compared the pattern across the depositional periods for changes and found no discernible trend.

Table 6.   Percentage of Different Body Parts of Anatidae, Alcidae, Loons, and Grebes

Body Parts	Taxa				Reference Percentage[c]
	Anatidae[a]	Alcidae[b]	Loons	Grebes	
Cranium	8.3	14.1	12.6	5.8	7.3
Body	49.8	41.4	32.0	32.6	63.6
Wing[d]	25.2	30.6	21.4	32.6	14.5
Leg[d]	16.7	13.9	34.0	29.0	14.5
Total %	100.0	100.0	100.0	99.9	99.9
N	828	382	103	138	55

[a]Includes ducks, geese, and swans.
[b]Includes murres, auklets, murrelets, and puffins.
[c]The reference percentage is the actual percentage found in a complete bird skeleton.
[d]Excludes the phalanges.

In all taxa except one, loons, wing elements are found in higher numbers than leg elements, although they are present in equal numbers in a whole carcass. Leg bones are usually somewhat smaller than wing bones—grouse and their relatives being an exception—but leg bones have more meat on them. During butchering the wings might be cut off and discarded separately, while much of the leg might be left on the carcass during cooking. Cooking might weaken the leg bones, and the meatier leg bones were possibly more likely to have been scavenged by dogs. The combination of these factors could create an underrepresentation of leg bones. All of this, however, is speculation. Data from other sites and work on the relative durability of different elements are needed for sorting it out further.

Summary

Examination of the bones has confirmed their progressively greater destruction as the depositional periods become older, particularly in the case of fish and probably of mammals, as well. The type of elements destroyed differs among the different species of fish and between fur seals and deer/elk. Any interpretation of change in resource use between the depositional periods will have to first take into account these factors.

A few species show butchering patterns that affect their representation in the site. Halibut elements are almost certainly very underrepresented because complete individuals were not being brought into the rockshelter. Also, it appears that sometimes fur seal forelimbs but not hindlimbs were brought into the shelter. This butchering pattern affects reconstruction of the fur seal contribution to the diet in particular.

SEDIMENTARY AND FAUNAL ATTRIBUTES OF DEPOSITIONAL PERIODS

Depositional Period 1 (DP–1)

The oldest, deepest deposits of DP–1 rest on mudstone bedrock. This period is characterized by a high frequency of naturally deposited, colluvial silty sand and gravel layers interbedded with cultural deposits. The overall frequency of different layer types (see Table 2) in DP–1 is different from that of the other periods. There is a low frequency of "living floors" (A) and shell refuse (D, E). Hearth-type layers (B) and refuse other than shell (H, I, J) are common, suggesting that resource processing was probably an important activity throughout the use of the shelter.

There are two probable hearth features in deposits from DP–1. Despite the abundance of hearth-type remains, no pit or stake molds were observed in the profiles at this depth. Absence of stakes and pits cannot be explained on the basis of lack of recognition of these features in the profiles, because the silty sand greatly increases the resolution of all cultural deposits.

Faunal materials were identified from only two adjacent excavation units in the southern area of the site. The three highest-density fish taxa are greenling, red Irish lord, and rockfish (Appendix A, Table A–2). They constitute 85 percent of the NISP and 66 percent of the MNI. Salmon, surfperch, and Pacific cod are of similar frequencies to each other, sharing a fourth-rank position in NISP and MNI. The total density of fishbone is low, 1,409 identified specimens. The MNI density is greater than in DP–3 and DP–8.

Only 2 identifiable and 32 unidentifiable mammal bones were recovered from DP–1 (Appendix A, Table A–3). Deer and sea lion are the only species identified. DP–1 has a lower density of deer bone than does any other depositional period. That sea lion is found at all in this period is surprising, because it is found in such a low density in the site.

The overall bird bone density in DP–1 is the lowest for any period in the site—21.2 bones and 7.5 MNI per cubic meter (Appendix A, Table A–6). The Anatidae (ducks, swans, geese) are found in the highest densities, followed by diving ducks and gulls and finally by the loons and grebes. In all taxa the DP–1 densities of NISP and MNI are the lowest in the site.

The paucity of deposits excavated from DP–1 makes difficult any generalizing about the character of site use when the shelter was first occupied. In general, though, the site seems to have been initially occupied intermittently, as evidenced by the interbedding of cultural remains among the silty-sand deposits. Occupations were probably for limited durations only and possibly for very specific reasons. This form of occupation would account for the low frequency of "floor" and shell refuse deposits. The lack of evidence of pits and stakes in DP–1 also suggests limited, possibly activity-specific or short-term occupation.

The data give no strong indication of a season of occupation. The sea lion bone suggests fall through spring, but we would not want to draw a conclusion on the basis of a single bone. The very low density of bone supports the interpretation of intermittent occupation suggested by the stratigraphy.

Depositional Period 2 (DP–2)

DP–2 is also characterized by a high concentration of natural deposits. However, the density of cultural layer types in DP–2 makes it more similar to the following periods than to DP–1. The frequency of different layer types conforms with expected values, except for refuse deposits other than shell (H, I, J), which were fewer than expected (see Table 4). Other important aspects of DP–2 include a fairly low volume (see Table 3) and a high frequency of pit and hearth features.

Fauna was identified from only two excavation units, the same units as in DP–1. The fauna in this period, however, is dramatically different from the fauna of DP–1 and from that of most of the other periods. The density of fishbone was the second-highest among the 8 periods—4,650 specimens and 149.5 MNI per cubic meter (Appendix A, Table A-2). Greenling NISP and MNI are the most dense of the fish in this period, and only in DP–5 is greenling more dense. Rockfish NISP and MNI are second-ranked in DP–2 and are at their highest densities in the site. Salmon, red Irish lord, and surfperch NISPs and MNI share third rank, at a density considerably below both rockfish and greenling (Appendix A, Table A–2).

Mammal bones do not show the very high density shown by the fish (Appendix A, Table A–4). Instead, at 30 specimens and 7 MNI per cubic meter, they have their second-lowest density in DP–2. Fur seal and harbor seal are the main mammals, followed by elk and deer. This depositional period contains one young harbor seal that died at 1–6 months. Its presence indicates that someone was residing at the site between July and November. The presence of fur seals is also of some help in determining the season of occupation; generally, fur seals are present in the region only in the fall through spring (Banfield 1974:360, Everitt et al. 1979:33–35).

Birds are present in a medium-high density, fourth-highest of all the periods, although well under DP–4, which is the most dense (Appendix A, Table A–6). The diving and dabbling ducks make up 60 percent of the NISP and 55 percent by MNI. They are both present in their highest density in this period.

Though the cultural deposits in this period are still interbedded with naturally deposited silty sand, many of the cultural deposits are thicker than those in DP–1. There are distinct floor and refuse deposits, and a high frequency of hearths and pit features. The second-highest density of fish remains found in any period was recovered from DP–2 (Appendix A, Table A–2). This high density of fishbones suggests that site use during this period was characterized by increasing intensity of activities. The presence of interbedded silty sand, however, suggests that the site was still being occupied seasonally or intermittently.

The relatively low density of mammal bones compared to the fish and bird bones possibly reflects a sampling problem; the larger mammal bones may have been discarded in an area we did not excavate. The low average weight of the mammal bones recovered, 1.12 gm, supports this interpretation.

Depositional Period 3 (DP–3)

The most commonly represented layers in this period are classified as hearth layers (B) and hearth refuse (F). However, hearth features were not observed in the unit profiles. Stake molds are also lacking. "Living floors" (A) and non-shell refuse deposits (H, I, J) are low in frequency. Shell refuse layers (D, E, G, K) are the only deposits that occur with expected frequency in DP–3 (see Table 4). Pit features are also common.

DP–3 is represented by the lowest volume of deposits of any period (see Table 3) and was recovered only from the central area of the rockshelter. The density of fishbone is second-lowest (Appendix A, Table A–2). Greenling and rockfish specimens are again the most frequent in the period, 30 percent and 24 percent of the NISP, respectively. Salmon in this period is in third rank among fish and considerably closer to the greenling and rockfish than is the case in DP–1 and DP–2. The fourth rank is difficult to establish because of conflicts between the NISP and MNI. The halibut NISP is higher than that of red Irish lord, but their MNIs are exactly the same. The halibut MNI is probably too low because of the scarcity of head bones, as previously mentioned. Halibut MNI reaches its highest density in this period.

The density of mammal bones is slightly higher than in DP–2 (Appendix A, Table A–4). Fur seals are the dominant mammals, with porpoise— appearing for the first time—at second rank. The single harbor seal element recovered from DP–3 is from an individual aged 6–9 months at death, which establishes season of death at mid-October to mid-February— overlapping the fur seal's fall through spring availability. The presence of both types of seals suggests human occupation of the site during most or all of this latter period.

The density of bird bones is 81.4 specimens and 25.7 MNI per cubic meter, the second-lowest NISP density and the highest MNI density (Appendix A, Table A–6). Diving seabirds have the highest density in DP–3, with the loons/grebes and the gulls tied for second-highest. The albatross/shearwater group is in third place. The shearwaters are present in the Strait of Juan de Fuca predominantly in the summer and fall (Whal et al. 1981: Tables C1–C4; Godfrey 1986:42–45), and their presence in DP–3 indicates hunting during one or both of these seasons.

In general, the character of deposition in this period is similar to that of DP–1. Features and "living floors" characteristic of prolonged or intensive use of the rockshelter are underrepresented. Naturally deposited silty sand and gravel layers are also less frequent than in the earlier periods, suggesting the slow infilling of the shelter and stabilization of the sloping shelter floor. A possible explanation of the apparent decline in activity during this time is that the main locus of activity had shifted to the north end of the shelter, which was not excavated. The higher density of artifacts in this period as compared to DP–1 and DP–2 suggests increasing use of the rockshelter.

DP–3 is from such a small area of the site that interpretations of it are particularly difficult. The density of fishbone has fallen dramatically from that of DP–2, although the dominant species present are the same. The density of mammal bones has risen slightly, but the proportions of species are the same. The bird density is similar, although the species dominating the assemblage are quite different. The mean weight of identified fish and mammal elements has risen, suggesting larger pieces of bone present. We believe that the best interpretation is a shift in use of this area of the shelter, resulting in a lower density of bone as well as different bones being deposited.

Depositional Period 4 (DP–4)

This period is characterized by an abundance of diverse deposits. In general, the different types of layers occur with expected frequencies. Hearths, pits, and stake molds are also common. DP–4 has the highest density of layers of all the depositional periods; the shelter appears to have been used intensively, with a wide variety of activities taking place, during DP–4. The density of rooffall layers (C2, C3) is higher than in DP–3. These deposits occur near the upper boundary of DP–4 and independently of the silty sand deposits (C1) with which they are normally associated in the lower depositional periods. Though these rooffall deposits do not form a distinct bed or concentration, their presence at high frequency may still indicate a period of moister conditions or possibly a hiatus in shelter occupation at the end of DP–4.

Fauna from DP–4 has been identified from six units, a much wider area than from any of the preceding depositional periods. Because these units are found within the rockshelter and down the slope, DP–4 offers a much better sample of the activities during its formation.

The density of fishbones is 3,066 elements and 102.1 MNI per cubic meter (Appendix A, Table A–1), much higher than in DP–3 and similar to the densities in succeeding DP–5 and DP–7. Greenling and salmon are the first- and second-ranked fish, although the salmon MNI is lower than that of the third-ranked group, red Irish lord and rockfish. Ratfish has a low density of elements, normal for this species, but the MNI is slightly higher than that of salmon.

The mammal density is higher than that of DP–1, DP–2, or DP–3, but much lower than that of any of the succeeding periods (Appendix A, Table A–4). Porpoise and fur seal are the dominant mammals, with deer ranking third.

DP–4 has the highest overall density of bird bone specimens and the third-highest bird MNI (Appendix A, Table A–6). The shearwaters and albatrosses are the dominant bird group here; they make up 38 percent of the elements and 14 percent of the MNI, their greatest density in the site. The loons, grebes, and diving sea birds have higher MNI densities than the shearwaters but much lower NISP densities. The diving sea birds, mainly the common murre, are second-ranked in DP–4 and at their highest density in the site. The shearwaters are present in the Strait of Juan de Fuca from about March to October; they leave to breed on Pacific islands during the winter (Wahl et al. 1981:Tables C1–C4; Godfrey 1986:42–45). Their dominance among the bird remains of DP–4 implies human occupation of the rockshelter during at least some of these months. Additionally, Hurst's (n.d.:7) analysis of the shellfish indicates "an early to late summer period of shellfish processing."

Depositional Period 5 (DP–5)

DP–5 is very distinctive in the stratigraphic profiles because of its abundance of thick, concentrated shell layers (Figure 2, 8.70–9.20m). These shell deposits extend over most of the site in DP–5, which has only a small area devoted to habitation activities. DP–5 also contains a high density of other refuse deposits (Table 4). This collection of sediment provides a striking contrast to the predominance of "living floor" deposits found in the central activity zone in DP–4. The density of layers in DP–5 is very low, reflecting the fact that shell layers in this period are very thick and thus are less numerous than the thinner layers in other depositional periods. Most other layer types are present in DP–5 at expected frequencies. Hearth and pit features are common, and stake molds are especially abundant.

The density of fishbone in DP–5 is 5,632 specimens and 163 MNI per cubic meter, the highest in the site (Appendix A, Table A–2). The number of bones identified is the highest of any period. Greenling and salmon are again first- and second-ranked, which seems to be a consistent pattern in the upper periods. Rockfish and red Irish lord are third- and fourth-ranked.

Although the fish reflect a continuation of the previous pattern, the mammals show a dramatic increase in density in DP–5. Most of this increase occurs in the density of fur seal bones (Appendix A, Table A–4), which is 196 NISP/m^3, although their MNI is still a relatively low 3/m^3. Porpoise, whale, elk, and deer are the other main mammal species.

In contrast to the mammals, the birds show a medium density of 185 NISP and 24.8 MNI per cubic meter (Appendix A, Table A–6). The duck, swan, and goose group is first-ranked, while diving sea birds are in second rank. After their peak density in DP–4, the shearwaters and albatrosses drop to a low density of 10 NISP and 1.7 MNI per cubic meter in DP–5.

The age at death of some of the fur seals indicates hunting during the winter to early spring. The shellfish indicate late summer to fall harvest (Hurst n.d.). This season of collection is later than the spring to summer harvest indicated by shellfish in DP–4. The fur seal and shellfish remains thus suggest a shift from summer to fall/winter occupation of the rockshelter.

The high density of shellfish and mammal bones reflects an intensification of resource collection, possibly resulting from an increase in the number of people using the site. While all types of mammal remains increase somewhat, most of the increase occurs in fur seal density. The concentration of fur seals might be explained as a result of resource specialization concomitant with increasing site population (Christenson 1980).

The high concentrations of general refuse and dense shell in the central activity zone also indicate that an intensification in resource processing has probably occurred, reflecting an increase in resource collection. A possible explanation for an intensification of resource collection would be an increase in the duration of occupation of the rockshelter (from summer only to summer through winter occupation). However, the replacement of "living floors" by dense shell refuse in the central activity zone argues against this interpretation, because ethnoarchaeological studies have reported that, as duration of site occupation increases, more time is invested in maintaining distinct refuse disposal areas (Yellen 1977a). The data thus support the idea of more people for a shorter period of time and a change of season to winter occupation. The rate of deposition may have increased in DP–5 due to the inclusion of more bulky shells and general refuse; if so, the density of bones would be even higher than the figures suggest.

Depositional Period 6 (DP–6)

In DP–6, humus "floors" are especially abundant, as are stake molds. The high frequency of floors suggests that there was a change in the types of activities conducted during this period, because DP–6 presents a sharp contrast to DP–5, in which refuse is more common in the central portion of the shelter.

DP–6 has a lower density of fishbones than does DP–5 (Appendix A, Table A–2). Greenling and salmon are again found in the highest densities, followed by red Irish lord in third place and rockfish in fourth place. Most of the aggregate drop is caused by the dramatic fall in greenling density.

The density of the mammal NISP is the highest in the site, although the density of the MNI is slightly less than DP–5 (Appendix A, Table A–4). The densities of fur seal NISP and MNI are at their peak in DP–6. One harbor seal individual was aged 1–6 months, indicating that it was killed between July and November.

The density of bird NISP is slightly higher than in DP–5, while the MNI is lower (Appendix A, Table A–6). Diving seabirds, the duck/swan/goose group, and the diving ducks are ranked, respectively, first, second, and third. The common murre accounts for the majority of the diving seabirds and is the most frequently occurring bird in DP–6.

Shellfish indicate mid- to late-fall harvest, which is an even shorter period of harvest than in DP–5 (Hurst n.d.: 7).

In summary, the fauna shows the same general composition as in DP–5. The only difference is a drop in density of identified fishbones. The density of unidentifiable fish and mammal bone (Figure 5) is extremely high in DP–6. The ratio of unidentified to identified fish and mammal bone is the highest in the site. The high proportion of living floors suggests that the drop in density of identified specimens is probably the result of trampling, which would break the bones and lower the number of identifiable specimens. If so, the intensity of resource collection may have been maintained in DP–6.

A higher proportion of floors results when people invest more time in maintaining refuse areas. This suggests an increase in the duration of the seasonal occupation (see Yellen 1977a).

Depositional Period 7 (DP–7)

This period is characterized by a somewhat higher than expected concentration of refuse deposits. However, dense shell refuse (D) is almost absent in the exterior and intermediate zones. This scarcity of shellfish remains indicates a dramatic drop in shellfish processing at the site. Hearth features and pits are common and, as in DP–6, stakes are abundant.

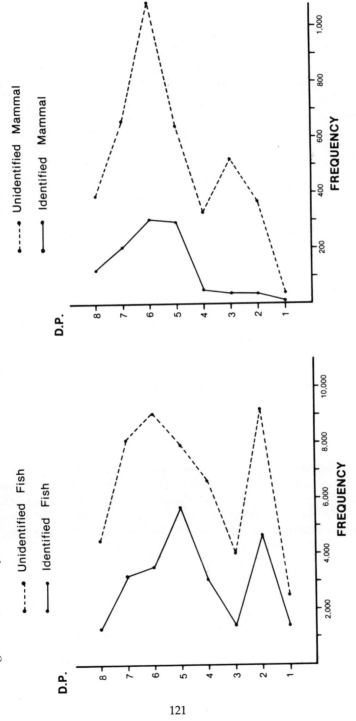

Figure 5. Density of Identified and Unidentified Fish and Mammal Bones, by Depositional Period (D.P.)

121

DP–7 has a fairly low volume of deposit, spread out over a wide area. Deposits of this period are absent in some excavation units. Individual layers are small, giving a patchy distribution of different types of layers.

The density of bone falls from the higher densities of DP–5 and DP–6 (Appendix A, Table A–2). Greenling and salmon are first- and second-ranked, as before, but the proportions have changed. Salmon makes up 30 percent of the NISP, the highest of any period. The salmon MNI rises considerably and is now higher than in any other period. Rockfish and red Irish lord again occupy third and fourth rank, and their densities remain fairly stable.

The density of mammal bones drops to about two-thirds of that in DP–5 and DP–6, as does the density of the fur seal NISP (Appendix A, Table A–4). Deer and elk densities are very similar to those of DP–6, although below those of DP–5.

Continuing its decline, the density of bird bones drops below that of any earlier period except DP–1. The diving seabirds, diving ducks, and duck/swan/goose categories are most common and so similar to each other as to make ordering them impossible.

DP–7 shows an overall decline in the density of the fish, bird, and mammal bones. The abundance of refuse deposits combined with the low volume of deposits also suggests a period of intermittent occupation. Radiocarbon dates from this period put it into the time of early European contact. The Spaniards had built a fort at Neah Bay by 1792 (Swan 1869:4), about 22 km from the site. Therefore, we may be seeing changes in residence patterns or the effect of disease on population size in response to this contact.

Depositional Period 8 (DP–8)

DP–8 encompasses those deposits within 20 cm of the surface. Stake molds, hearth features, and hearth-type deposits (B, F) are uncommon. Other refuse (H, I, J) and rooffall deposits are abundant. This assemblage of deposits suggests continued intermittent occupation of the site and its eventual abandonment. Deposits of DP–8 are spread over a wide area, expanding west of the shelter for the first time.

The fish density has dropped to less than half of that found in DP–4 through DP–7 (Appendix A, Table A–2). Salmon NISP is the most dense at 449 elements/m³. Greenling NISP is second-ranked, with a very low density of 338 elements/m³. The density of the greenling MNI is greater than that of salmon, although they are very close. Red Irish lord and rockfish again share third and fourth rank.

The density of mammal bone has dropped compared to DP–7. The drop in density of fur seal NISP and MNI is mainly responsible for the overall drop in mammal density. The densities of other mammal species are similar to levels in DP–7. Porpoise, deer, and elk are found in similar densities to each other, much lower than the density of fur seal. One very young fur seal has been recovered, definitely less than six months of age, possibly as few as ten weeks old. This age estimate places its death in October at the earliest and mid-December at the latest. One harbor seal was killed at 6–9 months of age, indicating it died between November and January.

The density of bird bones continues its progressive decrease from DP–4. The duck/swan/goose group is the most frequently occurring, while diving sea birds and diving ducks rank second and third.

The drop in density of fish, bird, and mammal bones supports the interpretation of gradual abandonment of the site.

CONCLUSION

The bone density of the depositional periods shows some interesting patterns (Figure 5). The low density of DP–1 is not surprising, considering the presence of noncultural layers and the probability that the bone in this period is the most decayed in the site. The noncultural layers probably account for about 30 percent of the volume of deposit. Reducing the volume figure by 30 percent and recalculating the bone density raises the fish density to about 1880 bones/m³ and mammal density to about 8 bones/m³. Neither density is very high; even considering great erosion of bone, we feel that human activity at the site was minimal in DP–1.

The extremely high density of fishbone in DP–2 is particularly marked, considering the low density in preceding DP–1 and the following DP–3 and DP–4. In addition, DP–2 has a large volume of noncultural deposits, possibly as much as 30 percent. Removal of this material from the volume calculation gives a density of some 7,360 fishbones, higher by a large margin than in any other period. On the other hand, the density of the mammal bone is very similar to that in DP–3 and DP–4, even if refigured, and not nearly as high as in DP–5 through DP–7. We are tempted to suggest that the site occupants were concentrating on fishing rather than hunting during DP–2, but consideration of the types of layers suggests another possibility. Excavated portions of DP–2 have very few refuse deposits, and mammal bones quite possibly were deposited in an area we did not excavate. We can conclude, however, that people were collecting fish in large quantities during DP–2. The very great change in density of fishbones from DP–1 implies an intensification of use of the rockshelter, i.e., occupation for a longer time or by a greater number of people.

The density of fishbones drops in DP-3, becoming similar to that of DP-1 and DP-4. The types of layers in DP-3 are similar to those of DP-2, although the volume of natural deposits is less, approximately 5 percent. Therefore, there appears to have been an actual drop in the quantity of fish collected. The density of mammal bones is similar to that of DP-2, probably again reflecting merely the absence of refuse layers. A shift in the locus of activity may also be affecting the observed densities of layers and bones.

In DP-4, density of fishbone rises somewhat, but the density of mammal bone remains similar to that of DP-3. Because the layers in this period are similar to those of DP-2 and DP-3, the low density of mammal bone is not surprising. The rise in fishbone density may be the beginning of the major rise in DP-5. Because destruction by decay should gradually decrease with decreased age of deposit, though, some of the increase in density may simply reflect better preservation.

DP-5 shows a major increase in density of both fish and mammal bones. The increase in fish density was seemingly foreshadowed in DP-4, but the increase in mammals is very sudden. Most of the increased density results from an increase in fur seal bones. The densities of other mammals either stay the same or increase only slightly. The simplest conclusion is that fur seal hunting has increased drastically. However, a high amount of general refuse is also present. Possibly the jump in volume of mammal bone results from the inclusion of refuse layers, which were absent in DP-1 through DP-4. On the other hand, if mammal bones were commonly discarded with general refuse, we would expect the density of all mammal bones to have increased. That this doesn't happen leads us back to our suggestion of increased exploitation of fur seals.

After DP-5, the density of identifiable fish and mammal bones drops steadily through DP-8. The density of unidentifiable bone reaches its peak in DP-6 and then drops. DP-5 through DP-8 all show both refuse and floor deposits, indicating that the drop is probably not related to the absence of particular types of deposits. The preservation of bone should be getting progressively better, resulting in a progressively greater bone density. Therefore, the progressive drop in density is best interpreted as a gradual decrease in intensity of site occupation.

Although generally the same species of fish supply the majority of identified elements in DP-1 through DP-8, the relative incidence of these species changes through the site. Greenling is the main fish present in almost all periods (Figure 6). However, salmon NISP and MNI steadily increase from DP-1 until they surpass greenling NISP and MNI in DP-8. The density figures show that some of this rise in the proportion of salmon results simply from the dramatic drop in the numbers of greenling bones from DP-5 onward, while salmon remains fairly steady or gains a bit (Appendix

Figure 6. Percent NISP and MNI for Red Irish Lord, Greenling, and Salmon, by Depositional Period (D.P.)

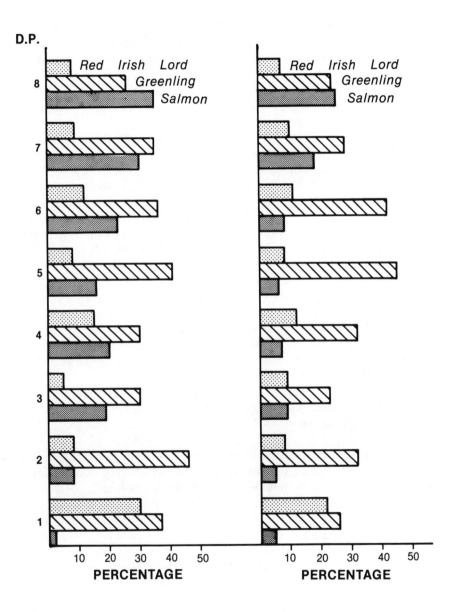

A, Table A–1). Evidently, some of this change in proportion reflects a problem inherent in reporting in percentages: as one thing drops, another *must* rise. It is still tempting to conclude that salmon contributed a larger quantity to the diet in the more recent periods, even though breakage analysis strongly suggests progressively greater destruction of salmon cranial bones in the lower periods. However, we would expect to see a progressive increase in density of both the NISP and MNI from the oldest to youngest depositional periods strictly as a result of the preservation factor. Therefore, the interpretation that salmon became progressively more important at Hoko cannot be proved from these data alone. Conversely, in the older periods salmon may have been more important than is suggested by their low numbers.

The proportions of the major mammal species show great similarity from period to period, with the exception of fur seals (Figure 7). The density and proportion of fur seal bones increases dramatically in DP–5, holds steady at a high density in DP–6, and then drops slightly in DP–7 and DP–8. The density and proportions of NISP and MNI of the other mammal species fluctuate somewhat but show no particular spatial or temporal pattern. Quite probably, most of these fluctuations reflect the small sample size rather than change in quantity of the animals themselves. DP–5 through DP–8 differ from the earlier periods in the presence of normal to high quantities of refuse layers. The absence of these layers in DP–1 through DP–4 could possibly explain the absence of fur seal bones there. However, neither the density nor the proportion of other mammals changes dramatically in DP–5, and we have no reason to believe that refuse deposits would contain only fur seal bones. Therefore, we believe this increase in fur seal bones reflects intensified hunting of fur seals or possibly a shift to winter/early-spring occupation of the site.

In summary, our examination of the stratigraphic and taphonomic factors influencing the faunal assemblage at the Hoko Rockshelter allows us to draw several conclusions:

1. The progressive increase in the quantity of salmon results from taphonomic factors, not from an increase in the collection of salmon. Conversely, salmon are underrepresented in the earlier periods.

2. The sudden rise in the fur seal NISP and MNI in DP–5 represents a real increase in the collection of fur seals. A possible explanation of these changes may be a rise in human population which necessitated intensification of resource collection.

3. Until DP–7 the rockshelter seems to have been used for short periods but possibly by larger groups of people through time. A decline in use starts in DP–7 and continues until the rockshelter is abandoned. The drop in use, indicated by lower densities of fauna, may be associated with the

Figure 7. Percent NISP and MNI for Porpoise, Fur Seal, and Deer/Elk, by Depositional Period (D.P.)

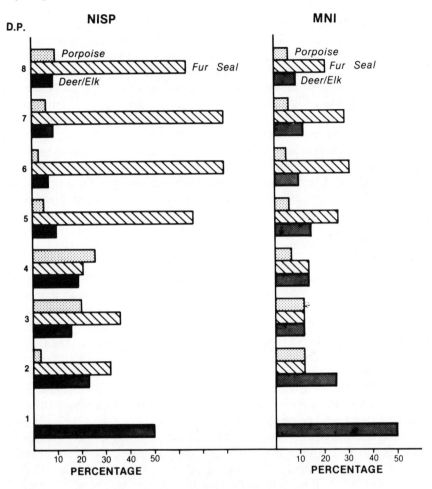

early European-contact period, when the native population was severely reduced by disease or seasonal routines were reorganized to take advantage of European settlements. Either or both situations could have led to the abandonment of the rockshelter.

4. Variations in layer type frequencies characterizing the different depositional periods could be a result of shifts in the season of site occupation and the number of people using the shelter. Although data for seasonal determination are limited, summer use of the shelter may have been prevalent in DP–4. Site occupation shifted to fall and winter in DP–

5. In DP–6 through DP–8, activities at the site may have been restricted more to the fall.

The importance of salmon in the diet of the prehistoric Northwest Coast people is a topic of debate among archaeologists (see, e.g., Matson 1983, Burley 1983). Obviously, the proportion of salmon bones in a site is particularly relevant in resolving this debate. At Hoko, we have shown that a temporal increase in the proportion of salmon bones, which might be seen as supporting the idea of progressively greater economic importance of salmon, was instead probably the result of taphonomic processes. In any site interpretation, taphonomic factors should be ruled out before an increase or decrease in bones of salmon (or any other taxa) is interpreted as resulting from an economic reason.

One aspect of taphonomy that we have examined is the variable durability of bone elements of different taxa. We have suggested that similar bones of various fish taxa have different patterns of survivability. Also, the pattern of seal elements recovered was quite distinct from that of deer and elk. Two factors that influence the pattern of elements shown in any site are inherent structure of the elements themselves and butchering patterns, both of which may vary between taxa. The Hoko Rockshelter appears to show a combination of both factors affecting the elements recovered. Intersite comparison of the patterns of elements recovered could be particularly useful in establishing the relative durability of different elements. This has not been done yet in the Northwest. It could be especially useful for fishbones, as no objective information on their durability is available.

Finally, we have attempted to combine the information gained from the stratigraphy and fauna to make a more complete interpretation. Changes in the fauna could possibly indicate changes either in the economic base of the rockshelter inhabitants or in the type of activities taking place in the rockshelter. The stratigraphy and fauna complement each other; in DP–6 the drop in density of identified fishbones is probably related to the high incidence of floor type deposits rather than to a drop in numbers of fish collected. Also, the ability to determine whether a layer type was under- or over-represented made comparisons between depositional periods more convincing. The sediments of any site can help establish the reasons for changes in the faunal assemblage.

APPENDIX A. NUMBER OF IDENTIFIED SPECIMENS (NISP) AND MINIMUM NUMBER OF INDIVIDUALS (MNI) OF FISH, MAMMALS, AND BIRDS, BY DEPOSITIONAL PERIOD (DP)

Table A-1.   Count of Fish NISP and MNI, by Depositional Period
Table A-2.   Density (per Cubic Meter) of Fish NISP and MNI, by Depositional Period
Table A-3.   Count of Mammal NISP and MNI, by Depositional Period
Table A-4.   Density (per Cubic Meter) of Mammal NISP and MNI, by Depositional Period
Table A-5.   Count of Bird NISP and MNI, by Depositional Period
Table A-6.   Density (per Cubic Meter) of Grouped Bird Taxa NISP and MNI, by Depositional Period

129

Table A-1. Count of Fish NISP (Number of Identified Specimens) and MNI (Minimum Number of Individuals), by Depositional Period (DP)

Taxa	DP-1 NISP	DP-1 MNI	DP-2 NISP	DP-2 MNI	DP-3 NISP	DP-3 MNI	DP-4 NISP	DP-4 MNI	DP-5 NISP	DP-5 MNI	DP-6 NISP	DP-6 MNI	DP-7 NISP	DP-7 MNI	DP-8 NISP	DP-8 MNI	Total NISP	Total MNI
Dogfish	23	1	22	2	12	1	62	2	365	11	250	11	22	2	225	9	976	39
Skate	4	1	3	1	—	—	1	1	9	1	9	1	9	1	25	1	60	7
Ratfish	5	1	5	1	4	1	42	11	68	16	29	7	15	3	41	11	209	51
Sturgeon	—		—		—		—		5	1	—		—		—		5	1
Herring	10	1	157	10	9	1	14	1	28	3	43	3	14	2	97	6	372	27
Anchovy	2	1	1	1	—		—		9	2	5	2	8	3	20	4	45	13
Salmon	22	3	358	7	184	4	866	10	1,792	19	2,176	18	1,079	17	3,300	64	9,777	142
Trout	—		1	1	—		—		2	1	5	1	—		4	1	12	4
Steelhead	—		—		—		—		1	1	3	1	—		1	1	5	3
Eulachon	—		—		—		3	1	—		—		6	1	—		9	2
Pacific Cod	30	2	44	3	—		8	1	17	1	13	1	35	2	177	9	324	19
Hake	—		3	1	—		1	1	1	1	84	6	33	1	171	2	293	12
Surfperch	34	3	240	8	19	1	315	9	494	15	45	3	2	1	12	1	1,161	41
Wolfeel & Prickleback	9	1	26	1	5	1	26	2	91	3	49	1	19	1	87	1	312	11
Rockfish	199	8	920	28	233	8	572	17	1,187	28	932	22	324	6	725	21	5,092	138
Sablefish	1	1	—		—		3	1	31	1	22	1	13	1	1	1	71	6
Greenling	446	15	2,034	46	299	10	1,309	46	4,604	148	3,406	100	1,237	26	2,482	67	15,817	458

Lingcod	3	_1_	72	_4_	40	_3_	122	_3_	619	_10_	548	_9_	185	_4_	623	_14_	2,212 _48_
Buffalo Sculpin	5	_1_	5	_1_	2	_1_	31	_3_	55	_3_	22	_1_	5		5	_1_	130 _12_
Red Irish Lord	315	_13_	350	_10_	50	_4_	642	_17_	962	_27_	1,186	_25_	317	_9_	788	_19_	4,610 _124_
Staghorn Sculpin	—		—		1	_1_	14	_1_	5	_1_	3	_1_	—		1	_1_	24 _5_
Great Sculpin	—		1	_1_	—		3	_1_	1	_1_	—	_4_	76	_3_	7	_6_	12 _4_
Cabezon	3	_1_	28	_2_	29	_2_	77	_4_	238	_5_	133	_2_	2	_1_	179	_5_	763 _27_
Sculpins	3		6		4		2		25	_3_	7		9		8	_1_	57 _15_
Arrowtooth Flounder	4	_1_	20	_1_	7	_1_	11	_1_	84	_3_	23	_1_	2		16	_2_	174 _9_
Petrale Sole			43	_4_	6		2		31	_3_	3		40		9	_4_	96 _13_
Halibut	6	_1_	7	_1_	62	_2_	41	_2_	204	_4_	117	_2_	11		237		716 _17_
Rock Sole			6						23	_3_	5	_1_			3		48 _7_
Starry Flounder			2				3	_1_	12	_1_	55	_3_	14		48	_3_	134 _10_
Sand Sole									7	_1_					1	_1_	8 _2_
Sanddab			2	_1_					—		—				—		2 _1_
Rex Sole									1	_1_	2	_1_			—		1 _1_
English Sole			1	_1_					8	_1_	1				5	_1_	16 _4_
Curlfin Sole									2	_1_	—				1		4 _3_
Flatfish	3	_1_	65	_3_	18	_1_	123	_5_	284	_7_	298	_6_	57	_2_	148	_5_	996 _30_
TOTALS	1,127	_58_	4,422	_142_	984	_44_	4,293	_143_	11,265	_326_	9,474	_236_	3,534	_92_	9,444	_265_	44,543 _1,306_
Unidentifiable	1,983		8,758		2,803		9,319		15,836		24,429		8,935		32,969		110,228

Table A-2. Density (per Cubic Meter) of Fish NISP (Number of Identified Specimens) and MNI (Minimum Number of Individuals), by Depositional Period (DP)

Taxa	DP-1		DP-2		DP-3		DP-4		DP-5		DP-6		DP-7		DP-8		Site	
	NISP	MNI	NISP	MNI	NISP	MNI	NISP	MNI	NISP	MNI	NISP	MNI	NISP	MNI	NISP	MNI	NISP	MNI
Dogfish	28.8	1.2	23.1	2.1	17.1	1.4	44.3	1.4	182.5	5.5	92.6	4.1	20.0	1.8	29.9	1.2	57.4	2.3
Skate	5.0	1.2	3.2	1.0	—	—	0.7	0.7	4.5	0.5	3.3	0.4	8.2	0.9	3.4	0.1	3.5	0.4
Ratfish	6.2	1.2	5.3	1.0	5.7	1.4	30.0	7.9	34.0	8.0	10.7	2.6	13.6	2.7	5.6	1.5	12.3	3.0
Sturgeon	—	—	—	—	—	—	—	—	2.5	0.5	—	—	—	—	—	—	0.3	0.1
Herring	12.5	1.2	165.3	10.5	12.9	1.4	10.0	0.7	14.0	1.5	15.9	1.1	12.7	1.8	13.2	0.8	21.9	1.6
Anchovy	2.5	1.2	1.0	1.0	—	—	—	—	4.5	1.0	1.9	0.7	7.3	2.7	2.7	0.5	2.6	0.8
Salmon	27.5	3.8	376.8	7.4	262.9	5.7	618.6	7.1	896.0	9.5	805.9	6.7	980.9	15.5	449.0	8.7	575.1	8.4
Trout	—	—	1.0	1.0	—	—	—	—	1.0	0.5	1.9	0.4	—	—	0.5	0.1	0.7	0.2
Steelhead	—	—	—	—	—	—	—	—	0.5	0.5	1.1	0.4	—	—	0.1	0.1	0.3	0.2
Eulachon	—	—	—	—	—	—	2.1	0.7	—	—	—	—	5.5	0.9	—	—	0.5	0.1
Pacific Cod	37.5	2.5	46.3	3.2	—	—	5.7	0.7	8.5	0.5	4.8	0.4	31.8	1.8	24.1	1.2	19.1	1.1
Hake	—	—	3.2	1.0	—	—	0.7	0.7	0.5	0.5	31.1	2.2	30.0	0.9	23.3	0.3	17.2	0.7
Surfperch	42.5	3.8	252.6	8.4	27.1	1.4	225.0	6.4	247.0	7.5	16.7	1.1	1.8	0.9	1.6	0.1	68.3	2.4
Wolfeel/Prickleback	11.2	1.2	27.4	1.0	7.1	1.4	18.6	1.4	45.5	1.5	18.1	0.4	17.3	0.9	11.8	0.1	18.3	0.6
Rockfish	248.8	10.0	968.4	29.5	332.9	11.4	408.6	12.1	593.5	14.0	345.2	8.1	294.5	5.5	98.6	2.9	298.5	8.1

Sablefish	1.2	1.2	—	—	2.1	0.7	15.5	0.5	8.1	0.4	11.8	0.9	0.1	0.1	4.2	0.4		
Greenling	557.5	18.8	2141.0	48.4	427.1	14.3	935.0	32.9	2302.0	74.0	1261.5	37.0	1124.5	23.6	337.7	9.1	930.4	26.9
Lingcod	3.8	1.2	75.8	4.2	57.1	4.3	87.1	2.1	309.5	5.0	203.0	3.3	168.2	3.6	84.8	1.9	130.1	2.8
Buffalo Sculpin	6.2	1.2	5.3	1.0	2.9	1.4	22.1	2.1	27.5	1.5	8.1	0.4	4.5	0.9	0.7		7.6	0.7
Red Irish Lord	393.8	16.2	368.4	10.5	71.4	5.7	458.6	12.1	481.0	13.5	439.3	9.3	288.2	8.2	107.2	2.6	271.2	7.3
Staghorn Sculpin	—				1.4	1.4	10.0	0.7	2.5	0.5	1.1	0.4	—	0.1	0.1		1.4	0.3
Great Sculpin	—		1.0	1.0	—		2.1	0.7	0.5	0.5	—		—	0.9	0.1		0.7	0.2
Cabezon	3.8	1.2	29.4	2.1	41.4	2.9	55.0	2.9	119.0	2.5	49.3	1.5	69.1	2.7	24.4	0.8	44.9	1.6
Sculpins	3.8	1.2	6.3	1.0	5.7	1.4	1.4	0.7	12.5	1.5	2.6	0.7	1.8	0.9	1.1	0.7	3.3	0.9
Arrowtooth Flounder	5.0	1.2	21.0	1.0	10.0	1.4	7.9	0.7	42.0	1.0	8.5	0.4	8.2	0.9	2.2	0.1	10.2	0.5
Petrale Sole	—		45.3	4.2	8.6	1.4	1.4	0.7	15.5	1.5	1.1	0.4	1.8	0.9	1.2	0.3	5.6	0.7
Halibut	7.5	1.2	7.4	1.0	88.6	2.9	29.3	1.4	102.0	2.0	43.3	0.7	36.4	0.9	32.2	0.5	42.1	1.0
Rock Sole	—		6.3	1.0	—		—		11.5	1.5	1.9	0.4	10.0	0.9	0.4	0.1	2.8	0.4
Starry Flounder	—		2.1	1.0	—		2.1	0.7	6.0	0.5	20.4	1.1	12.7	0.9	6.5	0.4	7.9	0.6
Sand Sole	—		—		—		—		3.5	0.5	—		—		0.1	0.1	0.5	0.1
Sanddab	—		2.1	1.0	—		—		—		—		—		—		0.1	0.1
Rex Sole	—		—		—		—		0.5	0.5	—		—		—		0.1	0.1
English Sole	—		1.0	1.0	—		—		4.0	0.5	0.7	0.4	—		0.7	0.1	0.9	0.2
Curlfin Sole	—		—		—		—		1.0	0.5	0.4	0.4	—		0.1	0.1	0.2	0.2
Flatfish	3.8	1.2	68.4	3.2	25.7	1.4	87.9	3.6	142.0	3.5	110.4	2.2	51.8	1.8	20.1	0.7	58.6	1.8
TOTALS	1408.8	72.5	4654.7	149.5	1405.7	62.9	3066.4	102.1	5632.5	163.0	3508.9	87.4	3212.7	83.6	1284.9	36.0	2620.2	76.8

Table A-3. Count of Mammal NISP (Number of Identified Specimens) and MNI (Minimum Number of Individuals), by Depositional Period (DP)

Taxa	DP-1 NISP	DP-1 MNI	DP-2 NISP	DP-2 MNI	DP-3 NISP	DP-3 MNI	DP-4 NISP	DP-4 MNI	DP-5 NISP	DP-5 MNI	DP-6 NISP	DP-6 MNI	DP-7 NISP	DP-7 MNI	DP-8 NISP	DP-8 MNI	Total NISP	Total MNI
Squirrel	—	—	—	—	—	—	—	—	—	—	1	1	1	1	2	1	4	3
Beaver	—	—	1	1	—	—	2	1	10	1	7	1	2	1	3	1	25	6
Small Rodents	—	—	—	—	—	—	—	—	4	2	3	1	2	1	7	2	16	5
Rabbit	—	—	—	—	1	1	5	2	9	2	4	1	—	—	2	1	21	7
Whale	—	—	—	—	—	—	6	1	50	1	3	1	—	—	27	1	86	4
Porpoise	—	—	—	—	5	1	21	1	47	2	40	2	16	2	96	2	226	10
Dog	—	—	—	—	1	1	5	1	22	1	24	2	—	—	38	1	90	6
Wolf?	—	—	—	—	—	—	—	—	—	—	2	1	—	—	—	—	2	1
Black Bear	—	—	—	—	—	—	—	—	—	—	—	—	—	—	1	1	1	1
Raccoon	—	—	—	—	—	—	1	1	16	2	4	2	3	1	2	1	26	7
Marten	—	—	—	—	—	—	—	—	—	—	—	—	—	—	1	1	1	1
Mink	—	—	—	—	—	—	—	—	—	—	—	—	—	—	1	1	1	1
River Otter	—	—	—	—	—	—	3	1	11	3	8	1	—	—	5	1	27	6
Sea Otter	—	—	2	1	2	1	1	1	3	1	7	2	—	—	22	2	37	8
Skunk	—	—	2	1	2	1	—	—	10	1	2	1	—	—	1	1	17	6
Cougar?	—	—	—	—	—	—	—	—	—	—	1	1	—	—	—	—	1	1
Fur Seal	—	—	10	1	9	1	17	2	588	9	928	12	195	5	586	7	2333	37
Sea Lion	1	1	—	—	1	1	—	—	11	2	10	3	1	1	15	3	39	11
Harbor Seal	—	—	9	2	—	—	5	1	20	3	46	3	3	1	23	3	106	13
Elephant Seal?	—	—	—	—	—	—	—	—	—	—	—	—	2	1	—	—	2	1
Elk	—	—	3	1	—	—	4	1	57	3	34	1	11	1	40	2	149	9
Deer	1	1	4	1	4	1	11	1	34	2	50	3	10	1	44	2	158	11
TOTALS	2	2	31	8	25	8	81	14	892	34	1174	39	247	17	916	33	3368	155
Unidentifiable Specimens	32		351		364		539		1918		4185		796		3015		11,200	

134

Table A-4. Density (per Cubic Meter) of Mammal NISP (Number of Identified Specimens) and MNI (Minimal Number of Individuals), by Depositional Period (DP)

Taxa	DP-1		DP-2		DP-3		DP-4		DP-5		DP-6		DP-7		DP-8		Site	
	NISP	MNI	NISP	MNI	NISP	MNI	NISP	MNI	NISP	MNI	NISP	MNI	NISP	MNI	NISP	MNI	NISP	MNI
Squirrel	—	—	—	—	—	—	—	—	—	—	0.3	0.3	0.8	0.8	0.3	0.1	0.2	0.2
Beaver	—	—	1	1	—	—	1	0.6	3.3	0.3	1.8	0.3	1.7	0.8	0.4	0.1	1.3	0.3
Small Rodents	—	—	1	1	—	—	—	—	1.3	0.3	0.8	0.3	1.7	0.8	0.9	0.3	0.8	0.2
Rabbit	—	—	—	—	—	—	3	1.2	3.0	0.7	1.0	0.3	—	—	0.2	0.1	1.1	0.3
Whale	—	—	—	—	—	—	4	0.6	16.7	0.3	0.8	0.3	—	—	3.5	0.1	4.3	0.2
Porpoise	—	—	1	1	7.0	1.4	13	0.6	15.7	0.7	10.4	0.5	13.3	0.8	12.5	0.3	11.4	0.5
Dog	—	—	—	—	1.4	1.4	3	0.6	7.3	0.3	6.2	0.5	—	—	5.0	0.1	4.5	0.3
Wolf?	—	—	—	—	—	—	—	—	—	—	0.5	0.3	—	—	—	—	0.1	.05
Black Bear	—	—	—	—	—	—	—	—	—	—	—	—	—	—	0.1	0.1	.05	.05
Raccoon	—	—	—	—	—	—	1	.6	5.3	.7	1.0	0.5	2.5	0.8	0.3	0.1	1.3	0.3
Marten	—	—	—	—	—	—	—	—	—	—	—	—	—	—	0.1	0.1	.05	.05
Mink	—	—	—	—	—	—	—	—	—	—	—	—	—	—	0.1	0.1	.05	.05
River Otter	—	—	—	—	—	—	2	0.6	3.7	1	2.1	0.3	—	—	0.7	0.1	1.4	0.3
Sea Otter	—	—	2	1	3.0	1.4	—	—	1.0	0.3	1.8	0.5	0.8	0.8	2.9	0.3	1.9	0.4
Skunk	—	—	—	—	3.0	1.4	1	0.6	3.3	.3	0.5	0.3	0.8	0.8	0.1	0.1	0.9	0.3
Cougar?	—	—	—	—	—	—	—	—	—	—	0.3	0.3	—	—	—	—	.05	.05
Fur Seal	—	—	10	1	13.0	1.4	10	1.2	196.0	3	241.0	3.1	162.0	4.2	76.6	0.9	117.8	1.9
Sea Lion	1.3	1.3	—	—	1.4	1.4	—	—	3.7	0.7	2.6	0.8	0.8	0.8	2.0	0.4	2.0	0.6
Harbor Seal	—	—	9	1	1.4	1.4	3	0.6	6.7	1	11.9	0.8	1.7	0.8	3.0	0.4	5.4	0.7
Elephant Seal	—	—	—	—	—	—	—	—	—	—	—	—	1.7	0.8	—	—	0.1	.05
Elk	—	—	3	1	—	—	2	0.6	19	1.0	8.8	0.3	9.2	0.8	5.2	0.3	7.5	0.4
Deer	1.3	1.3	4	1	6	1.4	7	0.6	11.3	0.7	13.0	0.8	8.3	0.8	5.8	0.1	8.0	0.5
TOTALS	2.6	2.6	33	8	36	11.4	49	8.5	297.0	11.3	305.0	10.1	205.8	14.2	120.0	4.3	170.1	7.8
Unidentifiable Specimens	40		369		520		327		639		1087		663		394		565.7	

135

Table A-5. Count of Bird NISP (Number of Identified Specimens) and MNI (Minimum Number of Individuals), by Depositional Period (DP)

Taxa	DP-1 NISP	DP-1 MNI	DP-2 NISP	DP-2 MNI	DP-3 NISP	DP-3 MNI	DP-4 NISP	DP-4 MNI	DP-5 NISP	DP-5 MNI	DP-6 NISP	DP-6 MNI	DP-7 NISP	DP-7 MNI	DP-8 NISP	DP-8 MNI	Total NISP	Total MNI
Common Loon	3	1	5	1	1	1	8	2	7	1	18	2	5	1	30	2	77	11
Small Loon	—	—	—	—	2	1	3	1	3	1	10	2	2	1	22	4	42	10
Red-necked Grebe	—	—	—	—	—	—	—	—	1	1	1	1	2	1	—	—	4	3
Western Grebe	—	—	5	1	2	1	6	2	2	1	9	1	1	1	6	1	31	8
Small Grebe	—	—	6	3	7	2	12	2	20	3	27	4	6	1	39	5	117	20
Albatross	—	—	—	—	1	1	4	1	16	2	12	2	4	1	36	3	73	10
Shearwater	—	—	1	1	8	2	107	3	9	2	13	2	5	1	55	3	198	14
Fulmar	—	—	—	—	—	—	—	—	—	—	6	1	—	—	20	3	26	4
Cormorant	—	—	—	—	—	—	—	—	39	2	32	4	5	1	57	2	133	9
Great Blue Heron	—	—	—	—	—	—	—	—	—	—	4	1	—	—	4	1	8	2
Swan	—	—	—	—	—	—	1	1	2	1	1	1	—	—	7	2	11	5
Small Goose	—	—	—	—	—	—	—	—	—	—	1	1	—	—	1	1	2	2
Medium Goose	—	—	—	—	—	—	—	—	10	1	6	1	2	1	8	1	26	4
Large Goose	—	—	—	—	—	—	—	—	5	2	5	1	2	1	3	1	15	5
Dabbling Ducks	—	—	—	—	—	—	—	—	2	1	4	1	5	1	3	2	14	5
Mallard	—	—	—	—	—	—	—	—	—	—	1	1	—	—	4	1	5	2
Gadwell	—	—	—	—	—	—	—	—	—	—	—	—	—	—	3	1	3	1
Wigeon	—	—	—	—	—	—	—	—	—	—	—	—	—	—	1	1	1	1
Diving Ducks	—	—	1	1	—	—	—	—	3	1	13	2	9	1	18	3	44	8
Goldeneyes	—	—	3	1	—	—	—	—	8	1	10	2	3	1	20	2	44	7
Common Goldeneye	—	—	—	—	—	—	—	—	2	1	1	1	1	1	1	1	5	4
Barrows Goldeneye	—	—	—	—	—	—	—	—	3	1	1	1	—	—	4	1	8	3
Bufflehead	—	—	—	—	—	—	—	—	2	1	2	1	2	1	8	2	14	5

136

Species																		
Oldsquaw	—	—	—	—	—	—	2	1	2	1	3	1	—	—	5	1	13	5
Scoters	4	2	32	3	—	1	12	2	48	4	76	6	12	1	55	5	240	24
Small Duck	—	—	4	1	—	—	—	—	4	2	13	1	—	2	7	2	28	6
Medium Duck	5	—	17	2	6	1	3	1	62	3	56	3	17	2	54	4	220	17
Large Duck	1	—	16	2	2	1	9	1	16	2	50	2	3	1	24	2	121	12
Merganser	—	—	—	—	—	—	—	—	—	—	1	—	—	—	1	1	3	3
General Duck	—	—	4	2	—	—	2	1	14	2	27	3	—	—	38	4	85	12
Hawks	—	—	—	—	—	—	—	—	3	1	1	1	1	—	2	1	7	4
Sharp-shinned Hawk	—	—	—	—	—	—	—	—	—	—	—	—	—	—	—	—	2	1
Bald Eagle	—	—	—	—	2	1	14	1	29	2	29	3	5	1	33	2	112	10
Falcon	—	—	—	—	—	—	—	—	—	—	1	—	—	—	—	—	1	1
Sandhill Crane	—	—	—	—	—	—	—	—	—	—	—	—	—	—	2	1	2	1
Sandpipers	—	—	—	—	—	—	—	—	1	1	—	—	—	—	2	1	3	2
Small Gull	—	—	—	1	—	—	4	1	15	2	8	1	2	—	12	1	42	7
Medium Gull	4	1	3	—	9	2	23	2	19	2	19	2	8	—	18	2	103	13
Large Gull	—	—	6	2	2	1	6	1	21	2	38	3	11	2	59	6	143	17
Black-legged Kittiwake	—	—	—	—	—	—	—	—	—	—	—	—	—	—	—	—	1	1
Common Murre	—	—	27	2	13	2	61	3	38	3	157	12	11	1	71	4	378	27
Pigeon Guillemot	—	—	—	—	—	—	—	—	—	—	—	—	—	—	—	—	1	1
Marbled Murrelet	—	—	1	1	—	—	6	—	11	2	4	2	—	—	4	—	26	7
Rhinoceros Auklet	—	—	—	—	—	—	3	—	—	—	—	—	—	—	—	—	4	2
Tufted Puffin	—	—	—	—	—	—	2	—	—	—	2	1	—	—	1	—	5	3
Songbirds	—	—	—	—	—	1	2	—	4	2	3	—	—	—	47	4	59	11
Raven	—	—	—	—	—	—	—	—	1	—	—	—	—	—	2	—	2	1
Crow	—	—	—	—	—	—	—	—	—	—	—	—	—	—	—	1	2	2
Pelican	—	—	—	—	—	—	—	—	1	—	—	—	—	—	2	—	2	1
TOTALS	17	6	133	26	58	19	290	30	425	57	667	79	126	28	791	89	2,506	334

Table A-6. Density (per Cubic Meter) of Grouped Bird Taxa NISP (Number of Identified Specimens) and MNI (Minimum Number of Individuals), by Depositional Period (DP)

Taxa	DP-1 NISP	DP-1 MNI	DP-2 NISP	DP-2 MNI	DP-3 NISP	DP-3 MNI	DP-4 NISP	DP-4 MNI	DP-5 NISP	DP-5 MNI	DP-6 NISP	DP-6 MNI	DP-7 NISP	DP-7 MNI	DP-8 NISP	DP-8 MNI	Site NISP	Site MNI
Loons & Grebes	3.75	1.25	16.8	5.3	17.0	7.1	23.2	5.6	14.3	3.0	19.1	2.9	13.3	4.2	12.8	1.6	14.9	2.9
Diving Seabirds	—	—	29.5	3.2	18.6	2.9	57.6	4.8	38.3	3.0	57.6	5.9	13.3	1.7	17.7	1.2	30.1	2.7
Diving Ducks	5.0	2.5	38.9	6.3	1.4	1.4	11.2	2.4	30.0	4.3	31.5	3.8	22.5	3.3	14.7	2.0	20.4	3.0
Dabbling Ducks, Swans & Geese	7.5	2.5	43.2	5.3	11.4	2.9	12.0	2.4	44.8	5.2	48.2	3.2	24.2	5.0	20.3	1.3	28.6	2.8
Shearwaters, Albatross & Fulmar	—	—	1.1	1.1	12.9	4.3	88.8	3.2	10.9	1.7	9.1	1.5	7.5	1.7	14.4	1.2	16.2	1.5
Gulls	0.5	1.25	9.5	3.2	17.1	5.7	26.4	3.2	23.9	2.6	19.4	2.1	17.5	3.3	11.8	1.2	15.9	2.1
Eagles & Hawks	—	—	—	—	2.9	1.4	11.2	0.8	14.8	1.3	9.1	1.5	5.0	1.7	4.6	0.4	6.7	0.8
TOTALS	21.25	7.5	138.9	24.2	81.4	25.7	230.4	22.4	177.0	21.3	194.1	20.9	103.0	20.8	86.4	8.9	132.9	15.8

138

APPENDIX B. DISTRIBUTION OF ELEMENTS OF FUR SEALS, DEER/ELK, AND BIRDS, BY DEPOSITIONAL PERIOD (DP)

Table B-1. Distribution of Fur Seal Elements, by Depositional Period (DP)

Elements	DP-1	DP-2	DP-3	DP-4	DP-5	DP-6	DP-7	DP-8	Total
Cranium	—	1	—	2	109	165	42	118	437
Mandible	—	—	—	—	18	35	6	16	75
Teeth	—	—	—	3	108	159	23	129	422
Hyoid	—	—	—	—	—	3	—	2	5
Vertebral Centrum	—	—	—	—	10	1	—	—	11
Cervical Vertebrae	—	—	—	1	13	51	8	7	80
Thoracic Vertebrae	—	—	—	—	7	33	8	11	59
Lumbar Vertebrae	—	—	—	3	2	17	3	2	27
Sacral Vertebrae	—	—	—	3	2	15	—	—	21
Caudal Vertebrae	—	—	—	—	1	4	—	1	6
Ribs	—	—	—	—	51	34	10	28	123
Sternbrae	—	—	—	—	13	23	5	17	58
Scapula, complete	—	—	—	1	8	23	3	5	40
Scapula, glenoid	—	—	—	—	—	3	—	—	3
Scapula, blade	—	—	—	—	19	22	2	22	65
Humerus, complete	—	—	1	—	6	9	2	8	26
Humerus, proximal	—	—	—	—	1	3	—	1	5
Humerus, proximal w/shaft	—	—	—	—	—	2	—	2	4
Humerus, shaft	—	—	—	1	13	14	7	17	52
Humerus, distal	—	—	—	—	2	6	2	1	11
Humerus, distal w/shaft	—	—	—	—	—	1	1	—	2
Radius, complete	—	—	—	—	4	4	2	2	12
Radius, proximal	—	—	—	—	2	—	—	—	2
Radius, proximal w/shaft	—	—	—	—	—	1	1	6	8
Radius, shaft	—	—	—	—	4	6	2	9	21
Radius, distal w/shaft	—	—	1	1	1	2	—	—	4
Ulna, complete	—	—	—	1	7	9	5	—	22
Ulna, proximal	—	—	—	—	1	—	—	1	2

									Total
Ulna, proximal w/shaft	—	—	—	—	—	4	—	3	7
Ulna, shaft	—	—	—	—	6	10	1	3	20
Ulna, distal w/shaft	—	—	—	—	1	3	2	1	7
Metacarpals	—	1	—	—	13	18	3	15	50
Carpals	—	—	1	—	1	6	—	—	8
Pelvis, complete	—	—	—	—	1	3	—	3	7
Pelvis, anterior	—	—	—	—	5	5	3	2	15
Pelvis, posterior	—	—	—	—	6	21	2	12	41
Femur, complete	—	—	—	—	3	6	3	—	12
Femur, proximal	—	—	—	—	1	1	—	—	2
Femur, proximal w/shaft	—	1	—	—	4	2	—	1	8
Femur, shaft	—	—	—	—	7	4	—	4	15
Femur, distal	—	—	—	—	2	4	—	—	6
Femur, distal w/shaft	—	—	—	—	—	—	—	3	3
Tibia, complete	—	—	—	—	1	2	2	—	5
Tibia, proximal	—	—	—	—	3	2	—	3	8
Tibia, proximal w/shaft	—	—	—	—	—	3	1	3	7
Tibia, shaft	—	—	—	—	—	5	—	5	10
Tibia, distal	—	—	—	—	—	—	—	1	1
Tibia, distal w/shaft	1	—	1	—	—	—	—	—	1
Fibula, complete	—	—	2	—	—	2	—	3	7
Fibula, proximal	2	—	—	—	—	2	—	4	2
Fibula, proximal w/shaft	—	—	—	—	—	3	—	—	6
Fibula, shaft	—	1	—	—	1	8	—	—	11
Fibula, distal	—	—	—	—	—	2	—	—	2
Fibula, distal w/shaft	—	—	—	—	—	—	—	1	1
Metatarsals	—	—	—	—	5	20	3	10	38
Tarsals	—	—	1	—	7	3	1	4	15
Phalanges	6	—	3	2	102	125	36	95	369
TOTALS	0	10	9	17	570	908	193	580	2287

Table B-2. Distribution of Deer and Elk Elements, by Depositional Period (DP)

Elements	DP-1	DP-2	DP-3	DP-4	DP-5	DP-6	DP-7	DP-8	Total
Cranium	—	2	1	—	12	5	3	6	29
Mandible	—	—	—	1	—	3	1	4	9
Teeth	—	—	1	1	14	15	5	4	40
Hyoid	—	—	—	1	—	1	1	—	3
Vertebral Centrum	—	—	—	—	—	—	—	1	1
Cervical Vertebrae	1	—	—	2	3	—	—	5	11
Thoracic Vertebrae	—	—	—	1	7	6	1	4	19
Lumbar Vertebrae	—	—	—	—	6	2	1	—	9
Ribs	—	1	—	—	5	5	1	4	16
Scapula, distal	—	—	—	—	—	1	—	—	1
Scapula, blade	—	—	—	1	—	1	—	—	2
Humerus, proximal & shaft	—	—	—	—	—	1	1	—	2
Humerus, shaft	—	—	—	—	—	—	1	3	4
Humerus, distal	—	—	—	—	1	—	—	1	2
Humerus, distal & shaft	—	—	—	—	—	—	—	2	2
Radius, proximal	—	—	—	—	1	—	—	3	4
Radius, proximal & shaft	—	—	—	—	—	—	1	—	1
Radius, shaft	—	—	—	—	—	—	—	1	1
Radius, distal	—	—	—	—	1	—	—	3	4
Ulna, proximal	—	—	1	—	—	5	—	2	8

	(1)	(7)	(4)	(15)	(82)	(72)	(20)	(84)	TOTALS
Ulna, shaft	—	—	—	—	—	—	1	1	2
Ulna, distal	—	—	—	—	—	—	—	1	1
Metacarpal, proximal	—	—	—	—	2	2	—	1	4
Metacarpal, proximal & shaft	—	—	—	—	3	1	—	1	4
Metacarpal, distal	—	—	—	—	—	2	—	2	3
Carpals	—	—	—	1	1	—	—	2	7
Pelvis, complete	—	—	—	—	1	—	1	2	4
Pelvis, anterior	—	—	—	—	—	—	—	—	3
Pelvis, posterior	—	—	—	—	1	—	—	3	3
Femur, proximal	—	—	—	—	—	—	—	—	1
Femur, distal	—	—	—	—	—	—	—	2	1
Tibia, shaft	—	3	—	—	2	—	—	1	8
Tibia, distal	—	—	—	—	1	1	—	3	2
Metatarsal, proximal	—	—	—	—	—	—	—	—	4
Metatarsal, proximal & shaft	—	—	—	—	—	—	—	3	1
Metatarsal, shaft	—	—	—	—	—	2	2	—	7
Metatarsal, distal	—	—	—	1	4	—	—	2	5
Tarsals	—	—	—	—	1	—	—	1	5
Metapodial, proximal	—	—	—	—	—	—	—	3	4
Metapodial, shaft	—	—	—	—	1	—	1	2	3
Metapodial, distal	—	—	—	—	—	—	—	1	3
Phalanges	1	1	—	6	11	14	1	13	46
TOTALS	1	7	4	15	82	72	20	84	285

Table B-3.   Distribution of Elements for Anatidae (Ducks, Geese, Swans), Loons, Grebes, and Alcidae (Murres, Murrelets, Auklets, Puffins)

Elements	Taxa			
	Anatidae	Loons	Grebes	Alcidae
Cranium	51	4	8	27
Mandible	17	3	—	27
Hyoid & Tongue	1	—	—	—
Cervical Vertebrae	113	2	15	23
Thoracic Vertebrae	74	3	6	42
Scapula	64	2	5	25
Coracoid	75	4	6	24
Furculum	26	—	2	19
Sternum	26	3	3	9
Pelvis & Synsacrum	34	4	8	16
Humerus	69	1	11	36
Radius	64	2	15	28
Ulna	39	4	11	32
Carpometacarpus	37	1	8	21
Wing Digits	43	3	—	20
Femur	31	4	18	24
Tibiotarsus	61	1	11	27
Fibula	8	2	3	1
Tarsometatarsus	38	5	8	1
Foot Digits	15	3	12	3
TOTALS	886	118	150	405

REFERENCES

Ascher, R. (1968) "Time's Arrow and the Archaeology of a Contemporary Community." Pp. 43–52 in K.C. Chang (ed.) *Settlement Archaeology*. Palo Alto, CA: National Press Books.

Banfield, A.W.F. (1974) *The Mammals of Canada*. Toronto: University of Toronto Press.

Behrensmeyer, A.K., and A.P. Hill (1980) *Fossils in the Making*. Chicago: University of Chicago Press.

Binford, L.R. (1977) *Nunamiut Ethnoarchaeology*. New York: Academic Press.

——— (1981) *Bones: Ancient Men and Modern Myths*. New York: Academic Press.

Binford, L.R., and J.B. Bertram (1977) "Bone Frequencies and Attritional Processes." Pp. 77–153 in L.R. Binford (ed.) *For Theory Building in Archaeology*. New York: Academic Press.

Brain, C.K. (1981) *The Hunters or the Hunted: An Introduction to African Cave Taphonomy*. Chicago: University of Chicago Press.

Burley, David V. (1983) "Cultural Complexity and Evolution in the Development of Coastal Adaptations among the Micmac and Coast Salish." Pp. 157–172 in R.J. Nash (ed.) *The Evolution of Maritime Cultures on the Northeast and Northwest Coasts of America*. Burnaby, BC: Simon Fraser University, Department of Archaeology, Publication No. 11.

Christenson, A. (1980) "Change in the Human Food Niche in Response to Population Growth." Pp. 31–52 in T. Earle & A. Christenson (eds.) *Modeling Change in Prehistoric Economies*. New York: Academic Press.

Cowan, I. McT., and C.J. Guiguet (1978) *The Mammals of British Columbia*. Victoria: British Columbia Provincial Museum Handbook 11.

Croes, D.R. (1985) "Hoko Rockshelter Bone Artifact Distribution." Attachment B in *Interim Annual Report, Hoko River Archaeological Project, Phase XIV*. Washington, DC: National Endowment for the Humanities.

——— (n.d.) "Working Paper: Hoko Rockshelter Bone Artifact Functional Types." Manuscript on file, Hoko Project, Washington State University, Pullman.

Everitt, R.D., C.H. Fiscus, and R.L. DeLong (1979) *Marine Mammals of Northern Puget Sound and the Strait of Juan de Fuca: A Report on Investigations, November 1 (1977)—October 31 (1978)*. Washington, DC: U.S. Department of Commerce, National Oceanic and Atmospheric Administration Technical Report, ERL MESA–41.

Franklin, J.F., and C.T. Dyrness (1973) *Natural Vegetation of Oregon and Washington*. Washington, DC: USDA Forest Service, General Technical Report PNW–8.

Fuchs, C., D. Kaufman, and A. Ronen (1977) "Erosion and Artifact Distribution on Open-air Epi-Paleolithic Sites on the Coastal Plain of Israel." *Journal of Field Archaeology* 4:171–179.

Gifford, D.P. (1981) "Taphonomy and Paleoecology: A Critical Review of Archaeology's Sister Discipline." Pp. 365–385 in M.B. Schiffer (ed.) *Advances in Archaeological Method and Theory, Vol. 4*. New York: Academic Press.

Gifford-Gonzales, D.P., J.P. Damrosch, D.R. Damrosch, J. Pryor, and R.L. Thunen (1985) "The Third Dimension in Site Structure: An Experiment in Trampling and Vertical Dispersal." *American Antiquity* 50:803–813.

Godfrey, W.E. (1986) *The Birds of Canada*. (Rev. ed.) Ottawa: National Museums of Canada.

Grayson, D.K. (1979) "On the Quantification of Vertebrate Archaeofaunas." Pp. 199–237 in M.B. Schiffer (ed.) *Advances in Archaeological Method and Theory, Vol. 2*. New York: Academic Press.

——— (1984) *Quantitative Zooarchaeology*. New York: Academic Press.

Hart, J.L. (1973) *Pacific Fishes of Canada*. Ottawa: Fisheries Research Board of Canada Bulletin 180.

Heulsbeck, D. (1983) *Mammals and Fish in the Subsistence Economy of Ozette.* Ph.D. dissertation, Washington State University.

Hurst, Gwen (n.d.) "Shell Middens: Seasonality and Exploitation." Paper presented at the 39th Annual Northwest Anthropological Conference, Moscow, ID, 1986.

Kent, S. (n.d.) "Potential Sources of Distortion in Artifact Spatial Distributions." Paper presented before the Society for American Archaeology, San Diego, CA, 1981.

Klein, R.G., and Cruz-Uribe, K. (1984) *The Analysis of Animal Bones from Archaeological Sites.* Chicago: University of Chicago Press.

Krause, R.A., and R.M. Thorne (1971) "Toward a Theory of Archaeological Things." *Plains Anthropologist* 16:245–256.

LeBlanc, S. (1971) "An Addition to Narroll's Suggested Floor Area and Settlement Population Relationship." *American Antiquity* 36:210–211.

Matson, R.G. (1983) "Intensification and the Development of Cultural Complexity: The Northwest versus the Northeast Coast." Pp. 125–148 in R.J. Nash (ed.) *The Evolution of Maritime Cultures on the Northeast and Northwest Coasts of America.* Burnaby, BC: Department of Archaeology, Simon Fraser University, Publication No. 11.

Miller, D.G. (1983) *The Hoko River Rockshelter: Intertidal Resources.* Master's thesis, Department of Anthropology, Washington State University.

Narroll, R. (1962) "Floor Area and Settlement Population." *American Antiquity* 27:587–589.

Phillips, E.L., and W.R. Donaldson (1972) *Washington Climate.* Pullman, WA: Washington State University, Pullman Cooperative Extension Service, College of Agriculture.

Samuels, S.R. (1983) *Spatial Patterns and Cultural Processes in Three Northwest Coast Longhouse Floor Middens from Ozette (Washington).* Ph.D. dissertation, Department of Anthropology, Washington State University.

Schiffer, M.B. (1972) "Archaeological Context and Systematic Context." *American Antiquity* 37:156–165.

——— (1976) *Behavioral Archaeology.* New York: Academic Press.

——— (1983) "Toward the Identification of Formation Processes." *American Antiquity* 48:675–706.

Stucki, B.R. (n.d.) "Geoarchaeological Investigations at the Hoko River Rockshelter (45CA21)." Manuscript, 1984.

Stucki, B.R., and R. Wigen (n.d.) "The Effects of Bone Element Loss on the Estimation of Past Activities and Resource Use." Paper presented before the Society for American Archaeology, Portland, April 1984.

Swan, J.C. (1869) *The Indians of Cape Flattery.* Washington, DC: Smithsonian Contributions to Knowledge 16.

——— (1971) *Almost out of the World: Scenes from Washington Territory, the Strait of Juan de Fuca 1859–1861.* Tacoma: Washington State Historical Society.

Wahl, T.R., S. Speich, D. Manuwal, K. Hirch, and C. Miller (1981) *Marine Bird Populations of the Strait of Juan de Fuca, Strait of Georgia and Adjacent Waters in 1978 and 1979.* Washington, DC: U.S. Environmental Protection Agency Report for the Interagency Energy/Environment Research and Development Program.

Weissner, P. (1974) "A Functional Estimator of Population from Floor Area." *American Antiquity* 39:343–350.

Woods, W.R., and D.L. Johnson (1978) "A Survey of Disturbance Processes in Archaeological Site Formation." Pp. 315–381 in M.B. Schiffer (ed.) *Advances in Archaeological Method and Theory, Vol. 1.* New York: Academic Press.

Yellen, J.E. (1977a) *Archaeological Approaches to the Present.* New York: Academic Press.

——— (1977b) "Cultural Patterning in Faunal Remains: Evidence from the !Kung Bushmen." Pp. 271–331 in D. Ingersol, J.E. Yellen & W. MacDonald (eds.) *Experimental Archaeology.* New York: Columbia University Press.

PART II

OZETTE VILLAGE

THE SURPLUS ECONOMY OF THE CENTRAL NORTHWEST COAST

David R. Huelsbeck

INTRODUCTION

The rich complexity of the Native American cultures on the Northwest Coast is often attributed to the production of surplus food, which freed individuals from the "day-to-day" food quest. Salmon is generally considered to be the most important resource in this context, along with the oil-yielding eulachon and sea mammals (Drucker 1965:10–15). Most discussions of Northwest Coast economy focus on the distribution of surpluses at potlatches, which textbooks characterize as redistributive exchange (Barnouw 1978, Harris 1985, Nanda 1984) or as reciprocal exchange (Ember & Ember 1985, Swartz & Jordan 1980). Analyses focusing directly on the potlatch have variously characterized it as a mechanism for achieving status (Codere 1950, Drucker & Heizer 1967), for clarifying status (Rosmen & Rubel 1971), for adapting to resource fluctuation (Piddocke 1965; Suttles 1960, 1968; Vayda 1961), or for attracting a sufficient labor force (Adams 1973, Langdon n.d.).

Research in Economic Anthropology, Supplement 3, pages 149–177.
Copyright © 1988 by JAI Press Inc.
All rights of reproduction in any form reserved.
ISBN: 0-89232-818-5

Although the production of surplus quantities of food is a critical factor in all discussions of Northwest Coast economy, the term "surplus" is used in the existing literature to refer to a variety of different conditions. Sometimes it denotes a quantity of foodstuffs that exceeds immediate needs but which is stored for consumption during "lean" months, when foodstuffs would otherwise be insufficient for optimal maintenance of the population. In other words, "surplus" in this sense disappears once the entire annual round is taken into consideration. "Surplus" is also used to refer to the food distributed at feasts and potlatches. Such food can indeed be viewed meaningfully as surplus if it was produced apart from and in addition to production for annual subsistence requirements. Of course, it would not be surplus in this sense from the standpoint of nonlocal (or other-stratum) guests who are experiencing concurrent food deficits. Finally, "surplus" can be conceived in a more general sense as *quantities of food that exceed subsistence and social requirements and which can be exchanged for other kinds of food or manufactured goods*. This last meaning of surplus is the definition used in this essay.

Analyses of Northwest Coast economies typically focus little attention on exchange, apart from the potlatch context. Oberg's (1973) analysis of Tlingit economy is an exception. He distinguishes between gift exchange and barter or trade. Gift exchange takes place within a network of social relationships, whereas in barter or trade "the individuals involved seek their own advantage through bargaining and tend to ignore the system of relationships which makes them members of a community" (Oberg 1973:93). Oberg maintains that pure barter did not exist prior to the arrival of Euroamericans, but he goes on to list a wide variety of essential commodities, such as food, clothing, and canoes, that were exchanged prehistorically among island, mainland, and interior peoples (Oberg 1973:107–109).

There is no doubt that some goods, such as dentalia shells, were exchanged over long distances prehistorically. Whether these exchanges took the form of gifts or barter is an important question in the study of prehistoric Northwest Coast economy, but a more fundamental question concerns the volume of prehistoric trade and the degree to which local groups depended on exchanging their surplus production for goods they did not produce. If commodities necessary for survival were exchanged prehistorically, then these societies cannot be characterized as having self-sufficient subsistence economies. The role of food production in the larger economy and the institutions that support production must assume a more prominent position in analyses of Northwest Coast culture (see Donald 1983, 1984; Donald & Mitchell 1975; Mitchell & Donald 1985) and analyses of maritime adaptation (see Osborn 1977, Schalk 1981, Yesner 1980).

This essay explores the question of the volume of exchange on the central Northwest Coast. The specific people under consideration are the Nootkan-speaking Makah, who occupy the northwest corner of the Olympic Peninsula in Washington state. Ethnohistoric information concerning the Makah and archaeological information from the Ozette site, one of their villages, will be compared with information on other Westcoast peoples (speakers of Nootkan languages) on the west coast of Vancouver Island in order to evaluate whether the Makah are a unique case. Because most of the items that would have been exchanged prehistorically were perishable animal or vegetal products, the volume of prehistoric exchange will be inferred by examining the magnitude of surplus food production.

EXCHANGE IN THE MAKAH ECONOMY

Historic Exchange

Several ethnohistoric sources describe the Makah as traders. The most elaborate description is that of James Swan (1869:30–31), who lived with the Makah during the mid-1800s:

They are emphatically a trading, as well as a producing people; and in these respects are far superior to the Clallams and other tribes on Fuca Strait and Puget Sound. Before the white man came to this part of the country, and when the Indian population on the Pacific coast had not been reduced in numbers as it has been of late years, they traded largely with the Chinooks at the mouth of the Columbia, making excursions as far as the Kwinaiult tribe at Point Grenville, where they met the Chinook traders; and some of the more venturesome would even continue on to the Columbia, passing through the Chihalis country at Gray's Harbor and Shoalwater Bay. The Chinooks and Chihalis would in like manner come north as far as Cape Flattery; and these trading excursions were kept up pretty regularly, with only the interruption of occasional feuds and rivalries between the different tribes, when the intercourse would be suspended, or carried on by means of intermediate bands; for instance the Chinooks would venture up as far as Chihalis, or perhaps Kwinaiult; they would go as far as the Kwilleyute, and these last in turn to Cape Flattery. After a while peace would be restored, and the long voyages again resumed. The Makahs took down canoes, oil, dried halibut, and hai-kwa, or dentalium shells. The large canoes were almost invariably made on Vancouver Island; for, although craft of this model are called "Chinook" canoes, very few in reality, except small ones, were made at Chinook, the cedar there not being of suitable size or quality for the largest sizes, and the best trees being found on the Island. The Makahs in return received sea otter skins from Kwinaiult; vermilion or cinnabar from the Chinooks, which they in turn had procured from the more southern tribes of Oregon; and such articles of Indian value as might be manufactured or produced by the tribes living south of the cape. Their trade with the northern Indians was for dentalium, dried cedar bark for making mats, canoes, and dried salmon; paying for the same with dried halibut, blubber, and whale oil. Slaves also constituted an important article of traffic; they were purchased by the Makahs from the Vancouver Island Indians, and sold to the coast Indians south.

The Makah occupied a location at the mouth of the Strait of Juan de Fuca that favored their activities as traders. Also, the Makah needed to engage in trade because good quality cedar for house planks and canoes was not readily available on Cape Flattery. Concerning cedar, Swan (1869:4) observed:

> The houses of the Makahs are built of boards and planks, split from the cedar. These are principally made by the Indians of Vancouver Island, and procured by barter with them. There is very little cedar about Cape Flattery, and such as is found is small and of inferior quality.

He (Swan 1869:35) noted that

> The largest and best canoes are made by the Clyoquots and Nitinats on Vancouver Island; the cedar trees being of a quality greatly superior to that found on or near Cape Flattery. Canoes of the medium and small sizes are made by the Makahs from cedar procured a short distance up the Strait or on the Tsuess River.

The Makah could obtain these necessities of Northwest Coast life through exchange because they produced surplus quantities of halibut and sea mammal products, particularly whale blubber and oil. Swan (1869:32) estimated the Makah's average annual oil production (whale oil and dogfish shark oil) at 5,000 gallons. This total might have included oil obtained in trade with other Native Americans but could have been their own production, because there are records of 16,000 (Swan 1869:32) and 20,000 gallons (cited in Lane n.d.:18) being sold to white traders. Five thousand gallons of oil represents approximately 5 whales (Rice & Wolman 1971, Wolman 1978) or fewer whales and a significant number of seals and sharks. Seals and sharks were plentiful in the area (see Brown 1895:352–399; Huelsbeck 1981, 1983a), and fisheries records indicate that the Makah did in fact kill more than one whale per year. In 1889–1892, when the whale population had already been decimated by American whalers (Scammon 1968:23), the Makah at Neah Bay averaged 5.5 whales per year (Wilcox 1895:290). At the same time, the Makah were also catching about 300,000 lb of halibut per year (Wilcox 1895:290). Given that the Makah then numbered fewer than 450, it is clear that they produced quantities of food significantly beyond their subsistence needs during the historic period. These surpluses were exchanged for commodities that they needed but did not produce themselves. Because of the dependence on surplus production and the concentration on sea mammals and halibut, the Makah economy can be characterized as a specialized rather than a generalized subsistence economy.

Prehistoric Exchange

The increasing availability of nonlocally-produced goods during the historic period could have stimulated the transformation of essentially generalized subsistence economies into specialized, surplus-exchanging economies. Analysis of the faunal remains recovered from the Ozette site indicates that animals from the offshore habitat, particularly sea mammals, were the focus of food production activities. Although the Ozette village is infrequently mentioned in the ethnohistoric literature cited above, the abundance of sea mammal remains indicates that the Ozette economy was specialized (see Table 1).

Table 1 illustrates the relative frequency of exploitation of different habitat zones near the Ozette site, based on the frequency of faunal remains (cf. Calvert 1980). The boundaries of the habitat zones are not absolute. The zones describe optimal habitats where the animals are most abundant. For the purposes of this paper, three general zones will be considered: offshore, nearshore, and stream/forest (see Appendix). The offshore zone extends inward from the open ocean to the point where water depth is about 20m. The nearshore zone extends from this point to the beach. The stream/forest zone includes dry land and freshwater habitats. More than 80 percent of the individual animals represented in the Ozette collection are from the offshore habitat. The forest near Ozette contains several natural prairies, and the forest habitat itself contains abundant animal resources; yet, the forest was exploited relatively little. Salmon, presumably from the Ozette River/Lake system, are the most commonly exploited inland resource. The dominance of one habitat zone in production activities can be viewed as a kind of specialization in food production.

If one considers the amount of food represented by the faunal remains,

Table 1. Relative Frequency (in Percentages) of Habitat Exploitation of Ozette[a]

Taxon	Offshore[b]	Nearshore	Stream/Forest	Total MNI
Mammals[c]	96.06	1.10	2.84	1,371
Fish	59.29	30.78	9.93	614
Birds	53.97	42.86	3.17	126
Site Mean	82.85	12.22	4.93	2,111

[a]Relative frequency is percentage of total MNI, Minimum Number of Individuals, shown in last column; data are from Huelsbeck (1983a). Percentages add by row.
[b]Offshore is water deeper than 20m; nearshore extends from the offshore zone boundary to the beach; stream/forest is fresh water and dry land.
[c]Excluding whales.

Table 2. Ozette Habitat Exploitation: Percentage Food Contribution[a]

Taxon	Offshore[b]	Nearshore	Stream/Forest
Mammals[c]	97.21	0.07	2.72
Fish	77.37	9.14	13.49
Birds	57.03	41.86	1.11
Site Mean	96.85	0.27	2.88

[a]Data from Huelsbeck (1983a). Percentages add by row.
[b]Offshore, nearshore and stream/forest are defined in note b in Table 1.
[c]Excluding whales.

the emphasis placed on the offshore zone is even more pronounced. Table 2 shows that more than 95 percent of the food represented by the faunal remains was derived from the offshore habitat zone. Tables 1 and 2 list those taxa from Ozette that also were analyzed in two other Westcoast studies (see below). When the amount of food represented by the whale and shellfish remains is added to the figures in Tables 1 and 2, sea mammals still account for more than 90 percent of all the food and the offshore habitat still accounts for more than 95 percent of the food represented by the faunal remains (see Table 3).

The Ozette population clearly produced an abundance of sea mammal products. Whether this constituted a surplus that was traded will be considered below.

Table 3. Faunal Remains and Represented Food From Ozette

Taxon	NISP[a]	MNI[b]	Quantity of Food	
			kg	%
Bird[c]	3,200	400	1,100	0.11
Land mammal[d]	1,067	54	2,141	0.22
Fish[e]	625,000	16,000	32,000	3.32
Shellfish[f]	540,183	300,100	4,050	0.42
Sea mammal (other than whale)[d]	47,040	1,317	77,857	8.08
Whale[g]	521	67	846,600	87.85
Total			963,748	100.00

[a]Number of Identified Specimens.
[b]Minimum Number of Individuals.
[c]Estimate based on DePuydt (1983) and the volume of unanalyzed bird remains.
[d]Huelsbeck (1983a), excluding dogs.
[e]Estimates based on Huelsbeck (1983a:79-81) and the volume of analyzed remains, correcting for recovery technique.
[f]Wessen (1982), correcting for recovery technique.
[g]Huelsbeck (1983b).

EXCHANGE AMONG OTHER WESTCOAST PEOPLES

Historic Exchange

The Makah are not unique among Westcoast peoples in being noted as traders during the historic period. Gilbert Sproat (1868:78–79), who lived on Vancouver Island from 1860 to 1865, describes the trading activities of the Ahts (his general term for all Nootkan peoples) as follows:

Commodities are obtained among the Ahts from one another by bartering slaves, canoes, and articles of food, clothing, or ornament; and from the colonists by exchanging oil, fish, skins, and furs. All the natives are acute, and rather too sharp at bargaining. . . . News about prices, and indeed about anything in which the natives take an interest, travels quickly to distant places from one tribe to another. If a trading schooner appeared at one point on the shore, and offered higher prices than are usually given, the Indians would know the fact immediately along the whole coast. An active trade existed formerly among the tribes of this nation, as also between them and the tribes at the south of the island and on the American shore. The root called gammass [camass], for instance, and swamp rushes for making mats, neither of which could be plentifully produced on the west coast, were sent from the south of the island in exchange for cedar-bark baskets, dried halibut, and herrings.

This trade was frequent, took place over long distances, and involved commodities necessary in Northwest Coast culture, particularly cedar canoes. Sproat (1868:85) recorded:

Vancouver Island and the immediately opposite coast of the mainland of British Columbia have always supplied the numerous tribes to the northward with canoes. The native artificers in these localities have in the cedar *(Thuja gigantea)* a wood which does not flourish so extensively to the north, and which is very suitable for their purpose, as it is of large growth, durable, and easily worked.

These exchange activities also were common earlier in the historic period, as reported by John Jewitt, armourer on the trading ship *Boston* and captive on Vancouver Island in 1803–1805. The list of items exchanged by his captors and other Native Americans is similar to those already discussed. Jewitt (1974:69) wrote:

The trade of most of the other tribes with Nootka was principally train-oil, seal or whale's blubber, fish fresh or dried, herring or salmon spawn, clams and mussels, and the yama [probably salal], a species of fruit which is pressed and dried, cloth, sea-otter skins, and slaves. From the Aitizzarts and the Cauyquets, particularly the former, the best Ife-whaw [dentalia shells] and in the greatest quantities was obtained. The Eshquates furnished us with wild ducks and geese, particularly the latter. The Wickinninish and Kla-iz-zarts [Makah] brought to market many slaves, the best sea-otter skins, great quantities of oil, whale sinew, and cakes of the yama, highly ornamented canoes, some Ife-whaw, red ochre and pelpelth [black mica] of an inferior quality to that obtained from the Newchemass, but particularly the so much valued metamelth [elk hide], and an excellent root called by the Kla-iz-zarts Quawnoose [camass]. . . . From the Kla-iz-zarts was also received, though in no great quantity, a cloth manufactured by them from the fur already spoken of, which feels like wool and is of a grey colour [probably dog hair].

Little indication of the volume of exchange is given in Jewitt's narrative, other than the imprecise phrase "great quantities." Some idea of the volume of exchange can be gained by examining Jewitt's (1976) journal, though. There, he lists 91 trading visits during the 21 months of regular entries. During 64 of these visits, foodstuffs were brought to Jewitt's captors, the Yuquotaht. Quantities are rarely mentioned, but the 64 visits involved 90 canoe-loads of goods and visitors. Including the nonfoodstuffs (dentalia, etc.), a total of 117 canoe-loads of goods and visitors were brought to Jewitt's captors. This is an average of 5.5 canoe-loads per month.

The main items that visitors received from the Yuquotaht were trade goods taken from Jewitt's ship when it was captured. Exchanging surplus food products for other desired commodities appears to have been common in the early historic period, but the frequency and volume of exchange easily could have been affected by historic-period events such as the fur trade. However, the ethnohistoric literature suggests that a degree of economic specialization did exist; each of the groups listed above typically traded a particular commodity. Did this specialization and surplus production also take place prehistorically? If so, was this trade relied on for goods not produced locally?

The ethnohistoric literature does not discuss these questions directly, but they can be investigated indirectly by examining local group rank (see Donald & Mitchell 1975). There are essentially two food resources on the west coast of Vancouver Island that could support intensive production— sea mammals and salmon. These animals are most abundant in two distinctly different areas. Locally, these areas are referred to as outside and inside or outer coast and inner coast (see Appendix). The outer coast is the western edge of Vancouver Island. It fronts directly on the open Pacific Ocean and is exposed to the full force of winter storms. The inner coast is located along the fiords and inlets that dissect Vancouver Island. The relatively sheltered inside area provides access to a different suite of salt-water resources. Sea mammals were most common near the outer coast. Salmon were most available in their spawning streams at the heads of fiords and inlets some distance inland from the outer coast. Local groups controlled access to resource exploitation areas, and the access of outside (outer coast) groups to salmon streams and other inside resources (and vice versa) was limited (Drucker 1951:226–227).

During the historic period, these differences were reduced to some extent among northern Westcoast peoples because of the development of confederacies linking a number of local groups whose territories were inside and at least one local group whose territory was outside, on the outer coast. Each local group controlled access to its own salmon fishing location (inside resource) and had access to sea mammal hunting areas (outside resource) by virtue of sharing the summer confederacy village located on or near the outer coast (see Drucker 1951:222–246). Local groups were ranked relative to one another within the confederacies. In each of the four confederacies, the group controlling the outside territory was or had been the highest ranking local group.

If a local group's rank reflects its resource base (see Donald & Mitchell 1975) and the dominance of outside groups predates the fur trade, then the sea mammal resource was rich enough to give the outside local groups an economic advantage over the inside groups. If sea mammals were such a valuable resource, then surpluses of sea mammal products probably were generated and exchanged for other products, such as salmon. Jewitt (quoted above) lists oil and blubber as principal trade items. If large volumes of sea mammal products were exchanged, then whaling must have been economically important, because seals, sea lions, and porpoises do not yield large quantities of oil and blubber.

Drucker (1951:50) maintained that whaling was of little economic importance, but several recent analyses suggest that it was very important (Arima n.d., Cavanagh 1983, Huelsbeck 1983b, Inglis & Haggarty n.d.). Whales were once much more common than they are now; even Jewitt's observations on whaling at Yuquot may reflect a situation altered by the fur trade. Nevertheless, the 2.5 whales taken per year in 1803–05, while Jewitt was with the Yuquotaht, represent 16.25–36.25 MT of meat and blubber per year (depending on whether gray whales or humpback whales were taken, and assuming average sizes). If there were 500 people living at Yuquot at the time, then the whales provided 32.5–72.5 kg of meat and blubber/person/year, or 0.7–1.4 kg/person/week (Inglis & Haggarty n.d.). If just a few of the whales that were struck and lost had been captured, the Yuquot whalers would have averaged 5 whales per year or about 0.25–0.5 kg of meat and blubber/person/day.

Sea mammal products were produced in large quantities and could have been produced in surplus quantities. Whether or not the exchange of sea mammal products by Westcoast peoples approached the economic importance suggested earlier for the Makah, is unclear in the ethnohistoric literature. Recent research suggests larger precontact Westcoast populations divided among more numerous, nearly sedentary local group villages (Haggarty 1985). If this was the case, many local groups may have lacked one or more desireable or necessary resources, a situation that would increase the likelihood of trade.

Prehistoric Exchange

Archaeological information on sites on the west coast of Vancouver
Island is limited. Major excavations have been conducted only at Yuquot
(Folan & Dewhirst 1980a, 1980b) and in Hesquiat Harbor (Calvert 1980,
Haggarty 1982) (see Figure 1). The Yuquot site is one of three occupied
seasonally during the historic period by the dominant local group in the
Moachat confederacy. It was the summer confederacy village. The Hes-
quiat Project excavated sites in the traditional territories of three different
local groups.

The artifacts and faunal remains recovered from the sites in Hesquiat
Harbor indicate that each local group exploited only a portion of the harbor

Figure 1.   The Central Northwest Coast

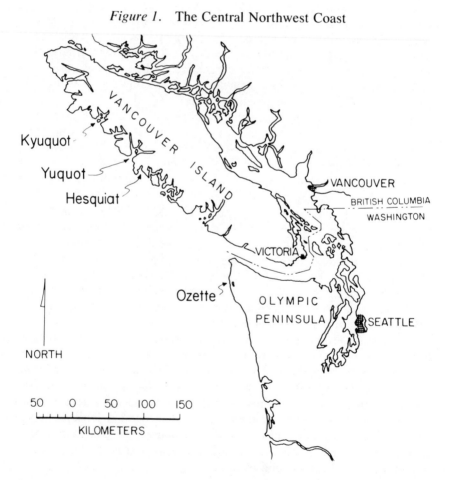

Table 4. Relative Frequency (in Percentages) of Habitat Exploitation at Hesquiat[a]

Site	Offshore[b]	Nearshore	Stream/Forest	Total MNI
DiSo 16	13.0	76.0	11.0	353
DiSo 9	32.5[c]	56.5	11.0	745
DiSo 1	56.0	35.5	9.5	1,098

[a]Relative frequency is percentage of Total MNI, Minimum Number of Individuals, shown in last column; data from Calvert (1980). Percentages add by row.
[b]Offshore, nearshore, and stream/forest are defined in note b of Table 1. The offshore entries do not include nonspecifically identified cetaceans.
[c]Consists primarily of harbor seals and sea otters, and includes few pelagic species.

environment, suggesting that the historic pattern of local group resource ownership existed prehistorically as well (Calvert 1980, Haggarty 1982). Table 4 shows that the net effect of the distribution of local group territories within Hesquiat Harbor for the three local groups examined (one site each) is specialization in resource exploitation: the group that lived at DiSo 16 focused on nearshore resources, the group at site DiSo 9 emphasized nearshore resources augmented by offshore resources, and the group that lived at DiSo 1 emphasized offshore resources. The difference between DiSo 9 and DiSo 1 is more pronounced than is suggested by Table 4, because the local group at DiSo 9 exploited only the inner edge of the offshore habitat, hunting sea mammals such as the harbor seal, whereas the local group at DiSo 1 also exploited truly pelagic sea mammals, such as fur seal and cetaceans. DiSo 1 is located on the outer coast and the other two sites are located inside Hesquiat Harbor.

If the amount of food represented by the faunal remains from different areas is considered, the difference among the three groups is even more striking (see Table 5). The first local group (DiSo 16) obtained their animal

Table 5. Hesquiat Habitat Exploitation: Percentage Food Contribution[a]

Site	Offshore[b]	Nearshore	Stream/Forest
DiSo 16	17.0	44.0	39.0
DiSo 9	53.5[c]	26.0	20.5
DiSo 1	82.3	8.1	9.6

[a]Data from Calvert (1980). Percentages add by row.
[b]Definitions of offshore, nearshore and stream/forest are provided in note b of Table 1. The entries under offshore here do not include nonspecifically identified cetaceans.
[c]Consists primarily of harbor seals and sea otters and includes few truly pelagic species.

Table 6. Percentage Food Contribution, by Taxon: Hesquiat[a]

Site	Sea Mammal[b]	Whale	Land Mammal	Birds	Fish	Total kg
DiSo 16	0.00	0.0	38.74	4.98	56.28	679
DiSo 9	48.39	0.0	17.54	3.07	31.00	4,377
DiSo 1	9.53	86.35	1.13	0.20	2.79	180,663

[a]Data from Calvert (1980). Percentages add by row.
[b]Excluding whale.

food resources mostly from the nearshore/forest habitat; the second local group (DiSo 9), mostly from the inner edge of the offshore habitat and the nearshore habitat; and the third local group (DiSo 1), mostly from the offshore habitat.

When the data on relative quantities of food are restructured to be more readily comparable with the Ozette data, and when whales are added to the picture, the extent of the specialization of the outside local group (DiSo 1) is clear (see Table 6). Whales represent more than 85 percent of the available food for the outside local group; all told, sea mammals represent more than 95 percent of the available food for this group. These proportions are very similar to those observed in the Ozette data.

The other major excavation in Westcoast territory was conducted at Yuquot, the outside site of the Moachat confederacy and the site where John Jewitt lived seasonally during his captivity. This site is a fairly sheltered "outside village site near the outside-inside interface at Nootka Sound" (Dewhirst 1980:12). A mixture of resources are available in the vicinity of Yuquot. In view of the preceding discussion—although lacking a rigorous habitat analysis—I would expect resources from all three habitat zones to be exploited but with the heaviest emphasis on outside resources, particularly sea mammals.

The faunal remains from Yuquot conform roughly to the foregoing expectation (see Table 7). Outside resources appear to have been slightly emphasized over inside resources, but if most of the salmon were caught trolling rather than in spawning streams, then the outside is favored decidedly. Sea mammals are more common than land mammals. I cannot calculate the relative amount of food represented by the animal bones from Yuquot, but such calculations should increase the relative frequency of sea mammals only slightly, because the seals represented in the collection are only a bit heavier than the most common land mammal, the coastal black-tailed deer. The addition of whale to the figures in Table 7 would bring the observed exploitation pattern much closer to the expected pattern, especially considering the amount of food represented by each

Table 7. Relative Frequency (in Percentages) of Habitat Exploitation at Yuquot[a]

Taxon	Offshore[b]	Nearshore	Stream/Forest	Total MNI
Mammals	50.3	8.9	40.8	191
Fish	59.7	3.7	37.6	896
Birds	64.5	28.8	6.7	299
Total	58.8	9.8	31.4	1,386

[a]Relative frequency is percentage of total MNI, Minimum Number of Individuals, shown in final column. Data are from Dewhirst (n.d.), based on Units II and III, 1000 B.C. to A.D. 1790. Percentages add by row.
[b]Offshore, nearshore, and stream/forest are defined in note b of Table 1. Entries under offshore here do not include whale.

whale. Whales definitely were exploited prehistorically, as evidenced by the presence of whale bones and whale barnacles (Dewhirst 1980, Fournier & Dewhirst 1980). Dewhirst (1980:340–344) suggests that whaling was not a very important activity at Yuquot because whaling harpoons occur relatively late (ca. A.D. 1000) and infrequently, and because whale bones are never very plentiful. Nevertheless, even a small number of whales constitute a large quantity of food.

The faunal data from Yuquot do conform to the expected pattern, showing a concentration on locally available resources. Whether the local resources were emphasized to the point of specialization, as was suggested for Ozette and Hesquiat, is unclear. However, if deposits closer to the beach and outside of houses had been excavated, whale and other large sea mammal bones might have been more common (see Dewhirst 1980:33–34), as was the case at Ozette (Huelsbeck 1983a, 1983b). If unexcavated deposits that contain significantly more sea mammal bones do exist at Yuquot, then sea mammals would dominate the measurable food production, indicating a degree of specialization and perhaps exchange.

Thus far, the ethnohistorical information suggests that local groups among Westcoast peoples produced surpluses of locally abundant resources, in addition to their general subsistence activities, and that they exchanged those surpluses for food and manufactured products that were difficult to obtain locally. The archaeological data concerning faunal exploitation indicate that local resources were emphasized. In the case studies reviewed here, sea mammals constituted more than 90 percent of the represented animal products, and as much as one-half of this is blubber (Pyke 1970). The monotony of this diet, the abundance of oil, and the nearby availability of other animals all suggest that outside groups traded sea mammal products for fish and other foods, but this is not certain. If more sea mammals than could possibly be consumed were harvested, then exchange is indicated. We are able to evaluate this question at the Ozette site because there we can associate a collection of faunal remains very closely with a particular population and time.

FOOD PRODUCTION AT OZETTE

The Ozette Site

The Ozette site is located on the west coast of the Olympic Peninsula, about 30 km south of Cape Flattery (see Figure 1). Excavation at Ozette concentrated on a small part of the village that was covered by a mudslide about 250 BP, based on tree-ring dates. The clay maintained anerobic, water-saturated conditions that preserved vegetal materials, such as wood and basketry (Croes 1977, Friedman 1975, Gleeson 1980b, Gleeson & Grosso 1976, Mauger 1978). Excavation of this "wet" part of the site (Unit V, Area B70) between 1970 and 1981 yielded more than 50,000 artifacts, 30,000 structural remains, and more than a million faunal remains (Gleeson 1980a, Samuels 1983).

In addition to preserving organic materials, the clayslide stratigraphically isolated a relatively brief period of occupation on top of an earlier clayslide (Samuels 1983:9–31). The excavation area encompassed two complete house platforms and an estimated 25 percent of a third (see Figure 2). House 1 was constructed no more than 450 years ago (440 ± 90 BP WSU 1778). House 5 was built shortly after this on the second house platform, located behind House 1; it was occupied for a short time and then was partially dismantled and abandoned. Following the abandonment of House 5, this second house platform was covered by a small mudslide; then House 3 was built on the third platform; a short time later, House 2 was constructed on top of the clay on the second house platform. Houses 1 and 2 were in use at the time of the slide; House 3 may have been recently abandoned (Gleeson 1982, Samuels 1983).

The difference between the radiocarbon date and tree-ring dates is 200 years. Stratigraphic analyses and rate of deposition studies are consistent with an estimated occupation of 100 years for House 1 (Samuels 1983:24). The rafter support posts of House 2 were replaced shortly before the mudslide and the House 1 posts had been replaced sometime earlier. The houseposts are cedar and average 16 cm in thickness (Mauger 1978). Representatives of several lumber companies have suggested to me that such posts should last some 25 or more years before needing to be replaced.

Figure 2. The Ozette Site

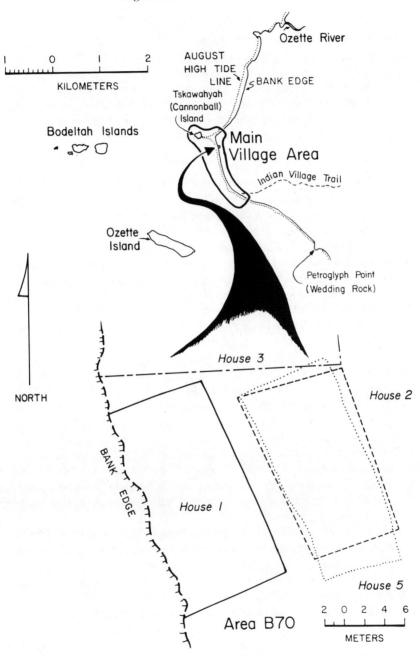

Thus, the Unit V stratum at Ozette represents between 50 and 200 years of activity. An estimate of 100 years will be used in this analysis.

A number of artifacts and faunal remains of nonlocal origin have been recovered from this part of the Ozette site. These include dentalia, red turban, and abalone shells from the north (Wessen 1982:179), Oregon ash bowls, coil basketry and baskets with bear grass imbrication from the south and/or east (Croes 1977, Friedman 1975), and several stone projectile points more characteristic of areas to the south or the interior. These artifacts demonstrate the existence of trade but shed little light its on magnitude, especially regarding foodstuffs.

Quantifying Production

The first step in the investigation of trade in foodstuffs at Ozette is to determine if quantities of food in excess of those required for survival were being produced. The amount of food represented by the faunal remains was calculated by multiplying the average useable weight of each species by the minimum number of individuals (MNI) represented by the faunal remains. Allowances were made for portions of the collection that have not yet been identified and quantified and for differential recovery of small items (see Huelsbeck 1983a, Wessen 1982). The results are listed in Table 3.

There are a number of points where inaccuracies can skew such calculations (see Grayson 1984, Lyman 1982), but these should not cause problems here. The unit of aggregation for the determination of MNI is the stratum as a whole or the sum of individual house floor deposits, whichever was larger (see DePuydt 1983; Huelsbeck 1983a, 1983b; Wessen 1982). All size classes of the various species are represented in the collection, so the use of average weight should not create significant error (see Stewart & Stahl 1977). The faunal evidence suggests that all parts of the animals in question were consumed, so the potential difference between consumed butchering units and complete animals should not be skewing the results (see Lyman 1979).

I used conservative estimates of live weight and useable weight. The average weight of the female was used in the cases of sexually dimorphic species, the average springtime weight during the northward migration after a winter of fasting was used for whales, and the proportion of useable food in each animal was usually set at only 50 percent of live weight (see DePuydt 1983; Huelsbeck 1983a, 1983b; Wessen 1982). Finally, it is likely that in all cases the MNI underrepresents the total number of utilized animals. Thus, the estimates of food production presented in Table 3 are conservative.

Production Needed for Subsistence

Table 3 shows clearly that the faunal remains recovered from this small portion of the site represent a considerable amount of food, but a large quantity of food would have been needed to feed the inhabitants of this part of the site for 100 years. In order to compare the amount of food represented and the amount of food needed, we must make several assumptions.

The houses that were excavated at Ozette were typical Northwest Coast multifamily "longhouses." House 1 contained 10 hearth areas and, therefore, could have been occupied by 10 nuclear families. House 2 contained 6 hearth areas. House 5, stratigraphically beneath House 2, contained 6 or 7 hearth areas (Samuels 1983). The physical stratigraphy of the floor deposits indicates that some hearth areas were not used continuously, so fewer than 10 and 6 nuclear families, respectively, probably occupied the houses at any one time.

In James Swan's (1869:2–3,6) census of the Makah villages in 1868, the average number of people per house varied from 12 to 16. Prior to the historical epidemics, the numbers were undoubtedly higher. Drucker (1951:281–286) illustrates two houses on Vancouver island and provides data on the occupants ca. 1890–1900. The houses contained 13 and 17 places, respectively, with 7 and 11 in regular use. The first household contained 40 people and the second contained 33 people. The number of people per living area in this limited sample ranges from 3 to 6. If we estimate that 8 of the 10 and 5 of the 6 living areas at Ozette were in regular use by an average of 4.5 people, then the two houses were occupied by some 60 people (actually, 58.5) during the time in question.

The area excavated at Ozette also included some 25 percent of a third house platform (see Figure 2). This house was occupied almost as long as House 1, based on stratigraphic correlations (Gleeson 1982), but the house platform behind House 1 was not occupied continuously. Analysis of the rate of deposition in the houses suggests that, if House 1 was occupied for 100 years, then House 2 was occupied for 55 years and the underlying House 5 was occupied for 19 years (Samuels 1983:116). The faunal remains recovered from the House 3 floor deposit should approximate the quantity of the faunal remains that would have accumulated on the House 5/House 2 platform if it had been occupied continuously for 100 years instead of around 74 years (House 5, 19 years; House 2, 55 years).

Clearly, then, food production at Ozette must have supplied an adequate diet for 60 people for 100 years. The estimated daily energy requirement for an active adult male is 3,000 kcal, and for an adult female, 2,200 kcal (Passmore et al. 1974). The requirements for adolescents range between these totals, while younger children require less than adult females. For purposes of this discussion, let us assume that the average person consumed an average of 2,750 kcal/day.

Northwest Coast peoples did not rely heavily on plant foods (Drucker 1951, 1965). Even with the good preservation of vegetal materials at Ozette, though, we cannot gauge the quantity of plant foods utilized. Nevertheless, a wide variety of plants were used (see Gill 1983, Gunther 1945, Turner 1975) and must have been consumed in sufficient quantities to compensate for deficiencies in such nutrients as iron and ascorbic acid in the heavily sea mammal and fish diet (see Pyke 1970). An average of 250 kcal/person/ day from plant foods, or less than 10 percent of the diet, can be used as a conservative estimate of plant food consumption. Therefore, the faunal remains need to account for approximately 2,500 kcal/person/day. I recognize that dietary requirements are far more complex than can be evaluated simply by counting calories. Calories are readily quantifiable and are used here to assess the magnitude of production, not nutritional status.

Archaeological Indications of Surplus

If the members of these Ozette households were generating food surpluses for exchange, can we expect the faunal remains to document this surplus? The techniques used to process blubber, oil, and fish often involve the removal of the animal's bones. If the amount of food represented by the bones is more than 2,500 kcal/person/day, a food surplus is indicated. However, in most studies of diet based on faunal remains, the bones represent too little food to support the known population of the site. For example, the faunal remains from Fort Ligonier, a British fort occupied in 1758–1766, represent only enough meat to sustain just two soldiers for that length of time. Historic records indicate that between 8 and 4000 soldiers were garrisoned at the fort at different times in 1758–1766 (Guilday 1977).

Generally speaking, a wide variety of forces act on the bones before and after they are deposited and eliminate some of the bones from animals that were utilized by the people living at the site. The minimum number of individuals (MNI) is a *minimal* estimate, whereas the actual number of animals utilized could range from the MNI up to or beyond the number of bones recovered. Therefore, if any surplus is indicated, it probably should be viewed as substantial.

Calculating Food Production

Table 3 indicates that the faunal remains represent nearly 1 million kg of food. Using a figure of 3 kcal/gram (see Denniston 1972, 1974; Osborn

1977; Pyke 1970), the million kg represent nearly 3 billion kcal, an average of 1,370 kcal/person/day (3 billion kcal/100 years/365 days/60 persons). This total is 45 percent (1,130 kcal) short of the estimated daily requirement.

Although 55 percent of the daily dietary requirement is a higher proportion than indicated at most archaeological sites, the faunal remains recovered from Ozette do not by themselves demonstrate the production of a food surplus. However, all of the remains from all of the animals consumed were not recovered, as noted earlier. There are clear indications that some of the midden eroded before excavation, that some faunal remains were destroyed before excavation, and that the MNI statistic seriously underrepresents those taxa whose bones are common in the deposit. Each of these points is considered below.

The midden that was excavated at Ozette is not all of the midden that was deposited during the occupation of the houses in question; the seaward portion of the midden, including the western edge of House 1, was lost to ocean erosion prior to excavation. The faunal remains from the missing midden would contribute substantially to the represented food supply. In the areas excavated to date, the midden deposits outside of houses (exterior midden) constituted 40 percent of the area excavated and yielded 65 percent of the smaller faunal remains and nearly 100 percent of the whale bones (see Huelsbeck 1983a, 1983b; Wessen 1982). Whale bones are particularly common along the beach edge of the midden in other parts of the site. Also, interior deposits near walls typically yield more faunal remains than other areas within houses. If the missing exterior midden between the house and the edge of the drop-off to the beach was just 2m wide, there would be 25 percent more exterior midden and about 25 percent more food represented (an additional 25 percent of total whale, plus 25 percent of the 65 percent of all other bones derived from exterior midden). This would add another 342 kcal/person/day/year, bringing the total to 1,712, or 68 percent of the daily requirement.

There are a number of animals that should have contributed more food than is indicated by the faunal remains. The herring definitely falls into this category. This small fish was captured using dip nets and/or the herring rake (see Drucker 1965:15–16), techniques designed to capture them in large numbers. Fragments of at least 6 herring rakes and 10 dip nets were recovered from the houses in question, indicating substantial exploitation (Gleeson 1980a), but the identified portion of the fish bone collection yielded only 3 herring (MNI). Herring were very common in the area (Collins 1892:246), and they probably contributed at least two weeks' worth of food each year. This translates to 96 kcal/person/day/year, bringing the total to 72 percent of the daily requirement.

A disparity between numbers of tools and animals is not evident for any of the other apparently underrepresented animals. Nevertheless, the number of individuals represented in the faunal collection is unreasonably low for all taxa except, perhaps, for whales. Annual per capita consumption figures to only 0.07 birds, 0.01 land mammals, 0.22 sea mammals other than whales, 2.67 fish, and 50 shellfish (see Table 3; divide MNI by 60 people/100 years or 6,000 person-years). Each person at Ozette undoubtedly consumed more than 3 fish and one-fifth of a seal during the average year.

One reason these numbers are low is the extremely conservative nature of the MNI statistic. Studies of the relationship between the MNI and the number of identified pieces of bone demonstrate that, as the number of identified specimens (NISP) per taxon increases, the relative number of individuals represented by those bones decreases (see Grayson 1984). In other words, in a small collection, 2 or 3 bones may contribute 1 MNI to the total, whereas in larger collections, 30–40 or more bones may be assigned to each minimum individual.

In the collection under consideration here, 12 right whale bones have been identified and assessed as representing a minimum of 6 individual whales (ratio: 2 bones/1 whale). Other examples are: humpback whale, 260 bones and 31 MNI (ratio: 8.39/1); harbor seal, 319 bones and 17 MNI (ratio: 18.8); fur seal, 44,563 bones and 1,240 MNI (ratio: 35.9/1); and salmon, 3,059 bones representing an MNI of 61 (ratio: 50/1). The butchering pattern for the two kinds of whales listed above is the same. There may have been slight differences in the butchering patterns of the two kinds of seals (see Huelsbeck 1983a), but these differences are not large enough to account for the fact that each fur seal in the collection is represented by 36 bones, whereas each harbor seal is represented by only 19 bones. Very probably, the MNI figures calculated from the faunal collection significantly underrepresent the actual number of animals utilized by the people living in the houses at Ozette—possibly by a factor of 2 (based on the seals) or 8 (based on the whales) or more. If the underrepresentation is only a factor of 2, then animal food production averaged 3,616 kcal/person/day. This would be 1,116 kcal/person/day above the daily requirement and would amount to 8,147 kg of surplus production per year for the two households.

In view of the statistical slight-of-hand used to obtain this estimated surplus, is it reasonable to assume that the required number of animals could have been captured? A brief examination of Table 8 demonstrates that the estimated harvest based on all of the calculations above is not only possible but is unreasonably low for all taxa except, possibly, whales. It is difficult to believe that only 6.77 fish/person/year were used, in light of historic descriptions of Makah fisherman returning from a one-day fishing trip with more than 100 halibut (Collins 1892, Wilcox 1895), or that less than one seal/person/year was taken, when it was possible to take 6

Table 8. Inferred Faunal Exploitation at Ozette

Taxon	MNI[a]	MNI + 25%[b]	2(MNI + 25%)[c]	Number of Animals Per Person/Year[d]
Bird	400	500	1,000	0.17
Land Mammal	66	83	166	0.03
Fish	16,000	20,000	40,000	6.67
Sea Mammal[e]	1,317	1,646	3,292	0.55
Whale	67	84	168	0.03
Shellfish	300,100	375,125	750,250	125.04

[a]Minimum Number of Individuals, calculated from the identified faunal remains, adding estimates for unprocessed portions of the collection.
[b]The additional 25 percent compensates for eroded midden.
[c]Multiplying by 2 compensates for the conservative nature of the MNI statistic.
[d]$\frac{2(MNI + 25\%)}{6,000}$. The denominator is the product of 100 years of occupancy × 60 persons.
[e]Excluding whales.

in one day even after the fur seal population had declined drastically (Brown 1895).

Some readers may be uncomfortable with the idea that the inhabitants of the two longhouses captured an average of 1.68 whales per year. However, Densmore (1939:63) reports that "in old times the average catch for a whaler was one or two whales a year, but a man often caught four and occasionally five in a season." If each longhouse contained one whaler, a combined average of 1.68 whales is not unreasonable. On the other hand, during the 1890s, the Makah captured an average of 5.5 whales per year (Wilcox 1895), or an average of one whale for every 80 people in the village. Because whale populations had declined by the 1890s and, thus, whaling should have been more successful prehistorically, this ratio can be used to calculate a minimal estimate of whaling success. Applying this rate to the assumed population of 60 persons for Ozette yields an estimate of 0.75 whales per year, or 75 in 100 years. Thus, the estimate of 168 whales calculated in Table 8 may be somewhat too high. On the other hand, it is clear from Table 8 that the faunal remains must represent less than the total exploitation for all taxa except, perhaps, for whales.

The question of food production can be examined from a different perspective by accepting the minimum number of whales represented by the bones and adding to that figure very conservative estimates for the other taxa (e.g., 2 fish/person/week; see Table 9). This procedure yields a total estimated production of more than 5,000 kcal/person/day (3,668,237 kg × 3,000 kcal/kg divided by 60 people/100 years/365 days = 5,025). This is more than double the daily energy requirement and represents a surplus of 0.84 kg of meat and blubber/person/day. This amounts to nearly 20,000

Table 9.   Minimal Estimates of Potential Exploitation at Ozette

Taxon	Rationale for Estimate	Number of Animals	Available Food (kg)[a]
Whale	observed MNI[b]	67	846,600
Fish	2/person/week[c]	624,000	1,248,000
Sea Mammal	2/house/week[d]	20,800	1,229,632
Shellfish	24/person/month[e]	1,728,000	233,202
Land Mammal	1/house/month[f]	2,400	77,803
Bird	1/person/year[g]	6,000	33,000
Total			3,668,237

[a]Available food is the product of the number of animals and average food yield per animal. Amounts were calculated using conservative estimates of the averge amount of useable food from representatives of each taxon. For example, fish represented in the colleciton range in size from 0.25 kg herring to 12.5 kg halibut but the "average" fish should have yielded 2 kg of food.
[b]From Table 8.
[c]2 × 60 persons × 52 weeks × 100 years
[d]2 × 2 houses × 52 weeks × 100 years
[e]24 × 60 persons × 12 months × 100 years
[f]1 × 2 houses × 12 months × 100 years
[g]1 × 60 persons × 100 years

kg of surplus production per year for the two longhouses. In view of the minimal production estimates given in Table 9, larger surpluses easily could have been produced.

Any attempt to infer amounts of food from faunal remains must be considered hypothetical at best. The production figures are used here to evaluate the relative magnitude of the potential surplus production, not to present precise indications of the actual amount of food produced.

The animal bones indicate that at least 67 whales are represented in the collection (see Table 8). Given that whales were butchered on the beach and that the MNI statistic probably underrepresents the actual number of all animals taken, it is likely that more than 67 whales were harvested by the residents of the two longhouses. The MNI figures for all other taxa drastically underrepresent the actual number of animals taken. Almost certainly, bones were burned, dumped on the beach, eaten by dogs, or otherwise destroyed. As a result, the faunal collection does not clearly indicate the production of food surpluses at Ozette. However, the documented harvest of whales, coupled with minimal projections of production in other taxonomic categories, suggests that the Ozette village produced a very sizeable food surplus. This surplus would have been large enough to support extravagant consumption and the acquisition of other commodities.

SUMMARY AND CONCLUSIONS

The ethnohistoric literature indicates that the Makah depended on the production of food surpluses that were exchanged for such needed commodities as canoes and house planks. The literature suggests that other Westcoast peoples also frequently exchanged large quantities of goods. Oil and blubber are frequently mentioned as exchanged commodities. The degree of dependence on this exchange is unclear in the literature, but whales and other sea mammals clearly could have been exploited in sufficiently large numbers to support regular exchange for necessary commodities.

The archaeological evidence from the Ozette, Yuquot, and Hesquiat Harbor sites clearly indicates the exploitation of resources available in the immediate vicinity of the site. For Ozette and Hesquiat Harbor, this pattern of exploitation results in production focused on a very narrow range of resources. There would be so little variety in the diet represented by the faunal remains that some exchange is extremely likely. This may or may not have been the case at Yuquot.

The volume of prehistoric exchange is difficult to estimate, particularly for such perishable commodities as foodstuffs. However, a combination of archaeological data and reasonable inferences based on these data suggest strongly that Ozette did produce a surplus of sea mammal products, especially whale blubber and oil. Such a determination is not possible for the Hesquiat Harbor sites, but given the similarities between the Hesquiat and Ozette faunal collections in the proportional exploitation of different habitat zones, surpluses probably were produced for exchange for other commodities.

This picture of Northwest Coast surplus economies should be treated as hypothetical. Production and distribution occur in a social/environmental context. Consideration should be given to variables such as the nature of the social institutions required to coordinate labor forces, the size of the labor force required to procure and process surplus quantities of foods that are available for limited periods of time, and whether the environment could support the indicated levels of production and consumption. It will be difficult to obtain new, independent evidence concerning these variables. However, information concerning prehistoric population levels may shed light on this question. Higher population levels imply smaller exploitation territories and increase the probability that critical resources will occur in limited quantities. If archaeological investigations indicate that precontact population levels were significantly higher than is currently acknowledged, then surplus economies may have been common.

Production and exchange of surpluses were regular and important aspects of Makah economy historically and almost certainly prehistorically. They probably were regular aspects of all Westcoast economies, but the volume of exchange may not have been as large in all cases as that inferred for the Makah. Oil and dried fish were staple foodstuffs on the Northwest Coast and are the two commodities most likely to have been exchanged in the manner proposed here. The ethnohistoric literature for the Coast as a whole suggests that production and exchange of surpluses may have been a characteristic of all central and northern Northwest Coast economies during the early historic period and very possibly prior to Euroamerican contact.

ACKNOWLEDGMENTS

The Ozette Project was conducted under contract with the National Park Service. The Makah tribe gave permission for the project and actively participated in the project. Their contributions and support are gratefully acknowledged. I also thank Gay Calvert and James Haggarty for permission to use the Hesquiat data and John Dewhirst for permission to use the Yuquot data. I have tried to represent those data accurately; responsibility for interpretations presented here is mine unless otherwise noted. The figures were drafted by Steve Samuels. Gary Wessen and John Dewhirst commented on an earlier draft of this essay. Finally, I would like to thank the editor of this volume for helping to make this essay more intelligible outside the circle of northwest faunal analysts.

APPENDIX: LOCAL PHYSIOGRAPHY

The west coast of Vancouver Island is cut by numerous fiords. A large portion of the total coastline is "inside" these inlets. This "inner coast" is protected from the full force of winter storms. The "outer coast" is located "outside" of these inlets. It is the area between fiords and harbors. This dichotomy in the local physiography has had a far-reaching impact on Westcoast peoples. Drucker (1951:7) states:

> It is apparent that the sounds and large inlets, major features of local physiography, played an important part in forming the sociopolitical divisions of the people. The obvious reason is that inhabitants of such a locality were thrown together and their outside contacts were interrupted by the frequent periods of bad weather when it was impossible to round the headlands to the next sound. It is noteworthy that each of these geographic divisions, that is, the people of a certain sound, had their characteristic intonation and speech mannerism-differences roughly comparable to the regional differences in the English of New England and the Southwest, for example.

> Between the sounds there are areas of low headlands fringed in many places by long, straight beaches on which the surf pounds endlessly. It is said that anciently there were a few groups of people who lived all the year on these "outside" coasts. They suffered many hardships during winter storms when the surf was too heavy for them to launch their canoes. Eventually they made alliances with people of the sounds and abandoned the outer coasts except for spring and summer camp sites.

The physiographic difference between outer coast and inner coast also affects the distribution of resources. For the purposes of this essay, three broad habitat zones are recognized. The *offshore zone* is deep-water, open ocean. Pelagic sea mammals and large, deep-water fish such as halibut are common in this zone. The offshore zone is arbitrarily divided from the *nearshore zone* at the point where the water is 20m deep. The nearshore zone extends from this point to the beach. Smaller fish and shellfish are common in this zone. Sea mammals such as harbor seal and sea otter are common within the nearshore zone, but they also frequent the boundary between it and the offshore zone. The *outer coast area* contains both offshore and nearshore habitat zones and has direct access to the offshore zone. The inner coast area has relatively little access to the offshore zone and much greater access to the nearshore zone. The stream/forest habitat zone consists of dry land and fresh water. Spawning salmon are the most important food resource in this zone. Streams and rivers typically occur at the inland end of the inside waters. Thus, any group of people living outside of one of the inlets on the outer coast would have limited access to salmon streams.

The problem of restricted access was solved in the ethnographic period by forming alliances among inside and outside groups and moving seasonally between the inside and outside areas. Drucker, in the quote above, attributes great time depth to these alliances. Recent analyses suggest that this seasonal round pattern may be a historic period phenomenon (Haggarty 1985).

REFERENCES

Adams, J. (1973) *The Gitksan Potlatch: Population Flux, Resource Ownership and Reciprocity*. Toronto: Holt, Rinehart & Winston.

—— (1981) "Recent Ethnology of the Northwest Coast." *Annual Reviews In Anthropology* 10:361–392.

Arima, E. (n.d.) "Notes on Nootkan Sea Mammal Hunting." Paper presented at the XIth International Congress of Anthropological and Ethnological Sciences, Vancouver, BC, 1983.

Barnouw, V. (1978) *An Introduction to Anthropology, Vol. 2, Ethnology*. 3rd ed. Homewood, IL: The Dorsey Press.

Brown, C. (1895) *Fur Seal Arbitration, Proceedings of the Tribunal of Arbitration, Volume III. Senate Executive Document 177, Part 3, 53rd Congress, Second Session.* Washington, DC: Government Printing Office.

Calvert, S. (1980) *A Cultural Analysis of Faunal Remains From Three Archaeological Sites in Hesquiat Harbor, British Columbia.* Ph.D. dissertation, University of British Columbia.

Cavanagh, D. (1983) *Northwest Coast Whaling: A New Perspective.* M.A. thesis, University of British Columbia.

Codere, H. (1950) *Fighting with Property: A Study of Kwakiutl Potlatching and Warfare, 1792–1930.* Seattle: University of Washington Press, American Ethnological Society Monograph 18.

Collins, J. (1892) *Report on the Fisheries of the Pacific Coast of the United States. Report of the Commissioner, U.S. Commission of Fish and Fisheries, for 1888.* Washington, DC: Government Printing Office.

Croes, D. (1977) *Basketry from the Ozette Village Archaeological Site.* Ph.D. dissertation, Washington State University.

Denniston, G. (1972) *Ashishik Point: An Economic Analysis of a Prehistoric Aleutian Community.* Ph.D. dissertation, University of Wisconsin, Madison.

——— (1974) "The Diet of the Ancient Inhabitants of Ashishik Point, An Aleut Community." *Arctic Anthropology* XI-Supplement:143–152.

Densmore, F. (1939) *Nootka and Quileute Music.* Washington, DC: Smithsonian Institution, Bureau of American Ethnology, Bulletin 124.

DePuydt, R. (1983) *Cultural Implications of Avifaunal Remains Recovered from the Ozette Site.* M.A. thesis, Washington State University.

Dewhirst, J. (n.d.) "An Archaeological Pattern of Faunal Resource Utilization at Yuquot, A Nootkan Outside Village: 1000 B.C.–A.D. 1966." Paper presented before the Society for American Archaeology, Vancouver, BC, 1979.

——— (1980) "The Indigenous Archaeology of Yuquot, A Nootkan Outside Village." Pp. 5–358 in W. Folan & J. Dewhirst (eds.) *The Yuquot Project, Vol. 1.* Ontario: Parks Canada, History and Archaeology 39.

Donald, L. (1983) "Was Nuu-chah-nulth-aht (Nootka) Society Based on Slave Labor." Pp. 108–119 in E. Tooker (ed.) *The Development of Political Organization in Native North America.* Washington, DC: The 1979 Preceedings of the American Ethnological Society.

——— (1984) "The Slave Trade on the Northwest Coast of North America." Pp. 121–158 in B. Isaac (ed.) *Research in Economic Anthropology, Vol. 6.* Greenwich, CT: JAI Press.

Donald, L., and D. Mitchell (1975) "Some Correlates of Local Group Rank among the Southern Kwakiutl." *Ethnology* 14:325–346.

Drucker, P. (1951) *The Northern and Central Nootkan Tribes.* Washington, DC: Smithsonian Institution, Bureau of American Ethnology, Bulletin 144.

——— (1965) *Cultures of the North Pacific Coast.* San Francisco: Chandler.

Drucker, P., and R. Heizer (1967) *To Make My Name Good.* Berkeley: University of California Press.

Ember, C., and M. Ember (1985) *Cultural Anthropology.* 4th ed. Englewood Cliffs, NJ: Prentice-Hall.

Folan, W., and J. Dewhirst, eds. (1980a) *The Yuquot Project, Vol. 1.* Ontario: Parks Canada, History and Archaeology 39.

——— (1980b) *The Yuquot Project, Vol. 2.* Ontario: Parks Canada, History and Archaeology 43.

Fournier, J., and J. Dewhirst (1980) "Zooarchaeological Analysis of Barnacle Remains from Yuquot, British Columbia." Pp. 59–102 in W. Folan & J. Dewhirst (eds.) *The Yuquot Project, Vol. 2*. Ontario: Parks Canada, History and Archaeology 43.

Friedman, J. (1975) *The Prehistoric Uses of Wood at the Ozette Archaeological Site*. Ph.D. dissertation, Washington State University.

Gill, S. (1983) *Ethnobotany of the Makah and Ozette People, Olympic Peninsula, Washington*. Ph.D. dissertation, Washington State University.

Gleeson, P. (1980a) *Ozette Archaeological Project, Interim Final Report, Phase XIII*. Pullman: Washington State University, Washington Archaeological Research Center, Project Report No. 97.

———— (1980b) *Ozette Woodworking Technology*. Pullman: Washington State University, Laboratory of Archaeology and History, Project Reports No. 3.

———— (1982) *Ozette Excavations, Phase XV*. Pullman: Washington State University, Laboratory of Archaeology and History.

Gleeson, P., and G. Grosso (1976) "The Ozette Site." Pp. 13–44 in D. Croes (ed.) *The Excavation of Water-Saturated Sites (Wet Sites) on the Northwest Coast of North America*. Ottawa: National Museum of Man, Mercury Series, Archaeological Survey of Canada Paper 50.

Grayson, D. (1984) *Quantitative Zooarchaeology*. Orlando: Academic Press.

Guilday, J. (1977) "Animal Remains from Archeological Excavations at Fort Ligonier." Pp. 121–132 in D. Ingersoll, J. Yellen & W. Macdonald (eds.) *Experimental Archeology*. New York: Columbia University Press.

Gunther, E. (1945) *Ethnobotany of Western Washington*. Seattle: University of Washington Publications in Anthropology.

Haggarty, J. (1982) *The Archaeology of Hesquiat Harbour: The Archaeological Utility of an Ethnographically Defined Social Unit*. Ph.D. dissertation, Washington State University.

———— (1985) *Review of* A Site Catchment Analysis of the Little Qualicum River Site, Di Sc 1: a Wet Site on the East Coast of Vancouver Island (Kathryn Bernick). *Canadian Journal of Archaeology* 9:91–93.

Harris, M. (1985) *Culture, People, Nature*. 4th ed. New York: Harper and Row.

Huelsbeck, D.R. (1981) *The Utilization of Fish at the Ozette Site*. Washington State University, Laboratory of Archaeology and History, Project Reports No. 11.

———— (1983a) *Mammals and Fish in the Subsistence Economy of Ozette*. Ph.D. dissertation, Washington State University.

———— (1983b) "The Economic Context of Whaling at Ozette." Report submitted to the Interagency Archaeological Service, National Park Service, Seattle.

Inglis, R., and J. Haggarty (n.d.) "Provisions or Prestige: A Re-evaluation of the Economic Importance of Nootka Whaling." Paper presented at the XIth International Congress of Anthropological and Ethnological Sciences, Vancouver, BC, 1983.

Jewitt, J. (1974) *The Adventures and Sufferings of John R. Jewitt, Captive Among the Nootka 1803–1805*. Toronto: McClelland & Stewart.

———— (1976) *A Journal Kept at Nootka Sound*. New York: Garland.

Lane, B. (n.d.) "Political and Economic Aspects of Indian-White Culture Contact in Western Washington in the mid-19th Century: Makah Economy." Ms. on file, Washington Archaeological Research Center, Washington State University, 1973.

Langdon, S. (n.d.) "The Development of the Nootkan Cultural System." Paper presented at the Northwest Coast Studies Conference, Simon Fraser University, 1976.

Lyman, R.L. (1979) "Available Meat From Faunal Remains: A Consideration of Techniques." *American Antiquity* 44:536–546.

—— (1982) "Archaeofaunas and Subsistence Studies." Pp. 331–393 in M. Schiffer (ed.) *Advances in Archaeological Method and Theory, Vol. 5*. New York: Academic Press.

Mauger, J. (1978) *Shed Roof Houses at the Ozette Archaeological Site: A Protohistoric Architectural System*. Pullman: Washington State University, Washington Archaeological Research Center, Project Report No. 73.

Mitchell, D., and L. Donald (1985) "Some Economic Aspects of Tlingit, Haida, and Tsimshian Slavery." Pp. 19–35 in B.L. Isaac (ed.) *Research in Economic Anthropology, Vol. 7*. Greenwich, CT: JAI Press.

Nanda, S. (1984) *Cultural Anthropology*. 2nd ed. Belmont, CA: Wadsworth.

Oberg, K. (1973) *The Social Economy of the Tlingit Indians*. Seattle: University of Washington Press.

Osborne, A. (1977) *Aboriginal Exploitation of Marine Food Resources*. Ph.D. dissertation, The University of New Mexico.

Passmore, R., B.M. Nicol, and M.N. Rao (1974) *Handbook on Human Nutritional Requirements*. Rome: Food and Agriculture Organization of the United Nations.

Piddocke, S. (1965) "The Potlatch System of the Southern Kwakiutl: A New Perspective." *Southwestern Journal of Anthropology* 21:244–264.

Pyke, M. (1970) *Man and Food*. New York: McGraw-Hill.

Rice, D., and A. Wolman (1971) *The Life History and Ecology of the Gray Whale (Eschrichtius robustus)*. Stillwater, OK: Special Publication Number 3, The American Society of Mammalogists.

Rosman, A., and P. Rubel (1971) *Feasting with Mine Enemy. Rank and Exchange Among Northwest Coast Societies*. New York: Columbia University Press.

Samuels, S. (1983) *Spatial Analysis of Three Nootkan Long House Floor Middens*. Ph.D. dissertation, Washington State University.

Scammon, C. (1968) *The Marine Mammals of the Northwestern Coast of North America, Together with an Account of the American Whale Fishery*. New York: Dover. (First published 1874.)

Schalk, R. (1977) "The Structure of an Anadromous Fish Resource." Pp. 207–249 in L. Binford (ed.) *For Theory Building in Archaeology*. New York: Academic Press.

—— (1981) "Land Use and Organizational Complexity among Foragers of Northwestern North America." Pp. 53–75 in Shuzo Koyama and D.H. Thomas (eds.) *Affluent Foragers*. Osaka, Japan: National Museum of Ethnology, Senri Ethnological Studies, No. 9.

Sproat, G. (1868) *Scenes and Studies of Savage Life*. London: Smith, Elder & Co.

Stewart, F., and P. Stahl (1977) "Cautionary Note on Edible Meat Poundage Figures." *American Antiquity* 42:267–270.

Suttles, W. (1960) "Affinal Ties, Subsistence, and Prestige Among the Coast Salish." *American Anthropologist* 62:296–305.

—— (1968) "Coping with Abundance: Subsistence on the Northwest Coast." Pp. 56–69 in R. Lee & I. Devore (eds.) *Man the Hunter*. Chicago: Aldine.

Swan, J. (1869) *The Indians of Cape Flattery*. Washington, DC: Smithsonian Contributions to Knowledge No. 220, Vol. 16, Article 8, Pp. 1–108.

Swartz, M., and D. Jordan (1980) *Culture: The Anthropological Perspective*. New York: John Wiley & Sons.

Turner, N. (1975) *Food Plants of British Columbia Indians, Part 1/Coastal Peoples*. Victoria: British Columbia Provincial Museum Handbook 34.

Vayda, A. (1961) "A Re-examination of Northwest Coast Economic Systems." *Transactions of the New York Academy of Science, Series 2* 23:618–624.

Wessen, G. (1982) *Shell Middens as Cultural Deposits: A Case Study from Ozette*. Ph.D. dissertation, Washington State University.

Wilcox, W. (1895) *Fisheries of the Pacific Coast*. Washington, DC: Report of the Commissioner, U.S. Commission of Fish and Fisheries for 1893.

Wolman, A. (1978) "The Humpback Whale." Pp. 46–53 in D. Haley (ed.) *Marine Mammals.* Seattle: Pacific Search Press.

Yesner, D. (1980) "Maritime Hunter-Gatherers: Ecology and Prehistory." *Current Anthropology* 21:727–750.

THE USE OF SHELLFISH RESOURCES ON THE NORTHWEST COAST:

THE VIEW FROM OZETTE

Gary C. Wessen

INTRODUCTION

The vast majority of all prehistoric archaeological sites on the Northwest Coast are shell middens, accumulations of cultural materials wherein marine shells are a principal component. While these deposits have been investigated since the earliest years of this century (Hill-Tout 1903, Smith 1909, Reagan 1917), studies focusing upon the shellfish remains themselves and the cultural behaviors represented by them have been relatively few. Thus, we know few details about the actual context and circumstances of the use of shellfish resources. Economic considerations of Northwest Coast cultures rarely address the role of these resources, and existing ideas about them are often undemonstrated and occasionally contradictory.

This essay discusses the use of shellfish resources at the Ozette, a large shell midden site on the northwest coast of Washington state. The essay

Research in Economic Anthropology, Supplement 3, pages 179–207.
Copyright © 1988 by JAI Press Inc.
All rights of reproduction in any form reserved.
ISBN: 0-89232-818-5

describes the nature and disposition of the Ozette shellfish remains and considers the character of the cultural behaviors responsible for their presence. Much of the data examined here was originally reported in a detailed study of the methodology of shell midden archaeology (Wessen 1982). The present essay does not repeat the methodological details of sample documentation and data processing. Rather, it focuses upon details of the range of cultural behaviors represented by them.

PERCEPTIONS OF THE USE OF SHELLFISH RESOURCES

Perceptions of the use of shellfish resources have been generated from two principal types of sources: (1) ethnographic and early historic materials and (2) contemporary archaeological investigations. Here, I provide a synoptic overview of the general scope and character of the perceptions provided by these sources, but not a detailed consideration of either.

Ethnographic and Early Historic Sources

These sources include the accounts and commentaries of explorers and other early travelers in the region, and descriptive ethnographies of individual ethnic groups. At least 35 such documents are available for the Northwest Coast,[1] but they are generally quite sparse with respect to the discussion of shellfish and most of them contain few specific details regarding their use. Taxonomic information is invariably limited; most sources refer directly to fewer than 10 taxa and few mention as many as 20. Most sources agree that shellfish were used primarily as a food resource and that the principal emphasis was on a relatively small group of bivalves. Other frequently cited shellfish foods include crabs and echinoids. While many references impart the impression that shellfish were collected in large quantities, actual quantitative data are quite limited.

Beyond basic taxonomic accounts, most sources provide a cursory description of collecting and processing activities. Collecting localities are often noted, and we can say that most collection was conducted by groups of women or women and children. The question of ownership of shellfish resource areas is rarely directly addressed, and the few available remarks include statements which both confirm and deny the existence of this type of resource regulation. Spring and summer are the most frequently cited collection seasons, although all seasons are mentioned and some groups are explicitly described as engaging in year-round collection. Procurement technologies were quite simple and usually included little more than a digging stick. Boiling, drying, and roasting appear to be the most common methods of food preparation; the consumption of raw shellfish meat was uncommon and limited to only a few taxa.

Archaeological Sources

These sources include both studies that are directly based upon particular archaeological data sets and studies that are more conceptual and speculative in scope (and less directly supported by empirical data). Until relatively recently, ideas about the prehistoric use of shellfish resources were closely tied to ideas about the character and significance of shell midden deposits. The deposits have traditionally been regarded as largely homogeneous refuse heaps, and the study of their structure and contents has often been generalized, simplistic, and of relatively limited scale. The lack of concern for detail has given rise to the impression that most shell middens constitute a single type of site representing a single type of cultural behavior. For the most part, archaeological shellfish studies have addressed three principal issues: environmental reconstructions, dietary reconstructions, and changes in shellfish use over time. The investigation of shellfish seasonality, predator-prey relationships, and intra-site contexts have become more frequent in recent years, but these important areas of study are still relatively uncommon.

Environmental reconstructions from shellfish remains are interpretations of the intertidal setting associated with a site, based upon the ecology of the represented animals. Such analyses do not directly address cultural behaviors, although they have often been the basis for limited inferences regarding shellfish collecting strategies.

Dietary reconstructions have been the major focus of cultural investigations of shellfish remains. Indeed, they are often the only focus of these studies. Dietary reconstructions identify the relative importance of the various prey species and attempt to assess the quantities of food resources represented by them. Such studies have been undertaken with widely varying levels of precision but have not usually produced quantifiable estimates directly comparable to those for other food resources. Thus, while virtually all archaeological sources agree that most shells in cultural deposits represent food residues, there is substantial uncertainty about their relative importance. Shellfish have been suggested to be both staples and very minor dietary elements used only as alternatives to starvation.

Change in shellfish use over time represents the only type of variation in shell presence that has been regularly examined in shell midden sites. A wide variety of cultural and non-cultural effects have been cited as explanations for such changes. Most of the explanations fall into one or a combination of three broad categories: environmental changes, cultural and/or technological changes, and changes in the shellfish resource itself.

Studies of this type usually rely upon relatively small samples, and they rarely include independent tests of the purported change mechanisms.

Archaeological investigations on the Northwest Coast include examples of all three of these types of shell midden studies, although it is fair to say that the excavation of shell middens in this region has never been primarily concerned with shellfish-related cultural behaviors. Thus, Northwest Coast studies have provided only limited insights into the issues of cultural behavior raised by shellfish studies conducted in other regions. Shellfish-based environmental reconstructions in this region have been both few in number and limited in focus; most have documented deltaic developments with only indirect cultural inferences. Some degree of dietary reconstruction is common in these studies, but most are quite limited in this regard; detailed assessments of shellfish foods, with direct comparisons to other food resources, are rare. The observation of temporal changes in shellfish is not uncommon in Northwest Coast sites, and all of the foregoing explanations have been offered. However, no effort has been made to integrate this last group of studies, despite the fact that they all report the same or similar changes. Most such studies report earlier shell faunas dominated by mussels changing to later shell faunas dominated by clams (see below).

THE OZETTE SITE AND THE OZETTE SHELLFISH COLLECTION

The Ozette archaeological site is a large complex of shell midden deposits and waterlogged deposits rich in organic materials located at Cape Alava, Washington (Gleeson and Grosso 1976). The site represents at least 2,000 years of occupation terminating in the early 20th century, when it was held by members of the Makah Tribe. In early historic times, Ozette was an important center of marine hunting (especially whaling and sealing) and fishing activities, and these pursuits appear to have considerable time depth here. Archaeological investigations at Ozette began in the mid-1960s and gained momentum in 1970 with the discovery of the waterlogged portion of the site. This latter area was the focus of an 11-year field program that produced an extensive and well controlled sample of cultural materials, including approximately 55,000 artifacts and more than one million faunal remains.

The waterlogged portion of the Ozette site is composed of at least four major cultural strata separated by culturally sterile masses that appear to represent the lag deposits of clay slides, which periodically interrupted occupation here (Samuels 1983:9–31). The uppermost stratum, Unit I, is considered to represent historic occupation between approximately 1850 and 1920 A.D. It is not waterlogged, and little information is available about its internal structure. The second cultural stratum, Unit III, is an early historic occupation thought to date prior to 1850 A.D. This deposit is partially waterlogged and contains the remains of at least one longhouse structure. Beneath this is Unit V, a waterlogged deposit containing the remains of five at least partially contemporaneous longhouses. Unit V represents approximately 100 years of occupation beginning ca. 1550 A.D. The lowermost cultural stratum, Unit VII, is a waterlogged deposit dating to ca. 1200 A.D. It has been subject to only very limited study.

Unit V was the principal focus of study at Ozette. The excavations exposed three complete longhouses, a portion of a fourth, and extensive exterior deposits in their immediate vicinity.[2] Far smaller though still sizable samples are also available for Units I and III.

The archaeological shellfish collection from the Ozette Site is a very broad and extensive sample collected by a variety of techniques. In total, it includes both piece samples of taxonomically identifiable mollusc and weight samples of arthropod and echinoid remains. The basic sampling unit for the collection was a two-meter excavation square within each depositional stratum. The vast majority of all recovered shell represents either representative or water-screen sample collection techniques. Representative samples were hand collected by each excavator; they are considered to be qualitative and semi-quantitative. Water-screened samples were obtained by washing the midden matrix through 7-millimeter hardware cloth. These latter samples represent the entire volume of each sampling unit and are considered to be both qualitative and quantitative. Density-dependent correction factors were generated for selected sub-sets of the representative samples in order to compensate for the reduced sensitivity of this technique.

Analysis of the Ozette shellfish materials required the conversion of the recovered samples into a data base capable of addressing a broad range of research questions in a controlled manner. To this end, a highly detailed computer code was developed in order to record a wide range of taxonomic, morphologic, provenience, and cultural/contextual information on a per-piece basis for most types of shellfish remains (Wessen 1982, Appendix A). The code descriptions allow the calculation of Minimum Number of Individuals (MNI) estimates for the various shell materials and support most analyses reported in this essay.

BASIC PARAMETERS OF THE OZETTE SHELLFISH SAMPLE

The coded shellfish data base from the Ozette site represents piece count data on 306,456 pieces of identified mollusc remains and weight data on 66,699 grams of identified arthropod and echinoid remains. Approximately

95 percent of the sample represents the Unit V occupation. The remainder of the materials represent Units III and I, with about 60 percent of these shells collected from the former stratum. While the latter two Unit samples are proportionally small, each contains several thousand pieces.

Taxonomic Diversity

The shellfish collection from Ozette contains a very broad taxonomic range—at least 89 species of marine and freshwater invertebrates, including 28 marine bivalves, 1 freshwater bivalve, 38 marine univalves, 4 chitons, 2 cephalopods, 9 barnacles, 4 crabs, and 3 sea urchins (see Table 1). The proportional occurrence of these various animals is highly skewed, how-

Table 1. Shellfish Present in Cultural Deposits at Ozette.

Taxon	*MNI*[a]	*FT*[b]
Glycymeris subobsoleta (Ark Shell)	27	Ic
Pododesmus macroschisma (Rock Oyster)	3	Ic
Mytilus edulis (Blue Mussel)	4,085	P
Mytilus californianus (California Mussel)	44,472	P,R,F
Pecten caurinus (Weathervane Scallop)	55	D
Hinnites multirugosa (Purple Hinged Rock Scallop)	27	S,M
Chlamys icelandicus (Icelandic Scallop)	6	D
Chlamys rubidus (Hinds Scallop)	20	D
Chlamys hastata (Pacific Spear Scallop)	22	D
Tellina bodegensis (Bodega Clam)	16	S
Macoma nasuta (Bent-nose Clam)	69	S
Macoma irus	31	S
Macoma secta (Whitle Sand Clam)	30	S
Semele rubropicta (Red Paint Semele)	1	Ic
Siliqua patula (Pacific Razor Clam)	23	P
Tresus nuttalli (Horse Clam)	16	P,R
Tresus capax (Horse Clam)	70	P,R
Clinocardium nuttalli (Basket Cockle)	126	S
Protothaca staminea (Littleneck Clam)	22,676	P
Saxidomus giganteus (Butter Clam)	5,307	P
Humilaria kennerleyi (Kennerley's Venus Clam)	7	Ic
Lyonsia sp.	1	Ic
Entodesma saxicola (Pacific Ugly Clam)	2	Ic
Mytilimeria nuttalli (Sea Bottle Shell)	1	Ic
Panope generosa (Geoduck Clam)	1	Ic
Hiatella pholadis (Nesting Saxicave)	3	Ic
Hiatella gallicana (Gallic Saxicave)	1	Ic
Penitella penita (Piddock Clam)	3	Ic
Margaritifera falcata (Freshwater River Mussel)	16	?
Acmaea digitalis (Finger Limpet)	110	S
Acmaea instabilis (Unstable Limpet)	5	Ic

Table 1. Continued

Taxon	MNI[a]	FT[b]
Acmaea mitra (Nootka Cap Limpet)	235	S
Acmaea pelta (Ridge Limpet)	1,417	P
Acmaea persona (Masked Limpet)	149	S
Acmaea t. scutum (Shield Limpet)	1,715	P
Haliotis kamtschatkana (Northern Abalone)	32	D
Diodara aspera (Rough Keyhole Limpet)	136	S
Tegula funebralis (Purple Turban Snail)	315	S
Tegula pulligo (Dusky Turban Snail)	3	Ic
Calliostoma ligatum (Blue Top Shell)	18	S
Astraea gibberosa (Red Turban Snail)	203	D
Littorina sitkana (Sitka Periwinkle)	55,137	P
Littorina planaxis (Flat Periwinkle)	40	S
Littorina scutulata (Checkered Periwinkle)	7	S
Lacuna variegata (Variegated Chink Shell)	543	S
Bittium eschrichtii (Threaded Bittium)	29	Ic
Hipponix cranoides (Flat Hoof Shell)	47	Ic
Crepidula adunca (Hooked Slipper Shell)	11	Ic
Crepidula nummaria (White Slipper Shell)	8	Ic
Polinices lewisi (Lewis's Moon Snail)	1	Ic
Natica clausa (Arctic Natica)	2	Ic
Opalia wroblewskii (Wroblewski's Wentletrap)	8	Ic
Fusitriton oregonensis (Oregon Triton)	11	S
Searlesia dira (Dire Whelk)	1,024	S
Nassarius fossatus (Channeled Dog Whelk)	6	Ic
Ceratostoma foliata (Leafy Hornmouth)	4	Ic
Ocenebra lurida (Lurid Rock Shell)	12	Ia,Ic
Ocenebra interfossa (Sculptured Rock Shell)	8	Ic
Thais lamellosa (Frilled Dogwinkle)	775	S
Thais emarginata (Emarginate Dogwinkle)	487	Ia
Thais lima (File Dogwinkle)	485	Ia
Thais caniculata (Channeled Dogwinkle)	130	Ia
Amphissa columbiana (Wrinkled Amphissa)	2	Ic
Mitrella sp. undetermined Dove Shell	11	Ic
Olivella biplicata (Purple Olive Shell)	63	D
Dentalium pretiosum (Dentalium)	256	D
Mopalia lignosa (Woody Chiton)	192	S
Mopalia muscosa (Mossy Chiton)	587	P
Katharina tunicata (Black Katy Chiton)	1,577	P
Cryptochiton stelleri (Steller's Chiton)	340	S
Octopus dofleini (North Pacific Octopus)	252	P,F
? undetermined cephalopod	2	?
Balanus cariosus (Acorn Barnacle)	*	P,Ia
Balanus rostratus (Acorn Barnacle)	*	S,Ia
Balanus balanus (Acorn Barnacle)	*	S,Ia
Balanus nubilus (Horse Barnacle)	*	S,Ia
Mitella polymerus (Sessile Goose-neck Barnacle)	3,023	P
Lepas sp. (undetermined Pelagic Goose-neck Barnacle)	42	S
Cryptolepas rachianecti (Gray Whale Barnacle)	29	Ia

Table 1. Continued

Taxon	MNI[a]	FT[b]
Coronula diadema (Humpback Whale Barnacle)	724	Ia
Coronula reinae (Humpback Whale Barnacle)	8	Ia
Cancer productus (Red rock Crab)	371	P
Cancer magister (Dungeness Crab)	2	S
Hemigrapsus spp. (Shore Crabs)	137	S
Pugettia producta (Kelp Crab)	164	S,M
Strongylocentrotus purpuratus (Purple Sea Urchin)	*	P,M
Strongylocentrotus drobachiensis (Green Sea Urchin)	*	P,M
Strongylocentrotus franciscanus (Red Sea Urchin)	*	P,M

[a]MNI is the uncorrected Minimum Number of Individuals. An asterisk indicates a weight data taxon without MNI.
[b]FT is Functional Type. Values are P (Primary Prey), S (Secondary Prey), F (Fishbait), D (Decorative/ Symbolic/Ceremonial), R (Raw Material), M (Medicinal), Ic (Incidental), and Ia (Inadvertant).

ever, and a relatively small number of taxa constitute the vast majority of the collection. The range of variation in absolute numbers is so great, in fact, that we can easily speak in terms of "major," "minor," and "trace" species. Major species account for more than 1 percent of the collection; minor species, from 1-.01 percent; and trace species, <.01 percent. The relative contribution of major species to the piece count data is summarized in Figure 1. Remains represented by weight data were identified only to the level of genera and thus are not recorded in Figure 1; 94 percent of this latter material represents barnacles, while 6 percent represents sea urchin.

While piece counts are the form in which the data were collected, this level of data description is poorly suited to most kinds of cultural questions. Discussion of the populations of animals represented by the pieces is far more useful. Conversion of the piece counts to MNI data indicates that the Ozette shellfish collection represents at least 160,419 animals. The relative contribution of major species to the MNI data is summarized in Figure 2. This conversion results in significant, though not major, changes in the relative contribution of taxa. We can still speak of "major," "minor," and "trace" species—here calculated as percentages of the overall animal total—and few assignments in these terms change as we go from Figure 1 to Figure 2. However, there are a number of changes in the absolute ranking of species. In general, bivalves and univalves increase in importance, whereas barnacles and chitons decrease.

Figure 1. Relative Contribution of Ozette Shellfish Species to the Piece Count Data.

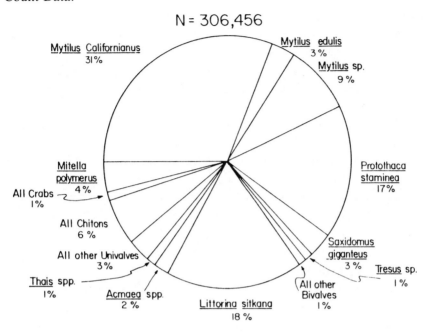

N = 306,456

Mytilus Californianus 31%

Mytilus edulis 3%

Mytilus sp. 9%

Mitella polymerus 4%

All Crabs 1%

All Chitons 6%

All other Univalves 3%

Thais spp. 1%

Acmaea spp. 2%

Littorina sitkana 18%

All other Bivalves 1%

Tresus sp. 1%

Saxidomus giganteus 3%

Protothaca staminea 17%

Functional Typology

A functional typology was developed in order to assess the behavioral significance of the taxonomic diversity and relative occurrence of the Ozette shellfish. Review of ethnographic and early historic sources, and other practical considerations, suggest that at least eight functional types may be recognized: primary prey, secondary prey, fish bait, medicinals, decorative/symbolic/ceremonial items, manufacturing raw materials, inadvertants, and incidentals. Primary and secondary prey species are those taxa which constitute human food resources. Primary prey are those species which were the targets of specific, conscious collection strategies; secondary prey were collected in more casual, fortuitous, and less systematic manners. The fish bait, medicinals, decorative/symbolic/ceremonial items, and raw materials types are all self-explanatory. Inadvertants are shellfish species that were not utilized systematically but which regularly entered the site as by-products of other activities. Incidental species also were not utilized systematically, but they appear to be random, for-

Figure 2. Relative Contribution of Ozette Shellfish Species to the MNI Data.

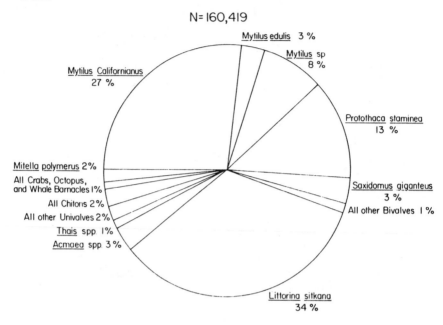

N= 160,419

Mytilus edulis 3 %

Mytilus sp 8 %

Mytilus Californianus 27 %

Protothaca staminea 13 %

Mitella polymerus 2%

All Crabs, Octopus, and Whale Barnacles 1%

All Chitons 2%

All other Univalves 2%

Thais spp. 1%

Acmaea spp. 3 %

Saxidomus giganteus 3 %

All other Bivalves 1 %

Littorina sitkana 34 %

tuitous, or idiosyncratic in their occurrence. These functional assignments are not mutually exclusive, and some species have multiple, though hierarchal, assignments.

A number of patterns are apparent in the relationships between functional assignments and the relative abundance of Ozette shellfish. For example, all major species are primary prey. Most secondary prey and nearly all inadvertants are minor species. All incidentals are trace species. Summarizing broadly from these distributions, we can say that more than half of the shellfish species present at the site were utilized as human food with some degree of frequency. Fully another third of the species occur without being the focus of any direct purpose.

The Represented Food Resource

Accepting the suggestion that shellfish were used primarily as a human food resource, how much food is actually represented by the Ozette shellfish collection? Estimates of the food resource presented here rely upon calculations of the live meat weight for the animals represented in the collection. I should note that this is not a nutritional assessment, but rather an estimation of the quantities of raw meat available based upon the numbers of animals and measurement of their actual or average body size. From a nutritional point of view, shellfish meats tend to be low in caloric value, although they offer significant amounts of protein and important minerals, such as calcium, iron, and iodine (Watt and Merrill 1963, Hooper n.d.).

This assessment of the food resource represented by the Ozette shellfish utilizes the live meat weight values for animal totals, using the density-dependent correction factors developed to compensate for the two different sample recovery techniques. The calculations indicate that at least 4,047 kg (approximately 4.5 tons) of shellfish meat are represented by the collection. The relative contributions of major species to the live meat weight total are summarized in Figure 3. Consistent with the suggestions of most references, bivalves are the single largest source of shellfish meat. In fact, the five bivalves most frequently cited in ethnographic documents (*Mytilus californianus, Mytilus edulis, Protothaca staminea, Saxidomus giganteus,* and *Tresus* spp.) account for almost all of the bivalve meat (see Figure 3). Note, however, that bivalves constitute only about half (45.6 percent)

Figure 3.   Relative Contribution of Ozette Shellfish Species to the Live Meat Weight Data.

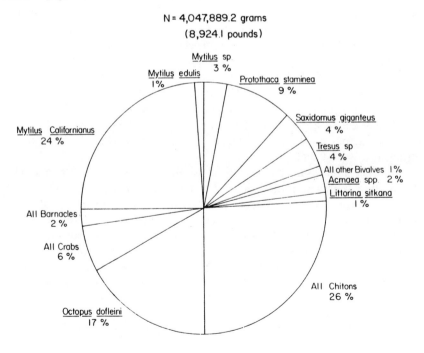

of the total shellfish. Other major sources are chitons and cephalopods. Univalves, while numerous as pieces and animals, are quite small in size and thus represent only a small quantity of meat. Similarly, barnacles are numerous as animals, but their small individual size results in a low meat total.

THE ROLE OF SHELLFISH IN THE ECONOMY

Evaluation of the role of shellfish in the Ozette economy may be approached in a number of ways, three of which will be examined here. First, shellfish are compared to other food resources represented at the site. Secondly, the timing of the use of shellfish resources is considered. Finally, the extent to which use of shellfish varied among contemporaneous households within the community is examined.

Shellfish in Comparison to Other Resources

While detailed studies at Ozette make possible the comparison of shellfish to other classes of represented fauna, it is important to briefly consider the limitations of this type of comparison. The main limitation is that the recovered collections are not directly equivalent to the represented diet for several reasons. First, there were probably significant seasonal changes in the population at Ozette, and many important resources may have been consumed elsewhere. Second, many resources consumed at the site may have been butchered and/or partially processed elsewhere, thereby biasing their apparent presence in the site. Third, different food residues have different survival potentials. Fourth, archaeological recovery techniques are not equally appropriate to all classes of food residues. Finally, the recovered sample is just that, a sample, and a substantial amount of material relevant to any quantitative reconstruction was not collected. All of these factors must be considered in evaluating archaeological reconstructions of past diets.

All food estimates used at Ozette are similar to those made for shellfish, that is, they represent useable meat estimates multiplied by the MNI value for each taxon present. Conservative estimates were used for all meat weight and individual count values (see Depuydt 1983; Huelsbeck 1983a, 1983b; Wessen 1982), and the resulting food estimates are considered to represent lower limits in all cases. Estimates for animal food resources from Ozette are presented in Table 2. A considerable quantity of plant food residues, mostly seeds representing various types of berries, were also identified at Ozette, but quantitative estimates for these materials are not available (Gill 1983).

Table 2 indicates that the recovered collection of animal food residues

Table 2. Estimates of Animal Food Resources Represented at Ozette.

	Estimated Animal Food	
Taxa Group	*Kilograms*	*Percent*
Birds	1,100	0.11
Terrestrial Mammals	2,141	0.22
Shellfish	4,048	0.42
Marine Fish	32,000	3.32
Marine Mammals (other than Whales)	77,875	8.08
Whales	846,600	87.85
TOTAL	963,764	100.00

from Ozette is heavily dominated by marine mammals, particularly whales. Fish are the next most important animal food resource at the site. While shellfish rank fourth, they appear to account for less than 0.5 percent of all the meat and fish represented in the site. Terrestrial mammals, such as deer and elk, and all birds account for even less.

Having complied these data, we must examine the question of their relationship to the actual diet. In doing so, it is important to consider the size of the human population that is probably represented. Recall that the Unit V deposit represents approximately 100 years of cultural deposition. The excavated area contains the remains of four large, shed roof longhouses, although only one of them was occupied for the entire period. Early historic data reported by Swan (1869:6) indicate that such structures were typically occupied by 12–16 individuals. Analysis of the house floor deposits from these particular houses suggests that the above estimates are probably low (Samuels 1983). Given these uncertainties regarding occupation duration and household size, 50 individuals is probably not too conservative an estimate for the number of residents represented in the excavated area at Ozette.

Accepting the rough parameters of 50 individuals and 100 years of occupation, the magnitude of resource underrepresentation begins to become apparent. These values, and the estimates reported in Table 2, suggest a shellfish meat consumption rate of less than 1kg/person/year. Such a rate indicates only one or two shellfish meals per year. I suggest that this is not a credible figure for the actual use of shellfish resources at Ozette. Other examples of underrepresentation are discussed by Huelsbeck (this volume). The foregoing figures probably mean that shellfish were not a staple resource at Ozette, but they provide only limited additional insight into what their role may have been. While they might be cited in support of the suggestion that shellfish were only a marginal resource used as a starvation alternative, the following discussion indicates that such an interpretation is also unlikely.

The Timing and Character of Shellfish Collection

Consideration of the timing and character of shellfish collection provides important additional perspectives to the question of their role in the diet at Ozette. In particular, if shellfish use was limited to the role of "starvation alternative," then their use would have been largely confined to annual lows in environmental productivity, that is, late winter and early spring (cf. Osborn 1977:173). Examination of the population characteristics of shellfish prey also relates to this question, because such data may reflect the degree of size-class selection exhibited by collectors. If collection occurred only as an alternative to starvation, little or no size-class selection would be apparent.

The following discussion of these conditions will be limited to a single shellfish taxon, *Protothaca staminea* (littleneck clam), which is the most common clam at the site and the second most important source of shellfish meat. However, I must stress that collection patterns that can be demonstrated for this animal do not necessarily apply to other varieties of shellfish. In fact, ethnographic documents and other considerations make it likely that they do not; thus, other taxa must be evaluated on a case-by-case basis.

Seasonality determinations on archaeological shellfish remains have become increasingly common during the last 20 years. Most such studies employ the investigation of annual growth cycles in order to infer the season in which the animal stopped growing (was collected). At Ozette, calibration of the growth rates for littleneck clams was achieved by controlled seasonal sampling of living populations. From these observations, a model of seasonal growth was constructed with the year divided into three periods: individuals with up to 40 percent of annual growth represent late winter through early spring, those with 41–70 percent represent mid-spring through summer, and those with 71–100 percent represent fall through mid-winter collection.

This seasonal growth calibration was applied to a sample of 110 shells recovered from Unit V deposits at Ozette. The results of that effort are summarized in Figure 4 and they indicate that, while intensity varied, these clams were being taken virtually year-round. The distribution suggests that the greatest use of these animals occurred during late winter and early spring (45 percent of the sample), but that it continued at a relatively high rate through the late spring and summer months (38 percent). Collection during the fall and early winter occurred at a decidedly lower rate (17 percent). Since the "starvation alternative" model of shell-

Figure 4. Seasonal Distribution for *Protothaca staminea* (little neck clam) from Unit V Deposits at Ozette.

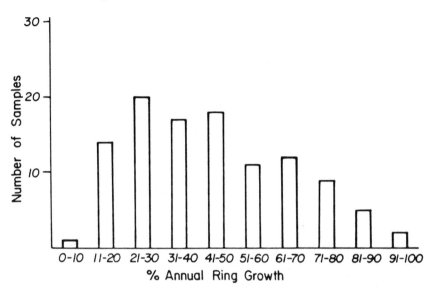

fish use argues that use was largely restricted to the first of these three periods, the data indicate that this model is not appropriate to Ozette.

Population size-class data for these same 110 littleneck clams provides insight into an additional dimension of the seasonal variation in their use. This investigation makes use of the observations that bivalve populations are characterized by high rates of reproduction and high mortality rates in the younger age classes (Rounsefell 1975: 365–374). Furthermore, the growth rates of bivalves slow considerably once they reach sexual maturity. Thus, the size-class distribution for a population of bivalves normally contains a large number of small individuals, a moderate number of medium-sized individuals, and a small number of large individuals. It follows that non-selective collection from a local bivalve population should approximate this type of size-class distribution.

All 110 clams used in the seasonality study were represented by whole values, and therefore plotting the size-class distributions of the above noted seasonal subsets (0–40 percent of annual ring growth, 41–70 percent, etc.) is relatively easy and straightforward. Figure 5 represents these same shell samples with their maximum dimension (in an anterior-posterior plane) recorded as the vertical axis of the plot. Simple visual inspection of this figure reveals substantially different size-class distributions for the late winter and early spring (0–40 percent) and late spring and summer (41–

Figure 5. Size Class and Seasonal Distributions for *Protothaca staminea* (Littleneck Clam) from Unit V Deposits at Ozette.

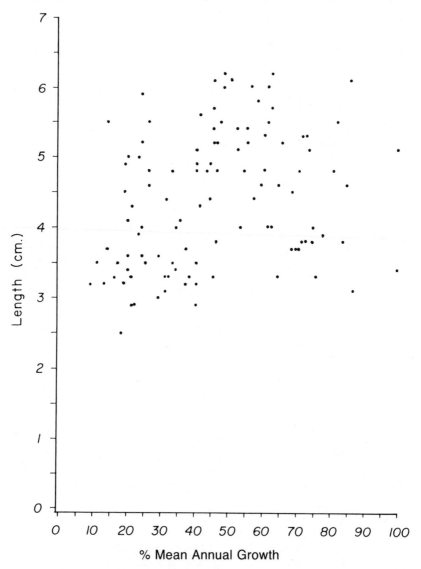

70 percent) groups. The former group has a distribution much like that expected for a natural population; in contrast, the latter group is heavily dominated by relatively large-sized individuals. The last of the three groups (71–100 percent) appears to have a distribution similar to that of the first, but its small sample size limits its value.

While the mean sizes of the first two groups overlap at one standard deviation (3.89 ± .82 and 4.95 ± .82, respectively), statistical examinations indicate that they are probably significantly different. A T-Test for means difference between these groups produced a T value of -6.16 with 92 degrees of freedom, indicating a very high probability that the groups are different. Similarly, a Kolmogrov-Smirnov Two Sample Test produced a D value of .438 and a critical value of .405 (at the .001 level of significance), again indicating a very high probability that the groups are different.

The size-class distributions for the two seasonal groups indicate that there is an important seasonal dimension in the selectivity of the exploiters of these clams. While humans are not the only predators that can affect the size range parameters of shellfish populations, the cultural provenience of this sample makes it is likely that humans played a major role in shaping these distributions. The size-class distribution for the late winter through early spring group is not inconsistent with the type of indiscriminate collecting that would occur if shellfish were being used to stave off starvation. However, during late spring and summer, individual size appears to be a significant factor and only relatively larger clams were harvested. This latter pattern is consistent with ethnographic sources which suggest that large quantities of shellfish meat were dried during these months (Collins 1974; Ellis and Swan 1981; Gunther 1927; Singh 1956; Stern 1934). Because shellfish meats shrink when they are dried, collectors prefer larger animals if storage is intended.

Intracommunity Variation in Shellfish Use

While all of the foregoing and virtually all other considerations of prehistoric shellfish use patterns imply a single adaptation for the group, data from Ozette indicate significant intracommunity variation in the use of these resources. Intracommunity variation may be considered in several ways: data from the site reflect differences in consumption patterns that appear to be related to individual household status, as well as differences in collection patterns that appear to be related to lineal affiliations of groups embracing more than one household.

Intracommunity variation in the use of shellfish resources is reflected in observed differences in the shell contents of the four excavated Unit V houses. Independently of their shell contents, the artifact inventories from these four structures also provide criteria for assessing social relationships. In this regard, several lines of evidence seem to indicate that House 1 was the residence of a relatively high-status household. Whaler's gear was well represented in House 1 and was uncommon in the other three houses. Similarly, House 1 contained carved wall panels, inlayed bench planks, and other house decorations not found in the other structures. At least two types of variation in shellfish materials appear to corroborate this observation of relatively higher status for the House 1 household.

The strongest shellfish-based indication of status differences among the houses is the distribution of decorative/symbolic/ceremonial shell. Animals in this functional group account for 4.41 percent of all shellfish in House 1, while they constitute 0.44–0.06 percent of the shell contents of the other three houses. This interhousehold difference is even more dramatic if we consider only the exotic taxa represented in the group. Three of these shellfish *(Dentalium pretiosum, Astraea gibberosa,* and *Haliotus kamtschatkana)* do not occur locally and were probably obtained in trade from Vancouver Island. House 1 contained 99.2 percent of all *Dentalium* recovered at the site, 58.1 percent of all *Astraea,* and 31.2 percent of all *Haliotus* from the site. Thus, among the sampled Houses, House 1 residents appear to have had much greater access to these shell materials.

This predominance of House 1 is also evident in actual shellfish food residues. Here, the observation is based on the diversity and emphasis of the animals in the total resource base represented in each house. In this context, I would argue that a relatively low species diversity, with a greater emphasis on primary prey, reflects a higher status household. While there is actually very little house to house variation in overall species diversity, the four houses differ in the relative contribution of the five major primary prey bivalves noted earlier as major sources of shellfish meat. These five animals account for 75.7 percent of all House 1 shellfish meat, while they range from 63.2 percent to 36.3 percent of the shellfish meat in the other three houses. In these latter three, much of the remaining food residues reflect much greater use of chitons and univalves, many of which are secondary prey.

A broader perspective on the variation in shellfish use may be obtained by considering the probable sources of the major taxa within each house. A summary of selected shellfish species, calculated by house, is presented in Table 3. These animals include representatives of at least five different nearby intertidal micro-environments, as well as the exotic taxa discussed above. (Note that Table 3 also shows House 1 dominance in exotic animals.) Examination of the relative presence of these major species, and of certain minor species, shows a broadly similar pattern of occurrence in Houses 1, 2, and 3. House 5 exhibits a somewhat different pattern. For example, *Mytilus edulis* constitutes 2–3 percent of all animals in the first three houses, but about 0.08 percent in House 5. In Houses 1, 2, and 3, *Protothaca staminea* outnumbers *Saxidomus giganteus* by approximately 3:1, whereas the proportions of these animals is reversed, to roughly 1:2, in House 5. Similarly, in the first three houses the chiton *Katharina tunicata* outnumbers the chiton *Mopalia muscosa* by ratios of from 4:1 to 10:1, but in House 5, *Mopalia* is slightly more abundant than *Katharina*.

Table 3.   Percent MNI Occurrence of Selected Shellfish in Houses in
Unit V at Ozette.

Taxon	H1	H2	H3	H5
Mytilus califorianus	16.23	23.35	30.98	13.99
Mytilus edulis	3.05	3.38	2.11	0.08
Protothaca staminea	7.04	9.06	13.12	3.38
Saxidomus giganteus	1.85	2.45	3.05	3.64
Tresus spp.	1.02	0.44	0.96	0.15
Littorina sitkana	50.24	39.15	25.83	57.44
Acmaea spp.	4.90	3.96	5.33	3.62
Dentalium pretiosum	2.73	—	—	—
Astraea gibberosa	1.24	—	0.05	0.03
Katharina tunicata	0.28	1.36	0.52	0.36
Mopalia muscosa	0.06	0.39	0.07	0.64
House MNI Total	9,577	39,581	6,655	6,140

This interhouse variation is probably due to more than one factor. I have already mentioned one of them, namely, the relative status of the occupying household. Another major source of interhouse differences appears to be variation in the collection emphasis among the local intertidal micro-environments. This factor is particularly evident in the case of *Mytilus edulis,* a mussel that is largely restricted to a small area approximately 3 km north of the site. Table 3 suggests that the residents of Houses 1, 2, and 3 regularly collected in this area, whereas House 5 collectors do not appear to have operated there. The species ratio differences noted in the preceding paragraph also seem to reflect differences in the collectors' emphases among the local beaches. Given that these variations repeatedly group Houses 1, 2, and 3, and separate House 5, a regular and systematic mechanism may be inferred. The most plausible explanation is that shellfish collection areas were owned and controlled by lineal groups in the same sense that fishing, seal hunting, or berry collecting sites were. If so, Houses 1, 2, and 3 were probably members of one lineal organization, while House 5 probably represented another.

TEMPORAL CHANGE IN SHELLFISH RESOURCE USE

Change in patterns of shellfish use over time is the most frequently cited variation in archaeological shellfish collections. Such changes are evident at Ozette and appear to be similar to those in shellfish reported at other Northwest Coast sites. I shall now describe the temporal changes at Ozette, examine the apparently similar changes elsewhere and their purported explanations, and then consider the applicability of these explanations at Ozette.

Temporal Change at Ozette

Temporal changes in the shellfish faunas at Ozette are evident when the relative occurrences of major species in the three major depositional units of the site are compared. Figure 6 shows that Units V and III are very similar to each other and somewhat different from Unit I in this

Figure 6. Major Shellfish Species Composition for Units I, III, and V at Ozette.

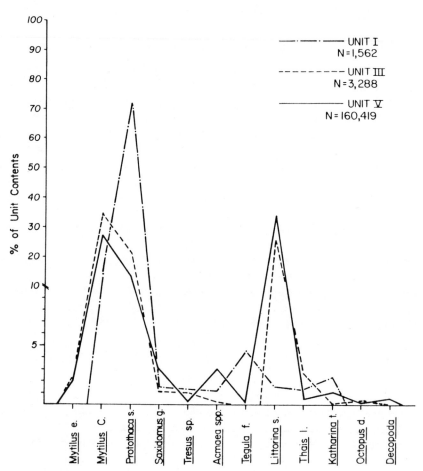

regard. The principal difference is the reversed dominance of *Mytilus cal-iforianus* and *Protothaca staminea* (clam dominance replacing mussel dominance); these animals are the two most important bivalves in all Units, but *Mytilus* dominates Units V and III while *Protothaca* dominates Unit I. A dramatically reduced presence of *Littorina* also characterizes Unit I. Although not reflected in Figure 6, a decrease in overall species diversity also appears to distinguish the Unit I deposit from earlier strata. (I caution that this last observation may be at least partially a product of the relatively smaller sample size for Unit I.)

These changes in shellfish use patterns occur between the early and later historic occupations at Ozette. While this portion of the site's history has not been well studied, we can safely assume that the changes noted in shellfish are associated with a much broader range of changes occurring at this time. The historic residents of Ozette were becoming increasingly involved in the Euro-American cash economy, and major changes in both activities and diet were occurring at the site (Lane n.d.). For example, cattle *(Bos taurus)* begin to appear at the site during the Unit I occupation.

Explanations of the Change from Mussels to Clams

The change from mussel to clam dominance at Ozette appears similar to changes reported elsewhere on the Northwest Coast and in California. However, many of these other cases are only superficially described, and it is often difficult to determine the extent of their actual similarity. Parallel changes in shellfish taxa other than mussels and clams are rarely reported and are difficult to evaluate. The timing of the mussel-to-clam change is more frequently recorded, and comparison of studies indicates that this shift in resource emphasis is not temporally consistent. At Ozette and some other sites, the shift occurs very late; elsewhere it occurs relatively early in the depositional sequence.

Environmental changes have often been cited as an explanation for the mussel-to-clam shift. For the Skagit Delta of Washington, Stilson (1972) ties the shift to changes in intertidal environments, particularly the siltation of rocky shores. Grabert et al. (1978) suggest the same condition at Sem-iahmoo Spit in Washington, and Ham (1976) describes a similar one at the Fraser Delta in British Columbia. They argue that epifaunal mussel communities declined with the reduction of their habitat and were gradually replaced by infaunal clam communities expanding with the growing sand and mud flats. Such changes would probably be gradual, and we should be able to relate intertidal changes to postglacial sea level adjustments.

A second type of environmental explanation for the mussel-to-clam shift has been proposed for Yuquot on Vancouver Island (Clarke and Clarke 1980). There, the change occurs during the historic occupation, and Clarke and Clarke have suggested that it is related to the local extermination of sea otter *(Enhydra lutris)* during the early fur trade period. This model argues that sea otter removal would significantly alter the varieties of shellfish available to human collectors.

Cultural explanations for the mussel-to-clam change have been relatively limited, and they usually are related to ideas about increasing sophistication about the maritime environment. The notion, first articulated by King (1950) at the Cattle Point site on San Juan Island, suggests that mussels were relied upon earlier because, as epifaunal animals, they are more readily visible; the targeting of clams, buried in the sediments, came later. This model is potentially compatible with ideas about changing intertidal environments, and it should reflect the resource shift relatively early in the occupation period.

A final type of explanation for the mussel-to-clam shift addresses the effect of human exploitation on shellfish populations. One of its clearest expressions was proposed by Botkin (1980) for a site in California, with shellfish species common in Northwest Coast sites. The model suggests that predators (in this case, humans) will exploit a particular prey species until its collection is no longer profitable, due to its reduction from predation pressure, and then they will shift to a different prey. A similar idea has recently been suggested at the Hoko Rockshelter in Washington (Croes and Hackenberger n.d.). This model recognizes the potential effect of exploitation on shellfish populations and could conceivably be used to predict cyclic changes in species use.

Explanations for Change at Ozette

To what extent do any or all of the foregoing explanations account for the mussel-to-clam shift observed at Ozette? First, while no general model is offered, I believe that the widely reported change from mussels to clams may actually represent a number of related, but not actually identical, conditions. It is not within the scope of this discussion to determine just how many conditions may be involved, but it is clear that some of these ideas have no relevance to the situation at Ozette.

Environmental change is not a likely explanation of the shellfish change at Ozette. In the first place, the total time period represented by the sample is small and relatively recent (ca. 1550–1920 A.D.). The shift in resource emphasis is quite late within this range, possibly less than 100 year ago. Although the mouth of the Ozette River is not far from the site, little sediment build up has occurred from it, and we have no other reason to suspect significant intertidal changes during the last 400 years.

The suggestion that the removal of sea otters may be a factor is tantalizing but probably not correct. While sea otters can have a marked effect on nearshore ecology, data reported by Palmisano and Estes

(1977:556–558) indicate that removing sea otters would expand, rather than reduce, mussel communities. In any event, based upon the frequency of their bones in the site, sea otters do not appear to have been common in the vicinity of Ozette.

Increased sophistication about the maritime environment is an equally unreasonable explanation for the change in shellfish emphasis. The sophisticated maritime activities pursued by the late prehistoric Ozette people have considerable antiquity in this area. Offshore marine mammal hunting has been conducted at Ozette for at least 2,000 years (Gustafson 1968), and offshore hook and line fisheries have been present at the nearby Hoko River for almost 3,000 year (Croes and Blinman 1980). Maritime adaptations appear remarkably stable over this period, and it is therefore unlikely that new insights regarding shellfish were obtained during the last 100 years.

The third type of explanation, the over-exploitation model, at first appears promising. While influenced by predator population size, the model is not dependent upon environmental or cultural changes, and the potentially large human population and long-term occupation of Ozette would seem to make over-exploitation of local resources a real possibility. The earlier observation that shellfish were probably not a staple resource hardly minimizes the risk. There are ample indications that large quantities of shellfish were being collected at the site, and the model concerns the relationship between predator and prey populations, not the relative contributions of particular prey.

Predation pressure on a population is manifest in a reduction in the mean size of individuals (Russell 1942). If over-exploitation is the mechanism responsible for the change in prey emphasis at Ozette, then *Mytilus californianus* should show a decline in size over time (see Botkin 1980). A summary of the mean size-classes of all major bivalves in each of the three depositional units at Ozette is provided in Table 4, which shows that no size reduction occurs in any of these animals there. The data sug-

Table 4. Mean Size (in centimeters) of Major Bivalves in Depositional Units at Ozette.[a]

Taxa	Unit I	Unit III	Unit V
Mytilus califorianus	7.3±1.6	7.6±2.3	7.1±2.5
Mytilus edulis	—	4.3±1.8	4.0±1.5
Protothaca staminea	5.0±0.7	4.8±0.8	4.7±0.8
Saxidomus giganteus	5.6±2.2	5.2±1.6	5.7±1.7
Tresus spp.	9.6±1.9	9.0±1.3	10.1±1.8

[a]Approximate temporal ranges for these deposits are: Unit I, ca. 1850-1920 A.D.; Unit III, ca. 1800-1850 A.D.; and Unit V, ca. 1550-1650 A.D.

gest that the observed change in shellfish use at Ozette is not a response to over-exploitation.

The failure to find evidence of size-class reduction of any major bivalve species at Ozette is both interesting and surprising, since the site's deposits indicate long-term use of shellfish resources. The apparent stability of these populations indicates that they were not subject to heavy pressure and suggests that some type of resource management mechanism was regulating the use of shellfish. Recall that house-to-house comparisons of shell contents suggested that different households collected from different local beaches, and that there appears to have been a consistent pattern of collection relationships among certain households. I have suggested that these circumstances of shell refuse occurrence reflect lineal group ownership of shellfish resource areas, and this perception of resource ownership also is relevant to the present observation. If shellfish collection areas were owned by particular individual lineage groups, local shellfish populations would never have been subject to the unregulated pressure of the entire community. Thus, lineal group management of shellfish resources is a credible explanation for the absence of evidence of predation pressure on shellfish at Ozette.

None of the existing ideas about changes in shellfish use are reasonable explanations of the shift from mussels to clams at Ozette. An adequate explanation is not currently available. Nevertheless, while a specific mechanism cannot be cited, this change in shellfish use was likely related to the much broader range of changes affecting the economy during the early historic period. The Unit I shell sample reflects a pattern of shellfish use very similar to that of the contemporary Makah Indians, and its adoption was probably associated with an absolute decline in the importance of shellfish in the overall diet.

SUMMARY AND CONCLUSIONS

This essay has examined a number of aspects of the cultural utilization of shellfish resources at the Ozette archaeological site. While the data presented here are derived from only a single site, a wider perspective on historic and prehistoric use patterns (Wessen n.d.) indicates that many conditions noted at Ozette were probably typical of much of the region. Data and discussions presented here suggest the following conclusions about the use of shellfish resources:

1. Archaeological and ethnographic treatments of shellfish resource issues are generally impoverished. Such sources are probably incomplete far more often then they are incorrect, although significant errors of both fact and interpretation also appear to be present.

2. While the vast majority of shellfish remains represented in archaeological sites are probably by-products of food preparation or consumption, a number of other mechanisms also contribute to the presence of shell materials. Some varieties of shells were routinely acquired while fishing or whaling. Random and/or idiosyncratic behaviors may also account for some shells.

3. A relatively small group of marine bivalves were probably the most important sources of shellfish meat, but a number of other groups of shellfish also were important, especially crabs, chitons, and cephalopods. While barnacles and univalves are also frequently noted in ethnographic sources, the small size of these animals minimizes their actual food contribution.

4. The relative quantities of represented food, as well as the timing and character of shellfish collection, suggest that these animals were neither dietary staples nor merely starvation alternatives. Although their high predictability and year-round availability make shellfish a dependable buffer against starvation, it is unlikely that their use was restricted to that circumstance. Rather, shellfish were likely a significant minor element in an economic structure that exploited a wide range of local resources.

5. While shellfish foods and non-food materials were available to all members of the community, there was considerable variation in their use. Social status appears to have been one important dimension of this variation. Higher status households had far greater access to exotic decorative/symbolic/ceremonial shell materials and also had different consumption patterns of local shellfish foods. In particular, shellfish consumption in higher status households appears to have been more tightly focused upon a few of the major bivalves; such households may also have had a smaller proportional use of shellfish relative to other food resources.

6. Lineal group affiliation may have been another important source of intra-community variation in the use of shellfish resources. Some of the evidence from Ozette suggests that local shellfish collection areas were controlled by such groups, and that, as a result, variation in the intertidal characteristics of the nearby beaches resulted in differential access to particular prey species. Ownership of collection areas appears to have been a significant resource regulation mechanism for minimizing the risk of over-exploitation of the local shellfish populations. In fact, the concern for resource regulation may have been a major incentive for the control of these areas.

7. The shift from earlier, mussel-dominated shellfish faunas to later, clam-dominated faunas, which has been reported at a number of Northwest Coast sites, appears to be the result of several different mechanisms rather than any single, widely occurring one. The available regional materials suggest that the timing and circumstances of this phenomenon vary and that better data would probably reveal still more differences. At Ozette, this shift occurs during the historic occupation and is probably related to

Euro-American aculturation influences rather than to any environmental, internal cultural, or resource characteristic changes.

ACKNOWLEDGMENTS

The Ozette Archaeological Project was conducted under contract to the National Park Service. The principal investigator for the project was Richard Daugherty. Permission to excavate the site was provided by the Makah Tribe, and their interest has supported many of the shellfish studies reported here. Illustrations in this essay were prepared by Stephan Samuels.

NOTES

1. Ethnographic sources include: Barnett (1955), Boaz (1921, 1966), Bouchard, Miranda, and Kennedy (1975), Collins (1974), De Laguna (1972), Drucker (1951), Duff (1952), Ellis and Swan (1981), Elemendorf (1960), Gunther (1927), Haeberlin and Gunther (1930), Jenness (n.d.), Kenyon (1980), Koppert (1930), Krause (1956), Oberg (1973), Olson (1936), Ray (1938), Singh (1956), Smith (1940), Stern (1934), Suttles (1951), Tweddell (1974), and Underhill (1945). Early historic sources include: Boit (1960), Dawson (1880), Eells (1889), Jewitt (1974), Kane (1925), Mayne (1862), Moziño (1970), Reagan (1917), and Swan (1869, 1972).

2. The excavated materials represent Houses 1, 2, 3, and 5; House 4 at Ozette has been left intact for future study.

REFERENCES

Barnett, Homer G. (1955) *The Coast Salish of British Columbia*. Eugene, OR: University of Oregon Press.

Boas, Franz (1921) *Ethnology of the Kwakiutl*. Washington DC: Thirty-fifth Annual Report of the Bureau of American Ethnology 1913–1914, Part 1.

—— (1966) *Kwakiutl Ethnography*. Chicago: University of Chicago Press.

Boit, John (1960) *Voyage of the Columbia Around the World, 1790–1793*. Portland, OR: Beaver Books.

Botkin, Steven (1980) "Effects of Human Exploitation on Shellfish Populations at Malibu Creek, California." Pp. 121–139 in T. Earle and A. Chistenson (eds.) *Modeling Change in Prehistoric Subsistence Economies*. New York: Academic Press.

Bouchard, Randy, Louis Miranda, and Doe Kennedy (1975) *Squamish Indian People*. Victoria: British Columbia Indian Language Project.

Clarke, Louise R., and Arthur H. Clarke (1980) "Zooarchaeological Analysis of Mollusc Remains from Yuquot, British Columbia." Pp. 37–58 in W. Folan and J. Dewhirst (eds.) *Archaeology and History*, 43. Hull, Quebec: Parks Canada.

Collins, June (1974) *Valley of the Spirits: the Upper Skagit Indians of Western Washington*. Seattle: University of Washington Press.

Croes, Dale R., and Eric Blinman, eds. (1980) *Hoko River: A 2500 Year Old Fishing Camp on the Northwest Coast of North America*. Pullman: Washington State University Laboratory of Anthropology Reports of Investigation, 58.

Croes, Dale R., and Steven Hackenberger (n.d.) "Predictive Modeling of Prehistoric Economic Patterns in the Hoko River Region." Paper presented before the 49th Annual Meeting of the Society for American Archaeology, Portland, OR, 1984.

Dawson, George A. (1880) *Haida Indians of the Queen Charlotte Islands.* Ottawa: Geological Survey of Canada, Report of Surveys and Explorations, Appendix A.

De Laguna, Frederica (1972) *Under Mount Saint Elias: the History and Culture of the Yakutat Tlingit.* Washington DC: Smithsonian Contributions to Anthropology, 7.

DePuydt, Raymond (1983) *Cultural Implications of the Avifaunal Remains Recovered from the Ozette Site.* M.A. thesis, Washington State University.

Drucker, Philip (1951) *The Northern and Central Nootkan Tribes.* Washington DC: Bureau of American Ethnology, Bulletin 133.

Duff, Wilson (1952) *The Upper Stalo Indians of the Fraser River of British Columbia.* Victoria: Anthropology in British Columbia, Memoir 1.

Eells, Myron (1889) *The Twana, Chemakum, and Klallam Indians of Washington Territory.* Washington, DC: Annual Report of the Board of Regents of the Smithsonian Institute for 1887.

Ellis, David W., and Luke Swan (1981) *Teachings of the Tides: Uses of Marine Invertebrates by the Manhousat People.* Nanimo, BC: Theytus Books Ltd.

Elmendorf, William (1960) *The Structure of Twana Culture.* Pullman: Washington State University Research Studies Monograph Supplement, 2.

Gill, Steven (1983) *Economic Botany of the Ozette Village Site.* Ph.D. dissertation, Washington State University.

Gleeson, Paul, and Gerald Grosso (1976) "The Ozette Site." Pp. 13–44 in D. Croes (ed.) *The Excavation of Water-Saturated Sites (Wet Sites) on the Northwest Coast of North America.* Ottawa: National Museum of Man, Mercury Series, Archaeological Survey of Canada Paper 50.

Grabert, G.F., J.A. Cressman, and A. Wolverton (1978) *Prehistoric Archaeology at Semiahmoo Spit, Washington.* Bellingham: Western Washington University, Reports in Anthropology 8.

Gunther, Erna (1927) *Klallam Ethnography.* Seattle: University of Washington Publications in Anthropology 1:5.

Gustafson, Carl E. (1968) "Prehistoric Use of Fur Seal: Evidence from the Olympic Coast of Washington." *Science* 161: 49–51.

Haeberlin, H., and E. Gunther (1930) *The Indians of Puget Sound.* Seattle: University of Washington Publications in Anthropology 4:1.

Ham, Leonard C. (1976) "Analysis of Shell Samples." Pp. 42–78 in R.G. Matson (ed.) *The Glenrose Cannery Site.* Ottawa: National Museum of Man, Mercury Series, Archaeological Survey of Canada Paper 52.

Hill-Tout, Charles (1903) "Kitchen Middens of the Lower Fraser." *The American Antiquarian* 25:180–182.

Hooper, Helen (n.d.) "A Nutrient Analysis of Foods Eaten by Indians Native to Southeastern Alaska." Paper presented before the 7th Annual Ethnobiology Conference, Seattle, WA, 1984.

Huelsbeck, David R. (1983a) *Mammals and Fish in the Subsistence Economy at Ozette.* Ph.D. dissertation, Washington State University.

—— (1983b) "The Economic Context of Whaling at Ozette." Report submitted to the Interagency Archaeological Service, National Park Service, Seattle, WA.

Jenness, Diamond (n.d.) "The Sannich Indians of Vancouver Island." Ms. on file, Archives of the National Museum of Man, National Museums of Canada, Ottawa.

Jewitt, John R. (1974) *The Adventures and Sufferings of John R. Jewitt, Captive Among the Nootka, 1803–1805.* Toronto: McClelland and Stewart.

Kane, Paul (1925) *Wanderings of an Artist Among the Indians of North America.* Toronto: The Raddisson Society of Canada.

Kenyon, Susan M. (1980) *The Kyuquot Way: A Study of a West Coast (Nootkan) Community.* Ottawa: National Museum of Man, Mercury Series, Canadian Ethnology Service Paper 61.

King, Arden R. (1950) *Cattle Point: A Stratified Site in the Southern Northwest Coast Region*. Menasha, WI: Society for American Archaeology, Memoir 7.

Koppert, Vincent A. (1930) *Contributions to Clayoquat Ethnology*. Washington, DC: Catholic University of America, Anthropology Series 1.

Krause, Aurel (1956) *The Tlingit Indians*. Seattle: University of Washington Press.

Lane, Barbara (n.d.) "Political and Economic Aspects of Indian-White Culture Contact in Western Washington in the Mid-19th Century: Makah Economy." Ms. on file, Washington Archaeological Research Center, Washington State University, 1973.

Mayne, Richard C. (1862) *Four Years in British Columbia and Vancouver Island*. London, UK: John Murray.

Moziño, Jose Marino (1970) *Noticias de Nutka, an Account of Nootka Sound in 1792*. (Iris Higbie Wilson, trans.) Toronto: McClelland and Stewart.

Oberg, Kalervo (1973) *The Social Economy of the Tlingit Indians*. Seattle: University of Washington Press.

Olson, Ronald (1936) *The Quinault Indians*. Seattle: University of Washington Publications in Anthropology 7:5.

Osborn, Alan J. (1977) "Strandloopers, Mermaids, and Other Fairy Tales: Ecological Determinants of Marine Resource Utilization—the Peruvian Case." Pp. 157–205 in L. Binford (ed.) *For Theory Building in Archaeology*. New York: Academic Press.

Palmisano, John F., and James A. Estes (1977) "Ecological Interactions Involving the Sea Otter." Pp. 527–567 in M.L. Merritt and R.G. Fuller (eds.) *The Environment of Amchitka Island, Alaska*. Washington, DC: U.S. Energy Research and Development Administration, TID-26712.

Ray, Verne F. (1938) *Lower Chinook Ethnographic Notes*. Seattle: University of Washington Publications in Anthropology 7:2.

Reagan, Albert B. (1917) *Archaeological Notes on Western Washington and Adjacent British Columbia*. San Francisco: Proceeding of the California Academy of Sciences 7:1.

Rounsefell, George A. (1975) *Ecology, Utilization, and Management of Marine Fisheries*. St. Louis: C.V. Mosby Co.

Russell, E.S. (1942) *The Overfishing Problem*. Cambridge, UK: Cambridge University Press.

Samuels, Stephan R. (1983) *Spatial Analysis of Three Nootkan Longhouse Floor Middens*. Ph.D. dissertation, Washington State University.

Singh, Raj Rai (1956) *Aboriginal Economic Systems of the Olympic Peninsula Indians*. Ph.D. dissertation, University of Washington.

Smith, Harlan I. (1909) *Shell-heaps of the Lower Fraser*. New York: American Museum of Natural History, Memoir 4:2.

Smith, Marion W. (1940) *The Puyallup-Nisqually*. New York: Columbia University Contributions to Anthropology 32.

Suttles, Wayne (1951) *The Economic Life of the Coast Salish of Haro and Rosario Straits*. Ph.D. dissertation, University of Washington.

Stern, Bernhard J. (1934) *The Lummi Indians of Northwest Washington*. New York: Columbia University Press.

Stilson, Malcom L. (1972) *Fluctuations in Aboriginal Environmental Utilization in Response to Delta Progration: Three Sites from Skagit County*. B.A. honors thesis, University of Washington.

Swan, James (1869) *The Indians of Cape Flattery*. Washington, DC: Smithsonian Contributions to Knowledge 16:220.

——— (1972) *The Northwest Coast or, Three Years Residence in Washington Territory*. Seattle: University of Washington Press.

Tweddell, C.E. (1974) "A Historical and Ethnological Study of the Snohomish Indian People." Pp. 475–694 in David Horr (ed.) *Coast Salish and Western Washington Indians*. New York: Garland Publishing.

Underhill, Ruth (1945) *Indians of the Pacific Northwest*. Riverside, CA: Sherman Institute Press.

Watt, B.K., and A.L. Merrill (1963) *Composition of Foods Raw, Processed, and Prepared*. Washington, DC: United States Department of Agriculture, Agricultural Handbook 8.

Wessen, Gary C. (1982) *Shell Middens as Cultural Deposits: A Case Study from Ozette*. Ph.D. dissertation, Washington State University.

———— (n.d.) "An Archaeological and Ethnographic Review of the Native Use of Marine Invertebrates in Western Washington." Paper presented before the 7th Annual Ethnobiology Conference, Seattle, WA, 1984.

PART III

LOWER SKEENA RIVER AND QUEEN CHARLOTTE STRAIT

PREHISTORIC ECONOMIC AND SOCIAL CHANGE IN THE TSIMSHIAN AREA

Gary Coupland

INTRODUCTION

This paper investigates the relationship between change in economic organization and the development of non-egalitarian social organization in the Tsimshian area. The research focusses on the prehistoric and early historic periods of the lower Skeena River area of the northern Northwest Coast.

Most researchers agree that at some point during the last 5000 years the social organization of the people of the Northwest Coast changed fundamentally from egalitarian to non-egalitarian (Borden 1970, Mitchell 1971, Fladmark 1975, Matson 1976, Burley 1980, Ames 1981). The traditional job of archaeology has been to determine *when* this transition occurred. Only recently have archaeologists begun to investigate systematically *how* and *why* ascribed social inequality developed on the Northwest Coast.

Research in Economic Anthropology, Supplement 3, pages 211–243.
Copyright © 1988 by JAI Press Inc.
All rights of reproduction in any form reserved.
ISBN: 0-89232-818-5

This concern with explanation coincides with the development of models of the evolution of social inequality that can be tested by archaeological data. In this paper, I examine two such models, evaluating them against archaeological evidence from the Tsimshian area, including the important prehistoric localities of Kitselas Canyon and Prince Rupert Harbour (Figure 1).

MODELS OF SOCIAL INEQUALITY

On the eve of European contact, much of Northwest Coast society was characterized by ascribed status differences, individual or family ownership of and differential access to wealth and food resources, permanent villages and dense population concentrations, warfare and slavery, and styles of art and architecture that have become world renowned.

How did this system evolve? As Matson (1983:127) asks: "What society would willingly go from a situation where everyone is considered in some way to be equal and thus worthwhile, to one in which only some could have high status, where a large part of the society is placed beyond the pale, and where much of these distinctions are made on the basis of birth?" The many models that have been advanced to deal with the origins of ascribed social inequality—on the Northwest Coast and elsewhere—may be subsumed under two major theoretical positions.

One such position, the functional-ecological perspective, has held sway for many years. It argues that hierarchical elites obtain their position because they provide services essential to the population as a whole. This model implies that hierarchical organization results in greater systemic efficiency and a higher standard of living for all. Archaeologists have been virtually unanimous in embracing functional-ecological explanations of social inequality (see Flannery 1972, Renfrew 1972).

The nonfunctionalist perspective on social inequality, while not new (Engels 1972 [1891]), has only lately found a prominent place in anthropology (see Friedman & Rowlands 1978). This perspective argues against the general adaptiveness of hierarchy, stressing instead its exploitative characteristics. Archaeological examples of this paradigm are few (see Earle 1977, Gilman 1981).

Were the hierarchical elites of the Northwest Coast "functional or fungal" (Rathje 1983:25)? Each argument has its proponents. The functional-ecological argument is most closely associated with Wayne Suttles (1960, 1968; see also Vayda 1961, Piddocke 1965); the nonfunctional argument, with Eugene Ruyle (1973; see also Drucker & Heizer 1967, Rosman & Rubel 1971).

Suttles (1960, 1968) argued that the potlatch and the prestige system served as systemic regulators that facilitated the adjustment of the pop-

Figure 1.   The Northern Northwest Coast, Showing the Location of
Prince Rupert Harbour and Kitselas Canyon

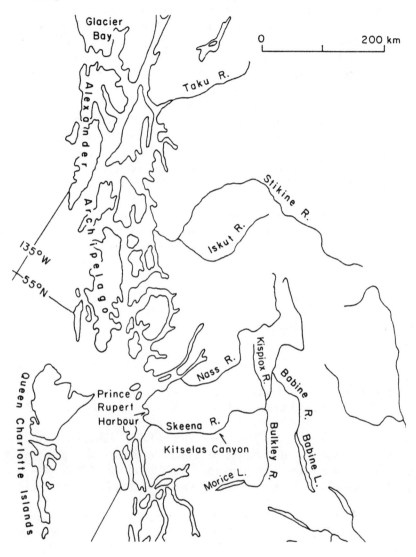

ulation as a whole to a physical environment characterized by local, seasonal, and annual fluctuations in productivity. This model, by now well-
represented in the Northwest Coast literature, stresses the beneficial
functions of the prestige system—the maintenance of high levels of production and the equalization of food consumption among local groups.
The system is seen by Suttles as an adaptive response to external stress,

the long-term evolutionary advantage of which was to allow the people of the Northwest Coast "greater biological success than they could have had each living as a self-sufficient community" (Suttles 1973:622). At the core of this argument is the notion that institutionalized hierarchy evolves as a long-term response to systemic stress. That social inequality could emerge simply because certain individuals in society want it to is, for Suttles, "the expression of some inexplicable ethos" (Suttles 1973:622).

Ruyle's (1973) model runs counter to Suttles'. Ruyle (1973:617) argues from a Marxist perspective that social stratification is a process in which economic surplus is funnelled out of the hands of the producers and into the hands of the ruling class. He sees the prestige system and the potlatch not in terms of adjustment to the physical environment, but rather as the "socio-cultural design of an exploitative class society" (1973:617). According to Ruyle (1973:628), the producing class may need the beneficial functions that the ruling class performs, but these could be performed by the producers themselves; the functions are necessary, not the ruling class.

In Ruyle's model, the potlatch was not a regulating mechanism for the distribution of wealth but instead the critical mechanism for channelling the flow of energy upwards through the system, into the hands of the elites. Ruyle (1973:617) argues that, through control of ritual, elites monopolized access to supernatural beings and the power that these beings imparted. The prestige system, according to Ruyle, provided an ideology that justified this differential access and legitimized the system of exploitation.

RESOURCE MANAGEMENT, LOGISTICAL MOBILITY, AND DELAYED CONSUMPTION

Although refined over the years (see Orans 1975), variants of the functional-ecological model continue to appear in the Northwest Coast archaeological literature. The common thread in much of this work is an emphasis on external systemic stress as a causal factor in the rise of social inequality.

For example, Burley (1979, 1980, 1983) argues that the emergence of social inequality in the Gulf of Georgia area was a direct response to demographic pressure, resulting from a population influx from the Fraser Canyon area at the beginning of the Marpole Phase (2500 BP). For Burley, this stress led directly to the rise of chiefs, who performed the dual roles of labor organizers and resource managers. The pre-Marpole culture is considered egalitarian by Burley, who describes it as being in "established density equilibrium" and as a "closed system" (Burley 1979:136, 140). In Burley's model, the pre-Marpole cultural system was forced out of equilibrium by the population influx, which created a need for more efficient management of resources and for improved production (see also Richardson 1982). Social ranking emerged in response to those needs. The implication is that ranking will not be adopted until the appropriate need arises. Whether population migration to the Gulf of Georgia represented the appropriate need is, of course, open to question. An alternate model to Burley's is that population migration did not place stress on resources, but rather created a labor surplus that emerging elites could exploit to increase production and finance their own political aspirations.

Schalk (1981) and Ames (1985) emphasize the importance of logistical mobility and delayed consumption as sources of stress contributing to organizational complexity on the Northwest Coast. Logistical mobility (Binford 1980) is a potential strategy for dealing with spatially and temporally incongruent resource distributions. Logistical hunter-gatherers make a limited number of settlement moves annually but make frequent task-group forays from residential bases to procure specific resources. In the middle and high latitudes, logistical hunter-gatherers often practise delayed consumption—food storage—to resolve the overwintering problem.

Schalk (1981) argues that delayed consumption, characteristic of Northwest Coast economies, is strongly associated with social complexity because of the need to manage and manipulate complicated resource-consumer relationships. Schalk demonstrates that logistical mobility, storage, and social complexity all increase on the Northwest Coast in a south-to-north gradient as the spatial and temporal distribution of resources becomes more patchy and overall biotic abundance declines. His argument is that northern groups had to organize more complexly in order to maintain a standard of living roughly equivalent to that of the southern groups (see also Suttles 1962). The implication is that logistical mobility, storage, and social complexity were a triumvirate on the north coast. Evidence for one implies existence of the other two.

Testart (1982) also notes the strong association between storage and social complexity but differs from Schalk with regard to the nature of the relationship between the two. Testart (1982:534) distinguishes between small-scale storage—for example, use of temporary caches—and large-scale storage, in which the bulk of winter food comes from storage. According to Testart (1982:157), only large-scale storage is associated with social complexity, because only large food stores represent a source of potential individual wealth. Thus, for Testart (1982:527), the existence of large, collective stores "provides the opportunity for the emergence of . . . exploitation." What remains is for someone to seize the opportunity. The implication of Testart's argument is that large-scale storage is a necessary condition for the emergence of social inequality. The actual transformation to inequality results from changes that are internal to the cultural system.

Ames (1985) also emphasizes the importance of internal systemic change. In his model, stress results from the organizational requirements of logistical mobility, delayed consumption, and intensification of production. Vertical hierarchies will emerge when this stress cannot be resolved by the various strategies available to egalitarian groups (see Ames 1985:160). According to Ames (1985:159), the advantage of vertical hierarchies lies in their efficient information-processing and decision-making capabilities.

While I do not dispute the efficiency of hierarchies, I would argue against the notion that egalitarianism will necessarily persist until sufficient stress arises, whether internal or external, to bring about a non-egalitarian transformation. My view, implicit in Ruyle's model, receives empirical support from Cashdan (1980). Cashdan argues that egalitarianism among the !Kung is not simply a natural condition but rather a strategy for dealing with the constraints of high spatial and temporal variability in food supply. The !Kung maintain strong social sanctions to reinforce sharing and egalitarianism. Cashdan (1980:116) argues that, in the absence of a storing economy, sharing is the principle means by which the !Kung cope with environmental variability. By contrast, Cashdan (1980:118) notes that the //Gana Bushmen are characterized by social inequality. The //Gana have a storing economy and practise limited cultivation and goat husbandry. According to Cashdan, these economic buffers reduce the importance of sharing and inevitably result in the lifting of constraints that produce strict egalitarianism.

Delayed consumption and logistical mobility are strategies regularly employed by hunter-gatherers to buffer environmental stress. These strategies result in greater household self-sufficiency and reduce the importance of sharing. Cashdan's evidence suggests that these strategies do not necessarily require vertical hierarchies; rather, they merely permit them. As Testart (1982:527) notes: "The longer the period of conservation [storage], the more opportunities there are to divert the product from its producer."

In the //Gana case, headmen have no formal political power, and there is an absence of any formal organization of ranking or stratification. How might social inequality become institutionalized? Two recent case studies are relevant to this question.

In his model of the origin of social stratification in Bronze Age Europe, Gilman (1981) argues that an important means by which egalitarian societies maintain their social organization is local group segmentation. If a leader displeases his followers, through self-aggrandizement or an attempt to make his authority hereditary, dissidents can simply abandon him (Gilman 1981:4). Segmentation ceases to be a viable option, however, if the dissidents have nowhere to go or if the cost of leaving is too great. In Bronze Age Europe, there was extensive, unoccupied, habitable land, according to Gilman. What tied people to an unwanted leader was their increasing energy investment, as a result of subsistence intensification, in the land they already occupied. The greater the investment in a particular locality, the more unattractive segmentation became, because it would lead to a lower standard of living, at least initially. "Segmentation is only easy if those who leave can readily produce in the manner and at the level to which they are accustomed" (Gilman 1981:5). Gilman (1981:7) posits that disgruntled individuals, dependent upon continued access to their existing subsistence investments, are more than likely to submit to the excessive exactions of an emerging elite.

An important archaeological implication of Gilman's study is that evidence of an investment of energy in a particular locality, in terms of more permanent settlement and intensified subsistence techniques, should precede evidence for stratification (Gilman 1981:7).

Legros' study of the 19th-century Tutchone, an Athapaskan-speaking hunting and gathering society of the upper Yukon drainage, is even more illuminating (Legros 1981, 1982, 1985). Here, social stratification emerged in one of the harshest environments in the world. Despite low population density, a lack of redistributive exchange, and simple production techniques, Tutchone society separated rich families from poor families and subjected the latter to brutal exploitation and eventual enslavement by the former (Legros 1985:37–38). According to Legros, this stratification was based on a resource structure in which abundant and predictable resources (fish, mainly) were available in only a few restricted locations (lake narrows). Not surprisingly, the Tutchone local groups who habitually used these locations were larger and better-off than other local groups (Legros 1985:46). Each local group had a headman. In the smaller groups, this individual was a temporary leader *(dan čo)* who lacked real power or accumulated wealth. For the larger groups, however, this individual was a permanent, hereditary leader *(dan noži?)*, a "rich man" who owned the resource location and came to own other critical resources, had tangible personal wealth, including slaves, and who could have "up to twenty wives" (Legros 1985:50). These were the social elites of Tutchone society. They lived in clusters of 3–4 closely related nuclear families, also called *dan noži?*, or *dan noži?* clusters. Legros (1985:51) refers to remaining members of rich local groups as "dependent poor." These could include 6–7 families whose labor was exploited by the *dan noži?*. No one could use the prime resource locations without permission of the *dan noži?* owner; such permission usually had its price in the form of tribute.

All poor Tutchone depended on the *dan noži?* in one way or another. Through exclusive control of the best resource locations and a monopoly on trade, the *dan noži?* had

the power to provide or to withdraw help, the power to put into circulation or to withdraw from the trade networks some of the most demanded use-values, and, thus, some control over other people's behavior through the promise to help or the threat to withdraw or withhold such help (Legros 1985:52).

How did the *dan noži?* hold their social position? Legros (1985:51) is quite specific about this: "Whenever necessary, they *[dan noži?]* resorted to organized violence to maintain their claims or privileges." Legros cites numerous examples of seemingly random violence by *dan noži?* (1985:55, 57–59, 61), demonstrating to poor Tutchone that *dan noži?* were willing and able to use force to maintain their prerogatives. According to Legros (1985:54), a *dan noži?* family cluster constituted a powerful coercive force through its ability to practice direct cross-cousin marriage. In a matrilineal society such as the Tutchone, this marital pattern would have the effect of insulating the corporate interests of the *dan noži?* from those of the remainder of the population (Legros 1985:55). Further, it meant that a *dan noži?* family cluster took on the structure of an "action group" that was organized to do whatever was necessary to protect its interests.

An important archaeological implication of Legros' study is that evidence for social stratification and the use of coercive force should co-occur in the archaeological record.

ARCHAEOLOGY OF THE LOWER SKEENA AREA

The Tsimshian area of the northern Northwest Coast includes the lower Skeena River valley and its tributaries and the coastline adjacent to the mouth of the Skeena. Within this area, two localities have undergone extensive archaeological investigation: Prince Rupert Harbour, near the mouth of the Skeena, and Kitselas Canyon, 150 km upriver from the mouth (Figure 1). The archaeology of these localities provides an opportunity to test the implications derived from the functional and nonfunctional models of the evolution of social inequality.

Prince Rupert Harbour

Intensive archaeological investigations were conducted at Prince Rupert Harbour in the 1960s by the National Museum of Canada's North Coast Prehistory Project, directed by George MacDonald. A total of 200 sites were recorded; 11 were excavated (Figure 2), and over 18,000 artifacts

Figure 2.   Archaeological Sites at Prince Rupert Harbour

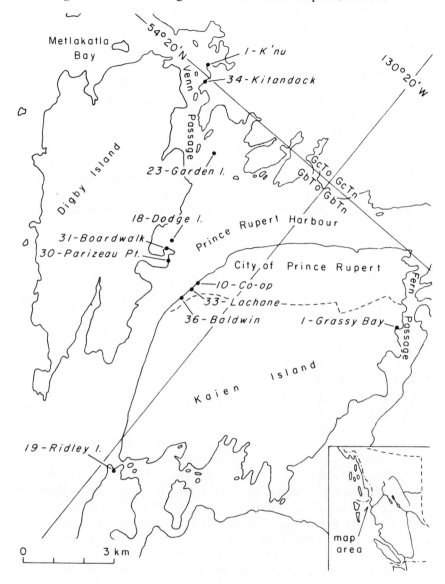

were recovered (MacDonald & Inglis 1981). To date, the results of this work have been reported only in brief overviews (MacDonald 1969, MacDonald & Inglis 1981, MacDonald 1983). At this time, a comprehensive report is being prepared by Kenneth Ames of Portland State University.

The known prehistoric occupation of Prince Rupert Harbour spans the last 5000 years (MacDonald 1969, MacDonald & Inglis 1981). MacDonald & Inglis (1981:42–52) propose a three-period sequence, the basic theme of which is cultural continuity with a gradual accretion of elements through time.

Period III, 5000–3500 BP

This period is characterized by "shallow midden accumulations and restricted site areas." Faunal remains indicate use of land and sea mammals. Mussel shell is present in the middens, but clams and cockles, which become abundant later, are absent at this time (MacDonald & Inglis 1981:42). Despite extensive excavation at numerous sites, "no house-pit structures have been recognized" (MacDonald & Inglis 1981:45). Post molds from this period are small in size, which probably reflects the use of temporary dwellings rather than the substantial post-and-plank structures seen later.

Period II, 3500–1500 BP

During this period, there is "rapid midden build-up" (MacDonald & Inglis 1981:45), including more intensive and diversified use of intertidal resources. Ames (1986) states that salmon, among the fish, and white-tailed and black-tailed deer, among the land mammals, stand out as critical resources. MacDonald & Inglis (1981) infer village occupation, large house construction, and substantial population increase during this period. At the Grant Anchorage site, on the coast just south of Tsimshian territory, Simonsen (1973:72) found evidence of plank house construction, similar to that of the historic period, dated to ca. 2100 BP. The first evidence of the use of drying racks occurs in this period, suggesting processing and storage of food for later consumption. Tidal stone fishtraps, which can involve a substantial investment of construction labor, may have been in use at this time (Simonsen 1973:75). Rostlund (1952:102) infers great antiquity for the use of these facilities in North America, and Pomeroy (1976:173) suggests that fishtraps in the Bella Bella area may be up to 3000 years old. It is possible, then, that tidal traps and their fresh water counterparts, weirs, were used in the lower Skeena area from the beginning of Period II.

The second millenium of Period II, beginning about 2500 BP, shows the first evidence of ranked social status (MacDonald & Inglis 1981:52). At Prince Rupert Harbour, grave goods from some burials include copper ornaments, amber beads, dentalium beads and gorgets, sea otter teeth, and large quantities of obsidian and jet—all of which had to be imported over considerable distances (MacDonald 1983:102). Whether these high-status burials crosscut age and sex lines is not yet clear. Most archaeologists accept the 2500 BP date, however, as marking the earliest evidence of ranked society on the north coast (see Ames 1981:795, 797) and farther south in the Gulf of Georgia area (Borden 1970:102, Mitchell 1971:54, Burley 1980:61).

Period I, 1500–150 BP

At Prince Rupert Harbour, this period marks a culmination of the trends noted in the second millenium of Period II. In MacDonald & Inglis' (1981:52) words, "the Northwest Coast pattern is in full stride by this period."

Kitselas Canyon

Kitselas Canyon, located 150 km upriver from Prince Rupert, is 2 km long. It is the first major constriction of the Skeena encountered as one proceeds upriver (Figure 3). The local environment is mountainous rain-forest. The prehistoric cultural deposits lack shell, and organic preservation is poor.

Like the occupation of Prince Rupert Harbour, the known prehistoric occupation of Kitselas Canyon spans the last 5000 years. Initial investigation focussed on the prehistory of the canyon as seen from the Gitaus site (Allaire 1978, 1979). An historic village, Gitlaxdzawk, was also test-excavated and mapped (Allaire & MacDonald 1971; Allaire et al. 1979). Later investigation centered on the Paul Mason site, located less than 1 km upriver from Gitaus (Coupland 1985a). Another historic village site, Gitsaex, was also mapped at this time (MacDonald & Coupland n.d.; Coupland 1985a, 1985b). Both Gitaus and the Paul Mason site have multiple prehistoric components. Integration of these components has produced a five-phase local sequence for the canyon (Coupland 1985a:322–340).

Bornite Phase, 5000–4300 BP

This period is characterized by small site size and a lack of evidence of permanent dwellings. It yielded a limited assemblage characterized by the presence of a microcore and blade technology. In all cases, microblade modification is restricted to the acute lateral edge, which suggests that blades were used as fine cutting implements, perhaps for processing fish (see Flenniken 1981:84). Implements associated with land mammal hunting (projectile points, bifaces, formed unifaces) are not represented in the Bornite Phase. Also absent are microcores; only two rejuvenation flakes from microcores were recovered. Whereas microblades may be used expediently and without maintenance, microcores would likely be curated. The absence of curated implements and site furniture suggests that the

Figure 3.   Archaeological Sites at Kitselas Canyon

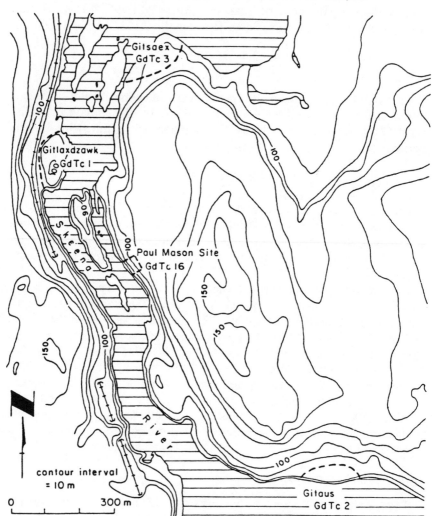

canyon was used at this time for temporary camps by small groups of perhaps 2–3 families.

Substantial mobility in the settlement pattern of the lower Skeena may be inferred at this time, since early Period III components from Prince Rupert Harbour are thought to have had similar site functions (MacDonald & Inglis 1981:42).

Gitaus Phase, 4300–3600 BP

Allaire (1979:45–46) interprets this phase as a purely coastal manifestation, probably representing a summer fishing camp. No remains of permanent winter dwellings were recovered. The dates place the Gitaus Phase within the latter part of Period III at Prince Rupert Harbour.

The coastal similarities include high proportions of cobble core tools and cortex spalls, and groundstone implements such as unshaped abraders, rubbed-slate points, and stone saws (Figure 4). Formed chipped-stone tools occur rarely. Obsidian is present in small amounts. Microblades are absent.

The paucity of formed chipped-stone tools suggests that land mammal hunting was of minor importance at this time. Evidence for the importance of summer fishing at Kitselas Canyon during the Gitaus Phase is seen in the following: an abundance of cortex spalls, which may have functionally replaced microblades as fish-processing implements; the remains of birch bark rolls (Allaire 1979:31), which may have been used as torches for night fishing; and a carved fish effigy.

The Skeena Phase, 3600–3200 BP

This phase shows an important change in subsistence orientation at Kitselas Canyon. Allaire (1979:47) states that the Skeena Phase reflects an adaptation toward "riverine and forest efficiency." A greater occurrence of implements typically associated with land mammal hunting is the most important change in the Skeena Phase. Compared to the Gitaus Phase, the artifact profile shows substantial increases in the proportions of formed chipped-stone tools, including bifaces, formed unifaces, and a distinctive lanceolate, Plano-like projectile point.

As in the previous phases, there is no evidence here for winter habitation. The presence of elements of subadult fisher *(Martes pennanti)* and salmon (Allaire 1978:157–58, 297) is consistent with summer-fall use of the canyon.

The Skeena Phase component at Gitaus appears to represent a base-camp occupation, given the presence of various curated items and multiple hearth features. The numerous small post molds may represent drying racks (Allaire 1979:37) or, alternatively, crude summer dwellings. Either interpretation supports the summer base-camp model.

The Paul Mason Phase, 3200–2700 BP

Important changes in technology, subsistence, and settlement at Kitselas Canyon occur during this time. The major change in the tool assemblage is the reduced proportion of formed chipped-stone tools, including bifaces

Figure 4. Artifact Profile for the Prehistoric Sequence at Kitselas Canyon

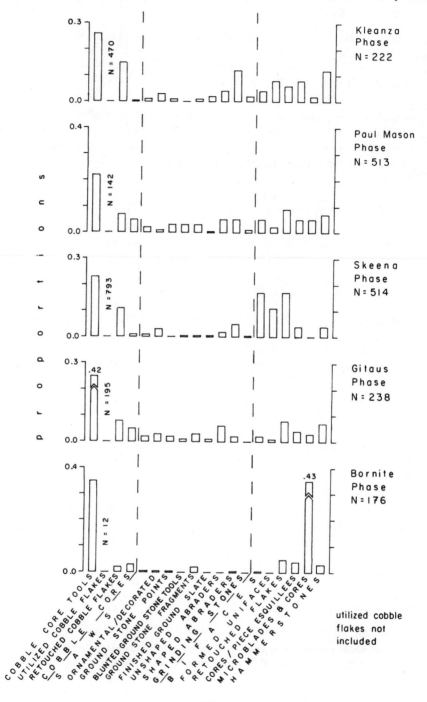

and formed unifaces, relative to the Skeena Phase. The lanceolate, Plano-like points are now absent. The proportion of groundstone tools also increases in this phase. Hexagonal, ground-slate points and blunted, rod-like implements, commonly referred to as "pencils" (Drucker 1943:57, MacDonald 1969:251), appear for the first time. Both types also appear in the Prince Rupert Harbour middens at about this time (MacDonald 1969:251, MacDonald & Inglis 1981:46).

The reduced proportion of chipped stone tools probably reflects a decline in the economic importance of land mammals at this time. Mammal elements now constitute only 18.1 percent of the assemblage (Roberts n.d.). The presence of a single hearth feature over 4m long, multiple hearths within dwellings, cache pits for food storage, and widespread scatters of fire-cracked rock reflect intensive processing of foodstuffs.

A conspicuous new element in the upper component at the Paul Mason site is a series of elongate, prepared dwelling floors that reflect permanent house construction. Defined by surface contours cut into the slope of the site, these floors are arranged side by side in two rows, facing southwest toward the river (see Figure 5). Two floors were excavated (see Coupland 1985a:396–98). The internal patterns were similar; each had two hearths, one centrally located, the other near the front or downslope end of the floor (see Figures 6 and 7). Post molds, oriented along the midline of the floors, suggest support of a central roof beam or ridge pole. Finally, each floor had raised earth benches on either side. These may have been used for sleeping, as the recovery of lithic material on these platforms was lower than on the sunken central section of the floor. The main activity area of the dwellings was the central floor section, a 3–4m strip that ran the length of the floor between the lateral benches.

The Kleanza Phase, 2500–1500 BP

Although this phase shows assemblage similarities to the Paul Mason Phase, the differences are sufficient to warrant separate periodization. The similarities include low proportions of formed chipped-stone tools, high proportions of groundstone and cobble implements, and widespread litters of fire-cracked rock. No clear remains of permanent dwellings appear at Kitselas Canyon during this time. However, Allaire (1979:48) argues that the fire-cracked rock and the outline of a large post reflect permanent house construction. If so, this would be another similarity to the Paul Mason Phase.

The foregoing general similarities between the Paul Mason and Kleanza Phases suggest little or no change in subsistence and settlement. The main difference is the addition in the Kleanza Phase of new artifact forms related to the outward display of personal status. These include a T-shaped labret,

Figure 5.   The Paul Mason Site

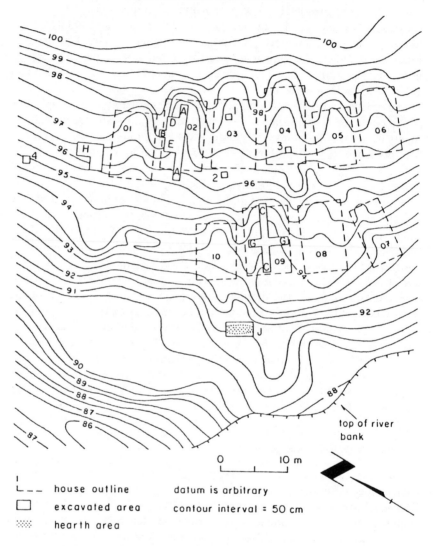

I
L _ _   house outline   datum is arbitrary

☐   excavated area   contour interval = 50 cm

▓   hearth area

slate mirrors, and slate daggers recovered from the midden. Groundstone adzes and celts are also present for the first time, which suggests that fine woodworking was being done.

These new elements may be associated with change in the sociological realm, but the evidence is admittedly weak. Only one labret was recovered (Allaire 1979:49). The symbolic importance of this artifact class as a status

Figure 6. Excavated Dwelling Floor at the Paul Mason Site

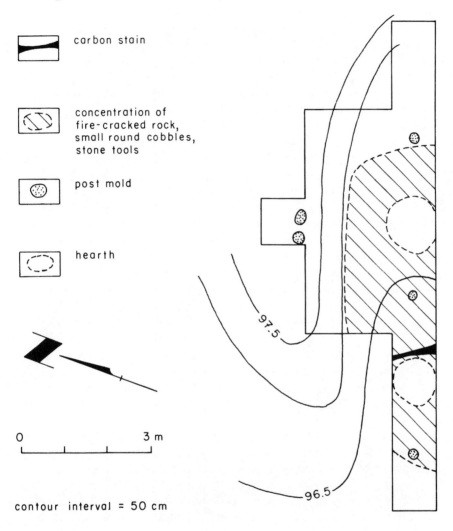

carbon stain

concentration of
fire-cracked rock,
small round cobbles,
stone tools

post mold

hearth

0   3 m

contour interval = 50 cm

marker is, moreover, not well-understood by Northwest Coast archaeologists. Slate mirrors were worn historically by Tsimshian women of high
status (McNeary 1976:68), but we do not know if this custom existed prehistorically. Since prehistoric burial contexts have not been recorded at
Kitselas Canyon, it is not clear if possession of status markets in the
Kleanza Phase crosscut age and sex lines. We may note, however, that
the emergence of social ranking occurred at Prince Rupert Harbour coeval

Figure 7. Excavated Dwelling Floor at the Paul Mason Site

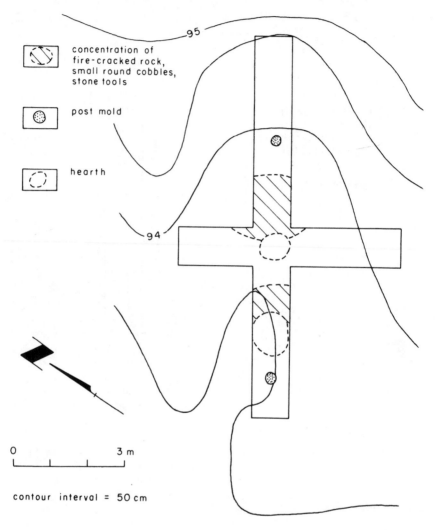

with the Kleanza Phase. In summarizing the evidence from Prince Rupert Harbour at ca. 2500 BP, MacDonald (1983:102) states:

> the emphasis on weaponry noted at this time coincides with the brief appearance of status grave goods that may be related to increased differentiation of rank. The development of ranked social status may also explain the concentration of materials imported over considerable distances, such as copper, obsidian, jet, amber and dentalium.

If Kitselas Canyon and Prince Rupert Harbour were incorporated in the same general cultural system (see Coupland 1985a:321–40), then we may infer that social ranking also developed at Kitselas Canyon during the Kleanza Phase.

The archaeological data from Prince Rupert Harbour and Kitselas Canyon may now be used to test the implications of the functionalist and nonfunctionalist models of the evolution of social inequality in the lower Skeena area.

EVIDENCE FOR SOCIAL RANKING

As stated above, the earliest archaeological evidence for social ranking in the lower Skeena area occurs at ca. 2500 BP. Could ranked society have evolved earlier along the lower Skeena? Two lines of evidence from the Paul Mason Phase suggest not.

First, there is a complete absence in the Paul Mason Phase artifact assemblage of status-markets that might reflect social differentiation. Exotic raw materials from distant sources, such as copper, amber, or dentalium, were not recovered.

Second, there is no reflection of status differentiation in the house floors at the Paul Mason site. A comparison of Paul Mason Phase house floor size to historic house floors from Gitsaex and Gitlaxdzawk (Coupland 1985b) revealed substantially more homogeneity in the prehistoric period. Briefly, the argument here is as follows. Historic chiefs lived in large, elaborate dwellings. They entertained more than did other people, and their dwellings were used for public gatherings (Garfield 1951:11). McNeary (1976:127) estimates that, for every chief's dwelling, there were 3–5 smaller dwellings for commoners in Niska villages from the Nass River area. The historic dwelling floors from Kitselas Canyon reflect such a distribution (Figure 8). Five dwelling floors were unusually large (each greater than 140m^2) and incorporated high-status features such as dug out floors and raised rear platforms (see Allaire et al. 1979:109, Coupland 1985b:49–50). The remaining 22 historic house floors were smaller than 120m^2 and lacked distinguishing features. The inferred ratio of commoners' to chiefs' dwellings is 4.4:1 (Coupland 1985b:48), which is consistent with McNeary's estimate. The range in Kitselas Canyon historic house floor size is from 53.07m^2 to 187.69m^2, a difference of 253.7 percent. The coefficient of variation, a measure of relative homogeneity within a data set, for historic house floor size at Kitselas Canyon is 0.29. (As the homogeneity of a data set increases, the value of the coefficient of variation approaches zero.) For the Paul Mason site, the coefficient of variation is 0.15 (Coupland 1985b:47), reflecting greater homogeneity in house floor size than in the historic sites. The range in house floor size at the Paul

Figure 8. Sizes of Historic and Paul Mason Phase Dwelling Floors at Kitselas Canyon.

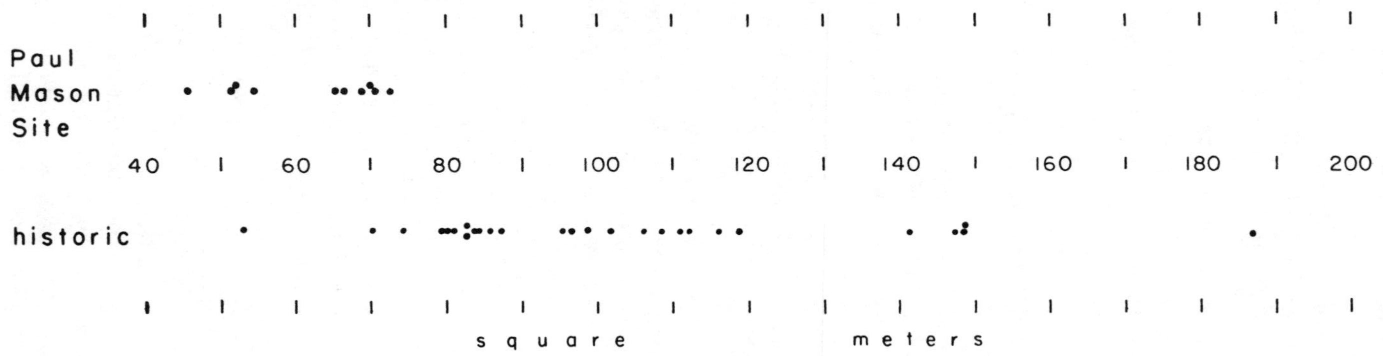

Paul Mason Site

historic

40   60   80   100   120   140   160   180   200

square meters

	coefficient of variation	range	difference in range
Paul Mason Site	0.15	45.76 - 72.60	58.65 %
historic	0.29	53.07 - 187.69	253.70 %

Mason site is from 45.76m^2 to 72.6m^2, a difference of only 58.6 percent. There is no bimodal separation of house floors according to size at the Paul Mason site (see Figure 7).

If wealthy, high-ranking individuals did live at Kitselas Canyon during the Paul Mason Phase, their dwellings were basically no different in size from those of other people. This negative evidence generally supports the argument that social ranking had not emerged along the lower Skeena prior to 2500 BP.

ANALYSIS OF PREHISTORIC STANDARD OF LIVING

Using data from Kitselas Canyon, we may now test the implication derived from Suttles' (1960, 1968) functional model. To determine whether the evolution of the prestige system was associated with an improved standard of living, data from the Kleanza Phase (2500–1500 BP) and the historic period, representative of ranked society, may be compared to data from the Paul Mason Phase (3200–2700 BP). I use two lines of evidence to test the functional argument: (1) differences in the amount of stored resources and (2) differential access to utilitarian goods obtained from distant sources. If the prestige system did result in an improved standard of living for everyone, greater per capita storage capacity and generally improved access to distant sources would be expected in the social ranking period. If the prestige system did not affect standard of living, no change would be expected in storage capacity or access to distant resources.

Differential Storage

Both the Paul Mason Phase villagers and the historic villagers used cache pits for food storage. MacDonald (personal communication 1981) states that cache pits were the primary food-storage facilities used by individual families along the lower and middle Skeena. These probably were not the only facilities used, but they are the only ones remaining in the archaeological record.

Because villagers of both periods occupied the canyon during winter, they likely had similar individual requirements for food storage. Comparison of per capita cache-pit storage capacity provides a rough indicator of which population was able to store more food.

Thirty-nine cache pits were recorded within the immediate vicinity (250m) of the Paul Mason site (Coupland 1985a:353). Some of these are located directly behind the house floors, so I assume that they are associated with the Paul Mason Phase village. I measured each cache pit for rim diameter and depth.

The shape of cache pits at the time of use most closely approximates a cylinder, the volume of which is $\pi r^2 h$, where r = radius and h = height or depth of the cylinder. At the Paul Mason site, the resulting volumes were then multiplied by a constant of 1.5 to account for erosion or humus build-up in the bottom of the pits. The volumes were then summed, giving a total capacity of 38.05m^3 (see Table 1).

A total of 128 cache pits were recorded in the immediate vicinity of Gitsaex. (Cache pits near the historic village, Gitlaxdzawk, have been disturbed by railway construction.) Using the same procedure applied to the Paul Mason site, a volume total of 113.59m^3 was obtained (Table 1).

To determine per capita cache pit storage capacity for both villages, I divided the total volumes by the village population estimates. To determine population size for Gitsaex, I used the ethnographic model of dwelling and household size developed for the Tsimshian. Boas (1916:46–48) stated that Coast Tsimshian winter dwellings at Kitkatla averaged about 10m × 10m (100m^2). In an early visit to Gitsaex, Emmons (1912:469) estimated one house structure to be 36' × 36' (about 11m × 11m), which is close to Boas' figures. A total of 17 house floors were recorded at Gitsaex (MacDonald & Coupland n.d.). McNeary (1976:128) states that traditional Niska households averaged 25 people (cf. Donald & Mitchell 1975:333). When average dwelling size (100m^2) is divided by average household size (25), the amount of floor space per person is 4m^2. The total area of house floor space at Gitsaex is 1706.35m^2. At 4m^2 per person, a village population of 426.59 is obtained.

The ethnographic model has less applicability for the 3000-year-old Paul Mason Phase dwellings. These house floors are smaller than the historic floors, averaging 61.7m^2. Each excavated floor had two hearths, which suggests two nuclear families per household, or a total of 12 people, giving a village size of 120. The most appropriate floor space model for the Paul Mason Phase dwellings is that provided by Cook & Heizer (1968:92–93). This model was developed for aboriginal dwellings in northern California, which are remarkably similar in size, structure, and shape to the Paul Mason Phase dwellings (see Gould 1978:131). The regression formula,

Table 1.   Food-Storage Pit Volumes at Gitsaex Village and the Paul Mason Site (in m^3)

Village/Site	Mean	Median	Range	Total
Gitsaex (128 pits)	0.89	0.58	0.11–5.13	113.59
Paul Mason Site (39 pits)	0.95	0.75	0.19–2.85	38.05

$y = a + bx$ is used by Cook & Heizer (1968:93), where y = the amount of floor space per person, a = a constant value of 1.485, b = the slope 0.0549, and x = the dwelling area in square meters. Dwelling space per person was calculated for each of the 10 house floors at the Paul Mason site using this formula (see Table 2). Each floor was then divided by its y-value to arrive at a household population estimate. The sum of these estimates is the village population, 125.14, which is very close to the previous estimate based on hearths.

Per capita cache pit storage capacity is the total storage capacity for each village divided by its population estimate. For Gitsaex, per capita cache pit storage capacity is 0.266m^3; for the Paul Mason site, 0.304m^3. These figures suggest that the inferred egalitarian villagers of the Paul Mason Phase were actually storing more resources per capita than the ranked historic villages, although the difference is slight.

The accuracy of these results could be debated, since a number of assumptions are incorporated. I assume, for example, that the villages were occupied for roughly equal lengths of time, that resources in the vicinity of Kitselas Canyon have not changed substantially in the last 3000 years, and that the use of other types of storage facilities was proportional to the use of cache pits. Deviations from any of these assumptions could alter the above figures, but I think not significantly. At any rate, present results do not support the functional argument that standard of living improved after the introduction of the prestige system.

Table 2. Floor Measurements and Household Population Estimates for Ten Dwellings at the Paul Mason Site, Based on Cook & Heizer (1968)

Dwelling Floor Size (m²)	Floor Space/ Person (m²)	Household Population Estimates
70.70	5.73	12.34
66.30	5.12	12.95
68.68	5.26	13.06
72.60	5.47	13.22
51.20	4.30	11.91
54.56	4.48	12.18
45.76	4.00	11.44
65.28	5.07	12.88
70.00	5.33	13.13
52.00	4.34	11.98
617.08	4.93	125.14

Access to Raw Materials from Distant Sources

Access to tools or raw materials to manufacture tools from distant sources has been cited by Rathje (1983:29) as a measure of material well-being. At Kitselas Canyon, tools manufactured from obsidian occur in the assemblages of all five phases (Figure 9). These are primarily retouched and utilized flakes and, less frequently, bifaces and formed unifaces. Two sources of obsidian are represented at Kitselas Canyon—Mt. Edziza and Anahim Peaks (Godfrey-Smith 1984). The Mt. Edziza obsidian source is located in north-central British Columbia, 400 km north of Kitselas Can-

Figure 9. Proportions of Obsidian Tools in the Kitselas Canyon Prehistoric Sequence, by Phase

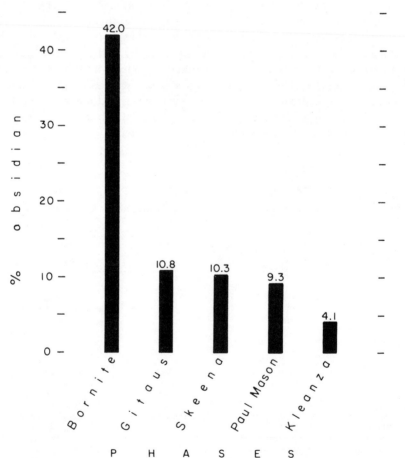

yon. The Anahim Peaks source is in south-central British Columbia, 330 km south of Kitselas Canyon. Access to both sources for the canyon inhabitants was through long-distance trade networks.

The high proportion of obsidian tools in the Bornite Phase at Kitselas Canyon may be accounted for by the high frequency of microblades. The Gitaus, Skeena, and Paul Mason Phase assemblages have very similar proportions of obsidian, roughly 10 percent in each case. There is a substantial decline in the proportion of obsidian tools in the Kleanza Phase, to less than half that of the previous phases. Only nine obsidian tools are represented in the Kleanza Phase (Allaire 1978:287), compared to 48 in the Paul Mason Phase. This decline indicates that access to obsidian was more restricted in the Kleanza Phase than in the previous phases.

One possible explanation of this restricted access is that obsidian ceased to be a utilitarian material in the Kleanza Phase, becoming instead a prestige resource that distinguished social status. This possibility is supported by the presence of obsidian only in high-status burials at Prince Rupert Harbour (MacDonald 1983:102). The decrease in proportion of obsidian in the Kleanza Phase reflects diminished access to raw materials from distant sources. This does not support an argument for improved standard of living for everyone, and suggests, if anything, a decline in the material well-being of nonelites.

EVIDENCE FOR ECONOMIC CHANGE

The Bornite and Gitaus Phases reflect seasonal use of Kitselas Canyon, probably coinciding with the summer salmon runs. The Skeena Phase represents an increase in resource diversity and perhaps in niche width. Christenson (1980:34) defines resource diversity as the number of different resources consumed, regardless of their proportional contribution. Niche width refers to the differing proportions or "evenness" with which food resources are consumed (Christenson 1980:34).

At Kitselas Canyon, during the Skeena Phase, land mammal hunting may have become as important as fishing. If so, this change suggests procurement of a greater variety of resources (increase in resource diversity) and greater evenness in procurement (increase in niche width). The evidence from Prince Rupert Harbour suggests a similar condition. With the onset of Period II, there was a substantial increase in the use of intertidal resources, especially clams, while land mammal and sea mammal hunting continued to be important (Stewart 1974:25, Calvert n.d.:96).

The combined evidence from Kitselas Canyon and Prince Rupert Harbour suggests a widening of resource diversity and niche width at ca. 3500 BP throughout the lower Skeena area. New species were exploited (e.g., clams, cockles), and the procurement of other species increased (e.g., land mammals). MacDonald & Inglis (1981:45) have argued for substantial population growth during Period II, which is a likely explanation for the broadening of the subsistence base.

These changes are consistent with Christenson's (1980) model of expanding resource diversity and niche width coupled with steady population growth. According to this model, a population with low density will select low-cost, high-yield resources. With steady population growth, higher-cost or lower-yield resources will be added on. This model may explain the presence of mussel shell and absence of clam shell in the Period III middens at Prince Rupert Harbour. Mussels tend to cluster in large numbers on rocky foreshores and can be easily gathered in large numbers in intertidal pools. They are a low-cost resource. Clams must be dug up, usually one at a time. Most clam species provide a higher yield than mussels but at greater cost.

The pattern of settlement along the lower Skeena at 3500 BP (Skeena Phase and early Period II) appears little changed from earlier times. There is still no evidence of permanent dwelling construction at either Prince Rupert Harbour or Kitselas Canyon.

This pattern changed substantially at Kitselas Canyon during the Paul Mason Phase. The most important change is the establishment of permanent residential structures and storage facilities at the Paul Mason site. The partially subterranean house floors, with multiple hearths and southwest exposure for maximum sunlight, provide the first evidence of winter village habitation at Kitselas Canyon. This is a significant departure from the settlement pattern described for the earlier phases. The canyon continued to be occupied during the summer months, as evidenced by salmon elements recovered from hearth features from both excavated house floors. In addition, a hearth feature over 4m long and 70cm deep was situated directly in front of the front row of house floors (see Figure 5). Salmon elements were also recovered from this feature, the size and depth of which suggest intensive food processing. (Again, there is no evidence of intensive food processing prior to the Paul Mason Phase.) This inference is supported by the litter of fire-cracked rock that occurs in the upper component of the site.

The presence of a winter village at Kitselas Canyon suggests that a small group of people, perhaps including those who already regularly used the canyon in summer, were no longer returning to the coast for the winter. The evidence suggests that the Paul Mason Phase villagers were procuring and processing a sufficient amount of food in summer to sustain their immediate needs and carry them through the winter. Two lines of evidence suggest that this food was predominantly fish. First, 79.9 percent of the faunal elements were fish; in all cases, identifiable fish elements were salmon (Roberts n.d.). Second, the reduction in the proportion of formed chipped stone tools reflects a decline in the economic importance of land mammals. Since the annual duration of occupation at Kitselas Canyon actually increased in the Paul Mason Phase, the decline in hunting must have been more than compensated by increased fishing. This suggests intensification of salmon fishing during the Paul Mason Phase.

In the lower Skeena area, salmon intensification may have resulted from over-exploitation of shellfish resources by the expanding population. This argument has been used by Croes & Hackenberger (n.d.) to explain intensification of fishing in the Gulf of Georgia/Puget Sound area at ca. 3000 BP.

Salmon intensification, in turn, helps to explain the settlement change during the Paul Mason Phase. With increasing dependence on salmon, control of critical fishing locations became important. Kitselas Canyon is perhaps the single most important fishing location on the lower Skeena. Year-round occupation is one way to ensure resource control.

Elsewhere, I have referred to the Kitselas Canyon villagers of the Paul Mason Phase as an "egalitarian corporate group" (Coupland 1985a, c). They were corporate in the sense that they were more or less permanent residents of the canyon, who collectively controlled the critical canyon fishery. As the above evidence suggests, they were also egalitarian. No individual or household was in a position to display wealth or prestige that might accrue from differential access to resources.

Egalitarian corporate groups at Kitselas Canyon probably operated on two levels, the household and the village. Individual households were probably the day-to-day units of production. They may have been analogous in size and function to the "fireside groups" of the Huron (Fenton 1978:303). At the village level, corporateness was probably expressed in the mutual defense and control of the canyon. That a small, egalitarian village group could maintain control of a critical resource territory does not seem unreasonable, since there is no basis for assuming that outside groups would be more highly organized or better prepared to wrest control of the canyon for themselves.

In terms of Gilman's (1981) model, the Paul Mason Phase reflects an "investment in Kitselas Canyon," not seen previously. People were now living in the canyon on a more or less permanent basis in well-built dwellings. They were logistical strategists who depended heavily on the critical resource that the canyon had to offer for their subsistence. They practised large-scale storage. As already demonstrated, these people had an egalitarian social organization, a feature that supports the following implication derived from Gilman's model: at Kitselas Canyon, evidence for subsistence intensification preceeds the earliest evidence for ascribed social differentiation.

THE CONSOLIDATION OF POWER

The third archaeological implication of this study is based on Legros' analysis of 19th-century Tutchone society. If social elites of the lower Skeena did not provide essential goods and services to improve the general standard of living, but rather came to power because dissidents within the group could no longer oppose them, then we should expect to see evidence for the use of coercive force coeval with the earliest evidence for social inequality.

Turning attention from Kitselas Canyon to Prince Rupert Harbour, the first evidence of high-status burials, with grave goods including exotic raw materials, occurs at ca. 2500 BP. At the same time, there are other burials, mass interments in the middens, with osteological evidence of considerable violence. Cybulski (n.d.) notes a high incidence of forearm "parry" fractures in these burials. These appear to relate to attempts to use the forearm to protect the head from a blow (MacDonald 1983:102). In other cases, there is evidence of blows to the head that caused severe depression fractures (MacDonald & Inglis 1976:77, MacDonald 1983:102). Bone clubs appear initially in the Prince Rupert Harbour middens at 2500 BP, and a basalt dagger, recovered from a high-status burial, also dates to this time (MacDonald 1983:101). The earliest evidence at Prince Rupert Harbour for the use of elaborately decorated stone clubs, which Duff (1963) called the "Skeena River club style," occurs at 2000 BP. MacDonald (1983:102) anticipates that future research will push this date back to 2500 BP, based on the recovery of a 2500-year-old stone club from the Blue Jackets Creek site on the Queen Charlotte Islands (Severs 1974), and also on a close match between the skull depression fractures from the mass graves and the knob-like butts of the later stone clubs (Cybulski n.d.).

Ames (personal communication, 1986) states that the mass graves at Prince Rupert Harbour probably do not represent a single event, such as a battle, but rather a series of interments over a period of time. If so, these burials, none of which represent individuals of high status, may reflect the use of force by a *dan noži?*-like individual to demonstrate his power or to keep dissidents in line. The close association between social inequality and the use of force is summed up by MacDonald (1983:102): "The emphasis on weaponry noted at this time coincides with the brief appearance of status grave goods that may relate to increased differentiation of rank."

Among the Tutchone, a superior extended-family organization, based on cross-cousin marriage, was the *dan noži?*'s actual means of coercion (Legros 1985:54). This may have also been the case for the Prince Rupert Harbour chiefs, since cross-cousin marriage with mother's brother's daughter is the ideal among the Tsimshian (Garfield 1951:23, Rubel &

Rosman 1983:8). In each case—Tutchone and Tsimshian—young men were under the direct authority of older men who were both fathers-in-law and maternal uncles. Legros (1985:55) states that this arrangement provided a *dan noži?* family cluster with a "powerful chain of command" to protect its interests. Resentments within the local group may have existed, but the *dan noži?* cluster was always well-prepared to deal with potential resistance. The potential of this marriage form for consolidating power and the fact that a similar marriage form exists among the ethnographic Tsimshian, establish the distinct possibility that the cross-cousin marriage preference developed at Prince Rupert Harbour 2500 years ago.

We can readily see how intergroup hostilities can escalate as a result of intragroup strife. It is in the emerging elites' best interest to redirect the group's hostility away from themselves and toward outside groups. By leading raids against such groups, the new chief can demonstrate his leadership qualities. This strategy has the additional effect of placing the chief in the position of coordinating group defense in case of retaliatory raids. In this way the chief can create a situation in which he provides a necessary service to his group in order to justify his exalted position. As long as intergroup aggression is maintained, the focus of intragroup hostility is weakened, and the chief's position of permanent leader/group defender remains vital. Further, the spoils of war can be distributed within the group as a means of appeasing the dissidents.

CONCLUSION: FUNCTIONAL OR EXPLOITATIVE ELITES

Two lines of evidence presented in this paper—intensification preceeding ascribed social inequality, and social inequality coinciding with the use of coercive force—support the "exploitation model" of the prehistoric lower Skeena cultural system. Further, following Gilman (1981) and Legros (1985), we now have some insight into how exploitation originated. Investment in the land, seen at Kitselas Canyon during the Paul Mason Phase, increasingly tied group members to specific resource/residence locations. Ames' (n.d.) evidence from Prince Rupert Harbour for the period 3000–1000 BP suggests a similar development. He notes that the harbor economy was localized, reflecting "intensive exploitation of microenvironments immediately adjacent to a site" (Ames n.d.:12). This investment in critical resource locations created an opportunistic situation for aspiring social elites to consolidate their positions, since group segmentation was now less likely. Building a tightly integrated extended-family unit, perhaps through first-degree cross-cousin marriage, provided the chief with a support force to maintain his position through intimidation or violence.

The evidence presented in this paper suggests that, contrary to the implications of the functional model, social ranking did not evolve to buffer systemic stress and did not result in an improved overall standard of living on the northern Northwest Coast. Wars were organized and waged, mainly by chiefs, for the acquisition of property (Ferguson 1983:133). Captives were enslaved (Mitchell & Donald 1985). Gormandizing and starvation coexisted. Marx and Engels, who argued that class societies are exploitative, would undoubtedly have been surprised to find such a social system among hunter-fisher-gatherers, but the archaeological evidence from the Tsimshian area suggests that this was in fact the case.

REFERENCES

Allaire, L. (1978) *L'archaeologie des Kitselas d'apres le site stratifie de Gitaus (GdTc2) sur la riviere Skeena en Colombie Britannique*. Ottawa: National Museum of Man, Archaeological Survey of Canada, Mercury Series No. 72.
—— (1979) "The Cultural Sequence at Gitaus: A Case of Prehistoric Acculturation." Pp. 18–52 in R. Inglis & G. MacDonald (eds.) *Skeena River Prehistory*. Ottawa: National Museum of Man, Archaeological Survey of Canada, Mercury Series No. 87.
Allaire, L., and G. MacDonald (1971) "Mapping and Excavations at the Fortress of the Kitselas Canyon, B.C.: Preliminary Report." *Canadian Archaeological Association Bulletin* 3: 49–55.
Allaire, L., G. MacDonald, and R. Inglis (1979) "Gitlaxdzawk: Ethnohistory and Archaeology." Pp. 53–166 in R. Inglis & G. MacDonald (eds.) *Skeena River Prehistory*. Ottawa: National Museum of Man, Archaeological Survey of Canada, Mercury Series No. 87.
Ames, K. (1981) "The Evolution of Social Ranking on the Northwest Coast of North America." *American Antiquity* 46:789–805.
—— (1985) "Hierarchies, Stress, and Logistical Strategies among Hunter-gatherers in Northwestern North America." Pp. 155–80, in T.D. Price & J. Brown (eds.) *Prehistoric Hunter-gatherers: The Emergence of Cultural Complexity*. Orlando: Academic Press.
—— (n.d.) "Prehistoric Subsistence Economy in Prince Rupert Harbour, British Columbia." Paper presented before the Canadian Archaeological Association, Toronto, 1986.
Binford, L.R. (1980) "Willow Smoke and Dog's Tails: Hunter-gatherer Settlement Systems and Archaeological Site Formation." *American Antiquity* 45:4–20.
Boas, F. (1916) *Tsimshian Mythology*. Washington, DC: Smithsonian Institution, 31st Annual Report of the American Bureau of Ethnology 1909–1910, Pp. 27–1037.
Borden, C. (1970) "Culture History of the Fraser-Delta Region: an Outline." *BC Studies* 6–7:95–112.
Burley, D. (1979) "Specialization and the Evolution of Complex Society in the Gulf of Georgia Region." *Canadian Journal of Archaeology* 3:131–43.
—— (1980) *Marpole: Anthropological Reconstructions of a Prehistoric Northwest Coast Culture Type*. Burnaby: Simon Fraser University.
—— (1983) "Cultural Complexity and Evolution in the Development of Coastal Adaptations among the Micmac and Coast Salish." Pp. 157–72 in R. Nash (ed.) *The Evolution of Maritime Cultures on the Northeast and Northwest Coasts of America*. Burnaby: Simon Fraser University.
Calvert, G. (n.d.) "The Co-op Site: A Prehistoric Midden Site on the Northern Northwest Coast." Unpublished report, Laboratory of Archaeology, University of British Columbia, 1968.

Cashdan, E. (1980) "Egalitarianism among Hunters and Gatherers." *American Anthropologist* 82:116–20.

Christenson, A. (1980) "Change in the Human Niche in Response to Population Growth." Pp. 31–72 in T. Earle & A. Christenson (eds.) *Modeling Change in Prehistoric Subsistence Economies*. New York: Academic Press.

Cook, S., and R. Heizer (1968) "Relationships Among Houses, Settlement Areas, and Population in Aboriginal California." Pp. 79–116 in K.C. Chang (ed.) *Settlement Archaeology*. Palo Alto: Stanford University.

Coupland, G. (1985a) *Prehistoric Cultural Change at Kitselas Canyon*. PhD dissertation, University of British Columbia.

—— (1985b) "Household Variability and Status Differentiation at Kitselas Canyon." *Canadian Journal of Archaeology* 9:39–56.

—— (1985c) "Restricted Access, Resource Control and the Evolution of Status Inequality among Hunter-gatherers". Pp. 217–26 in M. Thompson, M.J. Garcia & F. Kense (eds.) *Status, Structure and Stratification: Current Archaeological Reconstructions*. Calgary: University of Calgary.

Croes, D., and S. Hackenberger (n.d.) "Economic Modeling of Anadromous Fish Utilization in the Hoko River Region." Paper presented before the Society for American Archaeology, Portland, Oregon, 1984.

Cybulski, J. (n.d.) "Human Remains from the Boardwalk Site (GbTo 31), Prince Rupert, B.C." Unpublished report on file, National Museum of Man, Ottawa.

Donald, L., and D. Mitchell (1975) "Some Correlates of Local Group Rank Among the Southern Kwakiutl." *Ethnology* 14:325–46.

Drucker, P. (1943) "Archaeological Survey on the Northern Northwest Coast." Pp. 17–32 in *Bureau of American Ethnology Bulletin 133*. Washington, DC: Smithsonian Institution.

Drucker, P., and R. Heizer (1967) *To Make My Name Good: A Re-examination of the Southern Kwakiutl Potlatch*. Berkeley: University of California Press.

Duff, W. (1963) "Stone Clubs from the Skeena River Area." Pp. 2–12 in *Provincial Museum Annual Report for 1962*. Victoria: British Columbia Provincial Museum.

Earle, T. (1977) "A Reappraisal of Redistribution: Complex Hawaiian Chiefdoms." Pp. 213–29 in T. Earle & A. Christenson (eds.) *Exchange Systems in Prehistory*. New York: Academic Press.

Emmons, G. (1912) "The Kitselas of British Columbia." *American Anthropologist* 14:467–71.

Engels, F. (1971) *Origins of the Family, Private Property, and the State*. New York: International Publishers. [originally published in 1891].

Fenton, W. (1978) "Northern Iroquoian Culture Patterns." Pp. 296–321 in B. Trigger (ed.) *Handbook of North American Indians, Vol. 15*. Washington, DC: Smithsonian Institution.

Ferguson, B. (1983) "Warfare and Redistributive Exchange on the Northwest Coast." Pp. 133–47 in E. Tooker (ed.) *The Development of Political Organization in Native North America*. Washington, DC: The American Ethnological Society.

Fladmark, K. (1975) *A Paleoecological Model for Northwest Coast Prehistory*. Ottawa: National Museum of Man, Archaeological Survey of Canada, Mercury Series No. 43.

Flannery, K. (1972) "The Cultural Evolution of Civilizations." *Annual Review of Ecology and Systematics* 3:399–426.

Flenniken, J. (1981) *Replicative Systems Analysis: A Model Applied to the Vein Quartz Artifacts from the Hoko River Site*. Pullman: Washington State University, Laboratory of Anthropology, Report of Investigations No. 59.

Friedman, J., and M. Rowlands (1978) "Notes Toward an Epigenetic Model of the Evolution of Civilization." Pp. 201–79 in J. Friedman & M. Rowlands (eds.) *The Evolution of Social Systems*. London: Duckworth.

Garfield, V. (1951) "The Tsimshian and Their Neighbours." Pp. 3–70 in V. Garfield & P. Wingert (eds.) *The Tsimshian Indians and Their Arts*. Vancouver: Douglas and McIntyre.

Gilman, A. (1981) "The Development of Social Stratification in Bronze Age Europe." *Current Anthropology* 22:1–23.

Godfrey-Smith, D. (n.d.) "Obsidian x-ray Flourescence Analysis of Five Samples from the Paul Mason Site." Unpublished report on file, Laboratory of Archaeology, University of British Columbia, 1984.

Gould, R. (1978) "Tolowa." Pp. 128–36 in R.F. Heizer (ed.) *Handbook of North American Indians, Vol. 8*. Washington, DC: Smithsonian Institution.

Legros, D. (1981) *Structure socio-culturelle et rapports de domination chez les Tutchone septentrionaux du Yukon au XIXe siècle*. PhD dissertation, University of British Columbia.

——— (1982) "Réflexions sur l'origine des inéqualites sociales à partir du cas de Athapaskan Tutchone." *Culture* 2:65–84.

——— (1985) "Wealth, Poverty and Slavery among the 19th-Century Tutchone Athapaskans." *Research in Economic Anthropology* 7:37–64.

MacDonald, G. (1969) "Preliminary Culture Sequence from the Coast Tsimshian Area, British Columbia." *Northwest Anthropological Research Notes* 3:240–254.

——— (1983) "Prehistoric Art of the Northern Northwest Coast." Pp. 99–120 in R. Carlson (ed.) *Indian Art Traditions of the Northwest Coast*. Burnaby: Simon Fraser University.

MacDonald, G., and G. Coupland (n.d.) "Ethnohistorical and Archaeological Investigations at Kitselas Canyon." Unpublished report submitted to Parks Canada, Calgary, 1982.

MacDonald, G., and R. Inglis (1976) *The Dig: an Archaeological Reconstruction of a West Coast Village*. Ottawa: National Museum of Man.

——— (1981) "An Overview of the North Coast Prehistory Project." *B.C. Studies* 48:37–63.

McNeary, S. (1976) *Where Fire Came Down From: Social and Economic Life of the Niska*. PhD. dissertation, Bryn Mawr College.

Matson, R.G. (1976) *The Glenrose Cannery Site*. Ottawa: National Museum of Man, Archaeological Survey of Canada, Mercury Series No. 52.

——— (1983) "Intensification and the Development of Cultural Complexity: The Northwest Versus the Northeast Coast." Pp. 125–48 in R. Nash (ed.) *The Evolution of Maritime Cultures on the Northeast and Northwest Coasts of America*. Burnaby: Simon Fraser University.

Mitchell, D. (1971) *Archaeology of the Gulf of Georgia, a Natural Region and Its Cultural Types*. Victoria: Syesis 4 (Supplement 1).

Mitchell, D., and L. Donald (1985) "Some Economic Aspects of Tlingit, Haida and Tsimshian Slavery." *Research in Economic Anthropology* 7:19–35.

Orans, M. (1975) "Domesticating the Functional Dragon: An Analysis of Piddocke's Potlatch." *American Anthropologist* 77:312–29.

Piddocke, S. (1965) "The Potlatch System of the Southern Kwakiutl: A New Perspective." *Southwestern Journal of Anthropology* 21:244–64.

Pomeroy, A. (1976) "Stone Fish Traps of the Bella Bella Region." Pp. 165–73 in R. Carlson (ed.) *Current Research Reports*. Burnaby: Simon Fraser University.

Rathje, W. (1983) "To the Salt of the Earth: Some Comments on Household Archaeology among the Maya." Pp. 23–34 in E.Z. Vogt & R. Leventhal (eds.) *Prehistoric Settlement Patterns: Essays in Honor of Gordon R. Willey*. Cambridge Mass. and Santa Fe: University of New Mexico Press and Peabody Museum of Archaeology and Ethnology.

Renfrew, C. (1972) *The Emergence of Civilization: the Cyclades and the Aegean in the Third Millenium B.C.* London: Methuen.

Richardson, A. (1982) "The Control of Productive Resources on the Northwest Coast of

North America." Pp. 93–112 in N. Williams & E. Hunn (eds.) in *Ressource Managers: North American and Australian Hunter-gatherers.* Boulder, CO: Westview Press.

Roberts, L. (n.d.) "Faunal Analysis of the Paul Mason Site." Unpublished report on file, Laboratory of Archaeology, University of British Columbia, 1984.

Rosman, A., and P. Rubel (1971) *Feasting with Mine Enemy: Rank and Exchange among Northwest Coast Societies.* New York: Columbia University Press.

Rostlund, E. (1952) *Freshwater Fish and Fishing in Native North America.* Berkeley: University of California Press.

Rubel, P., and A. Rosman (1983) "The Evolution of Exchange Structures and Ranking: Some Northwest Coast and Athapaskan Examples." *Journal of Anthropological Research* 39:1–25.

Ruyle, E. (1973) "Slavery, Surplus and Stratification on the Northwest Coast: The Ethnoenergetics of an Incipient Stratification System." *Current Anthropology* 14:603–31.

Schalk, R. (1981) "Land Use and Organizational Complexity among Foragers of Northwestern North America." Pp. 53–75 in S. Koyama & D.H. Thomas (eds.) *Affluent Foragers.* Osaka: National Museum of Ethnology, Senri Ethnological Studies 9.

Severs, P. (1974) "Archaeological Investigations at Blue Jackets Creek, FlUa4, Queen Charlotte Islands, British Columbia." *Canadian Archaeological Association Bulletin* 6:163–205.

Simonsen, B. (1973) *Archaeological Investigations in the Hecate Strait-Milbanke Sound Area.* Ottawa: National Museum of Man, Archaeological Survey of Canada, Mercury Series No. 13.

Stewart, F. (1974) "Staff Research." Pp. 24–29 in G. MacDonald (ed.) *Archaeological Survey of Canada Annual Review 1973.* Ottawa: National Museum of Man, Archaeological Survey of Canada, Mercury Series No. 21.

Suttles, W. (1960) "Affinal Ties, Subsistence and Prestige among the Coast Salish." *American Anthropologist* 62:296–305.

—— (1962) "Variation in Habitat and Culture on the Northwest Coast." Pp. 533–37 in *Akten des 34 Internationalen Amerikanistenkongresses, Wien 1960.* Vienna: F. Berger.

—— (1968) "Coping with Abundance: Subsistence on the Northwest Coast." Pp. 56–68 in R. Lee & I. Devore (eds.) *Man the Hunter.* Chicago: Aldine.

—— (1973) "Comment on Ruyle's 'Slavery, Surplus and Stratification on the Northwest Coast: the Ethnoenergetics of an Incipient Stratification System'." *Current Anthropology* 14:622–23.

Testart, A. (1982) "The Significance of Food-storage among Hunter-gatherers: Residence Patterns, Population Densities and Social Inequalities." *Current Anthropology* 23:523–37.

Vayda, A. (1961) "A Re-examination of Northwest Coast Economic Systems." *Transactions of the New York Academy of Sciences* 23:618–24.

CHANGING PATTERNS OF RESOURCE USE IN THE PREHISTORY OF QUEEN CHARLOTTE STRAIT, BRITISH COLUMBIA

Donald Mitchell

INTRODUCTION

The archaeological data reported and examined in this paper come from the Queen Charlotte Strait area of the British Columbia central coast. Occupied exclusively by various southern Kwakiutl groups at the time of white contact, the area centers on and takes its name from the substantial body of water lying between northern Vancouver Island and the mainland (Figure 1). At its northwestern end, the Strait is separated from Queen Charlotte Sound, which is open water lying between Vancouver Island and the Queen Charlotte Islands, by a scattering of small islands and reefs. At its southeastern end, it seemingly dissolves in a welter of channels and

Research in Economic Anthropology, Supplement 3, pages 245–290.
Copyright © 1988 by JAI Press Inc.
All rights of reproduction in any form reserved.
ISBN: 0-89232-818-5

Figure 1.   Location of Excavated Queen Charlotte Strait Area Sites.
1, O'Connor; 2, Bear Cove; 3, Fort Rupert; 4, Hopetown Village; 5, Hornet
Passage fort; 6, Denham Island north; 7, Echo Bay; 8, Baker Island southeast; 9, Cramer Passage fort; 10, Retreat Passage northeast; 11, Davies
Island fort.

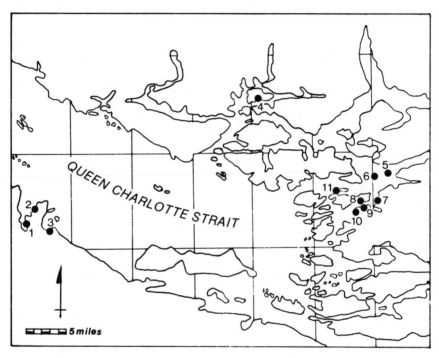

islands where some waterways lead towards the Strait of Georgia and
others run deep into the mainland's coast mountains.

Although there is evidence of occupation for at least 8000 years, data
restrictions have inclined us to be primarily concerned with the past 4500
or 5000 years. For this period, we have data bearing on some striking
changes in the character of artifact and faunal assemblages, and it is these
parallel, contrasting patterns that we want to examine.

Archaeological research in the Queen Charlotte Strait region is clearly
in an early stage of investigation. Shoreline surveys have provided us with
extensive lists of sites of differing sizes and varying formal or functional
categories and have disclosed areas of site concentration (e.g., Mitchell
1969). Little excavation work has been accomplished, however, and what
has been done is concentrated in three areas, near the modern-day set-

tlements of Port Hardy (since the mid-19th century, home territory of the Fort Rupert Kwakiutl), Echo Bay (in Kwicksutaineuk and, earlier, possibly Kwawwawaineuk territory), and Hopetown Indian Village (traditional winter settlement of the Kwawwawaineuk).

The Fort Rupert site (EeSu 1) was the first to be excavated in the Port Hardy vicinity and, in fact, the first in the Queen Charlotte Strait region. A test excavation conducted in 1960, it yielded about 20 artifacts (Capes 1964:72–77, 95). The O'Connor site (EeSu 5), on the east shore of Hardy Bay, was excavated in 1971 and 1973 with a resulting collection of almost 1600 items, 57 percent of which were obsidian flakes with little or no signs of working or use (Chapman 1982:114). Excavations at the Bear Cove site (EeSu 8) are the most recent in the Port Hardy vicinity. This 1978 salvage project produced about 470 artifacts (C. Carlson n.d.).

Test excavations in 1973 at eight sites to either side of Fife Sound in the vicinity of Echo Bay have yielded artifact collections of varying sizes (Mitchell 1981a). Excluding one very small midden from which no pre-contact-style artifacts were recovered, the sites and artifact sample sizes are as follows: Echo Bay site (EeSo 1), 133; Baker Island southeast (EeSp 48), 11; Cramer Passage fort (EeSp 12), 29; Retreat Passage northeast (EeSp 17), 6; Davies Island fort (EeSp 95a), 28; Denham Island north (EeSo 19), 32; and Hornet Passage fort (EeSo 14c), 60.

Extensive excavations in 1974 and 1976 at the Hopetown Village site (EfSq 2) have been the most productive for the area. In all, over 2250 artifacts were recovered (excluding several hundred shell beads from burials), about 40 percent of which were obsidian flakes (Mitchell 1979b).

Our picture of Queen Charlotte Strait prehistory is therefore based on three medium-sized excavations (two on Vancouver Island, one on an island near the mainland) and eight modest test excavations (one on Vancouver Island, seven on islands at the head of the Strait). The total number of artifacts involved is about 4650. Faunal remains, collected from all excavated sites, have been analyzed in detail only for those located at Hopetown Village and in the vicinity of Echo Bay.

ARTIFACT ASSEMBLAGES

The few excavations listed above include some stratified multicomponent, segregated multicomponent, and single component sites. With some creative reclassification and reallocation of reported component collections, it is possible to discern at these sites evidence of at least three culture types, identifiable by distinctive assemblages characteristic of broad periods of occupation. Brief descriptions of these culture types follow.

Old Cordilleran Culture Type

Represented in the Queen Charlotte Strait region by material from the lowest levels of the Bear Cove site in Hardy Bay (C. Carlson 1979), this culture type (Figure 2), widespread in the Pacific Northwest, is characterized by substantial, occasionally well-made, leaf-shaped points; bifaces; and an accompanying assemblage of crude primary flake tools, some retouched, some simply used as produced. Unifacial pebble tools and implements based on split pebbles and on cortex spalls are also prominent.

Obsidian Culture Type

The four components belonging to this form include part of Bear Cove III (C. Carlson 1979, n.d.), the early part of O'Connor II (Chapman 1982), Hopetown I (Mitchell 1979b), and the lower levels of the Echo Bay site (Mitchell 1981a). Regrouping of the Bear Cove and O'Connor site collections was attempted to isolate assemblages with a high incidence of ob-

Figure 2.   Old Cordilleran Culture Type Artifact Assemblage.
a–c, flaked stone points; d, cortex spall tool; e, pebble tool. (Bear Cove site, after illustrations in C. Carlson 1979: Figures 5, 6, and 11).

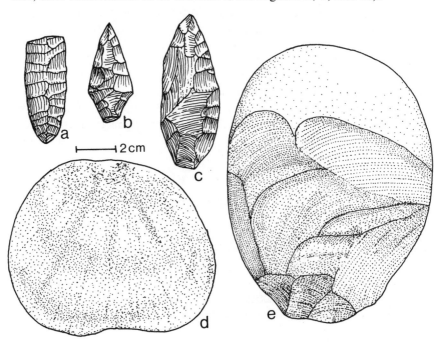

sidian. The resulting components are stratified and segregated at Bear Cove—on an elevated terrace—and stratigraphically separated at the O'Connor site, there comprising the lower levels of a distinct soil zone. In both cases, the newly identified "obsidian" components are distinguished as well by other artifactual and faunal characteristics.

Artifact categories distinctive of this culture type (Figure 3) include the following (from Mitchell n.d.a):

- Leaf-shaped flaked stone points
- Very few formed flake tools but numerous obsidian microflakes, mainly produced by bipolar techniques
- Hammerstones
- Irregular abrasive stones
- Bone composite toggling harpoon valves
- Bone bipoints
- Bone singlepoints
- Ulna tools
- Mussel shell celts
- Mussel shell knives

If there is one property that defines the type, it is the decided presence of flaked obsidian, much of which shows the distinctive characteristics of bipolar percussion. Obsidian items are mainly small flakes, although larger flakes and cores are also represented. Thanks in large measure to the prominence of obsidian flake technology, assemblages of this culture type are markedly different from their successors in relative proportions of bone and flaked stone. For example, Hopetown I (an Obsidian culture type component) has an artifact assemblage that is 12 percent bone items and 74 percent flaked stone. Hopetown III (a Queen Charlotte Strait culture type component) is 56 percent bone and only 1 percent flaked stone.

Queen Charlotte Strait Culture Type

To date, there are 11 or 12 excavated assemblages of this form. These include the upper levels of the Echo Bay site, Hornet Passage fort, Denham Island north, Cramer Passage fort, Retreat Passage northeast, Baker Island southeast, and Davies Island fort (Mitchell 1980); Fort Rupert (Capes 1964); the upper levels of the O'Connor site (Chapman 1982); the late part of Bear Cove III (C. Carlson 1979); and Hopetown III (Mitchell 1979b). Hopetown II, a burial assemblage, may also belong to this culture type.

The main distinguishing archaeological characteristics (after Mitchell n.d.a) are as follows (Figure 4):

Figure 3.   Obsidian Culture Type Artifact Assemblage.
a, b, leaf-shaped flaked stone points; c, fragment of sea mussel shell celt;
d–g, obsidian bipolar flakes; h, bone single-point; i, bone bipoint; j, ventral
view of bone composite toggling harpoon valve; k, obsidian flake core;
1, irregular absasive stone. (a, h–k, Echo Bay I; b–g, 1, Hopetown I).

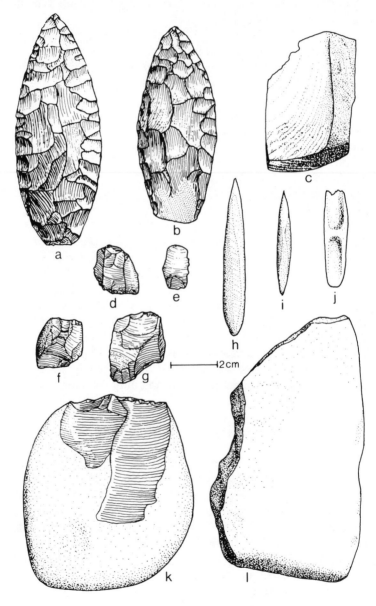

2 cm

Figure 4.   Queen Charlotte Strait Culture Type Artifact Assemblage.
a, b, bone single-points, probably arming points for composite toggling
harpoon heads; c, composite toggling harpoon valve; d, bone bipoint, e,
blanket or hair pin; f, unilaterally barbed bone point; g, non-toggling bone
harpoon head; h, deer ulna tool; i, sea mammal bone spindle whorl; j,
fragment of sea mussel shell celt; k, ground stone celt; 1, flat-topped hand
maul; m, pecked stone disc; n, sea mammal bone bark beater. (a–c, i,
Davies Island fort; d, j, Echo Bay II; e, k, m, n, Hopetown III; g, O'Connor
site [after Chapman 1982: Figure 3.18]; l, Southern Kwakiutl area [after
Boas 1909: Figure 36b]. l–n drawn to different scales than other items).

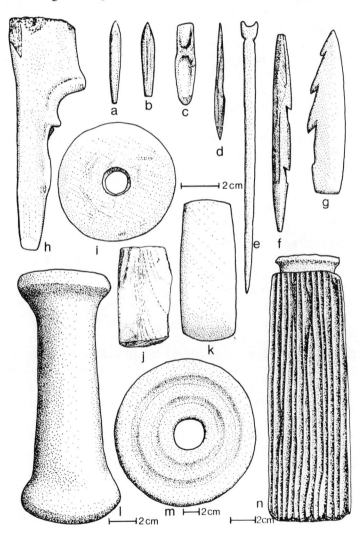

- Flat-topped hand mauls
- Stone discs
- Hammerstones
- Irregular and shaped abrasive stones
- Ground stone celts
- Unilaterally barbed bone points
- Unilaterally barbed, nontoggling bone harpoon points
- Bone composite toggling harpoon valves
- Bone bipoints
- Bone singlepoints
- Bone splinter awls
- Ulna tools
- Whalebone bark beaters
- Bone spindle whorls
- Bone blanket or hair pins
- Sea mussel shell celts
- Sea mussel shell knives

Bone items comprise upwards of 45 percent of each assemblage. For Hopetown III, bone, as mentioned earlier, amounts to 56 percent of the total. Bone and shell together account for 96 percent.

CHRONOLOGY

Less than satisfactory data are available for working out the chronological relationships of Queen Charlotte Strait components, but they at least offer a reasonably consistent and credible picture. At three sites (O'Connor, Echo Bay, and Hopetown), what may be distinguished as Obsidian culture type materials are contained in strata lying beneath deposits of Queen Charlotte Straits form. At Bear Cove, they overlie the Old Cordilleran layer. At the Bear Cove site, too, the shell-bearing Obsidian deposits are segregated on a bench elevated and inland from those shell deposits containing Queen Charlotte Strait materials. The terrace dating method would interpret the location of the Obsidian deposits as indicating greater age for those raised, "inland" assemblages than for their lower, more coastal counterparts.

In all, there are seven radiocarbon age estimates to consider (Table 1), most of which relate to the early, Obsidian culture type. Unfortunately, the one age estimate provisionally attributed to the Queen Charlotte Strait culture type is associated with a burial complex, and this assemblage is grouped with the Queen Charlotte Strait components on the basis of probable age rather than similarity. Thus, all that the radiocarbon data disclose

Table 1. Radiocarbon Age Estimates for Queen Charlotte Strait Area Site Components

Estimate	Component	Culture Type	Source
AD 340±130 (GaK 7345)	Hopetown II	Queen Charlotte Strait	author's own research
420 BC±100 (GaK 7346)	Hopetown I	Obsidian	author's own research
520 BC±120 (GaK 7344)	Hopetown I	Obsidian	author's own research
590 BC±120 (GaK 3901)	O'Connor II Lower Levels	Obsidian	Chapman 1982:126
740 BC±90 (GaK 4918)	O'Connor II Lower Levels	Obsidian	Chapman 1982:126
950 BC±90 (GaK 4917)	O'Connor II Lower Levels	Obsidian	Chapman 1982:126
6070 BC±110 (WSU 2141)	Bear Cover III Area 2 Shell	Old Cordilleran	C. Carlson 1979:177

is that Obsidian culture type components are ascribed to a comparatively restricted span of years, generally prior to 500 BC but later than 3000 BC, and that those of the Queen Charlotte Strait culture type pertain to the period after about AD 300. The one Old Cordilleran assemblage is demonstrably much earlier, with a radiocarbon age estimate of 6070±110 (C. Carlson 1979:177).

Finally, it can be noted that the one site component containing significant numbers of post-contact period trade goods (Hornet Passage fort) was in other respects of typical Queen Charlotte Strait form. This obviously suggests a late placement of the culture type.

FAUNAL ASSEMBLAGES

Only a partly completed faunal analysis has been reported for the Bear Cove Old Cordilleran component (C. Carlson 1979:188), and bone preservation in what were essentially non-shell deposits was described as very poor. The principal fish remains were those of the rockfishes (72 percent), with salmon being a remote second. Mammal bones were dominated by porpoise and dolphin. The analysis of bird remains has not been reported.

Better data are available from sites in the southeastern part of the strait, although our examination of even these must be incomplete because strictly comparable samples were not obtained for shellfish. A summary analysis of mammal, bird, and fish remains follows, with site assemblages grouped according to the culture types described above.

In this summary, the main statistic used is minimum "live" weight. This figure results from multiplying the minimum number of individuals (MNI) by an average weight for live or, more correctly, recently killed and uneviscerated specimens of both sexes and various ages (Table 2). Weight information is reasonably good for species or groups that are of current economic importance but is particularly difficult to acquire for other categories. Salmon and waterfowl averages are based on numerous observations and are therefore most reliable. Others may be calculated from but a few specimens. The weights used are listed in Table 2 along with sources from which values have been taken or calculated. I have recorded only weights of adults and have averaged male and female. Where sources have given only ranges, I have taken the mid-point.

Minimum edible meat weight would initially seem to be a more informative statistic to use. However, suitable conversion factors are available for only some species or genera (see, e.g., Albright 1984, White 1953, Ziegler 1973). There is also, admittedly, a subjective aspect to the decision of what is edible and what truly inedible. Further, an animal may be important for products in addition to meat. Bladders, bones, horns, antlers, and hides may well have been used and yet their value would not be reflected in any edible meat weight statistic. For these reasons, and because the study is not solely concerned with diet, I have elected to use weight of the whole animal.

The MNI statistic has been calculated for the Hopetown site by 2 × 2m excavation unit and by 30cm depth. For the Echo Bay vicinity sites, it is by 2 × 2m excavation unit and 10cm depth. This dissimilarity in the size of analytical units will produce lower MNI values for Hopetown I and III than for the other assemblages, but because I have used proportions rather than frequencies in my analysis, the difference in methods will have no effect on the outcome of this study. I have omitted from consideration here and in later comparisons any MNI figure based on only a single element in a site or site component.

Not all species or specimens in an archaeological faunal assemblage represent food or material resources, but most probably do. This study eliminates only canids from the list. Most of these specimens are likely domestic dog, a species not traditionally eaten on the Northwest Coast and, excepting the southern Gulf of Georgia Salish wool dogs, not known to have been routinely used as a source of raw material.

As an objective measure of the apparent dependence on one or a few species or on groups of species, I have used a diversity index based on qualitative variance and described in Mueller et al. (1977:179–181).[1] This

Table 2. Average Weights for Species and Groups

Common Name	Scientific Name	Weight[a] (kg)	Source
MAMMALS			
Beaver	Castor canadensis	20.00	Banfield 1974
Deer mouse	Peromyscus maniculatus	.03	Banfield 1974
Small rodents		.03	(averaged)[b]
Voles	microtus spp.	.02	Banfield 1974
Porcupine	Erethizon dorsatum	6.40	Banfield 1974
Porpoises	Delphinidae	78.75	Banfield 1974
Raccoon	Procyon lotor	8.05	Banfield 1974
Mink	Mustela vison	1.48	Banfield 1974
River otter	Lontra canadensis	7.48	Banfield 1974
Sea otter	Enhydra lutris	27.07	Banfield 1974
Lynx	Lynx rufus	8.20	Banfield 1974
Northern fur seal	Callorhinus ursinus	117.25	Banfield 1974
Northern sea lion	Eumatopias jubata	690.00	Scheffer 1958
California sea lion	Zalophus californianus	162.50	Nowak & Paradiso 1983
Harbor seal	Phoca vitulina	65.25	Banfield 1974
Coast deer	Odocoileus hemionus	92.13	Banfield 1974
Mountain goat	Oreamnos americanus	73.40	Banfield 1974
BIRDS			
Common loon	Gavia immer	3.40	Teres 1980
Arctic loon	G. arctica	2.61	Teres 1980
Red-throated loon	G. stellata	1.74	Teres 1980
Red-necked grebe	Podiceps grisegena	1.04	Teres 1980
Western grebe	Aechmophorus occidentalis	1.47	Teres 1980
Shearwater, medium	Puffinus spp.	.48	Teres 1980
Brandt's cormorant	Phalacrocorax pencillatus	2.43	Teres 1980
Pelagic cormorant	P. pelagicus	2.04	Teres 1980
Great blue heron	Ardea herodias	2.95	Teres 1980
Tundra swan	Cygnus columbianus	6.78	Bellrose 1980
Trumpeter swan	C. buccinator	10.94	Bellrose 1980
Canada goose	Branta canadensis	4.13	Bellrose 1980
Geese, medium	Anserinae	2.65	(averaged)
Mallard	Anas platyrhynchos	1.18	Bellrose 1980
Gadwall	A. strepera	.90	Bellrose 1980
Dabbling ducks	Anatidae	.75	(averaged)
Bay ducks	Aythya spp.	1.00	(averaged)
Common goldeneye	Bucephala clangula	.93	Bellrose 1980
Barrow's goldeneye	B. islandica	.78	Bellrose 1980
Bufflehead	B. albeola	.42	Bellrose 1980
Goldeneyes	Bucephela spp.	.71	(averaged)
Oldsquaw	Clangula hyemalis	.87	Bellrose 1980
Scoters	Melanitta spp.	1.13	(averaged)

Table 2.   (Continued)

Common Name	Scientific Name	Weight[a] (kg)	Source
Mergansers	Merginae	.95	(averaged)
Ducks, large		1.30	(averaged)
Ducks, medium		.82	(averaged)
Ducks, small		.60	(averaged)
Ducks		.83	(averaged)
Bald eagle	Haliaeetus leucocephalus	4.65	Teres 1980
Birds of prey	Falconiformes	1.07	(averaged, without eagle)
Plovers	Charadriidae	.12	(averaged)
Gulls, large	Laridae	2.27	(averaged)
Gulls, medium	Laridae	1.03	(averaged)
Gulls, small	Laridae	.35	(averaged)
Common murre	Uria aalge	1.01	Teres 1980
Marbelled murrelet	Brachyramphus marmoratus	.23	Teres 1980
Cassin's auklet	Ptychoramphus aleuticus	.17	Teres 1980
Rhinoceros auklet	Cerorhinca monoceraba	.54	Teres 1980
Tufted puffin	Lunda cirrhata	.76	Teres 1980
Alcids	Alcidae	.53	(averaged)
Great horned owl	Bubo virginianus	1.59	Palmer 1949
Northwestern crow	Corvus caurinus	.24	Uvic records[c]
Raven	C. corax	1.23	Teres 1980
Perching birds	Passeriformes	.04	(averaged)

FISH

Common Name	Scientific Name	Weight (kg)	Source
Spiny dogfish	Squalus acanthias	4.54	Hart 1973
Skates	Raja spp.	6.50	Wigen 1980[d]
Ratfish	Hydrolagus colliei	1.22	Wigen 1980
Pacific herring	Clupea harengus pallasi	.14	Wigen 1980
Northern anchovy	Engraulis mordax mordax	.10	(estimated)[e]
Pacific salmons	Oncorhynchus spp.	4.77	Hart 1973
Eulachon	Thaleichthys pacificus	.04	Uvic records
Codfishes	Gadidae	.89	Wigen 1980
Pacific cod	Gadus macrocephalus	2.27	Wigen 1980
Pacific hake	Merluccius productus	1.23	Wigen 1980
Pacific tomcod	Microgadus proximus	.17	Uvic records
Walleye pollock	Theragra chalcogramma	.92	Wigen 1980
Surfperches	Embiotocidae	.52	Wigen 1980
Rockfishes	Sebastes spp.	1.24	Uvic records
Sablefish	Anoplopoma fimbria	2.27	Clemens & Wilby 1949
Greenlings	Hexagrammos spp.	.31	Uvic records
Kelp greenling	H. decagrammus	.31	Uvic records
Lingcod	Ophiodon elongatus	4.11	Wigen 1980
Sculpins	Cottidae	.21	Uvic records
Buffalo sculpin	Enophrys bison	.15	Uvic records
Red Irish lord	Hemilepidotus hemilepidotus	.30	(estimated)
Staghorn sculpin	Leptocottus armatus	.14	Uvic records

Table 2.   (Continued)

Common Name	Scientific Name	Weight[a] (kg)	Source
Great sculpin	Myoxocephalus polyacanthocephalus	.43	Uvic records
Cabezon	Scorpaenichthys marmoratus	.50	Uvic records
Righteye flounders	Pleuronectidae	.49	Wigen 1980
Pacific halibut	Hippoglossus stenolepis	16.00	Hart 1973
Rock sole	Lepidopsetta bilineata	.49	Wigen 1980
Slender sole	Lyopetta exilis	.14	Wigen 1980
English sole	Parophrys vetulus	.20	Uvic records
Starry flounder	Platichthys stellatus	.11	Uvic records
Sand sole	Psettichthys melanostictus	.40	Uvic records

[a]Weights are for adults only and represent an average of male and female. Where sources give only ranges, the mid-points are recorded here.
[b]The notation (averaged) indicates a value that is the mean of weights reported for species grouped in the category.
[c]The notation "Uvic records" indicates data from specimens processed by the faunal laboratory of the University of Victoria's Department of Anthropology.
[d]Figures from Wigen (1980) were compiled from specimens at the British Columbia Provincial Museum, Victoria, Canada.
[e]The notation (estimated) indicates the value is derived from weights for species of comparable size and body form.

index scales from 0 to 1 and increases in value as the dependence on one or a few species increases. Following the lead of Mueller et al., who only suggest a possible name for the statistic, I have identified this as the Index of Qualitative Uniformity (IQU).

Discussion of the importance of species or groups of species is confined to comparison of taxa within each of the major faunal categories: mammals, birds, and fish. In theory, the minimum live weight statistic should provide a basis for evaluating the relative contributions of species or groups across the category boundaries. However, such comparison is meaningless if the level of identification is neither high nor approximately equivalent in all categories. As Table 3 indicates, these conditions are not met for the faunal assemblages under study. To take the extremes, it has been possible to identify 94 percent of the fish elements from Echo Bay I but only 19 percent of the mammal bones from Hopetown I.

Obsidian Culture Type

Faunal assemblages from the Hopetown I and Echo Bay I components are summarized in Figures 5, 6, and 7. Regarding the mammals (Figure 5), we find considerable dependence on land species, with deer clearly

Table 3. Percentage of Total Specimens Identified

Component	Mammals	Birds	Fish
Hopetown I	19	55	77
Echo Bay I	20	—	57
Hopetown III	32	47	88
Echo Bay vicinity	45	57	92

paramount—70.4 percent in Hopetown I, 56.1 percent in Echo Bay I. Of secondary importance amongst the mammals are harbor seal in Hopetown I (17.5 percent) and, at Echo Bay, porpoise (24.0 percent), followed closely by harbor seal (19.9 percent). At .48 (for Hopetown I), the Index of Qualitative Uniformity (IQU) is moderate. The Echo Bay I IQU is much lower (.12), in part reflecting a smaller sample with its fewer reported taxa.

Fish (Figure 6) show a more even distribution of remains amongst the species or groups of species. The salmons, as a group, predominate (36.4 percent in Hopetown I, 51.9 percent in Echo Bay I), but other categories are important, too. For both Hopetown I and Echo Bay I, ratfish and dogfish rank second and third, with rockfishes and codfishes vying for the next two places. As might be expected, the IQU is quite low—.17 at Hopetown and only a bit higher (.24) at Echo Bay.

Even greater diversity is found among the birds (Figure 7), although

Figure 5. Obsidian Culture Type Mammal Assemblages.
Proportions for Hopetown I are: 70.4% deer, 17.5% harbor seal, 4.6% mountain goat; 7.5% other. Echo Bay proportions are 56.1% deer, 24.0% porpoise, 19.9% harbor seal.

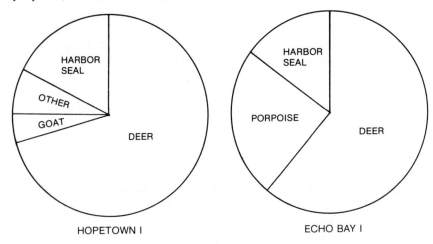

Figure 6. Obsidian Culture Type Fish Assemblages.
Proportions for Hopetown I are: 36.4% salmons, 24.9% ratfish, 15.1%
dogfish, 12.2% rockfishes, 5.5% codfishes, 5.9% other. Echo Bay I proportions are: 51.9% salmons, 24.0% ratfish, 9.9% dogfish, 7.3% codfishes,
6.9% rockfishes.

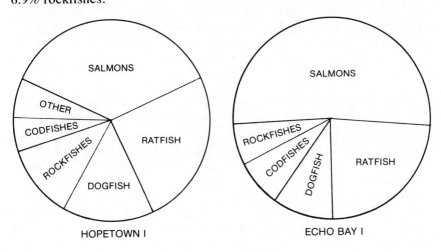

Figure 7. Obsidian Culture Type Bird Assemblage (Hopetown I only).
Proportions are: 23.3% ducks, 20.1% loons, 14.8% gulls, 13.8% bald eagle,
10.9% grebes, 8.7% great blue heron, 5.5% cormorants, 2.9% other.

too few specimens were recovered from Echo Bay I to permit a useful analysis. For Hopetown I, the various ducks rank first (23.3 percent) but are only marginally more significant than loons (20.1 percent). Of ducks, the sea duck category has the most representatives (8.4 percent), followed by dabbling ducks and bay ducks.[2] After loons, the next most important are gulls, bald eagle, grebes, great blue heron, and cormorant. The low IQU (.07) indicates how little dependence there is on any one species or category.

Queen Charlotte Strait Culture Type

Fauna from Hopetown III and a "pooled" assemblage of the seven sites investigated in the vicinity of Echo Bay (including the Echo Bay II component) are presented in Figures 8, 9, and 10. For the mammals, Figure 8 clearly shows a strong emphasis on sea taxa. In both Hopetown III and the Echo Bay sites, sea species comprise over 80 percent of the fauna, measured by minimum live weight. The three most important species or groups are sea lions (mostly northern sea lion, although a few smaller specimens may be Californias), harbor seal, and porpoise.[3] Harbor seal (40.4 percent) are most prominent at Hopetown, followed by sea lion (30.4 percent) and dolphins (9.0 percent). In the Echo Bay vicinity sites, sea

Figure 8. Queen Charlotte Strait Culture Type Mammal Assemblages. Proportions for Hopetown III are: 40.4% harbor seal, 30.4% sea lion, 15.1% deer, 9.0% porpoise, 5.1% other. Echo Bay vicinity proportions are: 20.1% harbor seal, 42.6% sea lion, 18.5% deer, 13.4% porpoise, 5.4% other.

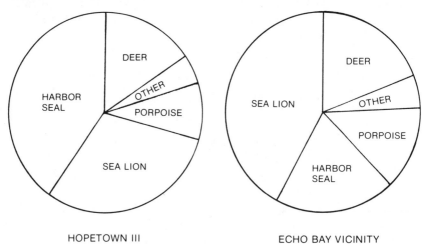

HOPETOWN III   ECHO BAY VICINITY

Figure 9. Queen Charlotte Strait Culture Type Bird Assemblages. Proportions for Hopetown III are: 26.2% ducks, 21.6% loons, 12.3% geese, 12.2% gulls, 9.6% grebes, 5.9% bald eagle, 4.8% great blue heron, 7.4% other. Echo Bay vicinity proportions are: 21.8% swans, 19.1% ducks, 18.2% loons, 12.1% gulls, 10.6% bald eagle, 10.3% geese, 4.5% great blue heron, 3.4% other.

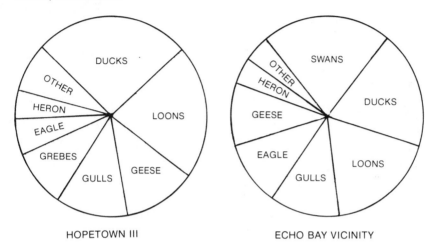

HOPETOWN III   ECHO BAY VICINITY

lions rank first (42.6 percent), harbor seal second (20.1 percent), and porpoise third (13.4 percent). Of land mammals, coast deer is the only species represented in significant numbers. They constitute 15.1 percent of the Hopetown III and 18.5 percent of the Echo Bay area assemblages. The IQUs for mammals are similar: .26 for Hopetown III, .21 for those at the Echo Bay sites.

With birds (Figure 9) there is little dependence on single species or groups of species. This is indicated by the IQUs which are alike and very low—.07 for the Echo Bay vicinity sites and .10 for Hopetown III. At Hopetown, ducks (26.2 percent) are most common, with the sea ducks being the principal category represented (12.2 percent). Other important birds include the loons (21.6 percent), geese (12.3 percent), gulls (12.2 percent), grebes (9.6 percent), bald eagle (5.9 percent), and great blue heron (4.8 percent). The Echo Bay sites place swans first (21.8 percent) with the trumpeter swan accounting for 16.7 percent. Following this is an order much like that for Hopetown III: ducks, 19.1 percent (sea ducks, 13.0 percent); loons, 18.2 percent (common loon, 15.5 percent); gulls, 12.1 percent; bald eagle, 10.6 percent; geese, 10.3 percent; and great blue heron, 4.5 percent.

Salmon are especially prominent among the fish (Figure 10). In Hope-

Figure 10. Queen Charlotte Strait Culture Type Fish Assemblages. Proportions for Hopetown III are: 72.7% salmons, 14.5% halibut, 6.8% dogfish, 6.0% other (including 3.0% rockfishes). Echo Bay Vicinity proportions are: 75.7% salmons, 7.5% halibut, 5.7% dogfish, 3.7% rockfishes, 7.4% other (including 4.0% ratfish).

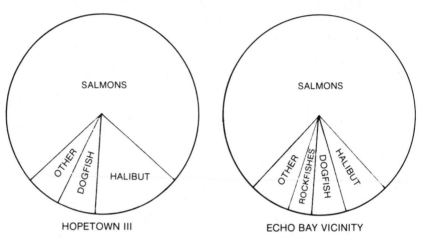

town III, they constitute 72.7 percent and in the Echo Bay vicinity sites, 75.7 percent of the fish fauna. The next most common fish remains at Hopetown are halibut, followed by dogfish, and rock fishes. For the Echo Bay sites, the order following salmon is halibut, dogfish, ratfish, and rockfishes. The IQUs are .52 for Hopetown III and .54 for the Echo Bay sites.

COMPARISON OF FAUNA FROM QUEEN CHARLOTTE STRAIT AREA COMPONENTS

Faunal assemblages may vary in the range, rank order, and "mix" of species present and in their degree of emphasis on one or a few species. For the Queen Charlotte Strait area sites we have been considering, the range of species is indicated by Table 4 and Figures 5–10. If we compare the quantities in Table 4 with those in Table 5 (number of specimens identified) it becomes clear that as the number of identified specimens increases, so (generally) does the number of species represented in the sample. However, if the relationship is graphed for each major faunal category, what is at first a steep rise in the number of categories soon begins to level off so that the addition of specimens adds fewer and fewer new categories. With the mammals, this perceptible decrease in category increments occurs when the sample reaches 300–400 specimens; with the birds,

Table 4. Number of Species or Groups Identified

Component	Mammals	Birds	Fish
Hopetown I	11	30	25
Echo Bay I	4	—	9
Hopetown III	16	43	28
Echo Bay vicinity	14	19	16

500–800 specimens; and with the fish, for which a linear relationship is less clearly evident, perhaps 3000–5000. Beyond these ranges, the importance of sample size is greatly reduced.

As indications of rank order, mix, and proportion, lists of the principal species are portrayed in Figures 5–10. We can expect that sample size will affect the qualitative composition of faunal assemblages because rarely collected species are less likely to be represented as the sample size decreases. For the variables being considered, though, at least the major species or groups should be fairly accurately reported.

Apart from the graphic depiction of proportions, my chosen measure of the degree of emphasis on species is the IQU, the values for which are summarized in Table 6. As both minimum live weight (derived from the MNI, which in turn is influenced by the number of specimens present) and the number of categories enter into the calculation of this statistic, it is obviously affected by the sample size. As pointed out when discussing the range of species, however, the effect of sample size is not likely to be important above the indicated amounts.

Having outlined the bases for comparison, we can next consider assemblages within the Obsidian and Queen Charlotte Strait culture types and then examine the differences between these forms.

Differences between our two Obsidian culture type components in the range of species represented and in IQU values, although pronounced, are most likely attributable to the differences in sample size. While Hopetown I has an adequate fish sample, it is only marginal with respect to mammals and has an inadequate bird sample. Echo Bay I has very small samples for all categories. We could expect that augmenting the sample

Table 5. Total Number of Specimens Identified

Component	Mammals	Birds	Fish
Hopetown I	359	310	5,885
Echo Bay I	45	—	958
Hopetown III	5,151	1,055	49,115
Echo Bay vicinity	2,172	135	8,216

Table 6. IQU Values, Queen Charlotte Strait Area Sites[a]

Component	Mammals	Birds	Fish
Hopetown I	.48	.07	.17
Echo Bay I[b]	*	*	.24
Hopetown III	.23	.10	.52
Echo Bay vicinity	.21	.07	.54

[a]IQU = Index of Qualitative Variability. Its values range from 0 to 1, increasing as the dependence on one or a few species increases (after Mueller et al. 1977:179–181). See my Note 1 for further explanation.
[b]The asterisk in this row denotes that the Number of Individual Specimens (NISP) identified was too low to yield a reliable IQU.

from each site component would increase the indicated range of species and alter the IQUs, with a more pronounced effect on Echo Bay I than on Hopetown I. About the only sound comparisons, then, that can be made between the two assemblages concern the mix, rank order, and proportions of prominent species.

Both Obsidian components show a dominance of coast deer and an apparently secondary importance of sea mammals, of which the most important at each site are harbor seal and porpoise. The differences in emphasis—harbor seal being decidedly more important than porpoise in Hopetown I, porpoise being slightly more important than seal in Echo Bay I—cannot presently be explained. The presence of mountain goat exclusively in Hopetown I may reflect the fact that Hopetown Village is on a small island very close to the mainland mountain habitat of goats, while Echo Bay, on the northwestern shore of a large island, is more distant from the mainland mountains.

The fish assemblages are very similar. There is a slightly higher proportion of salmon at Echo Bay and codfishes and rockfishes compete for 4th and 5th places of importance, but other than these minor peculiarities, there is little to distinguish between the two components in their fish assemblages. No comparison of bird assemblages can be made, as the one from Echo Bay I was too limited to permit analysis.

Because sample sizes are larger, more can be said from comparisons between components of the Queen Charlotte Strait culture type. Harbor seal and sea lion are the two most important mammals in both Hopetown III and the grouped Echo Bay vicinity components, with seal placing first in Hopetown III and second in the other group. The proportional differences are not great, however, and combined they represent a very similar dependence on these two marine mammals (see Figure 8). For both components, coast deer and porpoise rank third and fourth—again, with very similar proportions.

There is more difference amongst the birds (Figure 9). Swans (mostly trumpeter) are of first importance in the Echo Bay group of components but are absent from Hopetown III. In this latter component, grebes are present in significant numbers, while they are missing from the other sites. There are not major differences in the order or proportions of other main species or groups. The swan/grebe distinction is not easily interpreted. A relatively small sample size might account for the absence of grebes from the Echo Bay sites, but it is less easily invoked as a reason for the omission of swans from the much larger Hopetown assemblage. Explanation of both differences most likely lies in regional or seasonal availability, although all information needed for such interpretation is not presently available.

The two fish assemblages are quite similar, differing only in the proportions and rank order of some minor species and groups (Figure 10). In both cases, salmon form the bulk of the remains. Hopetown III places somewhat more emphasis on halibut than does the Echo Bay group of sites, although for both, these fish rank second in importance. Ratfish are rather more prominent in the Echo Bay sites than in Hopetown III.

In summary, there is relatively little difference between faunal assemblages within the Obsidian culture type category or among those of the Queen Charlotte Strait culture type. Where sample sizes are reasonably large, as with most of the Queen Charlotte Strait culture type, a comparison of IQU statistics may be considered reliable. For each faunal category distinguished in Table 6, the values for Hopetown III and Echo Bay components are seen to be very similar. Of the Obsidian culture type assemblages, only the fish approach a satisfactory sample size for both components. Here, too, the IQUs are close.

A quite different picture emerges when we compare components of one culture type with those of the other. At both Hopetown and Echo Bay the same transformation in mammal and fish assemblages occurs. For mammals, the shift is from heavy reliance on coastal deer and minor use of seal and porpoise to even heavier dependence on seal, sea lion, and porpoise and only minor use of deer. The change in fish is less dramatic but nevertheless pronounced. Salmon become very much more important in the later period and halibut, absent from Obsidian culture type components, assume second place in the later list. Bird assemblages are the most similar, although even here distinctions can be drawn. Between Hopetown I and III, the changes include addition of geese (mainly Canadas) to the list of prominent species or groups and a noticeable increase in importance for sea ducks.

Comparing IQUs for components in general reinforces the picture of dissimilarity. Between earlier and later culture types, there is a shift towards less dependence on a single species of mammal and more dependence on a single species of fish. By this measure, the bird assemblages do not change.

It is important to note that these changes occur between components at the same sites. They may be observed between Hopetown I (Figures 5 and 6) and Hopetown III (Figures 8 and 9), Echo Bay I (Figures 5 and 6) and Echo Bay II (Figure 11), and thus are not likely related to the archaeologist's chance selection of sites occupied during different seasons. We must look elsewhere for an explanation of this distinctive faunal differentiation, which, we have already seen, is linked with an equally distinctive change in the artifact assemblages.

COMPARISON WITH NEIGHBORING AREAS

We next ask if changes over time described for the Queen Charlotte Strait area are paralleled in assemblages from neighboring areas: the Strait of Georgia, the west coast of Vancouver Island, and the northern part of the central coast (see Figure 12). For each area, we look first at the relative prominence of flaked stone and worked bone in the artifact assemblages, paying particular attention to the presence of small flake tools or detritus, and then at the fauna.

Only a few faunal assemblages have been reported in sufficient detail to permit comparison with the Queen Charlotte Strait analysis. In addition, the use of various measures of quantification means that proportions reported are sometimes only roughly comparable. If MNI data have been

Figure 11. Echo Bay II Mammal and Fish Assemblages.
Proportions for mammals are: 46.4% sea lion, 21.4% porpoise, 12.4% deer, 8.8% harbor seal, 7.9% fur seal, 3.3% other. Proportions for fish are 93.3% salmons, 6.7% other (including 4.5% ratfish).

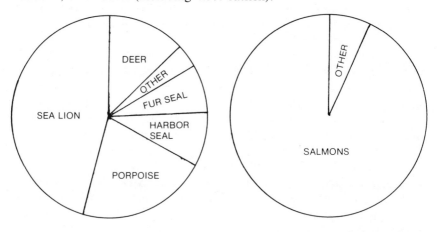

Figure 12. Locations of Sites Referred to in Artifact and Faunal Assemblage Comparison.
1, Grant Anchorage; 2, Roscoe Inlet; 3, McNaughton Island; 4, Kisameet Bay; 5, Namu; 6, Nutlitliquotlank; 7, Port Hardy vicinity sites (O'Connor, Bear Cove, Fort Rupert); 8, Hopetown Village; 9, Echo Bay vicinity sites (see Figure 1); 10, Yuquot; 11, Hesquiat Harbor vicinity sites (Hesquiat Village, Loon Cave, Yaksis Cave); 12, Shoemaker Bay; 13, Rebecca Spit fort; 14, Bliss Landing; 15, J. Puddleduck; 16, Millard Creek; 17, Buckley Bay; 18, Tsable River Bridge; 19, Deep Bay; 20, Little Qualicum River; 21, Saltery Bay; 22; Belcarra Park; 23, Glenrose Cannery; 24, St. Mungo Cannery; 25, Crescent Beach; 26, Dionisio Point; 27, Active Pass vicinity sites (Montague Harbor, Georgeson Bay, Helen Point); 28, Bowker Creek and Willows Beach; 29, Kitty Islet; 30, Fort Rodd Hill Park.

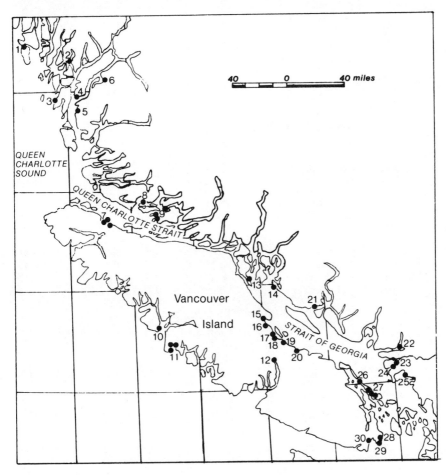

published, I have converted them to minimum live weight. Discussion is confined to mammals and fish, the two categories containing significant differences in the Queen Charlotte Strait study. Dog bones and those of unidentified specimens have not been included. IQUs (see Table 7) have been calculated only for those assemblages and faunal categories in which the identification of species appears to have been reasonably comprehensive.

Table 7.　IQUs for Selected Faunal Assemblages[a]

Area and Component	Basis[b]	Mammals	Fish
Gulf of Georgia Area			
A.　Charles culture type			
Glenrose Cannery II	MLW	.32	.36
St. Mungo Cannery I	MLW	.23	—
B.　Locarno Beach culture type			
Buckley Bay	MLW	.31	.11
Tsable River Bridge II	MLW	.23	.14
Puddleduck II	NISP	.35	.31
C.　Gulf of Georgia culture type			
Saltery Bay	BW	.91	.33
Little Qualicum River	BW	.83	.19
Crescent Beach, late	BW	.61	.05
Kitty Islet	NISP	.49	.20
St. Mungo Cannery III	MLW	.50	—
West Coast of Vancouver Island			
Yuquot II	MLW	.17	.33
Yuquot III	MLW	.16	.41
Hesquiat Harbor vicinity	MLW	.20	.14
Shoemaker Bay I	MLW	.24	.17
Shoemaker Bay II	MLW	.24	.21
Northern Part of the Central British Columbia Coast			
Roscoe Inlet	NISP	.60	—
Namu II/III	NISP	.24	—
Namu IV/V	NISP	.41	—
Namu VI/VII	NISP	.19	—
Kisameet Bay	NISP	.28	—
McNaughton Island III/IV	MLW	.12	—
	NISP	—	.82

[a]IQU = Index of Qualitative Uniformity (see Table 6, note a, and Note 1).

[b]NISP = Number of Individual Specimens. BW = weight of bone recovered. MLW = Minimum Live Weight (the product of MNI—Minimum Number of Individuals represented by identified bone remains—and the mean weight of recently-killed and uneviscerated specimens of both sexes and various ages).

Strait of Georgia

Assemblages contemporaneous with the Obsidian culture type are those of the Charles and Locarno Beach culture types (Borden 1975, Mitchell 1971b, n.d.a). Those of similar age to the Queen Charlotte Strait culture type are of the Gulf of Georgia culture type (Mitchell 1971b, n.d.a). Between components of these forms, there are obvious differences in the proportions of bone and flaked stone artifacts in the total assemblage (Table 8). These differences disclose a shift in emphasis between Locarno Beach and Gulf of Georgia. The transformation is the same as that observed in

Table 8. Gulf of Georgia Artifact Assemblages

Site Component	Source	Flaked Stone %	Bone %
Charles Culture Type			
Glenrose Cannery II	Matson 1976	51.5	29.7
St. Mungo Cannery I	Boehm 1973	29.8	46.7
Locarno Beach Culture Type			
Puddleduck II	Mitchell n.d.b	55.4	14.3
Millard Creek	Capes 1977	59.7	16.1
Buckley Bay	Mitchell 1974	34.3	26.9
Deep Bay I	Monks 1977	93.0	1.8
Belcarra Park I	Charlton 1980	52.5	5.1
Crescent Beach II	Trace 1981	48.3	12.3
Montague Harbor I	Mitchell 1971b	26.3	25.4
Georgeson Bay I	Haggarty & Sendey 1976	48.5	7.3
Willows Beach I	Kenny 1974	76.6	3.9
Bowker Creek	Mitchell 1979b	60.1	15.4
Gulf of Georgia Culture Type			
Rebecca Spit Fort	Mitchell 1968	2.9	65.0
Deep Bay III	Monks 1977	7.7	40.4
Little Qualicum	Bernick 1983	7.3	55.5
Belcarra Park II	Charlton 1980	19.5	46.6
St. Mungo Cannery III	Boehm 1973	29.1	28.5
Dionisio Point IIb	Mitchell 1971a	5.2	41.4
Crescent Beach late	Ham 1982	11.0	40.0
Montague Harbor III	Mitchell 1971b	4.1	52.3
Georgeson Bay II	Haggarty & Sendey 1976	12.8	41.4
Helen Point III	McMurdo 1974	8.8	49.8
Fort Rodd Hill Park	Mitchell 1981	22.3	51.0
Willows Beach II	Kenny 1974	21.6	37.6
Kitty Islet	Mitchell 1980	0.6	57.1

the Queen Charlotte Strait area—from a high proportion of flaked stone to bone in the earlier period to a higher ratio of bone to flaked stone in the later.

Small cryptocrystalline and fine-grained flakes are prominent in many Strait of Georgia area components of Charles or Locarno Beach form. Of Locarno Beach assemblages, for example, Millard Creek (Capes 1977) has 2.1 times as many such flakes as flaked stone artifacts; Willows Beach I (Kenny 1974), 3.8 times as many; Puddleduck II (Mitchell n.d.b), 4.3 times; Crescent Beach II (Trace 1981), 1.4 times; and Deep Bay I (Monks 1977), an amount equal to 60 percent of the flaked stone category. Although no strictly comparable measures of the abundance are available, there are references to prominence of flaked stone debitage in Charles culture type assemblages, as, for example, Glenrose Cannery (Matson 1976), Bliss Landing (Beattie 1972:30), and Helen Point Ia (McMurdo 1974). At the last two, the presence of small flakes was particularly noted. In contrast, flaked stone debitage of any size is much less common in Gulf of Georgia culture type assemblages, and the small quartz crystal or obsidian varieties so evident earlier are virtually absent.

Faunal analyses are available for two Charles culture type components (Table 9). Both come from sites situated at what was the mouth of the Fraser river at the time of their occupancy.

After converting the data reported by Imamoto (1976:30) to minimum live weight figures, the mammals recovered from the St. Mungo (Charles) component of the Glenrose Cannery site rank as follows: elk are first at 60.1 percent, deer next (19.0 percent), and seal (10.4 percent) third. Deer and elk combined come to 79.1 percent. For fish (Casteel 1976:85), the sum of listed and calculated live weights place salmon in first position (57.0 percent), followed by sturgeon (40.4 percent) (represented, however, by only two scutes from a single level), and eulachon at 1.7 percent.

For the similar component, St. Mungo I, at the nearby St. Mungo Cannery site (Boehm 1973:40), we can calculate minimum live weight. On this basis of quantification, the mammals rank as follows: elk, 71.9 percent; deer, 17.5 percent; (deer and elk together, 90.4 percent); harbor seal, 5.2 percent; beaver, 4.7 percent. The fish sample was not analyzed.

There are five Locarno Beach assemblages to consider (Table 9), all concentrated on the Vancouver Island shore of the northern part of the Strait of Georgia. Two of these, Buckley Bay and Tsable River Bridge II, have been analyzed using the same measure used in this study: minimum live weight.

At Buckley Bay (Wigen 1980:87–88), the most prominent mammals are sea lions (57.1 percent) and deer (21.7 percent). Sea mammals altogether account for 67 percent of the assemblage, deer and elk, 31.6 percent. Salmon (32.9 percent) are the most common fish, followed by herring

Table 9. Summary of Selected Proportions of Faunal Categories[a]

Area and Component	Deer/Elk %	Sea Mammal %	Salmon %
Queen Charlotte Strait Area			
Hopetown I	70.4	23.0	36.4
Echo Bay I	56.1	43.8	51.9
Hopetown III	15.1	82.6	72.7
Echo Bay vicinity	18.5	79.1	75.7
Strait of Georgia Area			
A. Charles Culture Type			
Glenrose Cannery II	79.1	10.4	57.0
St. Mungo Cannery I	90.4	5.2	—
B. Locarno Beach Culture Type			
Puddleduck II	58.6	18.6	50.0
Millard Creek[b]	92.0	6.9	80.0
Buckley Bay	31.6	67.0	32.9
Tsable River Bridge II	46.4	42.5	9.1
Deep Bay I	85.0	15.0	—
C. Gulf of Georgia Culture Type			
Deep Bay III	43.7	53.5	2.3
Saltery Bay[b]	93.2	1.2	16.9
Little Qualicum River[b]	99.7	0.0	43.7
St. Mungo Cannery III	75.2	16.6	—
Crescent Beach, late[b]	90.7	7.8	13.0
Kitty Islet[c]	83.3	4.8	20.0
West Coast of Vancouver Island			
Shoemaker Bay I	46.3	16.1	23.3
Shoemaker Bay II	48.1	44.1	19.8
Yuquot II	31.7	65.3	51.7
Yuquot III	28.2	68.8	63.4
Hesquiat Harbor vicinity	9.7	86.5	26.2
Northern Part of the Central British Columbia Coast			
Namu II/III[c]	53.2	22.5	—
Roscoe Inlet[c]	81.9	9.7	—
Namu IV/V[c]	67.5	12.0	—
Namu VI/VII[c]	47.4	44.2	—
Kisameet Bay[c]	57.7	29.9	—
McNaughton Island III/IV	13.0	87.0	92.7
Grant Anchorage[b]	—	64.5	—

[a]Except as noted, all figures are based on Minimum Live Weight (MLW)—the product of MNI (Minimum Number of Individuals represented by identified bone remains) and the mean weight of recently-killed and uneviscerated specimens of both sexes and various ages.
[b]Based on bone weight.
[c]Based on Number of Individual Specimens (NISP).

(18.3 percent), dogfish (15.7 percent), rockfishes (10.9 percent), skates and rays (7.5 percent), and sculpins (7.4 percent).

The proportions for Tsable River Bridge II (Wigen 1980: 94–95) mammals are: sea lion, 41.9 percent; deer, 31.9 percent; elk, 14.5 percent; and black bear, 10.1 percent. Deer and elk total 46.4 percent, sea mammals, 42.5 percent. With fish, the most prominent category is herring (38.4 percent), followed by dogfish (20.9 percent), rockfishes (10.2 percent), salmon (9.1 percent), and sculpins (6.5 percent).

Capes (1977:63) reports bone weight for major categories of fauna at the Millard Creek site. For the mammals, the fraction represented by deer is 92 percent, by sea mammals, 6.9 percent. Fish, quantified as grams of vertebrae, are simply described as salmon and "other." Salmon amount to 80 percent of the sample.

The few faunal remains from Deep Bay I (Monks 1977:203) give deer 85.0 percent of the minimum live weight and harbor seal the balance for mammals. No fish remains were recovered.

Minimum live weight estimates are available for the Puddleduck II assemblage (Mitchell n.d.b). On this basis, deer rank first among mammals at 58.6 percent. Black bear are next at 21.4 percent, followed by sea mammals (18.6 percent). Fish are as follows: salmon, 50.0 percent; herring, 13.4 percent; dogfish, 12.1 percent; rockfishes, 8.1 percent; and sculpins, 5.2 percent.

Gulf of Georgia culture type faunal assemblages available for comparison are more widely distributed. We have six to summarize (Table 9).

Minimum live weight figures can be calculated for Deep Bay III mammals using data reported by Monks (1977: Tables 24 and 28). Sea lions amount to 50.3 percent (seal and sea lion, 53.5 percent) and deer to 43.7 percent. Deer and elk combined equal 46.6 percent. Of the identified fish (Monks 1977: Tables 24 and 28), herring (96.7 percent) were first by bone weight. Salmon totalled 2.3 percent and dogfish, 1 percent.

Minimum live weight figures derived from data reported for St. Mungo III (Boehm 1973:40), give elk (51.7 percent) the first position. They are followed by deer (23.5 percent), harbor seal (16.6 percent), and beaver (7.7 percent). Elk and deer amount to 75.2 percent of the identified species. As noted in the discussion of St. Mungo I, fish remains were not analyzed.

Based on bone weight, the most important mammal in the Saltery Bay assemblage (Monks 1980:130) is the deer. It amounts to 93.2 percent. Sea mammal totals 1.2 percent. Rockfishes (59.2 percent) are most common, followed by salmon (16.9 percent), ratfish (9.2 percent), and pile perch (7.7 percent).

Bone weight was also used for reporting the faunal material from the Little Qualicum River site (Bernick 1983:360–362). For the dry portion of the site, deer top the list of mammals (86.9 percent). Deer and elk together equal 99.7 percent. With fish, the ranking is the following: salmon, 43.7 percent; dogfish, 23.8 percent; rockfishes, 9.7 percent; flatfishes, 5.7 percent, and sculpins, 5.5 percent.

In the late portion of the Crescent Beach site (Ham 1982:265), elk account for 78.4 percent of the weight of mammal bone recovered. This is followed by deer (12.3 percent) and sea mammals (harbor seal and sea lion) at 7.8 percent. Deer and elk together total 90.7 percent. By the same measure, the most prominent fish are flatfishes (25 percent) and herring (22 percent). Others are salmon and midshipmen at 13 percent each, dogfish (11 percent), sculpins (8 percent), and sturgeon (6 percent).

Kitty Islet's faunal data (Mitchell 1980: Table 3) are published as a simple element count. By this statistic, deer constitute 73.8 percent of the mammal collection, and deer and elk, 83.3 percent. Sculpins (45.7 percent) are the most plentiful fish, followed by salmon (20 percent) and by rockfishes and ratfish at 11.4 percent each.

West Coast of Vancouver Island

Few sites have been excavated and reported for the west coast or "Nootkan" portion of Vancouver Island. Of these, the Shoemaker Bay site (McMillan & St. Claire 1982), situated at the head of Alberni Inlet, has two components which resemble quite closely assemblages from the Strait of Georgia area. Shoemaker Bay I has radiocarbon age estimates ranging from 2080 BC to AD 220. While it may consist of two or more components (Mitchell n.d.a), the 1536 artifacts attributed to the unit by the excavators are 37.4 percent flaked stone and 11.5 percent bone. If Zone B artifacts are removed from this count (on grounds they comprise a distinct cultural assemblage), the proportion of flaked stone rises to 74.2 percent and that of bone falls to 1.6 percent. The flaked stone category includes substantial numbers of small crystal quartz and obsidian flakes—mostly in Zones C and D.

Shoemaker Bay II, with radiocarbon estimates of AD 500 and 850, is equated by McMillan & St. Claire (1982) to the Gulf of Georgia culture type. It has a very low incidence of flaked stone (2.1 percent) and a correspondingly large proportion of worked bone (47.8 percent).

Although the Alberni Valley and head of Alberni Inlet were held from the early historic period by the Opetchesaht and Tseshaht, Nuchahnulthaht ("Nootka") groups, McMillan & St. Claire (1982) conclude they have evidence of an earlier Strait of Georgia Salish affiliation for the area's occupants. Such a possibility was raised by several earlier investigators (Boas 1891:584; Drucker 1951:93; Sapir 1914:77). The archaeological data now seem to give the Salish occupation considerable time depth.

The Yuquot sequence (Dewhirst 1980) covers an even longer span of time. The early period (Yuquot I, pre-2300–1000 BC) is represented by a small assemblage that is about 1.0 percent flaked stone and 14.8 percent bone. The middle period (Yuquot II, 1000 BC–AD 800) runs 0.3 percent flaked stone and 42.7 percent bone, and the late period (Yuquot III, AD 800–1790), with no items of flaked stone, is 41.2 percent bone.

The several sites excavated in the Hesquiat Harbor vicinity (Calvert 1980, Haggarty 1982) date from the period beginning about AD 140 and are thus contemporaneous with only the Queen Charlotte Strait culture type. Three sites for which faunal assemblages were examined in detail share very low proportions of flaked stone and comparatively high ratios of worked bone. For Hesquiat Village the figures are 2.8 percent and 46.1 percent; for Loon Cave, 0.6 percent and 72.7 percent; and for Yaksis Cave, 3.0 percent and 64.7 percent (Calvert 1980:135).

Shoemaker Bay I is the only westcoast component with a faunal assemblage coeval with those of the Obsidian culture type. The early period at Yuquot had such poor preservation of organic material that no analysis has been included in preliminary reports (Dewhirst n.d.). The first five centuries of Yuquot II overlap with the postulated Obsidian span of existence, but the assemblage is considered here along with others of the same age as the Queen Charlotte culture type.

Mammalian faunal material attributed to Shoemaker Bay I (Calvert & Crockford 1982)—mainly contemporaneous with the Obsidian culture type—can be converted to minimum live weight. Using this statistic, deer are most prominent (46.3 percent), followed by black bear (33.9 percent) and harbor seal (14.9 percent). For the fish, also converted to minimum live weight, the order is dogfish (30.9 percent), salmon (23.3 percent), halibut (15.6 percent), and rockfishes (6.1 percent).

Site components concurrent with the Queen Charlotte Strait culture type, and for which faunal analyses are available, include Shoemaker Bay II, Yuquot II and III, and Hesquiat Village, Loon Cave, and Yaksis Cave—all at Hesquiat Harbor.

The Shoemaker Bay II faunal assemblage (Calvert & Crockford 1982) gives deer first position among the mammals with 42.6 percent of the minimum live weight. Deer and elk together are 48.1 percent (see Table 9). Northern sea lions place second at 32.1 percent; all sea mammals total 44.1 percent. Tuna lead the list of fish species (46.0 percent) but it should be recognized that although large and therefore strongly affecting minimum live weight proportions, they were probably rarely caught. After tuna come salmon (19.8 percent), halibut (7.4 percent), and herring (5.0 percent).

We can consider Yuquot II separately from Yuquot III because the former partially overlaps Obsidian culture type components in time. Of the Yuquot II mammals, deer rank first (31.7 percent) when the MNIs (Dewhirst n.d.) are recast as minimum live weight (Table 9). They are followed by northern fur seal (26.5 percent), northern sea lion (22.2 percent), and harbor seal (5.6 percent). Sea mammals altogether account for 65.3 percent. For fish, the order is: salmon, 51.7 percent; ling cod, 33.8 percent; and rockfishes, 13.4 percent.

Yuquot III (Dewhirst n.d.) gives a similar picture (Table 9). Deer are still first (28.2 percent), with northern sea lion next (27.0 percent), followed by northern fur seal (22.2 percent), and porpoises (7.7 percent). Sea mammals total 68.8 percent. The proportions for fish are salmon, 63.4 percent; ling cod, 22.8 percent; and rockfishes, 12.5 percent.

Data from three Hesquiat Harbor sites (Calvert 1980) have been pooled and used to calculate minimum live weights (Table 9). Exclusive of whales, the mammals rank as follows: northern sea lion, 40.7 percent; northern fur seal, 25.7 percent; deer, 9.7 percent; California sea lion, 6.9 percent; and harbor seal, 5.8 percent. Sea mammals (other than whales) equal 86.5 percent. Calvert (1980) notes that, in the various components of the Hesquiat Village site, whale bone amounts to 31–51 percent of the mammal bone count; thus, if MNIs had been determined and these converted to minimum live weights, sea mammals in general and whales in particular would certainly have reduced all other groups or species to insignificant proportions. The fish assemblage here has a much more balanced distribution of species and groups. Dogfish are 30.3 percent, followed by salmon (26.2 percent), rockfishes (12.1 percent), ling cod and other greenlings (9.1 percent), tuna (6.5 percent), and halibut (5.2 percent).

Northern Part of the Central British Columbia Coast

Of the several sites excavated in this area, six are reported in sufficient detail to be of use in comparing artifact or faunal assemblages. These are Namu, Kisameet Bay, and Roscoe Inlet (Hester & Nelson 1978); Nutlitliquotank (R. Carlson 1972); McNaughton Island (R. Carlson 1976); and Grant Anchorage (Simonsen 1973).

Artifacts from the first three sites are reported in such a way that neither site nor component assemblages can be distinguished. However, analysis of a chart portraying the duration of artifact classes grouped from the three sites (Luebbers 1978:66) discloses that 14 of the 15 flaked stone categories have disappeared from the sequence by AD 150 and that all are gone by AD 750. Eleven of the 14 bone categories appear no earlier than about 1350 BC, eight of them, no earlier than 850 BC. About 17 percent of the flaked stone items are classed as microflakes. When microblades (all pre-1350 BC) and microcores are added, the small tool and flake categories reach 54 percent of the flaked stone industry. Judging by the illustrations and information contained in captions, most of these small artifacts are made of obsidian.

On the basis of several beach site collections, R. Carlson (1972) defined a Cathedral phase for the Bella Bella and Bella Coola areas (Apland 1982), provisionally dated at 3000–500 BC. I have not calculated assemblage proportions because only stone has survived in these beach locations. There is a lot of flaked stone at these sites, however, with many items made of a fine-grained basaltic rock and some of obsidian.

For sites of the same general age as the Queen Charlotte Strait culture type, we have more informative assemblages. McNaughton Island's components III and IV combined show flaked stone at 1.5 percent and worked bone 61.1 percent of the pre-contact items (R. Carlson 1976:104–105). The Nutlitliquotlank site (R. Carlson 1972:49), of particular interest because of its location in a boundary zone between Bella Coola (Salishan) and Heiltsuk (Wakashan) territories at contact, is 5.4 percent flaked stone and 31.1 percent worked bone. Among the flaked stone artifacts, quartz and obsidian flakes are particularly prominent.

The Grant Anchorage site (Simonsen 1973) spans the years from about 1500 BC to the time of European contact at the close of the 18th century. There do not appear to be significant changes over time in the assemblage. Bone artifact categories account for 79.6 percent and flaked stone 8.7 percent of the pre-contact items. Some of the "utilized flake" category are made from obsidian, and judging from the illustrations, these would seem to include many of the smaller examples.

Faunal data relevant to this study are available only for mammals for the Namu, Kisameet Bay, Roscoe Inlet, and Grant Anchorage sites, and for mammals and fish for McNaughton Island. The reporting statistic is the simple element count for all sites and categories except mammals at McNaughton Island, for which MNI figures have been published, and for the Grant Anchorage material, for which bone weight is given.

Faunal assemblages of approximately the same age as the Obsidian culture type include Roscoe Inlet, Namu II and III, and the early part of the Grant Anchorage occupation. Conover (1978:96) reports a mammalian faunal assemblage that combines material from Namu II and III (see Table 9). The proportions are as follows: cervids (mostly deer), 53.2 percent; phocids (mostly harbor seal), 11.7 percent; river otter, 6.5 percent; and sea otter, 6.5 percent. The total for sea mammals is 22.5 percent. In the small sample from Roscoe Inlet, cervids rank first at 81.9 percent, followed by phocids and porcupine at 5.6 percent each. In this case, sea mammals amount to but 9.7 percent of the assemblage. As the Grant Anchorage fauna show little change over their 3500 year span, they are discussed when we consider the later period.

For that later period, we have Namu IV and V (930 BC–AD 970), Namu VI and VII (AD 970–1833), and Kisameet Bay (Conover 1978:96); McNaughton Island III/IV (R. Carlson 1976); and Grant Anchorage (Simonsen 1973 and personal communication). The combined Namu IV/V is 67.5 percent cervid and 7.2 percent porcupine (Table 9). All sea mammals (harbor seal, northern fur seal, northern sea lion, sea otter, and porpoises) total 12.0 percent. Namu VI/VII gives cervids first place (47.4 percent), followed by phocids at 24.7 percent, porpoises (8.2 percent), and sea otter (7.2 percent) with sea mammals totalling 44.2 percent. Kisameet Bay is 57.7 percent cervid, 13.4 percent phocid, and 11.3 percent sea otter. All sea mammals amount to 29.9 percent. After conversion to minimum live weight and elimination of species represented by only a single element, the data from McNaughton Island's combined components III and IV (R. Carlson 1976:107) indicate northern sea lion are in first place (39.0 percent), followed by northern fur seal (29.8 percent), and deer (13.0 percent). All sea mammal total 87.0 percent. By element count, salmon are the most important fish (92.7 percent). Data from Grant Anchorage are not identified beyond the categories bird, land mammal, sea mammal, and fish. By bone weight, sea mammals outrank land mammals (64.5 percent to 35.5 percent). This is in contrast to what is reported for Roscoe Inlet and Namu II and III, with which early components the Grant Anchorage occupation overlaps, but is similar to the later McNaughton Island.

Summary of Comparisons

We have seen that in the Strait of Georgia area (including the head of Alberni Inlet) and the northern part of the central British Columbia coast, there are many assemblages within which small, cryptocrystalline flake tools and debitage are prominent. These flake-bearing assemblages are generally early (of approximately the same age as Queen Charlotte Straits' Obsidian culture type) and wherever they occur in the study area, they are later replaced by assemblages in which the flakes are either lacking or of very low incidence.

In most of these same areas, only partly owing to this small flake complex, flaked stone technology is generally prominent and worked bone is generally less significant in the early assemblages. To a more marked degree, the opposite holds true for later assemblages. For the Strait of Georgia and head of Alberni Inlet sites (hereafter referred to simply as Strait of Georgia sites) the average ratio of flaked stone to worked bone is 3.5:1 for Charles and Locarno Beach culture type assemblages and 1:4.2 for the Gulf of Georgia culture type.

For most of the early components in the northern part of the central coast, it is not possible to calculate the above ratio, although flaked stone items obviously either outnumber bone items or are at least abundant. In this as in other characteristics, the Grant Anchorage site differs. Even in the early years of its 35-century occupation, there is a relatively low proportion of flaked stone. By approximately AD 500, other north-central coast artifact assemblages had grown more similar to the one from Grant Anchorage. For the last 1500 years of the precontact sequence, the overall flaked stone to bone ratio of the area is 1:11.

Of our major comparative areas, the west coast is the most aberrant. The flaked stone to bone ratio for the earliest period at Yuquot is 1:14.8; for the middle period at the same site (overlapping both the Obsidian and Queen Charlotte Strait culture types), it is 1:142.3; and for the later site components at Yuquot and Hesquiat Harbor, 1:44.3.

With a change in average flaked stone to bone ratios from 12:1 for the Obsidian culture type to 1:12.1 for the Queen Charlotte Strait culture type, and with high prominence of microflake categories in the early but not the late components, the Queen Charlotte Strait artifact assemblages form a prehistoric sequence that, in pattern, is similar to those of the Strait of Georgia and northern part of the central coast (except for Grant Anchorage) but is different from the west coast. For the late period, the ratios place Queen Charlotte Strait and the northern part of the central coast in a position intermediate between the Strait of Georgia and west coast.

Review of the faunal assemblages reveals a somewhat different pattern. As Table 9 indicates, the proportions of deer (and elk) and sea mammal, although quite variable from site to site, are similar for both early (Charles and Locarno Beach) and late (Gulf of Georgia) culture types of the Strait of Georgia area. The ratio of deer and elk to sea mammals is 3:1 for the early period and 4.2:1 for the late. The overall ratio is 3.5:1.

Components from the northern part of the central coast present a mixed picture. The Namu, Roscoe Inlet, and Kisameet Bay set of sites is fairly consistent over time (Table 9) in that deer and elk dominate sea mammals throughout the sequence. For components contemporaneous with the Obsidian culture type, the ratio is 4.2:1 in favor of cervids; for those of about the same age as the Queen Charlotte Strait culture type, 2:1. The overall ratio is 2.6:1. On the basis of data available (expressed as bone weight), Grant Anchorage, throughout its 3500 years, strongly favors sea mammals. McNaughton Island's Components II and IV also give sea mammals a decided edge (87.0 percent) when the minimum live weight is employed as a measure.

As with its artifacts, the west coast is different in its faunal assemblages. Here, from the start of the sequence, the sea mammal portion of the faunal assemblage dominates the deer/elk part. In this case, the overall ratio is 1:3.2.

In their deer/elk to sea mammal ratios, the Queen Charlotte Strait components are the only ones to exhibit a clear reversal in dominance through time. The Obsidian culture type ratio (1.9:1) is most like those of the Strait of Georgia and the eastern part of the north central coast, while the Queen Charlotte Strait culture type ratio (1:4.8) most closely resembles those of the west coast and the western or "outer" portion of the north central coast.

The relative importance of salmon is a major difference between the early and late occupancies. They rise from an average of 44.2 percent of the Obsidian fish fauna assemblages to 74.2 percent of the Queen Charlotte Strait culture type assemblages. No similar change is apparent in the Strait of Georgia or west coast areas, the only other neighboring regions for which data are available. Indeed, for the Strait of Georgia sites, the proportion is actually reduced—from 43 percent for the combined Charles and Locarno Beach culture types to 19.3 percent for the later Gulf of Georgia culture type.

The extent to which a group concentrated on one or a few resource species or groups of species, as measured by the Index of Qualitative Uniformity, can be summarized as follows. Within the Queen Charlotte Strait area, there is, for the mammals, a reduction in species concentration between the Obsidian and Queen Charlotte Strait culture types (from an IQU of .48 for Hopetown I to one of .22—averaging the Hopetown III and Echo Bay vicinity assemblages) and a somewhat greater increase in concentration for fish (from .21 for the Hopetown I/Echo Bay I average to .53 for the Hopetown III/Echo Bay vicinity average). For the northern part of the central coast, for which only mammalian data are available, there is a similar decline in single-species dependence between earlier components ($\overline{X} = .42$) and later ($\overline{X} = .25$).

A contrast is provided by the Strait of Georgia area. Rather than rising in concentration, fish species dependence remains more or less level between the early (Charles and Locarno Beach culture types) and late (Gulf of Georgia culture type) components. The IQUs, quite variable between sites (Table 7), have a mean of .22 for the early period, .19 for the late. However, mammals show a striking rise in species dependence, going from a mean of .28 for the early components to .60 for the later. As examination of Table 8 shows, the change occurs with comparative uniformity among components within the periods.

Once again, the west coast of Vancouver Island stands out as different. The single-species dependence for mammals (excluding whales, as noted earlier) goes from an IQU of .17 for Yuquot II to a mean of .18 for later components. For fish, the corresponding figures are .33 and .27. The west coast, one would conclude, has seen little or no change over the period surveyed.

INTERPRETATIONS, CONCLUSIONS, AND SPECULATIONS

We have seen that, coincident with marked changes in the character of artifact assemblages, there are major transformations evident in faunal assemblages associated with the Queen Charlotte Strait areas' Obsidian

(3000–500 BC) and Queen Charlotte Straits (AD 300–European contact) culture types. The specific changes are a pronounced shift from deer and other land mammals to seal, sea lion, and other sea mammals (accompanied by a decrease in single-species dependence) and a significant rise in importance of salmon as a food source.

Variation between faunal assemblages of different age can be explained in a number of ways, including chance fluctuation in the samples recovered; inequality in preservation characteristics of the faunal materials or site soils; variation in the season of site occupancy; differences over time in the availability of particular species; and differences in site inhabitants' preferences for or technical ability to acquire particular species.

In accounting for the Queen Charlotte Strait changes, random sample variation can be ruled out, both because sample sizes are reasonable in all cases except Echo Bay I mammals and because comparable shifts are observable in different sites: at Hopetown between components I and III and at Echo Bay between I and II. It is unlikely such parallel changes would occur by coincidence alone. Differential preservation is also an improbable source of major variation within the time span covered. Deer and sea mammal bone are not known to differ significantly in their resistence to decay, and each category is present in both early and late components of the two sites. Salmon, so prominent in the later assemblages, are less common in the earlier. This difference, too, is not likely the result of differential preservation. While the standardized frequency of occurrence of salmon bone does increase greatly between the early and late components at Hopetown (rising from 76.1 to 1030.1 pieces/m^3), that of all other fish remains does not change appreciably. The density in Hopetown I is 103.3/m^3 and in Hopetown III, 106.0. Also, there is no reason to believe the bones of salmon preserve less well than those of other fish.

An alteration in the seasonal pattern of site use could conceivably explain differences over time in faunal assemblages. However, this does not seem a probable cause in the cases under consideration, as it would require proposing a parallel and coincident change in seasonal use at two sites some 30 km apart. And, in any event, the species indicating greatest variation are not subject to major seasonal differences in likelihood of being added to site deposits. Most salmon, although caught during a restricted season, were preserved for later consumption; thus, their bones might enter site deposits at any time. Deer on coastal islands, and seals, sea lions, and porpoises in coastal waters, were essentially available year-round.

If seasonal accessibility is not a likely factor, change in availability of species over a longer run of time is more plausible. Unfortunately, it is difficult to draw many firm conclusions from the available data. We can

say that the decline in relative importance of deer between the Obsidian
and Queen Charlotte Strait culture types is not attributable to scarcity of
deer in the later period. The decline in importance is a *relative* one. When
the occurrence of deer remains is standardized by calculating the number
of elements per cubic meter of site deposit, there is actually an increase
between the two components of the Hopetown site. Density of deer bone
rises from 3.9 elements/m^3 in Hopetown I to 12.7 in Hopetown III. The
lessening in relative importance of deer is entirely attributable to the great
increase in sea mammal remains. At the same site and for the same periods,
harbor seal, for example, rise from .5 to 86.2 elements/m^3.

The growth in salmon and sea mammal remains in the late period is,
however, a real and not just a relative phenomenon, as the already cited
seal and salmon density figures indicate. Unfortunately, so little attention
has been paid to reconstructing the history of northwest coast animal populations that the meaning of the changes is near impossible to interpret.
The most comprehensive summary of regional palaeoenvironments (Fladmark 1975) serves mainly to emphasize how little we know. Fladmark
(1975:204, 209, 293) does conclude, however, that salmon and such predator populations as seal and sea lion in all probability reached "climax
productivity" shortly after 3000 BC, by which time sea levels and various
other environmental factors had attained "dynamic equilibrium."

This suggested date corresponds to the very beginning of the Obsidian
culture type, some 3000 years before the observed expansion in sea mammal and fish remains. While we cannot ignore the possibility that populations of these particular resources did not reach contemporary levels
until less than 2000 years ago, it does seem unlikely. "Modern" clima-
tological conditions, floral communities, sea levels, and river gradients
all seem to have developed much earlier (Fladmark 1975, Heusser 1960),
and we can reasonably assume that marine and riverine fauna would have
developed along with them.

Almost by a process of elimination, we are left with essentially "cultural" explanations for the inter-assemblage variation. Such explanations
are of two main forms: (1) the early and late human occupants differed
in their preference or desire for specific resources; or (2) these populations
differed in their technical or organizational ability to harvest or preserve
the resources. In either case, the distinction could result from alteration
of the local population's habits or capabilities, or from substitution of one
population by another of different culture. With investigation of Queen
Charlotte Strait prehistory only just beginning, it is prudent to avoid definitive choice among these possibilities. I will offer some comments and
speculations, though.

Review of the artifact assemblages reported to date reveals no obvious
technological advantages held by the recent occupants that would permit

them to capture or preserve more salmon or sea mammals than their predecessors. This does not mean such advantages may not have existed; only
that, if they did, no mark seems to have been left in the archaeological
record. With salmon, for example, it is quite conceivable that the adoption
of efficient river traps and more effective drying procedures could appreciably increase the importance of the resource. Equally, the incor-
poration of new means of organizing labor (as, for example, the adoption
of slavery) could have a similar result. In the case of sea mammals, it is
not so easy to suggest what technological or organizational improvements
could have enlarged the harvest. Toggling harpoons, the very effective
sea mammal hunting devices used by the Kwakiutl and all their neighbors
at the time of European contact, are, in fact, characteristic of both the
Obsidian and Queen Charlotte Strait culture types (see ARTIFACT AS-
SEMBLAGES).

The adoption of innovations in resource extraction may have played a
part in producing the faunal assemblage differences we have seen. It is
also possible, though, that new or old occupants of the Queen Charlotte
Strait area for some reason simply desired or required more salmon and
more sea mammals and therefore increased their take over that of their
predecessors. Population pressure could be behind such a drive to expand
the resource base. Alternatively, a way of life that valued a wider range
and greater quantities of resources may simply have become established
in the area. We do not yet have information adequate to choose among
these or other possible explanations for the observed differences.

Nonetheless, I shall offer a very tentative depiction of regional prehistory
to "explain" the distribution of artifact and faunal assemblages in time
and space, although I must emphasize the speculative nature of this reconstruction. The advent of the Queen Charlotte Strait culture type between 500 BC and AD 300 can be interpreted as the arrival in that period
of a "Wakashan" pattern of resource use, and the Obsidian culture type
that it replaces can be seen as an early variant of a "Salishan" pattern.

As a starting point, we can look at the distribution and relationship of
languages of the southern and central British Columbia coast at the time
of European contact (Figure 13). Within this area were five Wakashan
and six Salishan languages, as well as one Tsimshian language (possibly
spoken by those at the Grant Anchorage site). Of prime interest is the
position of the Salishan languages. The northernmost of these, Bella Coola,
in the northern part of the central coast, is separated from the others, all
in the Strait of Georgia area, by two Wakashan languages: Oowekyala,
of the Rivers Inlet Owikeno; and Kwakwala, language of the Southern
Kwakiutl of Queen Charlotte Strait and northern Vancouver Island (Lincoln & Rath 1980:2).

As Suttles & Elmendorf (1962) and Jorgensen (1969) have concluded,

Figure 13. Distribution of Languages of the Central and Southern British Columbia Coast.

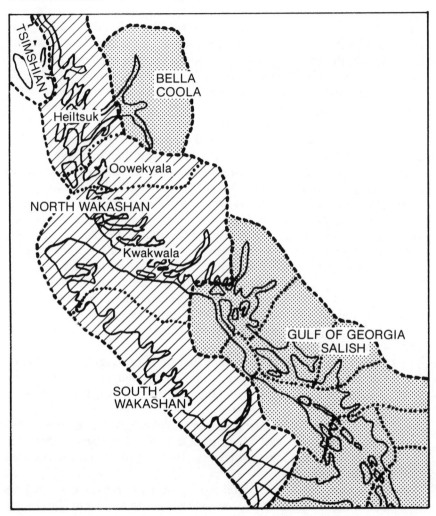

contrary to earlier suggestions, the Bella Coola isolate is more closely related to other coastal Salish languages than to any of the interior Salish forms. Bella Coola is not, therefore, to be explained as a detachment from nearby inland Salish. Bella Coola's closest linguistic congenor is Comox, spoken by those Salish in the northern portion of the Strait of Georgia. The intervening Oowekyala and Kwakwala languages, as part of the North Wakashan branch of the Wakashan stock, are closely related to and, in the case of Kwakwala, contiguous with the South Wakashan or Nootkan languages of Vancouver Island's west coast. These North Wakashan-speaking populations can be viewed as a late expansion of people or languages from the northern end of Vancouver Island into the Queen Charlotte Strait and Queen Charlotte Sound areas.

Jorgensen (1969:52) suggests that the Bella Coola moved into their present location from a homeland to the south. On the other hand, it is possible to see the linguistic isolation as the result of Wakashan intrusion into what was once a Salish continuum extending from at least Bella Coola to the Strait of Georgia (Suttles & Elmendorf 1962:47–48).

Although the linking of linguistic and archaeological data must be undertaken warily and can probably never be more than tentative, the archaeological data I have presented for the area between the Bella Coola and the Strait of Georgia Salish do seem to support the "Wakashan intrusion" interpretation. Put most simply, the early, Obsidian culture type has artifact and faunal assemblages that resemble those of contemporary and later components from the Strait of Georgia and eastern part of the north central coast but not those from the west coast of Vancouver Island or the western part of the north central coast. The late, Queen Charlotte Strait culture type, on the other hand, in its general artifact and faunal characteristics resembles the earlier and contemporary components of the west coast and the western portion of the north central coast but neither the early nor late parts of sequences for the Strait of Georgia or the eastern part of the north central coast.

A changing pattern of relationships like this fits reasonably well with Suttles & Elmendorf's (1962) reconstruction of linguistic history for the area. The trail of supposition leads, then, to the following reconstruction of central northwest coast prehistory in which, for sake of completeness, I include conjecture about developments in the western portion of the north central coast—an area whose prehistory is particularly unclear but may be enlightened more by an understanding of events to the north than to the east or south.

For some time prior to the period 500 BC–AD 300, populations speaking languages of the Salishan stock occupied the eastern portion of Vancouver Island and the adjacent mainland northward at least to the area of Dean and Burke channels and the Bella Coola valley, while populations speaking languages of the Wakashan stock were to be found at least on the west coast of Vancouver Island—perhaps only on the central part of that shore, perhaps along the entire western shore and even on the outer islands to the north of Queen Charlotte Sound. Sometime between 500 BC and AD 300, Wakashan languages, culture, and, most likely, populations expanded from the northern part of the west coast (and possibly as well from the western islands of the north central coast) at the expense of resident Salishan languages, culture, and, likely, populations. This expansion eastward and, for some, perhaps northward, eventually separated the Bella Coola from other Salishan-speaking peoples and left them with only Wakashan as their coastal neighbors.

Much needs to be accomplished before this possible interpretation can become a probable reconstruction—or before it can be effectively refuted. We need more data from sites on the west coast of Vancouver Island— especially from the northern part of that coast where, to date, not a single site has been excavated. We need information on the presently unknown and perhaps critically important 500 BC–AD 300 period in the Queen Charlotte Strait area. And, above all, we need to recover and examine human skeletal material from all periods and regions to explore the likelihood of population expansion and replacement. This essay has established that there were significant changes through time in the Queen Charlotte Strait area's artifact and faunal assemblages and in apparent patterns of resource use. We need now to discover how and why these changes occurred.

ACKNOWLEDGMENTS

Field work at Hopetown Village was led in 1973 by Sharon Keen and by me in 1975. In both seasons, the crew consisted mainly of members of the Kwawwawaineuk band. Elsie Williams, of Hopetown, was instrumental in obtaining Department of Indian Affairs cultural grants for both years of work, and she ably assisted in guiding the project. The Echo Bay vicinity sites were excavated in 1973 as an exercise involving the men and officers of C Company, 3rd Battalion, Princess Patricia's Canadian Light Infantry. I was assisted in field direction and technical support by members of the British Columbia Provincial Museum's Archaeology and Conservation Divisions and employees of what was then the Archaeological Sites Advisory Board.

Analysis of the faunal remains has been a protracted affair involving many people and diverse sources of funds. Of prime importance and a "constant" in the process has been Becky Wigen, who has guided a succession of student screeners and sorters through the steps of faunal analysis and who has been personally responsible for the bulk of the identification and the MNI calculations. The Echo Bay vicinity analysis was a separate subproject, under Becky Wigen's direction, handled by Bob Hogg.

Analysis has been funded by University of Victoria faculty research grants, a British Columbia Heritage Trust Student Employment Program grant, and several seasons of the Province of British Columbia's summer employment and winter work study programs.

I am grateful to Bjorn Simonsen and John Dewhirst for providing additional, unpublished data from sites they excavated and to Leland Donald for pointing the way to the IQU.

NOTES

1. The invention of indices of diversity or "evenness" has been a fertile field for statistically-minded ecologists, sociologists, and linguists (see, e.g., Greenberg 1956, Legendre & Legendre 1983:97–112, Lieberson 1969, Pielou 1975:5–18). Grayson (1984:158–167) discusses several of the ecological indices; while it might be desirable to use one already established in the archaeological literature, unfortunately, the ones he has selected are open-ended—thus producing values that do not lend themselves easily to comparison. Perhaps more important, the resulting numbers are not intuitively interpretable.

I have chosen, instead, the Index of Qualitative Uniformity (IQU), a measure based on variance that is discussed but only indirectly named by Mueller et al. (1977:179–181). Because IQU is standardized, the problem of differing sample sizes is eliminated and the measure is given a fixed scale on which to range.

The use of standard deviation was considered, in the light of Ray & Singer's (1973:429) discussion, but as use of variance will be more sensitive to concentration of counts in a single category, and as this would seem to be a desirable feature of any index selected for this study, I have stayed with variance.

The general formula for the index of qualitative uniformity is $\frac{\sigma_o^2}{\sigma_m^2}$ where o = observed values and m = maximum possible value. The working formula is

$$IQU = \frac{\frac{1}{k} \Sigma (Ni - \overline{N})^2}{(k-1)\overline{N}^2}$$

where N = number of units, i = the ith category, and k = number of categories.

2. After Bellrose (1980:29–33), identified duck specimens are grouped into the following "tribes":

(1) Dabbling ducks (tribe Anatini), including mallard, pintail, gadwall, widgeon, shoveller, and teals.
(2) Bay ducks (tribe Aythyini), including scaups and canvasback.
(3) Sea ducks (tribe Mergini), including oldsquaw, harlequin, goldeneyes, mergansers, bufflehead, and scoters.

3. I have used the term "porpoise" as a short way of referring to the delphinidae—porpoises, dolphins, and blackfish. The species most likely represented in sites south of the northern end of Vancouver Island, including the Hopetown and Echo Bay sites, is the harbor porpoise *(Phocoena phocoena)*, and north of this area, the Dall porpoise *(Phocoenoides dalli)*.

REFERENCES

Albright, S.L. (1984) *Tahltan Ethnoarchaeology*. Burnaby: Department of Archaeology, Simon Fraser University, Publication 15.

Apland, B. (1982) "Chipped Stone Assemblages from the Beach Sites of the Central Coast."
    Pp. 13–63 in P. Hobler (ed.) *Papers on Central Coast Archaeology*. Burnaby: Department
    of Archaeology, Simon Fraser University, Publication 10.
Banfield, A.W.F. (1974) *The Mammals of Canada*. Toronto: University of Toronto Press.
Beattie, O.B. (1972) "Salvage Archaeology at Bliss Landing." Pp. 23–39 in R.L. Carlson
    (ed.) *Reports on Salvage Archaeology undertaken in British Columbia in 1971*. Burnaby:
    Department of Archaeology, Simon Fraser University, Publication 1.
Bellrose, F.C. (1980) *Ducks, Geese & Swans of North America*. Harrisburg, PA: Stackpole
    Books.
Bernick, K. (1983) *A Site Catchment Analysis of the Little Qualicum River Site: A Wet Site
    on the East Coast of Vancouver Island*. Ottawa: National Museum of Man Mercury
    Series, Archaeological Survey of Canada, Paper 118.
Boas, F. (1891) "The Nootka." Pp. 582–604 & 668–679 in *Report of the Sixtieth Meeting
    of the British Association for the Advancement of Science*.
——— (1909) "The Kwakiutl of Vancouver Island." Pp. 307–515 in *Memoirs of the American
    Museum of Natural History*, 8.
Boehm, S.G. (1973) *Cultural and Non-cultural Variation in the Artifact and Faunal Samples
    from the St. Mungo Cannery Site, DqRr 2*. M.A. thesis, University of Victoria.
Borden, C.E. (1975) *Origins and Development of Early Northwest Coast Culture to about
    3000 B.C.* Ottawa: National Museum of Man Mercury Series, Archaeological Survey
    of Canada, Paper 45.
Calvert, S.G. (1980) *A Cultural Analysis of Faunal Remains from Three Archaeological
    Sites in Hesquiat Harbour, B.C.* Ph.D. dissertation, University of British Columbia.
Calvert, S.G., and S. Crockford (1982) "Appendix IV: Analysis of Faunal Remains from
    the Shoemaker Bay Site (DhSe 2)." Pp. 174–219 in A.D. McMillan & D.E. St. Claire
    *Alberni Prehistory: Archaeological and Ethnographic Investigations on Western Van-
    couver Island*. Penticton, BC: Theytus Books.
Capes, K.H. (1964) *Contributions to the Prehistory of Vancouver Island*. Pocatello: Oc-
    casional Papers of the Idaho State University Museum, 15.
——— (1977) "Archaeological Investigations of the Millard Creek Site, Vancouver Island,
    British Columbia." *Syesis* 10:57–84.
Carlson, C. (1979) "The Early Component at Bear Cove." *Canadian Journal of Archaeology*
    3:177–193.
——— (n.d.) Final Report on Excavations at Bear Cove. Unpublished draft manuscript,
    Heritage Conservation Branch, Victoria, BC, 1980.
Carlson, R.L. (1972) "Excavations at Kwatna." Pp. 41–57 in R.L. Carlson (ed.) *Reports
    on Salvage Archaeology undertaken in British Columbia in 1971*. Burnaby: Department
    of Archaeology, Simon Fraser University, Publication 1.
——— (1976) "The 1974 Excavations at McNaughton Island." Pp. 99–114 in R.L. Carlson
    (ed.) *Current Research Reports*. Burnaby: Department of Archaeology, Simon Fraser
    University, Publication 3.
——— (n.d.) "Prehistory of the Northwest Coast." Pp. 13–32 in R.L. Carlson (ed.) *Indian
    Art Traditions of the Northwest Coast*. Burnaby: Archaeology Press, Simon Fraser
    University.
Casteel, R.W. (1976) "Fish Remains from Glenrose." Pp. 82–87 in R.G. Matson (ed.) *The
    Glenrose Cannery Site*. Ottawa: National Museum of Man Mercury Series, Archaeo-
    logical Survey of Canada, Paper 52.
Chapman, M.W. (1982) Archaeological Investigations at the O'Connor Site, Port Hardy.
    Pp. 65–132 in P. Hobler (ed.) *Papers on Central Coast Archaeology*. Burnaby: De-
    partment of Archaeology, Simon Fraser University, Publication 10.
Charlton, A.S. (1980) *The Belcarra Park Site*. Burnaby: Department of Archaeology, Simon
    Fraser University, Publication 9.

Clemens, W.A., and G.V. Wilby (1949) *Fishes of the Pacific Coast of Canada*. Ottawa: Fisheries Research Board of Canada, Bulletin 68.

Conover, K. (1978) "Matrix Analysis." Pp. 67–99 in J.J. Hester & S.M. Nelson (eds.) *Studies in Bella Bella Prehistory*. Burnaby: Department of Archaeology, Simon Fraser University, Publication 5.

Dewhirst, J. (1980) *The Indigenous Archaeology of Yuquot, a Nootkan Outside Village*. Ottawa: National Historic Parks & Sites Branch, History & Archaeology 39.

—— (n.d.) "An Archaeological Pattern of Faunal Resource Utilization at Yuquot, a Nootkan Outside Village: 1000 B.C.–A.D. 1966." Paper presented before the Society for American Archaeology, Vancouver, 1979.

Drucker, P. (1951) *The Northern and Central Nootkan Tribes*. Washington, DC: Bureau of American Ethnology, Bulletin 144.

Fladmark, K.R. (1975) *A Paleoecological Model for Northwest Coast Prehistory*. Ottawa: National Museum of Man Mercury Series, Archaeological Survey of Canada, Paper 43.

Grayson, D.K. (1984) *Quantitative Zooarchaeology: Topics in the Analysis of Archaeological Faunas*. Orlando: Academic Press.

Greenberg, J. (1956) "The Measurement of Linguistic Diversity." *Language* 32:109–115.

Haggarty, J.C. (1982) *The Archaeology of Hesquiat Harbour: The Archaeological Utility of an Ethnographically Defined Social Unit*. Ph.D. dissertation, Washington State University.

Haggarty, J.C., and J.H.W. Sendey (1976) *Test Excavation at the Georgeson Bay Site, Gulf of Georgia Region, British Columbia*. Victoria: Occasional Papers of the British Columbia Provincial Museum, 19.

Ham, L.C. (1982) *Seasonality, Shell Midden Layers, and Coast Salish Subsistence Activities at the Crescent Beach Site, DqRr 1*. Ph.D. dissertation, University of British Columbia.

Hart, J.L. (1973) *Pacific Fishes of Canada*. Ottawa: Fisheries Research Board of Canada, Bulletin 180.

Hester, J.J., and S.M. Nelson, eds. (1978) *Studies in Bella Bella Prehistory*. Burnaby: Department of Archaeology, Simon Fraser University, Publication 5.

Heusser, C.J. (1960) *Late-Pleistocene Environments of North Pacific America*. New York: American Geographical Society, Special Publication 35.

Imamoto, S. (1976) "An Analysis of the Glenrose Faunal Remains." Pp. 21–41 in R.G. Matson (ed.), *The Glenrose Cannery Site*. Ottawa: National Museum of Man Mercury Series, Archaeological Survey of Canada, Paper 52.

Jorgensen, J.G. (1969) *Salish Language and Culture*. Bloomington: Indiana University Publications, Language Science Monograph 3.

Kenny, R.A. (1974) *Archaeological Investigation at the Willows Beach Site, Southeastern Vancouver Island*. M.A. thesis, University of Calgary.

Legendre, L., and P. Legendre (1983) *Numerical Ecology*. Amsterdam: Elsevier.

Lieberson, S. (1969) "Measuring Population Diversity." *American Sociological Review* 34:850–862.

Lincoln, N.J., and J.C. Rath (1980) *North Wakashan Comparative Root List*. Ottawa: National Museum of Man Mercury Series, Canadian Ethnology Service, Paper 68.

Luebbers, R. (1978) "Excavations: Stratigraphy and Artifacts." Pp. 11–66 in J.J. Hester & S.M. Nelson (eds.) *Studies in Bella Bella Prehistory*. Burnaby: Department of Archaeology, Simon Fraser University, Publication 5.

McMillan, A.D., and D.E. St. Claire (1982) *Alberni Prehistory: Archaeological and Ethnographic Investigations on Western Vancouver Island*. Penticton, BC: Theytus Books.

McMurdo, J. (1974) *The Archaeology of Helen Point, Mayne Island*. M.A. thesis, Simon Fraser University.

Matson, R.G., ed. (1976) *The Glenrose Cannery Site*. Ottawa: National Museum of Man Mercury Series, Archaeological Survey of Canada, Paper 52.

Mitchell, D.H. (1968) "Excavations at Two Trench Embankments in the Gulf of Georgia Region." *Syesis* 3:29–46.

———— (1969) "Site Surveys in the Johnstone Strait Region." *Northwest Anthropological Research Notes* 3:193–216.

———— (1971a) "The Dionisio Point Site and Gulf Culture History." *Syesis* 4:145–168.

———— (1971b) Archaeology of the Gulf of Georgia Area, a Natural Region and its Culture Types. *Syesis* 4, Supplement 1.

———— (1974) "Salvage Excavations at Site DjSf 13, Buckley Bay, British Columbia." Pp. 88–92 in W.J. Byrne (compiler), *Archaeological Salvage Projects 1973*. Ottawa: National Museum of Man Mercury Series, Archaeological Survey of Canada, Paper 26.

———— (1979a) "Bowker Creek: a Microblade Site on Southeastern Vancouver Island." *Syesis* 12:77–100.

———— (1979b) "Excavations at the Hopetown Village Site (EfSq 2) in the Knight Inlet Area of British Columbia." Pp. 87–99 in *Annual Report for the Year 1976, Activities of the Provincial Archaeologist's Office of British Columbia and Selected Research Reports*. Victoria: Ministry of Provincial Secretary and Government Services, Government of British Columbia.

———— (1980) "DcRt 1: a Salvaged Excavation from Southern Vancouver Island." *Syesis* 13:37–51.

———— (1981a) "Test Excavations at Randomly Selected Sites in Eastern Queen Charlotte Strait." Pp. 103–123 in K.R. Fladmark (ed.) *Fragments of the Past: British Columbia Archaeology in the 1970s (BC Studies* 48).

———— (1981b) "DcRu 78: a Prehistoric Occupation of Fort Rodd Hill National Historic Park." *Syesis* 14:131–150.

———— (n.d.a) "The Later Prehistory of the Southern Coast of British Columbia and Northwestern Washington." In W.P. Suttles (ed.) *Handbook of North American Indians, Volume 7, Northwest Coast*. Washington, DC: Smithsonian Institution.

———— (n.d.b) "The J. Puddleduck Site: a Northern Strait of Georgia Locarno Beach Component and its Predecessor." Unpublished manuscript, 1986.

Monks, G.G. (1977) *An Examination of Relationships between Artifact Classes and Food Resource Remains at Deep Bay, DiSe 7*. Ph.D. dissertation, University of British Columbia.

———— (1980) "Saltery Bay: a Mainland Archaeological Site in the Northern Strait of Georgia." *Syesis* 13:109–136.

Mueller, J.H., K.F. Schuessler, and H.L. Costner (1977) *Statistical Reasoning in Sociology*. Boston: Houghton Mifflin.

Nowak, R.M., and J.L. Paradiso (1983) *Walker's Mammals of the World*. Baltimore: Johns Hopkins.

Palmer, E.L. (1949) *Fieldbook of Natural History*. New York: McGraw-Hill.

Pielou, E.C. (1975) *Ecological Diversity*. New York: John Wiley & Sons.

Ray, J.L., and J.D. Singer (1973) "Measuring the Concentration of Power in the International System." *Sociological Methods & Research* 1:403–437.

Sapir, E. (1914) "A Girl's Puberty Ceremony among the Nootka Indians." *Proceedings and Transactions of the Royal Society of Canada* 3(2):67–80.

Scheffer, V.B. (1958) *Seals, Sea Lions & Walruses: a Review of the Pinnipedia*. Stanford: Stanford University Press.

Simonsen, B.O. (1973) *Archaeological Investigations in the Hecate Strait-Milbanke Sound Area of British Columbia*. Ottawa: National Museum of Man Mercury Series, Archaeological Survey of Canada, Paper 13.

Suttles, W., and W.W. Elmendorf (1962) "Linguistic Evidence for Salish Prehistory." Pp. 41–52 in V.E. Garfield (ed.) *Symposium on Language and Culture. Proceedings of the 1962 Annual Spring Meeting of the American Ethnological Society.* Seattle: University of Washington.

Teres, J.T. (1980) *The Audubon Society Encyclopedia of North American Birds.* New York: Alfred A. Knopf.

Trace, A.A. (1981) *An Examination of the Locarno Beach Phase as Reported at the Crescent Beach Site, DqRr 1, British Columbia.* M.A. thesis, Simon Fraser University.

White, T.E. (1953) "A Method of Calculating the Percentage of Various Food Animals Utilized by Aboriginal Peoples." *American Antiquity* 19:396–398.

Wigen, R.J.S. (1980) *A Faunal Analysis of Two Middens on the East Coast of Vancouver Island.* M.A. thesis, University of Victoria.

Ziegler, A.C. (1973) "Inference from Prehistoric Faunal Remains." Reading, MA: Addison-Wesley Publishing Co., Module in Anthropology 43.

PART IV

ARCHAEOLOGICAL OVERVIEW

ARCHAEOLOGY AND THE STUDY OF NORTHWEST COAST ECONOMIES

Donald Mitchell and Leland Donald

INTRODUCTION

This essay outlines dominant characteristics of Northwest Coast economic systems at the time of Euro-American contact and assesses the extent to which archaeological investigations have succeeded in reconstructing the region's earlier economies. The economic sector of a culture is taken to include all aspects of the production, distribution, and consumption of goods and services. More specifically, it concerns the acquisition of raw materials and their transformation into products desired by various segments of society. It also involves the storage of these products and their eventual distribution to consumers or exchange for other goods and services. What are commonly referred to as services are made available by the economy and to varied extent may be allocated by the same sector.

While we have attempted to cover a wide range of activities commonly considered economic, our description omits detailed discussion of sub-

Research in Economic Anthropology, Supplement 3, pages 293–351.
Copyright © 1988 by JAI Press Inc.
All rights of reproduction in any form reserved.
ISBN: 0-89232-818-5

sistence or manufacturing technology. Reasonably complete pictures of Northwest Coast technological variation are provided by the early culture element surveys (Barnett 1939, Drucker 1950) and by more recent analyses (Donald & Mertton 1975, Jorgensen 1980). Further descriptions of technology are to be found in Drucker (1963, 1965), Goddard (1945), and H. Stewart (1977). We have concentrated on some less commonly discussed aspects of economic activity: use of resources, the annual round, units of production, ownership of resources, preservation and storage of foods, wealth, distribution and redistribution, exchange and trade, and units of consumption.

ECONOMIES OF THE EARLY CONTACT PERIOD

In this essay, the term "Northwest Coast" includes all those groups who inhabited the north Pacific coast of North America from the vicinity of Yakutat Bay in southeast Alaska to the lower reaches of the Columbia River. For the most part, Northwest Coast groups were truly "coastal," having direct access to the sea or one of its inlets penetrating the largely mountainous coastline; nevertheless, groups inhabiting the lower portions of the great rivers of the region are also considered to belong to the culture area. As we define it, the Northwest Coast is bordered by four other major culture areas: Arctic, Mackenzie-Yukon, Plateau, and Oregon Coast-California.

The time of greatest interest here is the close of the 18th and opening of the 19th centuries—the period of earliest contact with Europeans for most Northwest Coast peoples. Some of the data available relate directly to this period, but most of the usable environmental and ethnographic information was collected much later. These data are used to make more or less secure inferences about resources and economic organization from about 1775 to 1825.

Although the Northwest Coast is fairly distinct from neighboring culture areas (Jorgensen 1980), there is also internal variation that should not be ignored (Donald & Mertton 1975; Jorgensen 1969, 1980). We have found the most desirable unit of analysis to be the local group: a set of people who shared a common winter village and who acted as a social unit at least part of each year. Many neighboring local groups shared a common language and culture, but there was still group to group variation, and each local group was an independent social and political unit. Unfortunately, little of the available information has focussed on a specific local group or its territory, and in our overview we have had to settle for a compromise. We offer details of economic life specific to the following groups, selected both for the quality or apparent completeness of their ethnographic record and with attention to broad geographic representation (Figure 1):

1. *Chilkat Tlingit:* There were four local groups in the lower Chilkat River valley of southeastern Alaska collectively referred to as the Chilkat. Each of the four villages was politically autonomous, but there were probably no major cultural differences among them. In any event, the principal ethnographers, Kalervo Oberg (1973) and Aurel Krause (1956), grouped them and we have followed suit.

2. *Metlakatla Tsimshian:* Some nine local groups that traditionally wintered in close proximity just north of the Skeena River mouth have been the subject of almost all Coast Tsimshian ethnographic accounts. The principal accounts are those of Franz Boas (1916) and Viola Garfield (1939, 1951). Each village community was independent. We can assume a high degree of cultural similarity among the nine.

3. *Fort Rupert Kwakiutl:* Similar to the Metlakatla Tsimshian situation, the bulk of what purports to be southern Kwakiutl ethnography actually pertains largely to those four local groups that assembled around the Fort Rupert trading post. However, these groups seem to have attained an additional degree of social cohesiveness (Donald & Mitchell 1975:328) that allows us greater confidence in treating them as a single unit. The main sources are Edward Curtis (1915) and Franz Boas (1897, 1909, 1921, 1935; and Codere 1966).

4. *Nuuchahnulth (or Nootka):* Philip Drucker's (1951) account of the northern and central "Nootka" provides a wealth of information on economic activities, although it does not permit ready identification of local group practices. Where practicable, we give details for the Hesquiat, a central Nuuchahnulth group whose five independent winter villages were situated on or near Hesquiat Harbor, and the Kyuquot, a "confederacy" of four local groups whose winter villages were at Kyuquot Sound in the northern Nuuchahnulth area. There was no significant overall political unity to the Hesquiat Harbor settlements, but those at Kyuquot Sound were seasonally united and in residence at a single summer village.

5. *Gulf of Georgia Salish:* From the large number of ethnic and local groups falling within this grouping, we have selected the Squamish for specific attention whenever possible. The Squamish people occupied 15 independent winter villages stretching up the Squamish River and its tributaries at the head of Howe Sound on the Strait

Figure 1. Archaeological Regions and Locations of Winter Settlements of Groups in Sample

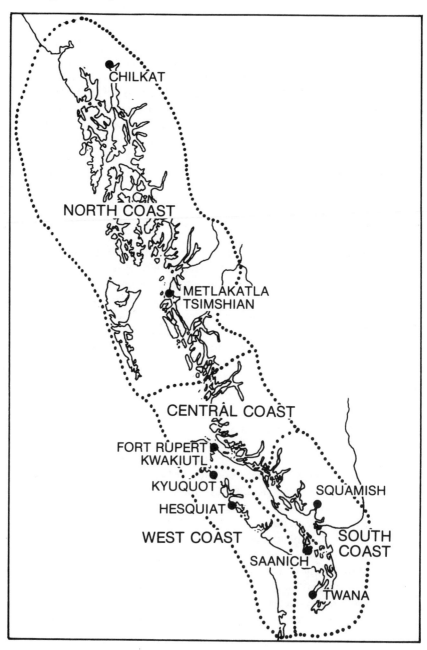

of Georgia's eastern shore. Homer Barnett (1939, 1955) is the principal ethnographer.

6. *Straits Salish:* When possible, we have tried to focus on the East Saanich, whose five or six independent settlements were at Saanichton Bay on southeastern Vancouver Island and on islands immediately to the east, and the nearby West Saanich, whose four villages were on the shores of Saanich Inlet (Barnett 1955:19; Suttles 1974:79). However, as the principal ethnographer, Wayne Suttles (1974), most often does not distinguish the Saanich from other Straits groups in his descriptions of the culture, we have necessarily resorted to more general discussion of Straits Salish economic behavior. Like Suttles (1974) and Barnett (1955), we omit the linguistically-related Klallam from our generalizations.

7. *Twana Salish:* A set of nine independent local groups, the Twana people spoke a different language from their neighbors. They lived on or near the shores of Hood Canal in the western part of Puget Sound. William Elmendorf (1960) is the main source on the traditional economy of the Twana.

Our most specific attribution of economic behavior is for the Chilkat Tlingit, Metlakatla Tsimshian, Fort Rupert Kwakiutl, and Twana Salish; our least specific is for the Gulf of Georgia Salish, Straits Salish, and Nuuchahnulth.

As some indication of the sizes of these local-group economies, we provide population estimates for the groups in our sample. Table 1 lists our results, based on the earliest available figures and modified by an entirely subjective process that includes inflating modestly to compensate for the probable effects of postcontact disease, ignoring counts that seem grossly high or improbably low, and judiciously rounding. In the only two cases in which our figures can be checked against early local group (or single settlement) counts independent of those used to develop the entries in Table 1, there is approximate agreement. Douglas (1853:14) gave 111 and 154 for two West Saanich local groups. Vancouver (1798:242) reported what is likely a Twana village or camp on Hood Canal that in May 1792 held about 60 people.

We can see that the politically autonomous Northwest Coast local groups represented small-scale domestic economies, seldom involving more than a few hundred people. Although these units were self-sufficient for the production of basic food, clothing, shelter, and transportation, they were nevertheless all tied into networks of exchange, gift-giving, and plundering that made each a part of larger, regional economies whose operation affected populations numbering in the thousands.

Table 1. Population Estimates for Local Groups

Group	Number of Local Groups	Estimate	Average Local Group Size
Chilkat	4	1500	375
Metlakatla Tsimshian	9	3000	390
Fort Rupert Kwakiutl	4	1500	375
Kyuquot	4	1000	250
Hesquiat	4	500	125
Squamish	15	1000	65
Saanich	9	1000	110
Twana	9	700	75

RESIDENTIAL UNITS

In this section, we describe the nature of some common and basic residential units: the independent household, extended household, and village. Other varieties, of more restricted distribution and lying between the extended household and village in scale, are also identified.

Independent households are the smallest residential units with at least some measure of autonomy in conduct of their economic activities. Included are both households that center on a nuclear family and those less common ones involving composite families produced by polygynous unions. We should also acknowledge that more distantly related kin (e.g., a grandparent, aunt, or nephew) and nonkin (e.g., slaves) may be part of these households. Residential units of this sort are found among all societies on the Northwest Coast. They have a great deal of economic independence among the central and southern Coast Salish and somewhat less in other groups.

Extended households are also evident throughout the Northwest Coast. These were true "households" in that they occupied a single dwelling unit, but in some places and at some times of the year there was little activity in which they collectively engaged. The independent member households were associated through kin ties, which would usually be close for the principal occupants but might be more distant for others. Frequently, the core independent household heads were brothers, although the families of brothers and their sons (on the south and central coast) or brothers and their sisters' sons (on the north coast) were also common. The bases of affiliation were more firmly defined for the northern matrilineal societies, with their phratries, clans, and lineages, as membership in these groups constrained residential association. For central and south coast groups, there is evidence of much greater flexibility and lower allegiance in extended household membership, although even here there is a relatively enduring core group. Extended households had 4–6 or more component independent households occupying fixed portions of the large dwelling. Each corner was usually defined as a separate residential area, often for the principal independent households. In larger houses, segments of the structure's long sides were allocated to additional individual households.

Each village consisted of several extended households, at least some of which would be allied by kin ties similar to but weaker than those that held together the extended household itself. By whatever process these loosely structured villages were formed, whether by amalgamation or fission, what has been described in the years since contact are social units with a comparatively minor economic role. Their main importance seems to have been for the conduct of ceremonial activity and for defence—although even here there was not always village unity in the face of an enemy.

Of somewhat more significance than villages were subunits consisting of groups of associated extended households. Where these existed, and there is little evidence for them among the Coast Salish, they were kin-based. Among groups of the central coast, the core was a nonunilineal descent group: the Kwakiutl *numaym* and its counterpart, the "local group" of Drucker (1951) and Kenyon (1980), among the Nuuchahnulth. For the north coast, matriclan affiliation provided the basis for association.

RESOURCES

Virtually every writer on the Northwest Coast culture area has commented on the richness of the resource base available to the region's aboriginal inhabitants, and there is no need for us to add to the paeans already made to rivers filled with fish, woodlands crowded with game. A lesser number of writers have argued that cyclical variation in availability, regional disparity in abundance, and local difference in species diversity are also important Northwest Coast resource characteristics (Piddocke 1965; Riches 1979; Suttles 1960, 1962; Vayda 1961). Systematic analysis of the character of this resource base is rare, however, and there is almost no detailed documentation of variation and its implications. A thorough and complete environmental analysis is obviously beyond the scope of this essay, but we can give some attention to these problems.

The most comprehensive analysis of environments exploited by native Americans known to us is in Jorgensen's (1980) *Western Indians*. Jorgensen rates 172 western Indian tribal territories on 132 environmental variables (including 70 faunal and 55 floral). Twenty-seven of his 172 tribal units are Northwest Coast groups as defined here. All but two of these

(Gitksan Tsimshian and Upper Stalo Salish) fall within a coastal environment that stretches from Yakutat Bay to northern California. The two exceptions belong to a "Northwest River" environment that reflects their distance from the sea. Of the 25 coast environment groups, 24 belong to what Jorgensen calls a Northwest Coast environment. These groups have an average of over 85 percent environmental similarity on the variables measured. The remaining tribal unit, the Lower Chinook, has an average of over 80 percent similarity with the Northwest Coast environments. Jorgensen (1980:20–28) places the Lower Chinook environment in a set of Oregon Coast environments that is transitional between the Northwest Coast and Northern California Coast. He shows that Northwest Coast environments are clearly distinct from those of surrounding culture areas, but his variables are too broadly defined to reveal much about environmental variation within the culture area. Additionally, only a few of his variables are attempts directly to assess resource potential.

The biologists' classifications of biotic areas or biogeoclimatic zones of the region are helpful, but they also tend to be too general, with usefulness further hampered by the fact that no classification system has yet been applied across modern political boundaries. There are three different prevailing schemes in Alaska, British Columbia, and Washington. One of the most useful outlines is that of Munro & Cowan (1947). It takes into account a wide range of plants and animals and has been applied to most of our area. They recognized 15 biotic areas within British Columbia, seven of which are found in the Northwest Coast culture area. Salient features of these seven zones are given in Table 2. Each is very large and there is obviously room for much internal variation. Plant and animal species listed in the table include only the most typical species and by no means exhaust the range present. There is also much overlap of species from area to area.

Most local group territories lie within one terrestrial biotic area, although some Tsimshian, Tlingit, and northern Wakashan groups had access to the northern or southern alplands, as well. In addition, most groups could make use of the coast littoral. Munro & Cowan (1947) and others who classify biotic areas also tend to ignore fish and all invertebrates—which, along with sea mammals, were undoubtedly the most important parts of the region's fauna for its aboriginal inhabitants.

The relative importance of fish and marine invertebrates emerges clearly from Fladmark's 1975 attempt to rank the value of faunal resources for the culture area. The top 15 categories in Fladmark's ranking—based on his interpretation of information in ethnographies for the Coast Salish, Nuuchahnulth, Coast Tsimshian, central Tlingit, southern Kwakiutl, and Haida—are: (1) salmon, (2) halibut, (3) herring, (4) other fish, (5) sea mammals, (6) eulachon, (7) bear, (8) shellfish, (9) deer, (10) wapiti, (11) small land mammals, (12) waterfowl, (13) sea urchins, (14) mountain goat, (15) mountain sheep. Although we are not convinced of the accuracy of some of the ratings—bear, for example, seeming too high, especially in relation to shellfish and waterfowl—the overall picture presented is clear: marine resources were especially important. The place of salmon as the leading resource is confirmed, and the fact that six of the top ten resources are fish or marine invertebrates highlights the importance of this aspect of the fauna for traditional exploitation patterns.

Although salmon are rightfully considered the most important single resource for the culture area as a whole, there was, in fact, considerable variation among local groups in the relative importance of these fish and of other resources (Table 3). Eulachon, herring, halibut, marine mammals, waterfowl, and shellfish all made significant, sometimes crucial contributions to the subsistence of one or another Northwest Coast groups (Folan 1984). Furthermore, although plants have received very little attention compared to fauna, their importance in the regional economies should not be overlooked. An indication of just how much Northwest Coast people desired plant foods is their enthusiastic adoption of the potato as a crop. Despite absence of any significant tradition of horticulture (except the tending of tobacco plants), the Haida were producing enough potatoes within a few years of their introduction to begin exporting them to mainland Tsimshian. Wherever introduced, the potato promptly became a staple (Suttles 1951).

Not only did the various berries, seaweeds, bulbs, and roots supply valuable foodstuffs, but the forests were the source of timber and bark—important raw materials for shelter, transportation, clothing, and subsistence technology. Access to a stand of red or yellow cedar was likely as important as access to a clam bed or herring spawning ground.

As a resource, salmon are the most singular feature of the Northwest Coast environment. All five species of Pacific salmon available in the region are anadromous. Aboriginal exploitation occurred largely in the rivers and streams as the salmon returned to their natal waters to spawn and sometimes in the narrow saltwater approaches to these spawning grounds. Major rivers had spectacularly large spawning populations, and even quite modest streams might have sizable runs. Even so, not all local groups had access to significant runs, and a very few possessed no salmon streams at all. For example, when the salmon resources of 79 Wakashan local group territories are assessed, three are found to contain no salmon streams and another four to have salmon runs too small to make important contributions to subsistence. Thus, for nearly ten percent of these territories, the taking of salmon could not have played a major role in procurement strategy. Non-Wakashan territories probably exhibited a similar pattern of variation in salmon availability. While salmon are without question the

Table 2. Characteristics of Selected Biotic Areas and Climatic Features (after Munro & Cowan 1947)

| Biotic Area | Annual Precipitation (cm) | Temperature (°C) | | Frost-free Days | Typical Flora | Typical Fauna |
		Mean Minimum	Mean Maximum			
Coast Forest	125 to 375	−2° to +2°	15° to 21°	200 to 250	Western hemlock, Western red cedar, Sitka spruce, mountain hemlock, Douglas fir, salal, red huckleberry, salmon berry	Columbia blacktail deer, Roosevelt elk, pileated woodpecker, hairy woodpecker, grey jay
Southern Alplands	100 to 125	−20° to −15°	20° to 21°	50 to 100	heaths, Alpine firs, dwarf willows	bog lemming, hoary marmot, mountain goat, Columbian ground squirrel, ptarmigan
Northern Alplands	Exact data are not available, but this area is colder and drier than the Southern alplands.				similar to Southern alplands	brown lemming, Parry ground squirrel, thinhorn sheep, gyrfalcon

Gulf Islands	60 to 90	−1° to +2°	21° to 24°	230 to 275	Garry oak, madrona, red alder	coast deer, widgeon, scoter, scaup
Puget Sound Lowlands	90 to 150	−7° to −1°	21° to 24°	230 to 275	red alder, broad leaf maple	(see Gulf Islands biotic area)
Queen Charlotte Islands	175 to 200	−2° to −1°	18° to 19°	165	Sitka spruce, Western red cedar, yellow cyprus, Western hemlock	wandering shrew, black bear, marten, Dawson caribou, Canada goose
Coast Littoral						harbour seal, northern sea lion, California sea lion, sea otter, harbour porpoise, Dall porpoise, killer whale, humpback whale, grey whale, double-crested cormorant

303

Table 3. Ranking of Ocean-based, Freshwater-based, Game, and Vegetative Resources

Group	Resource Types			
	Ocean-based	*Freshwater-based*	*Game*	*Vegetative*
Chilkat	1. Herring 2. Shell fish 3. Seal	1. Chum & Coho salmon 2. Eulachon	1. Deer 2. Mountain goat	1. Spruce & Hemlock 2. Berries, Seaweed & Algae
Metlakatla Tsimshian	1½. Halibut 1½. Seal & Sea lion	1. Eulachon 2. Sockeye & Spring salmon	1. Deer 2. Mountain goat 3. Bear	1½. Red cedar 1½. Yellow cedar 3. Berries
Fort Rupert Kwakiutl	1. Herring 2. Seal	1. Salmon 2. Eulachon	1½. Bear 1½. Mountain goat 3. Waterfowl	1. Red cedar 2. Berries 3. Seaweed
Kyuquot	1. Halibut 2. Seal & Sea lion 3. Herring 4. Whale	1. Chum salmon	1. Waterfowl 2. Deer	1. Berries
Hesquiat	1. Halibut 2½. Seal 2½. Herring 4. Whale	1. Chum salmon	1. Waterfowl	1. Berries
Squamish (Salish)	(unknown)	1. Sockeye salmon 2. Spring salmon 3. Sturgeon	1. Mountain goat 2. Deer 3. Birds	1. Red cedar 2. Berries
Saanich (Salish)	1. Sockeye salmon 2. Seal 3. Shellfish	1. Sockeye salmon 2. Spring salmon 3. Sturgeon 4. Eulachon	1. Elk 2. Deer 3. Birds	1. Red cedar 2. Berries 3. Camas
Twana (Salish)	1. Seal & Porpoise 2. Fish	1. Salmon	1. Waterfowl 2. Elk 3. Deer	1. Fern roots & Camas 2. Berries

most important Northwest Coast resource, their importance cannot be taken for granted for a particular local group.

To assist in assessing their significance, we identify four types of resources: ocean-based, freshwater-based, game, and vegetation. Table 4 shows the ranking of each of these types for each local group in our sample. Freshwater-based resources rank first or are at least tied for first position for eight of the nine units—because most salmon are caught in fresh water. The East Saanich used reef nets to take salmon in saltwater, raising the importance to them of ocean-based resources. These rankings emphasize the relative importance of food from each resource category. They tend to underplay the importance of wood in subsistence, transport, and shelter technology. If we could objectively compare resource importance across food and nonfood technologies, "vegetation" would likely come out ahead of "game" for all groups.

We are aware of two attempts to make comprehensive assessments of the proportion contributed to overall subsistence by the exploitation of different types of resources. These are Murdock's (1967:154) ratings of "the estimated relative dependence of the society on each of the five major types of subsistence activity" in the *Ethnographic Atlas* and Jorgensen's (1980) ratings of probable percentages of the diet contributed by various types of subsistence activities, in his *Western Indians*. Murdock provides codings for 19 and Jorgensen for 27 groups within the Northwest Coast culture area as we define it. All of Murdock's list is rated by Jorgensen. Table 5 shows these ratings. There is only modest variation from group to group. Murdock finds more differences than Jorgensen, probably because Murdock's ratings are purportedly more precise. For example, Jorgensen (1980:590) rates all 27 of his groups as having between 51 and 100 percent of their diets "contributed by fish, shellfish, and large aquatic animals procured locally." Murdock (1967:154) rates dependence on

Table 4.   Ranking of Resource Types

Group	Ocean-based	Freshwater-based	Game	Vegetation
Chilkat	4	1	2.5	2.5
Metlakatla Tsimshian	2.5	1	2.5	4
Fort Rupert Kwakiutl	2	1	4	3
Kyuquot	1.5	1.5	3	4
Hesquiat	1.5	1.5	3	4
Squamish	1.5	1.5	3	4
East Saanich	1	2	3	4
West Saanich	1.5	1.5	3	4
Twana	2	1	3	4

Table 5. Relative Dependence on Major Types of Subsistence Activities on the Northwest Coast, as Rated by Murdock (1967) and Jorgensen (1980)

Ethnic Unit	Gathering		Hunting		Fishing	
	Murdock[a]	Jorgensen[b]	Murdock[a]	Jorgensen[b]	Murdock[a]	Jorgensen[b]
N. Tlingit	–	2	–	2	–	4
S. Tlingit	1	2	3	2	6	4
Massett Haida	2	2	2	2	6	4
Skidegate Haida	–	2	–	2	–	4
Tsimshian	2	2	2	2	6	4
Gitksan	–	2	–	2	–	4
Haisla	2	2	3	2	5	4
Haihais	–	2	–	2	–	4
Bella Bella	2	2	3	2	5	4
Ft. Rupert Kwakiutl	3	2	2	2	5	4
Bella Coola	2	2	2	2	6	4
Clayoquot	2	2	2	2	6	4
Makah	2	2	2	2	6	4
Klahuse	–	2	–	2	–	4
Pentlatch	–	2	–	2	–	4
Squamish	2	2	3	2	5	4
Cowichan	2	2	3	2	5	4
W. Saanich	–	2	–	2	–	4
Upper Stalo	3	2	3	2	4	4
Lower Fraser Salish	–	2	–	2	–	4
Lummi	3	2	2	2	5	4
Klallam	1	2	3	2	6	4
Twana	1	2	3	2	6	4
Quinault	2	2	3	2	5	4
Puyallup	3	3	2	2	5	4
Quileute	1	2	3	2	6	4
Lower Chinook	2	2	2	2	6	4

[a]Murdock's ratings: 1 = 6%–15%, 2 = 16%–25%, 3 = 26% to 35%, 4 = 36%–45%, 5 = 46–55%, 6 = 56%–65%.
[b]Jorgensen's ratings: 2 = 5%–25%, 3 = 26%–50%, 4 = 51%–100%.

"fishing, including shellfishing and the pursuit of large aquatic animals" at 36–45 percent for one group, 46–55 percent for eight groups, and 56–65 percent for ten groups. Jorgensen's evaluations inspire more confidence, simply because they do not claim to be so precise. An examination of the sources cited for the Upper Stalo or Tait (Duff 1952; Hill-Tout 1902, 1904) makes one wonder how Murdock could have placed this group in so precise a range as 36–45 percent dependence on fishing. Indeed, in our judgment, the sources for no Northwest Coast group are sufficiently detailed to allow confidence in the application of Murdock's ten-point scale.

Other criticisms are required. We will not critique each rating for each group but will illustrate some of the general problems with a few examples. Wishing precise ratings and comparisons, Murdock attempted to establish a "focus" for each group, to locate both group and information applying to it as accurately as possible in space and time. The Haida focus, for example, was "1890," but no particular group of Haida was specified. In 1890, there were still at least three distinct groups of Haida: Masset, Skidegate, and Kaigani. Although usually minor, there were differences among the groups, including variation in resource bases offered by their respective environments. As well, by 1890 the Haida had been in contact with Europeans for over 100 years and some groups had been growing potatoes for several decades (Suttles 1951). Yet, Murdock reports a complete absence of agriculture for the Haida. It is correct, of course, that the Haida almost certainly did not practice agriculture before European contact, but this would dictate a time focus of 1790, not 1890. Interestingly, this is a group among whom Murdock (1934, 1936) did ethnographic fieldwork. Clearly, for the Northwest Coast, consultation of a few basic ethnographic sources will rarely allow the kind of detailed judgments about subsistence contributions that Murdock hoped to make.

The "fishing" contribution variable raises other problems. Both Murdock and Jorgensen include fish, shellfish, and large aquatic animals in this category. From almost any point of view, however, these are three very different kinds of resources—even ignoring differences between, say, salmon and halibut, clams and mussels, or seals and whales. This is true whether one concentrates on seasonal availability, the technology of procurement, storage possibilities and methods, the division of labor, or the amount of labor expended for each gram of protein or calorie obtained. They even lump together marine and riverine resources.

Altogether, Murdock's (1967) and Jorgensen's (1980) studies tell us very little about variation *on* the Northwest Coast. Thus, Schalk (1979:57) is perhaps not cautious enough when he suggests that even so broad a trend as the "general decline of gathering northward along the coast" is supported by Murdock's estimates. On the other hand, Jorgensen's ratings *do* clearly distinguish the Northwest Coast groups from the rest of Western North America (see his pp. 119–128). It is less clear that Murdock's will even accomplish this (see Driver et al. 1972).

Adjustment of seasonal activities to the cycle of resource availability can be seen in the amount of time spent on each type of resource procurement. Time spent is also an indicator of relative importance of resources. Unfortunately, there are few quantifiable data on time allocation in the literature. One notable exception is Oberg's (1973) Chilkat study, estimates from which are presented as Table 6. Although the reliability of these data and how well they might fit early contact times are difficult

Table 6.   Relative Amounts of Time Spent Each Month by Chilkat
Tlingit on Gathering Resources[a]

Resource Type	Month											
	Mar	Apr	May	Jun	Jul	Aug	Sept	Oct	Nov	Dec	Jan	Feb
Deep-sea fishing	34	30	36	14	—	—	—	10	—	3	3	6
Berry picking	—	—	—	3	8	31	9	—	—	—	—	—
Salmon fishing	—	—	—	—	24	14	80	4	10	—	—	—
Fur gathering	30	13	—	—	—	—	—	—	—	—	—	4
Bark gathering	—	—	20	—	—	—	—	—	—	—	—	—
Shellfish gathering	24	11	9	6	—	—	—	4	10	3	3	4
Hunting	—	18	8	7	—	—	—	29	9	3	3	4
Herb and root gathering	—	—	17	11	7	19	11	—	—	—	—	—
Seaweed gathering	—	28	—	—	—	—	—	—	—	—	—	—

[a]*Source:* Oberg 1973:75. Note that columns rarely add to 100%. For explanation, see text.

to determine, they are almost certainly the best estimates ever likely to
be available. Annoyingly, Oberg's percentages often do not add to 100
and his omissions are difficult to interpret. Nevertheless, the importance
of fish and particularly of salmon stands out.

As Oberg also provides estimates of time spent on major activities by
month, the place of food-getting can be seen within the overall pattern of
Chilkat activity. Table 7 summarizes these estimates and offers a forceful
reminder of the importance of food storage on the Northwest Coast. In
all but one month in which at least 30 percent of the Chilkat's time was
spent on gathering, nearly as much time was spent on storage. If we combine gathering and storage, there are five months when food procurement
takes over 50 percent (range = 65–100) of the time, whereas there are
another five months when food pursuits take less than 15 percent (range
= 2–13) of the time. For seven months, "ceremonialism and leisure"

Table 7.   Relative Amounts of Time Spent Each Month by Chilkat
Tlingit on Major Activities (Rounded to nearest %)[a]

Type of Activity	MONTH											
	Mar	Apr	May	Jun	Jul	Aug	Sep	Oct	Nov	Dec	Jan	Feb
Gathering food	44	55	44	10	31	34	50	24	2	4	2	5
Storing food	41	45	42	3	3	31	44	20	—	—	—	—
Trading	—	—	—	33	12	—	—	3	—	—	—	—
Manufacturing	10	—	—	4	4	6	4	3	18	27	33	35
Ceremonialism and leisure	4	—	15	50	50	30	—	50	80	69	65	60

[a]*Source:* Oberg 1973:77.

occupy 50 percent or more (range = 50–80) of the time. Note that there are two ceremonial "seasons": June/July and October–February.

This Chilkat pattern cannot be taken as representative of group schedules for the entire culture area, but is a reasonable estimate of how one set of local groups spent their time. The omission of one important category of activities should be noted: Oberg does not list time spent on warfare and raiding. In terms of both time and socioeconomic significance, warfare was probably as important an activity as trading. Although Tlingit sources (and those for most of the rest of the area) indicate considerable warfare, it is unlikely that each local group was involved in fighting each year.

THE ANNUAL ROUND

For most local groups on the Northwest Coast, the seasonal pattern of resource exploitation involved movement of people from one locale to another—to reside near the resource locus (or loci) they wished to use. No one annual round was common to the entire culture area, although for virtually all groups the winter village was regarded as the central residential focus of the year's cycle.

Some idea of the variations in seasonal settlements and the annual cycle can be obtained from Mitchell's (1983a) analysis of such patterns on the central Northwest Coast. This study distinguished "villages" (the basic local groups), "camps" (parts of a village population), and "village aggregates" (people from more than one village). Even within only a part of the culture area (southern Kwakiutl, Nuuchahnulth, Coast Salish north of the Strait of Juan de Fuca) there were at least 16 different combinations for a four-season year. The most common pattern was probably village occupation during the winter and spring, a summer move to a multi-village aggregation, and then dispersion to fall camps, usually for salmon fishing. We caution, though, that this pattern obtains in only 13 of the 69 local groups for which sufficient information on seasonal settlement arrangements exists. Six other patterns are each represented by 5–8 local groups (Mitchell 1983a:99). Even these seven most frequent versions leave the annual rounds of one-fourth of the 69 groups unaccounted for. Clearly, a local group's annual round was a product of the distribution, both spatial and temporal, of the accessible resources. A more detailed picture of the annual rounds of the groups in our sample is presented below and in Table 8.

Chilkat

Chilkat winter villages were occupied from October until the end of July. Late in that month or in early August, people dispersed to their salmon fishing streams along the upper reaches of Lynn Canal. Berry

Table 8. Summary of Annual Round

Group	Number of Annual Moves	Size of Annual Circuit (km)
Chilkat	at least 2	8–80
Metlakatla Tsimshian	4–5	290–450
Fort Rupert Kwakiutl	at least 4	252–276
Kyuquot	at least 3	5–55
Hesquiat	at least 3	16–18
Squamish	0–4	0–320
East Saanich	4–5	75–110
West Saanich	3–5	165–320
Twana	at least 3	48–70

grounds were located on the banks of these streams, so that an August berrying season usually preceded the intensive salmon processing of September. In October, Chilkat returned to their winter settlements. The distances from the winter locations were sometimes as great as 30 km but often much less. Although winter villages were occupied throughout the October–July period, small groups undertook trips away from the villages for up to 3–4 days for such productive activities as shellfish gathering, berrying, and mountain goat hunting. These round trips seem seldom to have covered more than 16 km (Goldschmidt & Haas 1946; Oberg 1973: 65–78).

Metlakatla Tsimshian

In February, inhabitants of the Tsimshian's Metlakatla Harbor winter villages moved 100–110 km to the Nass River eulachon fishery, where each local group had its own camping place. In April or May they made the return trip. By July, groups had left for salmon fishing camps along the Skeena River estuary, some 40–110 km away. There were separate settlements for each local group, although some villages may have divided into smaller, lineage-centered camps. In September, some Metlakatla Tsimshian returned to the winter village locations, while others went to hunting territories in the mountains before returning to Metlakatla in November (Boas 1916; Garfield 1951:15–16).

Fort Rupert Kwakiutl

From their winter villages, occupied from October or November until the end of March, the Fort Rupert Kwakiutl local groups travelled in early spring to Tsawitti at the head of Knight Inlet, a distance of some 96 km, where they caught and processed eulachon. All returned to the "winter" villages in June. We know the summer activities for only some Fort Rupert groups. The Kwiahkah went to Cluxewe River (42 km) for salmon, while the Walas Kwakiutl apparently travelled 30 km to the mouth of the Nimpkish River for the same purpose (Dawson 1887:72). Fall salmon fisheries were likely at a number of locations, but the details are not known.

Nuuchahnulth

The four Kyuquot winter villages were occupied from November until February. These four formed a federation and shared a common summer settlement on Village Island in Kyuquot Sound from February until August or September, when each of their 14 component descent groups travelled to its fall salmon station. All of these stations were within the Kyuquot Sound area. The distances from winter to summer village were 3–17 km. The distances from the summer villages to the fall salmon stations were 3.5–27 km, while the trip from fall fishing station to winter village was 1.5–14.5 km. From the summer settlement to the dentalium grounds was 13 km (Drucker 1951:222–224).

In early contact times, the Hesquiat formed at least five independent winter village groups, although all but one of these was little more than a few extended households in size. The larger settlement was a local group dominated by the Kiquinath, who, according to Drucker (1951:235), had their winter settlement in Hesquiat Harbor on the west shore near its entrance. In the summer they moved to Hitlwina, about 6 km across the harbor, for halibut and cod fishing. They had two fall salmon stations, each about 8 km from the summer village and about 2 km north of their wintering spot. Haggarty (1982:81) reports information provided by Hesquiat people in the 1970s that places the winter village of the Kiquinath and their associates at Hitlwina. Seasonal moves from this base would be different from some of those Drucker's informants described but would involve similar distances. Other Hesquiat groups also exploited primarily the harbor, although some groups did have summer sites on the open coast north of Estevan Point (Drucker 1951:236).

Gulf of Georgia Salish

Upriver Squamish left their winter villages in the spring, when the eulachon were running, and congregated at the mouth of the Squamish River near Stamas, the winter location of one local group. The people of Stamas, in fact, also spent the summer at their main village. Other Squamish villagers travelled more widely: to Port Moody (77 km from the winter village), Capilano Creek (56 km), English Bay (56 km), Jericho beach (61 km), and False Creek (55–58 km). Seven other villages probably spent the summer months on the Fraser River, returning to Howe Sound in late September and early October (Barnett 1955:31–32; Duff 1952).

Straits Salish

The seven Saanich winter villages located on the shores of Saanich Inlet and the Saanich Peninsula were occupied from at least November to March. During July, people from two West Saanich villages (Tsartlip and Tsekum) crossed the Strait of Georgia to a mainland village at Boundary Bay (72 km) to fish for salmon (sockeye and pink) and sturgeon. Some of these people later moved from Boundary Bay to a weir on the Salmon River, a small tributary of the Fraser River, about 40 km distant. At least some residents of these two Saanich villages moved to the Fraser River itself to fish in late August. People from Tsawout, an East Saanich village, did not cross to the mainland but took their salmon at South Pender Island (22 km from the winter village), halibut off Saturna Island (35 km), and seals and porpoises at D'Arcy, Chatham, and Discovery Islands (10 and 26 km). In the fall, Tsartlip's residents returned to Vancouver Island and then moved to camps on the Goldstream River (about 8 km away) to catch salmon (Barnett 1955:19–20).

Twana Salish

We can write in only general terms about the Twana annual round. The pattern followed was one of about 4–6 months of winter congregation and 6–8 months of spring, summer, and fall dispersion. Elmendorf (1960:260) describes the summer existence as "semimigratory." The dispersed villagers were engaged in "intensive fishing, hunting of land game and waterfowl, and gathering of edible plants." Occasionally during the summer, relatives of villagers or even people and groups from several different winter settlements would come together temporarily to exploit some seasonally abundant resource. A partial annual round and some indication of the distances involved can be reconstructed for the Skykomish division of the Twana. From their winter village in the Skykomish River valley, the group moved some 13 km to a summer location near the mouth of the river, but on Hood Canal. From here, many travelled for fall fishing to the mouth of the Hamahama River, about 22.5 km distant. The return trip to the winter village was a journey of 34 km. The fall trip for others took them only to Lilliwaup Bay (12 km) before they returned to the winter village (23 km).

UNITS OF PRODUCTION

With rare exception, the social units involved in the extraction and processing of food, raw materials, and commodities from the environment are not specialized economic organizations, but kin-based units, only one facet of whose operation is economic.

Although Northwest Coast groups show some variation in their organization for production, we can make four initial generalizations. First, in few places do units larger than extended-family or local lineage households operate as units of production. In fact, for most of the year's activities, a mere segment of the household based on a nuclear or composite family is the effective element.

Second, throughout the area there is a commonly observed gender division of labor. Women gather plant foods and shellfish, process fish and meats for storage, prepare meals, manufacture clothing and baskets, and weave nets, mats and fabrics. Men build traps (for fish, birds, and mammals), make and use the other hunting and fishing equipment, and carry out all aspects of woodworking required for the construction of houses, carving of canoes, and manufacture of boxes, utensils, and crest poles.

Third, as we have argued elsewhere (Donald 1983, 1984; Mitchell 1984, 1985; Mitchell & Donald 1985), slave labor was a significant—in some respects, critical—component of the regional economy. Slaves performed a great variety of menial, tedious tasks, thereby contributing to their owners' economic well-being and freeing title-holders, especially, for appropriate elite activities.

Fourth, when compared to other hunter-gatherers, the Northwest Coast residents show a fair amount of craft specialization. This is more evident for men than for women, but even for the latter there are elements of specialization in fine basket work and woven blanket production. Men might specialize as canoe-, mask-, or pole-carvers or as box-makers. Apparently, though, none of this should be considered full-time craft specialization. While an artisan and his family might be housed and fed by the person for whom he was carving a pole, he was freed from routine subsistence labors only until the job was done (Garfield 1951:16). It is doubtful if anyone made a living solely as an artisan.

Chilkat

For the Chilkat, the basic production unit was the lineage household—Oberg's (1973) "house-group." Men gathered firewood and harvested cod, halibut, herring, eulachon, and salmon. Women dug shellfish and gathered berries, roots, and other edible plant foods. Contrary to our generalization about the maximal productive unit, Chilkat men of several lineage house-groups might cooperate in hunting mountain goat, and all the house-groups of a clan in the village might work together at hunting and rendering seal. Nevertheless, "the fundamental food collecting activities are collectively performed by members of the house-group" (Oberg 1973:80).

Production of tools, weapons, and utensils by men and of baskets, blankets, or robes by women—whether for their own use or that of their independent household—were individual pursuits. A certain amount of "private" hunting or fishing for immediate consumption was acceptable, once the collective needs of the lineage household had been satisfied. The individual was also able to keep rewards gained from performance of services as a songwriter, carver, or shaman.

Oberg (1973:81) made a useful distinction between ceremonial and all other kinds of productive labor, and for the Chilkat he noted that many of the ceremonial labor task groups were based on moiety membership. "House-building, burial, . . . and lip, ear, and nose piercing and totem pole carving" (Oberg 1973:81) were conducted by moiety members "opposite" to those having the tasks performed. Collective tasks like house-building and burial might include a considerable number of these opposite moiety members as a producing unit, while other, perhaps more personal ritual activities—such as piercing or tattooing, or attending at childbirth, or carving a crest on a pole, helmet, or other object—would involve only individuals from that moiety.

Metlakatla Tsimshian

For Metlakatla Tsimshian, the only enduring groups which clearly operated as productive units were the independent family and lineage households. The independent family household was the food-producing unit during the fall period of hunting and gathering and probably also for the similar early summer activity. As well, it was very likely the productive unit at the eulachon, salmon, and halibut fisheries (Garfield 1951:15). Male members of the household would produce tools and wooden utensils and might also be canoe- or box-makers or mask- and pole-carvers. The women made clothing and baskets and might also produce woven blankets (Garfield 1951:16). The local matrilineage members formed the core of a single extended household that cooperated to construct the dwelling they would occupy (Garfield 1939:275).

In addition to these continuing social units, there were ad hoc groups formed as sealing and sea lion-hunting or raiding parties. Raiders appropriated the movable property of neighboring groups but also, as Mitchell (1984) suggests, "produced" slaves from captured members of the free population.

Fort Rupert Kwakiutl

Although there is no explicit description of Kwakiutl economic organization, some characteristics of the Fort Rupert Kwakiutl productive units
can be inferred from Curtis (1915). We conclude that the independent
family household was the basic production unit for collecting and processing herring, herring spawn, eulachon, halibut, coho and spring salmon,
hemlock cambium, and crabapples. Men working alone hunted mountain
goat and bear; women working alone (or perhaps with children) picked
salal and huckleberries and dug clover and clams.

One technique for fishing chum salmon—the bag net—required a crew
of three men and, thus, suggests a production unit drawn from different
independent households. Several techniques used for hunting deer and
ducks required pairs of hunters, probably also from different independent
households. Furthermore, elk hunting was accomplished by beaters and
a group of waiting hunters, perhaps more participants than even an extended household could provide.

When women gathered elderberries, they seem to have formed a unit
larger than an independent household, as the berries collected filled a
small canoe, in which they were then boiled. "Then everybody eagerly
crowds up to drink the juice down to the last drop" (Curtis 1915:40).

The building of a weir is described as a communal undertaking, but the
title-holder of the group controlling it had "the first right to take fish from
it; after him the others of rank, and finally the common people have their
turn" (Curtis 1915:28).

Rather different social units were formed for a sea otter hunt which,
as described by Curtis, was quite possibly a post-contact arrangement.
Each hunting vessel had a "captain" and two paddlers, obviously drawn
from three different independent households because, in preparation for
the event, they "slept apart from their wives" (Curtis 1915:30). Curtis
reported more than 40 canoes (120 adult males) would generally take part
in the hunt, making it likely the venture was of at least village scope.
Leadership of the flotilla was determined by a race to depart, with the
captain of the first canoe to get underway becoming the hunt commander.
Any sea otter skin belonged to the captain or captains whose arrow(s)
struck the animal. The hunt commander's advantage was that he had first
shot at each otter surrounded by the canoes.

Nuuchahnulth

Nuuchahnulth organization for production is very poorly described. The
impression gained from Drucker (1951) and Arima (1983) is that it must
have fairly closely resembled what we have reconstructed of the Kwakiutl

configuration. Much of the activity centered on the individual members of nuclear or composite family segments of an extended family household. Nevertheless, there seem to have been some occasions when the larger household cooperated in harvesting resources that at least in name belonged to the house's principal title-holder.

According to Drucker (1951:38–44), solitary pursuits of males included trapping for deer and fur-bearing land mammals, trolling for spring salmon, and fishing for halibut. A husband and wife might together fish for cod— but usually a man went out alone (Drucker 1951:38)—and might together gather marine invertebrates, although this was commonly a task for the wife alone. With a single partner or assistant a man hunted elk, hair seal, sea otter, and ducks, speared salmon, and gathered herring spawn. The butchering of a stranded whale would involve several extended households, but each seems to have been separately engaged in cutting up the specific portion of the animal allotted to its title-holder. The title-holder also sent the women of the household to make the first picking of his salmonberry, red huckleberry, and blackberry patches. With the harvest he gave a feast, and thereafter all could pick for themselves (Drucker 1951:56–57).

Drucker (1951:57) refers to groups of men cooperating in driving shiners or perch to the head of a small cove, where they could easily be scooped or raked out. He also notes that the Hopichisat (at the head of Alberni Canal) had "communal" deer drives (Drucker 1951:60).

Although we are not told how each canoe's crew was selected, Drucker (1951:50–51) does note that the one or more additional vessels in a whaling expedition might be captained by younger kinsmen of the head whaler. Each crew contained a harpooner, steersman, and six paddlers who had additional duties when the actual pursuit of a whale was underway. The expedition was accompanied by a fast sealing canoe with a crew of two or three to carry messages to shore.

Drucker (1951:47–48) specifically attributes the elaborate system of cooperatively hunting for sea otter, with its many canoes and detailed rules for allocating ownership of the pelts taken, to the postcontact period. Earlier, only a hunter and steersman went after these marine mammals.

Gulf of Georgia and Straits Salish

Sources do not permit separating Squamish and Saanich for much of our discussion of organization for production. Gulf of Georgia Salish generally had two identifiable productive units: the nuclear or composite family centered household group and the extended family household group. There were commonly four of the former included in the latter. The independent household seems to have been the principal productive unit for most foods and other goods (Barnett 1955:241; Suttles 1974:328). Exceptions would be the construction of the dwelling itself (a cooperative venture of the extended family household) and the use of such hunting technology as the deer net, when suitable males of the extended family group would all be engaged. As the large trawl nets for salmon fishing required two canoes and four adult males to operate, the extended family household may again have been involved.

Suttles (1974:328) indicates that "more productive subsistence activities" might require cooperation of several Straits Salish families, but that these were not necessarily associated as members of a single extended family. This statement likely applies primarily, if not exclusively, to the employment of reef-netting technology, when a strikingly different production unit was involved. As described by Boas (1891) and Suttles (1974), the reef-netting crew was not normally composed of related individuals but instead consisted of the best fishermen the crew leader or "captain" could hire for a share of the take. Crews for each of the two large canoes required and their nuclear families assembled in a special camp near the reef-netting location. For the fishing season, all who had hired on were under the control of the owner of that location (the captain), who guided the technical and ritual aspects of the fishery.

Twana Salish

Some elk and deer hunting was conducted by solitary Twana hunters, but another hunting method for both these land mammals was a group or "community" drive (Elmendorf 1960:93). For elk, at least, many members of the village might participate in the drive (Elmendorf 1960:117). Waterfowl, seal, and porpoise were taken by men working in pairs, one as steersman, the other as harpooner or, for waterfowl, spearsman or pole net wielder (Elmendorf 1960:102–112). Twana women picked berries, dug clams, and gathered roots in work parties, but such parties were formed for companionship and perhaps safety rather than for joint effort; thus, they cannot be considered units of production. According to Elmendorf (1960:152), an entire village cooperated to erect the plank house of an upper-class man. "Neighbors and fellow villagers" also assisted when a canoe-maker was ready to launch his vessel (Elmendorf 1960:182).

OWNERSHIP OF PRODUCTIVE RESOURCES

Our discussion of ownership of productive resources relies heavily on Richardson's (1982) comprehensive overview. The common alienable resource locations were those associated with the important salmon and eulachon fisheries and with a few plant species. In addition, there was regional ownership of certain land mammal hunting territories, of beaches on which sea mammals might strand, and of portions of the sea bed where halibut or dentalia were to be found.

Richardson's study of resource ownership identifies five regional variants, four of which fall within our area of interest. The southernmost of these includes the Chinook and southern Coast Salish—the Salish of Puget Sound and Washington State's ocean coast. These people seem to have had village rather than kin-group or individual control of the important resources. Fishing locations and weirs were considered property of the community, although stations or platforms on the weir were owned by the nuclear or polygynous family ("minimal family") or even by individuals (Richardson 1982:100). Jorgensen's (1980:406–408) analysis is in agreement for at least some of the Chinook groups, but he differs for the Puget Sound Salish. For most of these groups, he would add ownership by the patrihousehold of key gathering, hunting, and "aquatic animal" sites.

In some contrast, kin-group ownership is found among the central Coast Salish (Nooksack, Straits, Halkomelem, and Squamish), where it exists along with concepts of village community ownership and ethnic group territories. Extended families controlled such resource sites as those used for gathering "camas, 'wild carrots,' fern roots, wapato, cranberries, . . . butter clams, and horse clams; also owned were sites for raised duck nets and sturgeon, . . . traps, dip-net locations, and fishing streams" (Richardson 1982:101). To this list can be added, after Barnett (1955:251), sealing rocks and bird rookeries. Deer, duck, and fish nets, pits, and deadfalls were among the items owned by extended families. However, salmon traps and (as with their Salish neighbors to the south) weirs were considered village property. There was also a distinct, if poorly described concept of ethnic group (Barnett 1955:18) territory. As with the Puget Sound and outer coast Salish, Jorgensen (1980:406–408) records patrihousehold ownership of key gathering, land mammal hunting, and aquatic animal sites. In keeping with the distinctive organization of the Straits Salish reef-netting fishery (see discussion below), the fishing locales were reportedly owned by individuals (Stern 1934:126; Suttles 1974:270).

Richardson's Wakashan subarea includes Nuuchahnulth, Kwakiutl (except Haisla), Bella Coola, and possibly the northern Coast Salish—Pentlatch, Comox, Homalco, Klahuse, Sliammon, and Sechelt. "Virtually all land and water areas with resources of any value were owned by corporate ambilineal (nonunilineal) descent groups. There is no evidence of multi-kin-group communities or larger ethnic groups having any function in relation to the control of productive resources" (Richardson 1982:102–103).

According to Boas (Codere 1966:35–36), Southern Kwakiutl "numayms" owned mountain goat and other hunting territories, grounds for picking "all kinds of berries:—crab apples, viburnum, and salal . . . cranberries, elderberries, currants, salmon berries, huckleberries, sea milkwort," salmon rivers, salmon traps, and eulachon traps. To this list we can add clover beds, valued for the roots they produced (Curtis 1915:43).

The Northern Matrilineal subarea includes the Haida, Tsimshian, Haisla, Tlingit, and Eyak. For these groups, ownership of the principal resources was vested in the village subunits of the matrilineal descent groups. For the Tsimshian, these were matrilineages (or "houses"), for Tlingit and Haida, village segments of matriclans.

Among the Chilkat Tlingit, the matriclans owned the hunting grounds, salmon streams, most of the sealing rocks, berry patches, and trade route passes into the interior (Oberg 1973:55). Small berry, root, and clover patches, trees, and some sealing rocks were more commonly property of the lineage household (Oberg 1973:40, 59), as were the house itself—although the land on which it was situated seems rather to have been clan property—"slaves, large canoes, important tools and food boxes . . . and the food products of collective work" (Oberg 1973:62). Individual property of economic significance included tools, weapons, and small canoes (Oberg 1973:62). Tlingit clans owned *all* land and water areas but, within these territories, they only exercised control over specific resources. The Haida pattern is similar, with less valuable resources being excluded from clan control.

"Among the Tsimshian, corporate kin-groups, or their heads as individuals, owned virtually all territories and the productive resources within them" (Richardson 1982:105). Lineage properties were traditionally listed at the potlatch to install a new head. Most of these properties were lineage-owned, but some could be personal possessions of the head (Garfield 1951:14).

Garfield (1951:14) also indicates that, for the Haida, Tlingit, and Tsimshian, "by the time Europeans arrived, there were no unclaimed land or sea food resources of a kind important in the Indian's economy." According to Richardson (1982:104), the most important of these resources for his Northern Matrilineal area were "salmon streams, patches of crabapples and berries, sealing islands, mountain goat hunting areas, trap or deadfall sites, bird nesting sites, and salvage rights to dead sea mammals."

PRESERVED AND STORED FOOD

As many now appreciate, a key to realizing the potential of some highly productive hunting and gathering environments is the technology available for preservation (Schalk 1977) and storage (Ingold 1983, Testart 1982).

Northwest Coast cultures illustrate this well, although perhaps too much has been made of both the abundance and dependability of resources (Donald & Mitchell 1975) and the effectiveness of preservation technology. Matson (1985:250) further cautions that sedentary settlement, if one obvious potential of a beneficent hunting and gathering environment, is not necessarily realized by adoption of effective storage techniques.

Northwest Coast populations had a preservation technology that largely centered on drying animal or vegetable foods, storage of animal-origin oils, or storage of plant or animal foods in oil. Some dried plant and animal foods can be kept for 3–4 years under favorable conditions, although there is a pronounced decline in nutritional value after the first year (Wolf 1977:259). In the generally wet coastal winters, mold was likely a problem; it thrives unless close to 90 percent of the moisture has been removed in processing and is excluded during storage. Accordingly, as Jorgensen (1980:128) notes, dried fish rot after about six months. This comparatively short shelf life was likely one reason why, despite the sometimes greater abundance of midsummer salmon runs, the fall fishery was considered so important.

The principal resources yielding products that were stored included whales, sea lions, porpoise, seals, the salmons, halibut, cod, herring, eulachon, clams, mussels, berries, larger fruits, tree bark, roots, bulbs, and seaweeds. Oil, extracted from the sea mammals, eulachon, and some salmon, was stored in bentwood boxes, bladders, or kelp "bottles" or tubes. Salmon (including their roe), eulachon, halibut, cod, and herring (including spawn) were all preserved by smoking or, in certain locations, seasons, and weather conditions, by air drying. Large fish, such as salmon, halibut, and cod, were filleted with the skin on and intact at belly or back, so that the whole was spread out to dry or, in the case of halibut, cut into thin sheets of flesh. Dried fish were usually stored in wooden boxes or in baskets or for some time simply hung on poles high up in the house. Except among the Tlingit, northern Kwakiutl, and some Gulf of Georgia Salish, salmon roe was commonly stored in seal bladders hung in the house rafters. There it was allowed to "mature" until gaining the consistency of soft cheese (Barnett 1939:236; Drucker 1950:170). Clams were also hung in the rafters on long skewers or threaded onto cedar bark cords or withe hoops. They were sometimes also stored in baskets or boxes.

Most berries were air and sun dried after being lightly boiled and spread in thin layers. Such fruits as cranberries and crabapples were stored in boxes of fish oil. Seaweeds were air and sun dried and then stored in tight boxes. Roots and bulbs were first boiled or roasted and then dried for storage. Some groups (e.g., the Chilkat, Fort Rupert Kwakiutl) processed the soft white cambium layer of hemlock by cooking and pressing it into cakes for winter use.

WEALTH

All groups on the Northwest Coast identified some categories of product as wealth and treated them as other than ordinary consumables. This conception of wealth extended beyond the culture area and was the basis for an active precontact interregional trade in certain commodities, but even within the area high values were placed on some local products. Chief among these were fine woven blankets; choice pelts and hides; fancy baskets; bentwood boxes; canoes; dentalium shells; finely-carved spoons, dishes, and other ornate utensils and tools; "coppers" (large, shield-shaped objects made of the metal); and slaves. Wealth items were commonly distributed as gifts on ceremonial occasions and were sought as loot during raiding expeditions. Insofar as it existed, the formalized system of exchange involved items of the wealth category almost exclusively.

Wealth was concentrated in the hands of male members of an upper class and it was they, the title-holders or prominent men of each settlement, who struggled to amass wealth that they might distribute it to other men of prominence at potlatches in return for eventual recognition of their social standing. In discussing wealth and its relationship to the potlatch, Barnett (1968:88) noted that the "treasure wealth" had "an arbitrary value unrelated for the most part to physical human needs" and was "manipulated solely upon the prestige level."

Except in a more general sense than we are using the term here, wealth was not synonymous with surplus. Nevertheless, its formation and accumulation were very much dependent on the production of surpluses. In most years enough food could be gathered and preserved to satisfy subsistence requirements during periods of intensive food collection and during the balance of the year, when subsistence pursuits could take second place to other activities. The combination of a seasonally bountiful environment, efficient harvesting technology, and relatively effective preservation techniques permitted the freeing of labor for manufacture of wealth items. In addition, some groups with surpluses beyond what even they might consume in a year could exchange these excess foods for wealth items or for the raw materials of which such articles were made. Of surplus commodities we see being exported in this manner, processed eulachon oil would certainly be the most important.

What was considered wealth varies somewhat among the groups in our sample, with northerners apparently recognizing fewer categories of objects as wealth than did their counterparts to the south. Additionally, the exceptionally valuable coppers of the central and north coast were not found among the Nuuchahnulth (Drucker 1951:111) or Salish groups other than the Comox (Barnett 1939:269).

With the partial exception of blankets, our summary excludes any items of obvious European origin and, thus, of only postcontact importance. As fine blankets of native manufacture are known from all parts of the coast, the best probably were everywhere treated as rare and valuable. However, the use of large quantities of standard-quality blankets as wealth for potlatch distributions was almost certainly a postcontact practice. We are aware that a small sample of coppers proved all to have been of non-native metal (Couture & Edwards 1964) but do not yet regard these distinctive artifacts or the behavior associated with them as necessarily postcontact phenomena.

Chilkat and Metlakatla Tsimshian considered proper potlatch goods—our principal indication of what was considered wealth—to include slaves, coppers, sea otter skins, and blankets (Drucker 1950:233; Garfield 1951:26; Oberg 1973:118). Boas' (1916:435–436) list of Metlakatla Tsimshian potlatch items included elk skins (the "most commonly mentioned valuable objects"), marten and sea otter garments, raccoon skins, canoes, spoons made of elk antler and of horn, slaves, large coppers, abalone shells, and dancing blankets.

For the Fort Rupert Kwakiutl, potlatch goods include at least blankets, coppers, and canoes (Curtis 1915:132, 145) and probably also house boards and eulachon oil (Barnett 1968:86) as well as sea otter skins (Drucker 1950:233). Of Nuuchahnulth valuables recorded by Drucker (1951:110–111), big canoes, slaves, dentalia, goat wool and, possibly, blankets were likely considered wealth prior to the historic period. Elsewhere, Drucker (1950:233) reports skins as wealth, specifically citing sea otter pelts.

Suttles (1974:381) classifies as Straits Salish wealth those things used as potlatch goods and those acceptable as payment for debt. Included were "wool blankets, down and nettle fiber stuff, buckskin clothing and moccasins, dentalium and abalone shell ornaments, . . . canoes, bows and arrows, . . . slaves." Twana wealth articles consisted of slaves, canoes, "dog or goat wool blankets, fur robes, valuable pelts, particularly sea otter, . . . bone war clubs," and dentalia (Elmendorf 1960:331).

DISTRIBUTION AND REDISTRIBUTION

Although exchange, which is separately discussed below, played a part in the distribution of goods, the major role was assumed by gift-giving and obligations of kinship. A prevailing ethic of generosity left little room for any independent household to hoard what it had produced. Those in control of the most productive resources and those experiencing a windfall were both motivated to share their exceptional bounty.

Food in surplus to a family's needs was freely shared with other extended household members, with other relatives and friends in the village, and even, as described by Suttles (1960) for the central Coast Salish, with certain relatives beyond the village community. Food was also distributed to guests from the same village at feasts. At the most lavish affairs, the number of guests and the quantity of food consumed or taken away could be very large. Recipients were expected to share the distributed food with their own households.

Major intervillage gatherings were usually distinguished from these intravillage affairs and have become widely known as potlatches. The distinctive characteristics of potlatches have been summarized by Barnett (1938, 1968), whose descriptions ably convey their complexity and pervasiveness. We devote relatively little space to this important phenomenon because archaeology cannot contribute much to the topic. Potlatches varied considerably in scale, depending in part on the status, resources, and particular aspirations of the host and on the importance attached to the event being celebrated. They were true redistributive occasions in the sense that goods accumulated by the host group were given by its leader or title-holder to other group leaders or title-holders as guests. These people, in turn, distributed at least a part of what they received to their own groups.

Much discussion in recent years has turned on the question of whether the potlatch was or was not "primarily" a mechanism for regulating aberrations in the operation of regional economic systems. Piddocke (1965), Suttles (1960, 1962, 1968), and Vayda (1961) developed models for Coast Salish and Kwakiutl societies or for the Northwest Coast in general that placed potlatching activity in this regulating role. Drucker & Heizer (1967), Schalk (1977), Snyder (1975), Weinberg (1965), and others provided contrary views, arguing sometimes against the very existence of periodic resource scarcity and sometimes against the economic significance to the recipients of potlatch distributions.

Without entering this debate on the "true meaning" of potlatches, we will note that whatever other functions they may have served, the giveaways achieved wide distribution of food and other goods. Also, preparation for the event required a great deal of economic activity. Unlike the lesser, intravillage feasts, which were primarily mounted by extended households with a seasonal surplus of food, potlatches often involved larger social units in a long period of goods accumulation. The prospective host, his extended household and, on the central and northern coasts, his descent group, all participated directly in this task. Labor of many freemen and slaves was channelled for a number of years into production and acquisition of the potlatch materials. Women wove blankets and baskets and dressed hides; men made boxes, carved spoons and canoes, and trapped and hunted fur-bearing animals. In the season preceding the potlatch, great effort was put into building up a supply of those foods needed for the feast.

Oberg's (1973:87–88) discussion of Chilkat task allocation leads us to suggest that over the whole coast slave labor was particularly important during potlatch preparation. Slaves freed others from menial work for ceremonial labor and the production of wealth goods. And there is little doubt that for at least some groups, skilled artisans among the slave population contributed even more directly to the production of potlatch property (Donald 1983; Garfield 1951:29–30; Mitchell & Donald 1985).

At least during historic times, all groups on the coast appear to have been familiar with the concept of borrowing goods to increase the size of the giveaway. The idea of using goods as loan capital was also widespread. But only the Kwakiutl seem to have developed this means of goods accumulation into the complex financial transactions so thoroughly described by Boas (1897), Codere (1950), and Curtis (1915). We do not know if Kwakiutl practices were or were not a purely postcontact development, but there may well have been some influence from entry into the Euro-American cash and credit economy. As described, members of the host group loaned goods they had assembled during the early stages of preparation for a potlatch—in the historic era, usually trade blankets—at agreed rates of interest. When the time for the distribution approached, they called in these loans, receiving in the combined return of principal and interest substantially more than they had put out. Shortly before the potlatch, hosts might also borrow from other Kwakiutl who were themselves beginning the process of accumulation.

EXCHANGE AND TRADE

Since earliest contact, Northwest Coast economies were so thoroughly involved in the European fur trade that it may now be all but impossible to reconstruct major aspects of the precontact situation. Oberg (1973:105) concluded that pure barter did not exist among the Tlingit prior to arrival of commercial fur traders and that earlier "transactions" were in the form of reciprocal gifts. Drucker (1951:110) seems to come to similar conclusions about Nuuchahnulth exchanges. This may, indeed, have been the case along the entire coast, but while we will likely never know for certain, there is reason to suspect the existence of an early, sophisticated trading system.

Our information comes primarily from the testimony of those Europeans who made first contact with the coast occupants. As widely-separated people as the Haida, reached by Perez in 1774, and the Makah, contacted by Meares in 1788, were found to be quite familiar with the principle of exchanging goods (Fisher 1977:2; Gunther 1972:11, 57). Of the Meares contact, Gunther (1972:57) observes that, although obviously knowledgeable traders, they showed no sign of having yet obtained European goods. The implication is that trading familiarity was indigenous. Additional support for this view is provided by Vancouver's 1792 explorations. Vancouver (1798:348) discovered that the Nimpkish Kwakiutl, when first contacted, were "well versed in the principals of trade." This opinion is echoed by the expedition's botanist, Archibald Menzies, who reported the Nimpkish "well acquainted with traffic and the value of their own commodities" (Newcombe 1923:88).

Existence of a precontact system of standards for exchange of commodities or valuables would strengthen the case for barter rather than gift exchange alone. Unfortunately, almost all reported standards are so obviously linked with commonplace articles of the late 18th- and 19th-century fur trade that we can infer little about earlier conventions. Perhaps items such as a slave, a sea otter skin, or a good canoe could be described as worth set numbers of caribou hides, as Krause (1956:132) reports for the Tlingit, but whether these were generalized from some specific, remembered transactions or prevailed as acknowledged equivalents is not known.

The wide circulation of dentalia and standardization of value ascribed to these shells, especially in Northwestern California, have led some to view them as a form of currency. For a brief period in the early fur trade, they do appear to have served such a purpose, but there seems as much reason to argue their comparatively uniform value was a product of the fur trade as to assume they embodied a traditional standard adopted by that business.

We should note, as well, that Suttles' (1974:382) investigation of the Straits Salish economy found that, while dentalia and abalone shells were both valued as ornaments, there was no indication that either was a standard of value. Drucker (1951:110) was similarly convinced that the tokens of Nuuchahnulth wealth (luxury goods) "were not elaborately graded, and there were no standards of relative value." However, Elmendorf (1960:142) suggests for the Twana that sale of food "was in terms of equivalent values, definable by units of dentalium currency."

Similar uncertainties are encountered when we try to describe the movement of goods, whether by trade or gift. Demands of the commercial fur trade and the flow of pelts to the relatively few points of purchase unquestionably affected aboriginal patterns. What is unclear are the extent and manner in which they did so. In our summary of the trading activities of the sampled groups, we have not attempted to infer precontact circumstances but simply have outlined the situation as nearly as can be reconstructed for the early 19th century.

The Chilkat traded with other Tlingit groups residing on the coastal islands and mounted trading excursions to the interior and to villages of the Tsimshian and Haida. Expeditions were undertaken by the head of the extended household, who, with the aid of all members, assembled the goods required.

> The trader generally had definite trading connections with individuals at other villages or in neighboring tribes. On his arrival he would be met with a certain amount of ceremony and led to the house of his business associate. Exchanges were made publicly accompanied by a great deal of haggling. Each side set its prices high and then came down to a level where exchange was possible. Lesser traders and representatives of other house-groups bartered on the side. The whole proceeding smacked very much of a marketplace. When the party was small and the house chief bartered for the group as a whole, his every act was carefully watched by his kinsmen. Quite often a shrewd old woman was taken along who kept a check on exchange values. The two leaders would call out the values of the goods to be exchanged in rotation and, when the price suited the group behind each leader, a shout would go up signifying that exchange was agreeable at that point (Oberg 1973:110).

The main items offered by the Chilkat to their island neighbors included furs and hides for clothing—either in finished form as rabbit and marmot skin blankets, moose hide shirts and trousers, leggings, and moccasins, or as tanned hides (Oberg 1973:107). In addition, they proferred eulachon oil, dried eulachon, cranberries in oil, goat and sheep horn spoons, Chilkat blankets, and porcupine quill-decorated spruce root baskets (Oberg 1973:107).

In return, islanders gave

> dried venison, seal oil, dried halibut, dried king [spring] salmon, dried herring, dried algae, clams, mussels, sea urchins, preserved herring spawn, and numerous other sea products. They also produced cedar bark for the manufacture of the Chilkat blanket, yew wood for bows, boxes, and batons, water-tight baskets of cedar bark, green stone for tool making, and cedar wood, both red and yellow, for the making of ceremonial articles (Oberg 1973:108).

Trade with the interior was mainly conducted to acquire tanned caribou and moose hides, thongs and sinews, birchwood bows, and richly decorated moccasins (Oberg 1973:108). "The trade with the Tsimshian and Haida consisted chiefly of hides, Chilkat blankets, and copper, which were exchanged for large cedar canoes, slaves, and shell ornaments" (Oberg 1973:108).

Metlakatla Tsimshian leaders also controlled the main trading activity of each house and each village (Mitchell 1983b). There were expeditions to the interior (up the Skeena River) and to the south at least as far as Bella Bella. In addition, the annual spring assembly of Haida, Tsimshian, and Niska at the Nass River eulachon fishery was an important occasion for trade.

Figure 2 summarizes information available on the movement and nature of goods involved in the Metlakatla Tsimshian-centered portion of the

Figure 2. Diagram of Metlakatla Tsimshian Trade

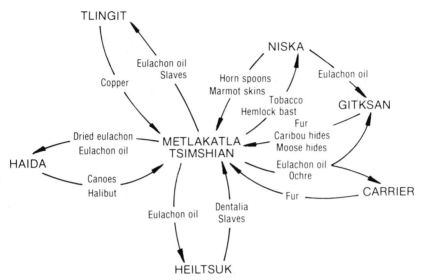

Northwest Coast trading network. Sources providing data include Garfield (1939:199), Morice (1904:209), Niblack (1890:338), and Tolmie (1963:314).

Insufficient information is available to reconstruct reliable patterns of trade for the Fort Rupert Kwakiutl or any single Nuuchahnulth local group. Nevertheless, there are enough recorded instances to indicate that the activity was at least familiar. Boas (1935:67–68) lists eight examples of "selling and buying" drawn from the large body of Kwakiutl texts. All appear to involve trade between Kwakiutl local groups. Curtis (1915:24) also reported trade among Kwakiutl in which some groups exchanged surplus eulachon oil for salmon, their partners having had no direct access to the eulachon fisheries. Examples of trade between Fort Rupert Kwakiutl and distant or non-Kwakiutl groups are provided by Barrett-Lennard (1862:84), Curtis (1915:9), Douglas (1841:58), and Tolmie (1963:299, 308). These sources show the Fort Rupert group engaged in purchasing slaves from the Lekwiltok in the south and trading them north to the Heiltsuk. With the Bella Coola, they traded oil for furs and with the Koskimo, via a short overland trail, they traded for sea otter pelts.

Straits Salish groups (Suttles 1974:374) exchanged their products—dried clams and possibly sun-dried salmon—for coiled baskets and plant fibers offered by people living up the Skagit and Fraser Rivers. "Flint" was obtained from Puget Sound suppliers and "woven root hats and possibly cedar-bark mats" from the Nuuchahnulth. To the latter, Straits Salish seem to have been providing in return roots or bulbs, baskets, reed mats, and woven wool blankets (Suttles 1974:375).

Elmendorf (1960:141) concluded for the Twana that any type of fresh or preserved food could be sold, but not to members of one's own village, with whom it was proper to be generous. "Food trade between communities was largely to secure diversity of diet or to obtain some specially prized delicacy, rather than a means of getting vitally needed foodstuffs" (Elmendorf 1960:310), as each winter village group was essentially self-sufficient in its subsistence economy. Among Twana communities, exchanges included dried molluscs and other saltwater food products given to inland settlements by those on the shore in return for deer or elk meat. Dried cockles were a "regular item of trade" to Puyallup–Nisqually of southern Puget Sound, whose return goods included hemp and mountain goat wool. A significant trade was also carried out over the Satsop trail linking the Twana with the Lower Chehalis of the Pacific coast. Twana exchanged local food products, furs, and baskets for whale meat, sea otter skins, dentalia, and slaves (Elmendorf 1960:288).

UNITS OF CONSUMPTION

Over much of the area and most of a typical year, the fundamental unit of consumption was the independent household. Day to day meals of ordinary food were prepared for and served to its members. Any food provided for a larger group was seen as some kind of feast or special occasion. Clothing, tools, utensils, ordinary baskets, dishes, and boxes were also produced by independent household members for the use of that household.

There were occasions, however, when the extended household or even some larger assembly of persons shared in the consumption of food and other products. It is repeatedly said, for example, that while ordinary, plentiful foods might be produced and consumed by the independent households, delicacies or rare foods should be shared with all in the dwelling—the extended household.

Seasonal and sporadic feasts, too, brought together villagers and, on occasion, an even wider group of neighbors. The latter case was that extraordinary kind of feast commonly referred to as a potlatch. To what we have already said about potlatches, we can add that guests received gifts, ate prodigious quantities of food, and carried home generous amounts of the remainder. Formal invitations would be extended to a select group of prominent men but they were expected to arrive accompanied by others. All would share in the food distributions. As obligations of reciprocity were established by participation in potlatches, over a period of years and through some considerable area the same people—often as guests, some-times as hosts—were involved in these affairs. Such potlatch groups or circles—of which there must have been many—formed a network of loosely-structured, overlapping consumption units along the whole north-west coast.

Chilkat

A partial exception to some of the foregoing generalizations is offered by the Chilkat, whose extended household or "house-group" shared use of a central fire and cooking box (Oberg 1973:30). Oberg (1973:114) ex-pressly notes that, just as it produced basic necessities in common, the house-group also consumed those necessities in common. While he does discuss individual ownership of some things, Oberg's depiction of Chilkat consumption leaves no apparent role for the independent household. Chil-kat potlatch feasts were of two kinds. The first, *xuʔix,* connected with house-building, burial, and coming of age, was confined to single villages and involved one phratry as hosts, another as guests. The consuming group was thusly limited to a portion of the village and delimited by phratry membership. The second was the *tutxuʔix,* larger in scope than the *xuʔix* and never designed to commemorate village social events. It was a clan function, given to honor its members but with guests coming from other settlements. "The underlying tone is that of competition and self-aggran-dizement" (Oberg 1973:121), and at least in its later years these motives led to flamboyant destruction of wealth.

Metlakatla Tsimshian

Among Metlakatla Tsimshian, the independent household operated as the principal consumption unit for that part of the year when it lived apart from the rest of the extended household. Even during winter, when the larger group was in residence, the independent household was still probably the most important consuming unit. The extended household was a unit of food consumption incidental to preparations for a potlatch (Garfield 1939:198) and perhaps on other occasions as well. Garfield (1939:278) has described a "typical" ancient plank house with a common open fire in the center. But she has also written of family cooking fires in the middle part of the house (Garfield 1951:10).

Guests gathered for feasts formed graded units of consumption related in size to the importance of the honor claimed at the event. The smallest affairs observed the first naming of children, when the mother's or both parents' relatives might be invited (Boas 1916:537). For more important occasions, all members of the village might be assembled (see also Garfield 1939:208), or persons from all nine Metlakatla villages or, on the most notable occasions, even members of outside groups would be brought together.

Fort Rupert Kwakiutl

The Fort Rupert Kwakiutl independent household maintained its own fire and "kitchen devices" (Curtis 1915:8) and was, thus, in all likelihood a basic unit of consumption. We have little information on whether extended households ever acted as such units. That they likely did so may be inferred from distribution practices at a potlatch. The title-holder who received food and goods at a feast was expected to be generous and pass food gifts on to members of his extended household. Size or composition of potlatch groups are not specifically described in the lengthy literature on the Kwakiutl, but from various accounts we can assume the existence of potlatching circles of multivillage scope.

Nuuchahnulth

As with the Fort Rupert Kwakiutl, the Nuuchahnulth independent household had its own fireplace within the large dwelling (Drucker 1951:71) and, preparing food on its own, it presumably consumed much of it separately. Whenever the title-holders of Nuuchahnulth society had an unusually large supply of a particular food—as when they received the first catch of salmon in their traps or the first harvest of fruit from their berry patches—the proper thing to do was to distribute it at a feast. Guests might be drawn from the whole village or might simply include other independent household heads of the host's extended household. Feasts of varying scale were offered for announced purposes, such as the decision to give a potlatch; the teething, weaning, or first successful hunt of a child; a wife's pregnancy; or simply because someone had requested the feast (Drucker 1951:370–372). Characteristically, a great deal of food was eaten by the guests and additional quantities were distributed on expectation that the recipient would himself hold a feast on his return home (Drucker 1951:372). Potlatches, in contrast, were even more elaborate feasts at which property as well as food was given away. The Nuuchahnulth potlatch might involve guests from the host's village or from different villages.

Salish Groups

All the Salish groups in our sample maintained separate fires for the various independent households of a large dwelling (Barnett 1955:38; Elmendorf 1960:162; Suttles 1974:327) and each member household prepared its own food at these. Nevertheless, for the Straits Salish at least there was within the extended household "considerable sharing of food and preparing of food for one another. It was felt that any surplus of fresh food ought to be shared, or any rare food, even if it were in small quantities" (Suttles 1974:330).

Elmendorf (1960:143) similarly indicates that the Twana strongly resented "stinginess of food within the household or within a group of relatives" and that, further, any large catch should properly be followed by invitations to fellow villagers to share through a feast. The Twana attitudes are but one expression of an underlying Northwest Coast ethic, most clearly expressed on the southern coast, that one should be generous with exceptional harvests of food.

Central Coast Salish groups, including the East and West Saanich and Squamish, distinguished among the smaller feasts given for members of extended households, larger ones involving members of a village community, and those grander affairs to which outsiders were invited (Barnett 1955:246–255). The large, important gatherings, or "klanaks," were the familiar potlatches of neighbors to the west and north. Invited guests brought other members of their households with them. While these additional guests did not directly receive gifts during the formal potlatch distributions, still they were fed, they could pick up something at the end of the event when leftover goods were thrown out in a "scramble," and their patron might share with them some of what he received as an invited guest (Suttles 1974:369–371). The Twana had the *sʔi'wad*, a similarly conducted occasion, which Elmendorf (1960:337) calls an intercommunity wealth-giving feast.

EARLY CONTACT ECONOMIES IN SUMMARY

Northwest Coast societies were based on extraction of resources from a distinctive, naturally prolific environment. The wide range of fishing, hunting, and gathering techniques employed included many specialized devices designed to take particular species under sometimes very specific conditions. While the list of plants and animals exploited is large, the economies are dominated by dependence on salmon, halibut, and herring, as storable foods; eulachon and such sea mammals as seal and whale for oil products; and red and yellow cedar for manufacturing material.

Many of these resources are particularly significant because of their concentration and abundance, but most of the important foods were also quite variable in their availability by season, locale, and numbers. An effective preservation technology based on drying permitted use of temporary surpluses during what would otherwise be seasons of shortage.

The annual round of economic activity, with its movement of local populations from one place to another, matched subsistence activities to the highly local nature of resources. There is still dispute about what mechanisms may have existed to remedy problems caused by year-to-year or longer-term variation in volume of resources. Many feel potlatch distributions may have played a role. Trade may also have been significant in this regard, as it likely also was for accommodating to persisting regional differences in productivity of the environment.

Organization of people for economic activity was constrained by the fact that these were kin-based societies. With rare exception (Straits Salish reef-netting being the most notable), units of production and consumption were defined by kinship. In this respect, Northwest Coast economies were like those of all other hunter-gatherers. There were also important differences, however, including the presence of economic classes and institutionalized slave labor.

The ideological basis of Northwest Coast economic activity is not well understood but was undoubtedly complex. It involved interplay of two dominant themes: personal aggrandizement and generosity. Each motive played an important part in operation of the economic system, on the one hand urging societies to harvest, produce, and accumulate more for the glorification of a few persons and, on the other, ensuring that many would share benefits of that greater productivity.

THE SEARCH FOR EARLIER NORTHWEST COAST ECONOMIES

The preceding description of Northwest Coast economic systems in the early part of the historic era provides a yardstick against which to measure the progress archaeology has made in reconstructing the area's prehistoric economies. Our review attempts to judge this progress by considering the extent to which archaeological research has focussed on economic aspects of Northwest Coast precontact cultures. It does so from a fairly general perspective, however, as too little work has been completed to permit anything like the comprehensive regional survey possible for cultures of the historic period. We also summarize briefly what is now known about prehistoric Northwest Coast economies.

It is useful to distinguish between work undertaken prior to 1970 and that which came later. Field reports from 1970 on have paid significant attention to the "non-artifact" portions of archaeological assemblages. Specifically, their routine reporting of faunal analyses has consistently provided a body of economic information largely lacking from publications of the earlier period.

What primarily characterizes the long early period of Northwest Coast archaeological investigation is its dominant concern with artifacts and features, identification of prehistoric cultures, estimates of their age, and discovery of sequences: the familiar materials and interests of culture history. Some conclusions from this era of investigation are not without interest to the economic prehistorian. Detailed site reports and typological studies—e.g., those by Drucker (1943), Laguna (1960), and Laguna et al. (1964) for the north coast; and Carlson (1960), Cressman (1960), Kidd (1969), King (1950), Mitchell (1971), Smith (1903), and Strong et al. (1930) for the south coast—have certainly contributed to the picture of prehistoric technology. Because plant materials and such animal parts as hides, hair, and horn were not preserved in the kinds of sites then being excavated, only limited contributions could be made to the study of such important industries as weaving, basket-making, hide-working, and woodworking. The presence of artifacts of kinds ethnographic sources identify with woodworking did permit some inferences about the age and development of this industry. Suppositions were possible here because of the distinctive character of the tools involved—hand mauls, adzes, chisels, and wedges—and the fact they were entirely or partly made of durable materials. Other perishable substances were either worked by tools of less distinctive character or by tools and on apparatuses that were subject to rapid decay.

What we have mostly gained from the pre-1970 era of investigation is knowledge of industries in stone-, bone-, antler-, shell-, and coal-working techniques. Indeed, it was an advancement simply to discover the importance of industries so seldom discussed by ethnographers.

With rare exception (e.g., the brief chapter by J.A. Freed & K.S. Lane in Laguna et al. 1964:77–84), little attention was paid to faunal remains in the sites. Most archaeologists provided nothing more sophisticated than a list of species identified, and few incorporated the results of even such rudimentary faunal analysis in their cultural reconstruction or culture histories.

The 1970s saw important changes in the kinds of data reported and used. Many innovations resulted from dramatic changes in fieldwork standards in the latter part of the preceding decade, but there was little or no impact on the published record until the early 1970s. The transformation almost certainly resulted from the great interest aroused in the sciences in matters concerning the environment. For anthropology, this concern took the form of renewed interest in the environment or habitat as an important factor to consider when attempting to explain cultural variability. Archaeologists now recognized that the debris through which they dug to obtain artifacts was itself a valuable class of data.

The celerity with which Northwest Coast archaeologists adopted the new interest is remarkable. Systematic collection of faunal materials formed an important objective of virtually every major project on the coast after the late 1960s, from George MacDonald's Prince Rupert Harbor and Queen Charlotte Islands investigations to Richard Daugherty's excavations at the Ozette site on Washington's Olympic Peninsula. Often the faunal analyses, in published, thesis, or dissertation form, long preceded reports on the artifacts found. In a few cases, *only* the faunal analyses have been produced.

Major or significant studies of archaeological fauna now available for the north coast include reports by Ferguson (n.d.), Savage (n.d.), and F. Stewart (n.d. a–e) for sites in the Prince Rupert Harbor area. For the central coast there are Conover (1978) on the Namu site and Carlson (1976) on the McNaughton Island site. The west coast of Vancouver Island and the Olympic Peninsula have Calvert (1980) and Haggarty (1982), who report several Hesquiat Harbor and vicinity assemblages; Calvert & Crockford (1982) on the Shoemaker Bay site; Clarke & Clarke (1980), Fournier & Dewhirst (1980), and McAllister (1980) for portions of the Yuquot Village faunal assemblage; and DePuydt (1983), Huelsbeck (1983), and Wessen (1982) on Ozette site faunal resources.

Much more is available for the Strait of Georgia, Puget Sound, and Strait of Juan de Fuca segments of the south coast. Among the highlights are Keen (1979), Monks (1977), and Wigen (1980), who deal with aspects of three Baynes Sound faunal collections; Boucher (1976) on the Helen Point site; Casteel (1976), Boehm (1973), Ham (1976), and Imamoto (1976) on the Glenrose and St. Mungo Cannery sites; Ham (1982) on the Crescent Beach site; Stiefel (1985) on Locarno Beach culture subsistence; and E. Friedman (1980), Gross (1980), Huelsbeck (1980), and Miller (1983) on various facets of Hoko River site complex fauna.

Most faunal studies to date have concentrated on evaluating the relative quantities of species or broader categories of animals represented in site deposits. Some attention has also been paid to the question of seasons of collecting shellfish (Clarke & Clarke 1980; Ferguson n.d.; Gross 1980; Ham 1976, 1982; Ham & Irvine 1975; Keen 1979; Miller 1983; Monks 1977)—investigations providing information that will be pertinent to reconstructing prehistoric annual rounds.

The faunal studies listed and an additional few of lesser scope have contributed to the developing picture of prehistoric Northwest Coast economies. That they have done so primarily with respect to limited aspects of economic life is no reflection on their importance. From faunal analyses we can eventually learn a great deal about those subsistence activities involving animals, including species selected, age and size of individuals taken, season of exploitation, butchering practices, and perhaps storage and cooking practices. We may also attempt to infer diet patterns and food-collecting activities based in different seasonal settlements.

Diets of prehistoric Northwest Coast populations were the subject of a small but highly interesting study by Chisholm et al. (1983). Using information derived from stable-carbon isotope ratios in the collagen of human bone, they feel they have estimated proportions of the diet drawn from marine-based and terrestrially-based plants and animals. The resulting ratios show very high fractions of marine food, which would include river-run salmon and eulachon. Estimates range from 81 to 100 percent (average = 90 percent) marine-based food for 37 mature individuals from sites distributed from the Nass to Fraser rivers. There is no discernible trend in the 5000-year span that was sampled and little difference between parts of the coast. Five specimens from the Prince Rupert Harbor sites averaged 95 percent; 13 from Namu, 99 percent; and 12 from Crescent Beach, in Straits Salish territory, 92 percent. The most aberrant measurement (omitted from the preceding calculations) was an immature individual from Namu—about 79 percent, raising at least the possibility of differences between diets of children and adults.

The 1970s also saw the beginning of a continuing flow of reports on plant materials and plant products. Water-saturated or "wet" sites have been the primary source of information on items that are highly perishable in common northwest coast site environments. At mid-decade, a volume edited by Croes (1976) reported excavations at 11 wet sites, distributed from Prince Rupert Harbor to the foot of Puget Sound. To date, however, comprehensive descriptions are available only from those situated on the southern coast. The most thoroughly reported are the Ozette site (Croes 1977, 1980a; J. Friedman 1975; Gill 1983), Hoko River site (Croes & Blinman 1980, Ecklund-Johnson 1984), and the Little Qualicum River site (Bernick 1983). Wet site assemblages have told us much already about the economic uses of various plant species and about the technologies involved in manufacturing wood products, baskets, mats, plant fiber clothing, and cordage. They have so far yielded little on the important question of food uses of plants.

Knowledge of subsistence and manufacturing technology have expanded since 1970, if only because more areas and periods have been sampled by the enlarged scope of archaeological investigations. Nevertheless, a glance at our review of these topics shows how far we are from filling in details for the prehistoric past. Some studies of specific technologies have also been produced. Pomeroy (1976) considers the distribution and use of stone fish traps in Heiltsuk territory and portions of adjacent areas. More recently, Easton (1985) has concluded an underwater archaeological study of two Straits Salish reef-netting locations. Hoff (1980) looked at wooden fishhooks from the Hoko River site. Gleeson (1980) examined woodworking technology evident at the Ozette site, and Paden (1980a) provided an analysis of Hoko River wood chip debitage. Flenniken (1981) described the production and possible uses of vein quartz microflakes, found in some abundance at the Hoko River site. Croes (1977, 1980a, 1980b, 1980c) has produced valuable studies of the basketry and cordage industries at the Ozette and Hoko River sites. For the former site, Paden (1980b) describes basketry waste material, as well.

In speculating on the sources of exotic materials found in the assemblages they are reporting, archaeologists have made at least some headway on the large and elusive topic of trade. The most promising and ambitious approach to this question so far has been the enquiry Roy Carlson and Erle Nelson initiated into the distribution of obsidian in archaeological sites (Carlson n.d.). Using an X-ray fluorescence technique for identifying the unique mix of elements composing each lava flow, they have traced hundreds of widely scattered archaeological specimens of obsidian to their source locations.

PREHISTORIC ECONOMIES IN SUMMARY

Archaeological inquiries have made some progress in reconstructing pre-contact Northwest Coast economies. Nevertheless, a research focus constrained by data, techniques, and goals, combined with sparse excavation, has resulted in an emerging picture that is of limited scope and selective emphasis. We have learned a fair bit about the broad outlines of evolving subsistence technology and faunal resource selection but relatively little about other aspects of the economies.

Let us review briefly what archaeology has accomplished to date. The areas considered are the south coast (Puget Sound and the Strait of Georgia), west coast (ocean shores of the Olympic Peninsula and Vancouver Island), central coast (Queen Charlotte Strait to Milbanke Sound and Dean Channel), and the north coast (Queen Charlotte Islands to the Alaskan panhandle) (Figure 1).

South Coast

The cultural sequence developed for this area includes the following culture types: Old Cordilleran (9000–6500 BP), Charles (6500–3200 BP), Locarno Beach (3200–2300 BP), Marpole (2300–1500 BP), and Gulf of Georgia (1500 BP to contact). Over this long span of time, the list of resources exploited remained remarkably constant and much like that at contact, but there were clearly some shifts in emphasis over time. While elk, deer, seal, salmon, sturgeon, and eulachon were all being taken from earliest times, presently available data suggest that the mammals—particularly the land mammals—were likely more important than other faunal food sources during the first 2500 years (Matson 1976:297, 1981). So few site components with good bone preservation are known from this time, however, that it is difficult say what would be the picture if data from the full range of seasonal sites were at hand. By the time the Charles culture is established, there is evidence of bird hunting and a "clear dominance of marine foreshore and riverine resources" (Matson 1976:299). This shift from land-based resources is largely accomplished by great increases in shellfish gathering (particularly of bay mussel), although fishing of salmon and other river species also grew in importance. The major difference between Charles and later parts of the sequence lies in the shellfish. For later culture types, clams become much more important than mussels. The occupation pattern throughout the sequence appears to be one of seasonal site use, but the details of any period's typical annual round have not yet been worked out.

Although faunal materials tell us that, for at least 8500 years, south coast occupants have been effective users of a wide range of sea and land resources, artifact assemblages are less instructive about subsistence technology. We know that flaked stone tools commonly identified by archaeologists with land mammal hunting are more prominent in earlier than later assemblages and that dogs, which possibly assisted hunters, are known from the Old Cordilleran on. Harpoons of sizes suitable for fish or smaller sea mammals are found beginning with Charles. Rather puzzlingly, they are in multi-barbed, nontoggling form during the Charles occupation, composite toggling form during Locarno Beach, predominantly nontoggling again in Marpole, and toggling once more in Gulf of Georgia. Small, bone single-points and bipoints of sizes and shapes that could have seen use on trolling hooks, bentwood hooks, and many other fishing devices, are present in the Charles and later components but are especially common in sites of the Gulf of Georgia type. Sinkers and weights that could have been used for nets or set lines or the distinctive halibut gear come from later parts of the sequence—from Locarno Beach on. From wet sites we have bentwood hooks dating back at least to Locarno Beach. Of many of the more productive land mammal and fishing techniques, we have as yet little evidence.

Based on underwater concentrations of anchorstones, Easton (1985) reasons a minimum age of several centuries for Straits reef-netting. Wet site deposits have yielded what appear to be fragments of latticework, of the kind used on weirs, from the Biederbost site in Puget Sound at about AD 100 (Nordquist 1976) and from the Little Qualicum River site in the northern Strait of Georgia from approximately AD 1000 (Bernick 1983). Munsell (1976) reports, also for Puget Sound, a weir structure at Wapato Creek that may date from the AD 900–1500 period. Large-gauge netting has been recovered from a wet site of Locarno Beach culture type. Thin, ground-slate knives of a form similar to those used at contact for preparing salmon for drying appear first in Locarno Beach sites but are vastly more common in some Marpole deposits.

Wet sites provide direct evidence of woodworking as early as Locarno Beach. Woodworking tools of the kinds used at contact, however, seem only gradually to make their appearance. The antler splitting wedge is first—from the very start of the sequence—followed by ground stone and sea mussel shell celts in Charles, wooden wedges in Locarno Beach, and stone hand mauls in Marpole, at which time there is also a proliferation of variously shaped and sized celts. Bone awls suitable for basketwork but not sufficiently distinctive to assume that this was their use, date from all periods. Early direct evidence of basketry and matting come from the Hoko River (Croes 1980b, 1980c) and Musqueam Northeast sites (Archer & Bernick n.d.). At Musqueam Northeast, the most common basketry technique, used in many open-work containers, is plaited wrapped twining—a style that seems not to have continued into the historic period. At Hoko River, the most common is open-wrapping. Other techniques at both sites include checker and twilled plaiting, plain twining, and diagonal twining. There are fragments of sewn rush matting from Hoko River.

Exotic materials such as nephrite (Fraser Canyon source), native copper (possibly from the Copper River, Alaska), dentalia (west coast of Vancouver Island), and obsidian (some from eastern Oregon), indicate establishment of a far-reaching trade network by at least Locarno Beach times. Obsidian—of as yet undetermined source—was being traded even earlier, by the time the Charles culture type was established.

West Coast

What strikes one about the West Coast sequence, which to date reaches back at least 4750 years (Dewhirst 1980), are its relative stability and continuity with the historic Makah and Nuuchahnulth occupants. All resources commonly exploited at contact are represented in the archaeological assemblages. Among the mammals, whales, seals, and porpoises were of greatest importance, with deer placing after these. Salmon, herring, and rockfishes were all used, as were many species of waterfowl. Clams and mussels were collected. Resource procurement was seasonally structured and, judging by the Hesquiat Harbor and Ozette data, likely involved at least some settlement moves for at least some portion of the population.

There are artifacts interpretable as whale, small sea mammal, and salmon harpoons (all of composite, toggling form); portions of composite fishhooks; knives suitable for preparing salmon, herring, or other fish and foods; woodworking tools; and tools for shaping the numerous bone artifacts. These tools and implements are represented in even the oldest components. Dog remains are present from at least the period 2900–1100 BP (Dewhirst n.d.).

By the time the Ozette site was occupied, the Northwest Coast woodworking tradition was fully developed. Not only are there examples of the full range of familiar tools, but also the site soils have preserved many quite spectacular wood products, both large and small. Some are even embellished with intricate shell inlay.

The archaeological evidence for trade is thin, as Huelsbeck reports in this volume. Yet, West Coast groups are believed to have been the principal collectors of dentalia, found in a great many site components throughout western North America.

Central Coast

For this largely Kwakiutl and Bella Coola area, we have two subregional sequences. Mitchell (this volume) outlines a south central coast set of culture types that begins with the Old Cordilleran (ca. 8500 BP) and, after a hiatus in our knowledge, runs through Obsidian (ca. 4750–2450 BP) and Queen Charlotte Strait (2450 BP to contact). Carlson (n.d:16) outlines a more complete sequence for the northcentral coast. It includes Namu I (9700–6000 BP), Namu II (6000–5000 BP), Namu III/McNaughton I (5000–2500 BP), Namu IV/McNaughton II (2500–1500 BP), Anutcix (1500–600 BP), and Kwatna (600 BP to contact).

From the earliest levels at which faunal materials are preserved, it is evident that a wide range of terrestrial, marine, and riverine resources was being harvested (Conover 1978). Deer, seal and porpoise, salmon, and shellfish form the major categories hunted, fished, or collected for the full 97 centuries. Initially, deer are particularly prominent and shellfish all but absent. During Namu II, mussels and barnacles became very conspicuous in the faunal assemblages. By the 5000–2500 BP period, mussels are no longer of first-rank importance, being replaced by clams. Mitchell (this volume) describes the post-2450 BP shift in resource emphasis that saw salmon and small sea mammals assume particular prominence in the southern subregion. The situation in the northern subregion is more complex. In the lengthy Namu site sequence, deer and elk dominate. At other sites, whose components range from about 3500 BP (Carlson 1976, Simonsen 1973) to contact, sea mammals are paramount. For the area as a whole, then, there may be a move from early predominance of land mammals to later prominence of sea mammals, but we will need better understanding of the annual round before we can be certain that sea mammals were any less significant in early times.

The earliest assemblages (until about 4500 BP) are primarily flaked stone—even in some deposits where bone preservation is apparently good

(Luebbers 1978). From 4500 BP onwards, bone, antler, and ground stone industries increase. Barbed, nontoggling harpoons appear after 4500 BP, and composite toggling forms, 3600 years later. Bone points, interpretable as parts of composite fishhooks, are present at least by 3500–3000 BP, and bentwood hooks date from at least the last 1300 years. Dog remains are present from the early part of the sequence to its end.

As with other areas surveyed, woodworking is the manufacturing technology about which we know most. Wedges and ground stone celts are found from 4500 BP on; hand mauls, much later—somewhere between 1550 and 750 BP. Products of woodworking technology are known from late in the sequence at Axeti in Kwatna Inlet (Hobler 1970) for the period 1300–200 BP. These include fragments of bentwood boxes and spoons. Cordage and checker work and twilled cedar bark baskets and mats come from the same deposits. Bark beaters and spindle whorls are known from several, widely distributed sites on the central coast.

An indication of the scope of coastal trade networks is provided by assemblages from the northcentral coast. Obsidian in these archaeological sites has been traced to sources on the Chilcotin Plateau (110–220 km distant), at Mt. Edziza near the upper reaches of the Stikine River (660 km), and in eastern Oregon (900–1100 km) (Carlson n.d.:23).

North Coast

This area includes the home territories of the Haisla, Tsimshian, Haida, and Tlingit. It has been the subject of several proposed subregional sequences, including ones by MacDonald & Inglis (1981) for Prince Rupert Harbor, Coupland (1985 and this volume) for Kitselas Canyon and the Lower Skeena River, and Fladmark (1975:238–239) for the Queen Charlotte Islands. The Queen Charlotte Islands sequence is so far accompanied by only limited faunal data, and the Skeena River series is adequately outlined in Coupland's contribution to this volume. Accordingly, we focus on the Prince Rupert Harbor developments, where MacDonald & Inglis (1981) distinguish three periods of occupation: Period III (5000–3500 BP), Period II (3500–1500 BP), and Period I (1500 BP to contact).

Essentially all faunal species considered economically important at contact were taken throughout earlier times. As on other parts of the coast, there is an initial dominance of mussels and other beach surface dwellers in the shellfish remains. Clams and other subsurface bivalves only become common in the Period II and later deposits—after 3500 BP.

Items of subsistence technology include nontoggling harpoons—either bilaterally- or unilaterally-barbed—in all periods and composite toggling harpoons from the last period. Small, single-pointed bone artifacts, like those used as barbs on composite fishhooks, are found throughout all deposits. Artifacts construed as sinkers occur after 3500 BP at Prince Rupert Harbor and after 2500 BP in the Skeena River's Kleanza phase. These could have been used on nets or as parts of other fishing gear. The Lachane site, a water-saturated component dating from Period II (Inglis 1976), has yielded several digging sticks.

Bone wedges or chisels and sea mussel shell celts, all woodworking artifacts, are present in small numbers from the start. By Period II, there are ground stone celts and, in the Lachane site, wooden wedges, chisel hafts, an elbow adze handle, and many wood products. These include kerfed boxes, canoe paddles, and carved bowls. There is also evidence of at least a small birch bark container industry. Not until Period I do grooved splitting adze and hafted maul heads appear. Bark shredders are found from Periods II and I. The wet site has also provided examples of basketry, cordage, and matting. All baskets were of cedar bark in checker weave, twill, plain twining, or twined open work. The mats, of cedar or alder bark, were all checker weave.

The exotic items—obsidian from all periods, and amber, copper, and dentalia from Periods II and I—indicate long-term participation in coastal and interior trade. The metal is likely from the Copper River in Alaska (1100 km away), dentalia from northern Vancouver Island (400 km), and the obsidian is from Mt. Edziza (400 km). The Chilcotin Plateau (250 km) is the source of obsidian in the Skeena River's Bornite phase (5000–4300 BP), while in the succeeding Gitaus phase (4300–3600 BP) it comes from Mt. Edziza (400 km).

LOOKING AHEAD

We will not dwell on the sizable temporal and spatial gaps in knowledge of Northwest Coast economic systems. If the length of coast and span of years since probable first occupation are considered, obviously only the sketchiest outline of the area's prehistory has been achieved. The predecessors of several hundred local economies have received no attention at all. Instead, we concentrate on those aspects of prehistoric economies that would seem to promise results if investigated by archaeological techniques.

As we have seen, the bulk of research has so far been directed, by opportunity or design, to determining resources exploited, subsistence and manufacturing technologies employed, seasons of collection, and evidence for trade. There is still much to be accomplished in all these areas and others.

A reconstruction of the postglacial history of those resources important in prehistory and at the time of contact would be useful. For one resource,

Hebda & Mathewes (1984) have produced the kind of study we have in mind. From pollen profiles, they charted the expansion of western red cedar in coastal forests, showing its rarity until about 6000 BP (south coast) or 4000 BP (north coast). After these dates there is a sharp increase in abundance until, by 5500–3500 BP, the species has reached its historic prevalence. The implications of this historical pattern for a resource so intimately tied to coastal economies are obvious: development of the woodworking industry must have been paced by the changing availability of mature red cedar trees.

Similar studies are needed for other raw material and food resources: yellow cedar, spruce, camas, salmon, herring, eulachon, halibut, deer, elk, seal, porpoise, whales, mussels, and clams—at the very least. Fladmark (1975) made an initial and general attempt over ten years ago. We now need the kind of focussed research that only specialists seem able to provide.

Analysis of faunal remains is an active area of research and publication, both with respect to substantive results and examination of analytical techniques. In course of time, refinements in quantification will no doubt permit reliable assessment of the importance of various faunal resources or categories to subsistence and manufacturing segments of economies. While we are still a long way from being able to include plants in these assessments, use of flotation in recent years has substantially increased the return of small plant and animal remains from a variety of northwest coast archaeological soils.

The seasonal round of subsistence and ceremonial activities, with its changing residence and periodic population concentration and dispersal, was a fundamental characteristic of Northwest Coast life at the time of contact. It will be important to determine if and how this differed in the past. A start has been made with shellfish seasonality research, but procedures so far involve a disturbing measure of subjectivity that will have to be reduced. Extension of the principle to other organisms with parts showing incremental growth is possible, and its application to northwest coast species and problems should be explored.

The direct historic approach, while guiding the research of a few archaeologists working on the coast (most notably, Laguna in southeast Alaska), has not received the attention it deserves. Its starting point— the archaeology of historic occupants—is particularly suited to investigation of the annual round. To make effective use of this strategy, one would discover what kind of archaeological assemblage is found at each site of *known* seasonal use for local groups from many parts of the coast. Such information would serve to some extent as a useful check on our seasonal indicators, but more important, would help to characterize a seasonal assemblage's artifacts and features. We could also gain information on faunal and floral assemblages associated with specific resource-processing sites. By dealing with known historic occupations, we can also supplement the ethnographic record with many details, e.g., the range of species actually exploited from a seasonal site.

Huelsbeck's essay in this volume opens an interesting avenue to the study of resource ownership and possibly also to the identification of units of production and consumption. When truly contemporaneous residential units are excavated, at least some interassemblage variability may be attributable to differences in access to specific resources. If combined with a catchment area approach, there is even the possibility of gaining insight into residential group territories.

Both subsistence and manufacturing technology studies stand to benefit from advances in organic residue analysis, whether of relict blood constituents (Loy 1987, Loy & Nelson 1986) or of amino acid crystals. Both sets of techniques reportedly make direct ties between artifacts and the species or category of organism on which they were employed. As distinctive amino acids are present in plants as well as animals, their study is of particular interest.

The final economic topic that would seem readily enlightened by archaeological research is trade. Actually, it may prove impossible to distinguish between "trade"—the exchange of specific goods and services—and gift-giving, but at least we can add to the examples of long-distance transport of some goods. As we have seen, a start has already been made on applying the X-ray fluorescence technique to locating sources of the obsidian found in archaeological sites. The procedure can be applied to some other rocks, as well, to give us a better picture of quarry locations and distances materials moved in various eras.

Other aspects of the Northwest Coast economic systems we have surveyed in this essay seem less promising for archaeological enquiry, but we may be surprised by the ingenuity of our colleagues in the discipline. As greater attention is channelled towards reconstructing the region's prehistoric economies and investigating its economic processes, more than we can presently imagine may prove accessible.

ACKNOWLEDGMENTS

We have been collaborating on Northwest Coast studies for well over a decade. Mitchell's interest in the culture area predates even his undergraduate work. Donald's involvement began at the University of Oregon, where he and Mitchell both participated in a series of graduate seminars run by David F. Aberle and focussing on northwestern North American cultural ecology. Portions of this paper have drawn on material assembled for the seminars. More important, Aberle's influence as scholar and teacher pervades all our work.

REFERENCES

Archer, D.J.W., and K. Bernick (n.d.) Perishable Artifacts from the Musqueam Northeast Site. Manuscript draft in possession of authors, 1986.

Arima, E.Y. (1983) *The West Coast People: The Nootka of Vancouver Island and Cape Flattery*. Victoria: British Columbia Provincial Museum, Special Publication 6.

Barnett, H.G. (1938) "The Nature of the Potlatch." *American Anthropologist* 40:349–358.

—— (1939) *Culture Element Distributions: IX, Gulf of Georgia Salish*. Berkeley: University of California, Anthropological Records 1(5).

—— (1955) *The Coast Salish of British Columbia*. Eugene: University of Oregon.

—— (1968) *The Nature and Function of the Potlatch*. Eugene: Department of Anthropology, University of Oregon.

Barrett-Lennard, C.E. (1862) *Travels in British Columbia, with the Narrative of a Yacht Voyage Round Vancouver's Island*. London: Hurst & Blackett.

Bernick, K. (1983) *A Site Catchment Analysis of the Little Qualicum River Site: A Wet Site on the East Coast of Vancouver Island*. Ottawa: National Museum of Man Mercury Series, Archaeological Survey of Canada, Paper 118.

Boas, F. (1891) "The Indians of British Columbia: Lku'ngen, Nootka, Kwakiutl, Shuswap; Sixth Report on the North-Western Tribes of Canada, 1890." Pp. 553–715 in *Report of the Sixtieth Meeting of the British Association for the Advancement of Science*.

—— (1897) *The Social Organization and Secret Societies of the Kwakiutl Indians*. Washington, DC: United States National Museum, Annual Report for 1895.

—— (1909) *The Kwakiutl of Vancouver Island*. Washington, DC: American Museum of Natural History, Memoir 8.

—— (1916) *Tsimshian Mythology*. Washington, DC: Bureau of American Ethnology, Thirty-first Annual Report, 1909–1910.

—— (1921) *Ethnology of the Kwakiutl*. Washington, DC: Bureau of American Ethnology, 35th Annual Report.

—— (1935) *Kwakiutl Culture as Reflected in Mythology*. New York: American Folk-lore Society, Memoir 28.

Boehm, S.G. (1973) *Cultural and Non-cultural Variation in the Artifact and Faunal Samples from the St. Mungo Cannery Site, DgRr 2*. M.A. thesis, University of Victoria.

Boucher, N. (1976) *Prehistoric Subsistence at the Helen Point Site*. M.A. thesis, Simon Fraser University.

Calvert, S.G. (1980) *A Cultural Analysis of Faunal Remains from Three Archaeological Sites in Hesquiat Harbour, B.C.* Ph.D. dissertation, University of British Columbia.

Calvert, S.G., and S. Crockford (1982) "Appendix IV: Analysis of Faunal Remains from the Shoemaker Bay Site (DhSe 2)." Pp. 174–219 in A.D. McMillan & D.E. St. Claire, *Alberni Prehistory: Archaeological and Ethnographic Investigations on Western Vancouver Island*. Penticton, BC: Theytus Books.

Carlson, R.L. (1960) "Chronology and Culture Change in the San Juan Islands, Washington." *American Antiquity* 25:562–586.

—— (1976) "The Excavations at McNaughton Island." Pp. 99–114 in R.L. Carlson (ed.) *Current Research Reports*. Burnaby, BC: Department of Archaeology, Simon Fraser University Publication 3.

—— (n.d.) "Prehistory of the Northwest Coast." Pp. 13–32 in R.L. Carlson (ed.) *Indian Art Traditions of the Northwest Coast*. Burnaby, BC: Archaeology Press, Simon Fraser University.

Casteel, R.W. (1976) "Fish Remains from Glenrose." Pp. 82–87 in R.G. Matson (ed.) *The Glenrose Cannery Site*. Ottawa: National Museum of Man Mercury Series, Archaeological Survey of Canada, Paper 52.

Chisholm, B.S., D.E. Nelson, and H.P. Schwarcz (1983) "Marine and Terrestrial Protein in Prehistoric Diets on the British Columbia Coast." *Current Anthropology* 24:396–398.

Clarke, L.R., and A.H. Clarke (1980) "Zooarchaeological Analysis of Mollusc Remains from Yuquot, British Columbia." Pp. 37–58 in W. Folan & J. Dewhirst (eds.) *The Yuquot Project, Volume 2*. Ottawa: Parks Canada, History and Archaeology 43.

Codere, H. (1950) *Fighting with Property: A Study of Kwakiutl Potlatching and Warfare 1792–1930*. Seattle: American Ethnological Society, Monograph 18.

Codere, H., ed. (1966) *Kwakiutl Ethnography* by Franz Boas. Chicago: University of Chicago Press.

Conover, K. (1978) "Matrix Analysis." Pp. 67–99 in J.J. Hester & S.M. Nelson (eds.) *Studies in Bella Bella Prehistory*. Burnaby, BC: Department of Archaeology, Simon Fraser University Publication 5.

Coupland, G.G. (1985) *Prehistoric Cultural Change at Kitselas Canyon*. Ph.D. dissertation, University of British Columbia.

Couture, A., and J.O. Edwards (1964) *Origin of Copper Used by Canadian West Coast Indians in the Manufacture of Ornamental Plaques*. Ottawa: Paper No. 6, Contributions to Anthropology 1961–62, Part II, National Museum of Canada, Bulletin 194.

Cressman, L.S. (1960) *Cultural Sequences at the Dalles, Oregon*. Philadelphia: American Philosophical Society, Transactions, New Series 50, Part 10.

Croes, D.R., ed. (1976) *The Excavation of Water-saturated Archaeological Sites (Wet Sites) on the Northwest Coast of North America*. Ottawa: National Museum of Man Mercury Series, Archaeological Survey of Canada, Paper 50.

Croes, D.R. (1977) *Basketry from the Ozette Village Archaeological Site: A Technological, Functional, and Comparative Study*. Ph.D. dissertation, Washington State University.

—— (1980a) *Cordage from the Ozette Village Archaeological Site: A Technological, Functional and Comparative Study*. Pullman, WA: Washington State University, Laboratory of Archaeology and History, Project Report 9.

—— (1980b) "Basketry Artifacts." Pp. 188–222 in D.R. Croes and E. Blinman (eds.) (1980) *Hoko River: A 2500 Year Old Fishing Camp on The Northwest Coast of North America*. Pullman, WA: Washington State University, Laboratory of Anthropology, Reports of Investigations 58.

—— (1980c) "Cordage." Pp. 236–257 in D.R. Croes & E. Blinman (eds.) (1980) *Hoko River: A 2500 Year Old Fishing Camp on The Northwest Coast of North America*. Pullman, WA: Washington State University, Laboratory of Anthropology, Reports of Investigations 58.

Croes, D.R., and E. Blinman, eds. (1980) *Hoko River: A 2500 Year Old Fishing Camp on The Northwest Coast of North America*. Pullman, WA: Washington State University, Laboratory of Anthropology, Reports of Investigations 58.

Curtis, E.S. (1915) *The North American Indian*, Vol. 10. New York: Landmarks in Anthropology. [Johnson Reprint Corporation, 1970]

Dawson, G.M. (1887) "Notes and Observations on the Kwakiool People of the Northern Part of Vancouver Island, and Adjacent Coasts, Made during the Summer of 1885, with a Vocabulary of about 700 Words." *Proceedings and Transactions of the Royal Society of Canada* 5:63–98.

DePuydt, R. (1983) *Cultural Implications of Avifaunal Remains Recovered from the Ozette Site*. M.A. thesis, Washington State University.

Dewhirst, J. (1980) *The Indigenous Archaeology of Yuquot, a Nootkan Outside Village. (The Yuquot Project, Volume 1)*. Ottawa: Parks Canada, History and Archaeology 39.

—— (n.d) "An Archaeological Pattern of Faunal Resource Utilization of Yuquot, a Nootkan Outside Village: 1000 B.C.–A.D. 1966." Paper presented before the Society for American Archaeology, Vancouver, 1979.

Donald, L. (1983) "Was Nuu-chah-nulth-aht (Nootka) Society Based on Slave Labor?" Pp.
    108–119 in E. Tooker (ed.) *The Development of Political Organization in Native North
    America*. Washington, DC: 1979 Proceedings of the American Ethnological Society.
——— (1984) "The Slave Trade on the Northwest Coast of North America." *Research in
    Economic Anthropology* 6:121–158.
Donald, L., and J. Mertton (1975) "Technology on the Northwest Coast: An Analysis of
    Overall Similarities." *Behavior Science Research* 10(2):73–100.
Donald, L., and D.H. Mitchell (1975) "Some Correlates of Local Group Rank Among the
    Southern Kwakiutl." *Ethnology* 14:325–346.
Douglas, J. (1841) Diary of a Trip to the Northwest Coast, April 22–October 2, 1840. Victoria:
    Public Archives of British Columbia, Manuscript A/B/CO/D75.2A.
——— (1853) Indian Populations and Statistics, Notes on Traditions and Populations of the
    Indians of the Northwest Coast. Private Papers, Second Series. Victoria: Public Archives
    of British Columbia, Manuscript B/20/1853.
Driver, H.E., J.A. Kennedy, H.C. Hudson, and O.M. Engle (1972) "Statistical Classification
    of North American Indian Ethnic Units." *Ethnology* 11:311–339.
Drucker, P. (1943) *An Archaeological Survey on the Northern Northwest Coast*. Washington,
    DC: Bureau of American Ethnology, Bulletin 133.
——— (1950) *Culture Element Distributions: XXVII, Northwest Coast*. Berkeley: University
    of California, Anthropological Records 9(3).
——— (1951) *The Northern and Central Nootkan Tribes*. Washington, DC: Bureau of
    American Ethnology, Bulletin 144.
——— (1963) *Indians of the Northwest Coast*. Garden City, NY: Natural History Press.
——— (1965) *Cultures of the North Pacific Coast*. San Francisco: Chandler.
Drucker, P., and R.F. Heizer (1967) *To Make My Name Good: A Re-examination of the
    Southern Kwakiutl Potlatch*. Berkeley: University of California.
Duff, W. (1952) *The Upper Stalo Indians of The Fraser Valley, British Columbia*. Victoria:
    Anthropology in British Columbia, Memoir 1.
Easton, N.A. (1985) *The Underwater Archaeology of Straits Salish Reef-netting*. M.A. thesis,
    University of Victoria.
Ecklund-Johnson, D. (1984) *Analysis of Macroflora from the Hoko River Rockshelter,
    Olympic Peninsula, Washington*. M.A. thesis, Washington State University.
Elmendorf, W.W. (1960) *The Structure of Twana Culture*. Pullman, WA: Washington State
    University, Research Studies 27(3) Supplement.
Ferguson, R.S.O. (n.d.) Seasonality of Shellfish Recovered from the Boardwalk Site (GbTo
    31), Prince Rupert, B.C. Ottawa: Archaeological Survey of Canada, National Museum
    of Man, unpublished manuscript No. 1117, 1975.
Fisher, R. (1977) *Contact and Conflict: Indian-European Relations in British Columbia,
    1774–1890*. Vancouver: University of British Columbia.
Fladmark, K.R. (1975) *A Paleoecological Model for Northwest Coast Prehistory*. Ottawa:
    National Museum of Man Mercury Series, Archaeological Survey of Canada, Paper 43.
Flenniken, J.J. (1981) *Replicative Systems Analysis: A Model Applied to the Vein Quartz
    Artifacts from the Hoko River Site*. Pullman, WA: Washington State University Lab-
    oratory of Anthropology Reports of Investigations No. 59, Hoko River Archaeological
    Project Contribution No. 2.
Folan, W.J. (1984) "On the Diet of Early Northwest Coast Peoples." *Current Anthropology*
    25:123–124.
Fournier, J., and J. Dewhirst (1980) "Zooarchaeological Analysis of Barnacle Remains from
    Yuquot, British Columbia." Pp. 59–102 in W. Folan & J. Dewhirst (eds.) *The Yuquot
    Project, Volume 2*. Ottawa: Parks Canada, History and Archaeology 43.
Friedman, E. (1980) "Analysis of Bird and Mammal Bone." Pp. 111–114 in D.R. Croes &

E. Blinman (eds.) (1980) *Hoko River: A 2500 Year Old Fishing Camp on The Northwest Coast of North America.* Pullman, WA: Washington State University, Laboratory of Anthropology, Reports of Investigations 58.

Friedman, J. (1975) *The Prehistoric Uses of Wood at the Ozette Archaeological Site.* Ph.D. dissertation, Washington State University.

Garfield, V.E. (1939) *Tsimshian Clan and Society.* Seattle: University of Washington Publications in Anthropology 7(3).

—— (1951) "The Tsimshian and their Neighbors." Pp. 1–70 in V.E. Garfield, P.S. Wingert & C.M. Barbeau, (eds.) *The Tsimshian: Their Arts and Music.* New York: American Ethnological Society, Publication 18.

Gill, S. (1983) *Economic Botany of the Ozette Village Site.* Ph.D. dissertation, Washington State University.

Gleeson, P. (1980) *Ozette Woodworking Technology.* Pullman: Washington State University Laboratory of Archaeology and History, Project Report 3.

Goddard, P.E. (1945) *Indians of the Northwest Coast.* New York: American Museum of Natural History, Handbook Series 10.

Goldschmidt, W.R., and T.H. Haas (1946) *Possessory Rights of the Natives of Southeastern Alaska.* Washington, DC: Commissioner of Indian Affairs.

Gross, B.T. (1980) "Analysis of Mollusk Remains." Pp. 117–124 in D.R. Croes & E. Blinman (eds.) (1980) *Hoko River: A 2500 Year Old Fishing Camp on The Northwest Coast of North America.* Pullman, WA: Washington State University, Laboratory of Anthropology, Reports of Investigations 58.

Gunther, E. (1972) *Indian Life on the Northwest Coast of North America as Seen by the Early Explorers and Fur Traders during the Last Decades of the Eighteenth Century.* Chicago: University of Chicago.

Haggarty, J.C. (1982) *The Archaeology of Hesquiat Harbour: The Archaeological Utility of an Ethnographically Defined Social Unit.* Ph.D. dissertation, Washington State University.

Ham, L.C. (1976) "Analysis of Shell Samples." Pp. 42–78 in R.G. Matson (ed.) *The Glenrose Cannery Site.* Ottawa: National Museum of Man Mercury Series, Archaeological Survey of Canada, Paper 52.

—— (1982) *Seasonality, Shell Midden Layers, and Coast Salish Subsistence Activities at the Crescent Beach Site, DqRr 1.* Ph.D. dissertation, University of British Columbia.

Ham, L.C., and M. Irvine (1975) "Techniques for Determining the Seasonality of Shell Middens from Marine Mollusc Remains." *Syesis* 8:363–373.

Hebda, R.J., and R.W. Mathewes (1984) "Holocene History of Cedar and Native Indian Cultures of the North American Pacific Coast." *Science* 225:711–713.

Hill-Tout, C. (1902) "Ethnological Studies of the Mainland Halkomelem." Pp. 355–490 in *Report of the Seventy-second Meeting of the British Association for the Advancement of Science.*

—— (1904) "Ethnological Report of the StEelis and Sk.aulits Tribes of the Halkomelem Division of the Salish." *Journal of the Royal Anthropological Institute of Great Britain and Ireland* 34:311–376.

Hobler, P.M. (1970) "Archaeological Survey and Excavations in the Vicinity of Bella Coola." Pp. 77–94 in R.L. Carlson (ed.) Archaeology in British Columbia: New Discoveries. *BC Studies* 6–7.

Hoff, R. (1980) "Fishhooks." Pp. 160–188 in D.R. Croes & E. Blinman (eds.) (1980) *Hoko River: A 2500 Year Old Fishing Camp on The Northwest Coast of North America.* Pullman, WA: Washington State University, Laboratory of Anthropology, Reports of Investigations 58.

Huelsbeck, D. (1980) "Analysis of Fish Remains." Pp. 104–111 in D.R. Croes & E. Blinman (eds.) (1980) *Hoko River: A 2500 Year Old Fishing Camp on The Northwest Coast of North America.* Pullman, WA: Washington State University, Laboratory of Anthropology, Reports of Investigations 58.

—— (1983) *Mammals and Fish in the Subsistence Economy of Ozette.* Ph.D. dissertation, Washington State University.

Imamoto, S. (1976) "An Analysis of the Glenrose Faunal Remains." Pp. 21–41 in R.G. Matson (ed.) *The Glenrose Cannery Site.* Ottawa: National Museum of Man Mercury Series, Archaeological Survey of Canada, Paper 52.

Inglis, R. (1976) " 'Wet' Site Distribution—The Northern Case: GbTo 33 The Lachane Site." Pp. 158–185 in D.R. Croes (ed.) *The Excavation of Water-saturated Archaeological Sites (Wet Sites) on the Northwest Coast of North America.* Ottawa: National Museum of Man Mercury Series. Archaeological Survey of Canada, Paper 50.

Ingold, T. (1983) "The Significance of Storage in Hunting Societies." *Man* 18:553–571.

Jorgensen, J.G. (1969) *Salish Language and Culture: A Statistical Analysis of Internal Relationships, History, and Evolution.* Bloomington: Indiana University, Language Science Monograph 3.

—— (1980) *Western Indians: Comparative Environments, Languages, and Cultures of 172 Western American Indian Tribes.* San Francisco: W.H. Freeman.

Keen, S.D. (1979) *The Growth Rings of Clam Shells from Two Pentlatch Middens as Indicators of Seasonal Gathering.* Victoria: Heritage Conservation Branch, Occasional Paper 3.

Kenyon, S.M. (1980) *The Kyuquot Way: A Study of a West Coast (Nootkan) Community.* Ottawa: National Museum of Man Mercury Series, Canadian Ethnology Service, Paper 61.

Kidd, R.S. (1969) *The Archaeology of the Fossil Bay Site, Sucia Island, Northwestern Washington State, in Relation to the Fraser Delta Sequence.* Ottawa: Paper No. 2, Contributions to Anthropology VII: Archaeology, National Museum of Canada, Bulletin 232.

King, A.R. (1950) *Cattle Point, a Stratified Site in the Southern Northwest Coast Region.* Menasha: Society of American Archaeology, Memoir 7.

Krause, A. (1956) *The Tlingit Indians.* (Trans. E. Gunther) Seattle: University of Washington Press. [Written 1885]

Laguna, F. de (1960) *The Story of a Tlingit Community.* Washington, DC: Bureau of American Ethnology, Bulletin 172.

Laguna, F. de, F.A. Riddell, D.F. McGeein, K.S. Lane, and J.A. Freed (1964) *Archaeology of the Yakutat Bay Area, Alaska.* Washington, DC: Bureau of American Ethnology, Bulletin 192.

Loy, T.H. (1987) "Recent Advances in Organic Residue Analysis." *Proceedings of the Second Australian Archaeometry Conference.* Canberra: Australian National University.

Loy, T.H., and E. Nelson (1986) "Potential Applications of Prehistoric Organic Residue Analysis." Pp. 127–135 in J. Owen & J. Blackmun (eds.) *Proceedings of the Thirteenth International Archaeometry Symposium.* Washington, DC: Smithsonian Institution.

Luebbers, R. (1978) "Excavations: Stratigraphy and Artifacts." Pp. 11–66 in J.J. Hester & S.M. Nelson (eds.) *Studies in Bella Bella Prehistory.* Burnaby, BC: Department of Archaeology, Simon Fraser University Publication 5.

McAllister, N.M. (1980) "Avian Fauna from the Yuquot Excavation." In W. Folan & J. Dewhirst (eds.) *The Yuquot Project, Volume 2.* Ottawa: Parks Canada, History and Archaeology 43.

MacDonald, G.F., and R.I. Inglis (1981) "An Overview of the North Coast Prehistory Project (1966–1980)." Pp. 37–63 in K.R. Fladmark (ed.) *Fragments of the Past: British Columbia Archaeology in the 1970s. BC Studies* 48.

Matson, R.G., ed. (1976) *The Glenrose Cannery Site*. Ottawa: National Museum of Man Mercury Series, Archaeological Survey of Canada Paper 52.

—— (1985) "The Relationship between Sedentism and Status Inequalities among Hunters and Gatherers." Pp. 245–252 in M. Thompson, M.T. Garcia & F.J. Kense (eds.) *Status, Structure, and Stratification: Current Archaeological Reconstructions*. Calgary: Proceedings of the Sixteenth Annual Conference of the Archaeological Association of the University of Calgary.

Miller, D.G. (1983) *The Hoko River Rockshelter: Intertidal Resources*. M.A. thesis, Washington State University.

Mitchell, D.H. (1971) *Archaeology of the Gulf of Georgia Area, a Natural Region and its Culture Types*. *Syesis* 4, Supplement 1.

—— (1983a) "Seasonal Settlements, Village Aggregations, and Political Autonomy on the Central Northwest Coast." Pp. 97–107 in E. Tooker (ed.) *The Development of Political Organization in Native North America*. Washington, DC: 1979 Proceedings of the American Ethnological Society.

—— (1983b) "Tribes and Chiefdoms of the Northwest Coast: the Tsimshian Case." Pp. 57–64 in R.J.T. Nash (ed.) *The Evolution of Maritime Cultures on the Northeast and Northwest Coasts of America*. Burnaby, B.C.: Department of Archaeology, Simon Fraser University, Publication 11.

—— (1984) "Predatory Warfare, Social Status, and the North Pacific Slave Trade." *Ethnology* 23:39–48.

—— (1985) "A Demographic Profile of Northwest Coast Slavery." Pp. 227–236 in M. Thompson, M.T. Garcia & F.J. Kense (eds.) *Status, Structure, and Stratification: Current Archaeological Reconstructions*. Calgary: Proceedings of the Sixteenth Annual Conference of the Archaeological Association of the University of Calgary.

Mitchell, D., and L. Donald (1985) "Some Economic Aspects of Tlingit, Haida, and Tsimshian Slavery." *Research in Economic Anthropology* 7:19–35.

Monks, G.G. (1977) *An Examination of Relationships between Artifact Classes and Food Resource Remains at Deep Bay, DiSe 7*. Ph.D. dissertation, University of British Columbia.

Morice, A.G. (1904) *The History of the Northern Interior of British Columbia, Formerly New Caledonia, 1660 to 1880*. Toronto: William Briggs.

Munro, J.A., and I. McT. Cowan (1947) *A Review of the Bird Fauna of British Columbia*. Victoria: British Columbia Provincial Museum.

Munsell, D.A. (1976) "The Wapato Creek Fish Weir Site 45PI47 Tacoma, Washington." Pp. 45–57 in D.R. Croes (ed.) *The Excavation of Water-saturated Archaeological Sites (Wet Sites on the Northwest Coast of North America)*. Ottawa: National Museum of Man Mercury Series. Archaeological Survey of Canada, Paper 50.

Murdock, G.P. (1934) *Our Primitive Contemporaries*. New York: Macmillan.

—— (1936) *Rank and Potlatch among the Haida*. New Haven: Yale University Publications in Anthropology 13.

—— (1967) "Ethnographic Atlas." *Ethnology* 6:108–236.

Newcombe, C.F., ed. (1923) *Menzies Journal of Vancouver's Voyage*. Victoria: Archives of British Columbia, Memoir 5.

Niblack, A.P. (1890) *The Coast Indians of Southeastern Alaska and Northern British Columbia*. Washington, DC: Report of the U.S. National Museum for the Year ending June 30, 1888.

Nordquist, D. (1976) "45SN100—The Biederbost Site, Kidd's Duval Site." Pp. 186–200 in D.R. Croes (ed.) *The Excavation of Water-saturated Archaeological Sites (Wet Sites on the Northwest Coast of North America)*. Ottawa: National Museum of Man Mercury Series. Archaeological Survey of Canada, Paper 50.

Oberg, K. (1973) *The Social Economy of the Tlingit Indians*. Seattle: University of Washington Press.

Paden, M. (1980a) "Woodchip Debitage." Pp. 273–289 in D.R. Croes & E. Blinman (eds.) (1980) *Hoko River: A 2500 Year Old Fishing Camp on The Northwest Coast of North America*. Pullman, WA: Washington State University, Laboratory of Anthropology, Reports of Investigations 58.

——— (1980b) "Basketry Waste Materials." Pp. 188–222 in D.R. Croes & E. Blinman (eds.) (1980) *Hoko River: A 2500 Year Old Fishing Camp on The Northwest Coast of North America*. Pullman, WA: Washington State University, Laboratory of Anthropology, Reports of Investigations 58.

Piddocke, S. (1965) "The Potlatch System of the Southern Kwakiutl: a New Perspective." *Southwestern Journal of Anthropology* 21:244–264.

Pomeroy, J.A. (1976) "Stone Fish Traps of the Bella Bella Region." Pp. 165–173 in R.L. Carlson (ed.) *Current Research Reports*. Burnaby, B.C.: Department of Archaeology, Simon Fraser University Publication 3.

Richardson, A. (1982) "The Control of Productive Resources on the Northwest Coast of North America." Pp. 93–112 in N.M. Williams & E.S. Hunn (eds.) *Resource Managers: North American and Australian Hunter-Gatherers*. Washington, DC: American Association for the Advancement of Science Selected Symposium 67.

Riches, D. (1979) "Ecological Variation on the Northwest Coast: Models for the Generation of Cognatic and Matrilineal Descent." Pp. 145–166 in P.C. Burnham & R.F. Ellen (eds.) *Social and Ecological Systems*. London: Academic Press, A.S.A. Monograph 18.

Savage, H. (n.d.) Faunal Material from the Boardwalk Site (GbTo 31), Prince Rupert, B.C. Ottawa: Archaeological Survey of Canada, National Museum of Man, unpublished manuscript No. 843, 1972.

Schalk, R.F. (1977) "The Structure of an Anadromous Fish Resource." Pp. 207–249 in L. Binford (ed.) *For Theory Building in Archaeology*. New York: Academic Press.

——— (1979) "Land Use and Organizational Complexity among Foragers of Northwestern North America." Pp. 53–75 in S. Koyama & D.H. Thomas (eds.) *Affluent Foragers: Pacific Coasts East and West*. Osaka: National Museum of Ethnology, Senri Ethnological Studies 9.

Simonsen, B.O. (1973) *Archaeological Investigations in the Hecate Strait-Milbanke Sound Area of British Columbia*. Ottawa: National Museum of Man Mercury Series, Archaeological Survey of Canada, Paper 13.

Smith, H.I. (1903) *Shell Heaps of the Lower Fraser, British Columbia*. New York: American Museum of Natural History, Memoir 3, Part 4.

Snyder, S. (1975) "Quest for the Sacred in Northern Puget Sound: An Interpretation of Potlatch." *Ethnology* 14:149–161.

Stern, B.J. (1934) *The Lummi Indians of Northwest Washington*. New York: Columbia University Contributions to Anthropology 17.

Stewart, F. (n.d.a) Faunal Analysis of a Sample Collection from the GbTo 33 Site, Prince Rupert Harbour, B.C. Ottawa: Archaeological Survey of Canada, National Museum of Man, unpublished manuscript No. 859, 1972.

——— (n.d.b) Faunal Material Identification from the British Columbia Site GbTo 34. Ottawa: Archaeological Survey of Canada, National Museum of Man, unpublished manuscript No. 878, 1972.

——— (n.d.c) Faunal Artifact Identification: Boardwalk Site, GbTo 31, B.C. Ottawa: Archaeological Survey of Canada, National Museum of Man, unpublished manuscript No. 997, 1973.

——— (n.d.d) Faunal Specimens with Butchering Marks and with Evidence of Burning from the Boardwalk Site (GbTo 31). Ottawa: Archaeological Survey of Canada, National Museum of Man, unpublished manuscript No. 1018, 1974.

—— (n.d.e) GbTo 31—Identification of Faunal Material by Excavation Units. Ottawa: Archaeological Survey of Canada, National Museum of Man, unpublished manuscript Nos. 1024, 1111–1114, 1975.

Stewart, H. (1977) *Indian Fishing: Early Methods on the Northwest Coast*. Vancouver: J.J. Douglas.

Stiefel, S.K. (1985) *The Subsistence Economy of the Locarno Beach Culture (3,300–2,400 BP)*. M.A. thesis, University of British Columbia.

Strong, W.D., W.E. Schenck, and J.H. Steward (1930) *Archaeology of the Dalles-Deschutes Region*. Berkeley: University of California Publications in American Archaeology and Ethnology 29(1).

Suttles, W.P. (1951) "The Early Diffusion of the Potato among the Coast Salish." *Southwestern Journal of Anthropology* 7:272–288.

—— (1960) "Affinal Ties, Subsistence and Prestige among the Coast Salish." *American Anthropologist* 62:296–305.

—— (1962) "Variation in Habitat and Culture on the Northwest Coast." Vienna: *Akten des 34 International Amerikanisten-kongresses*.

—— (1968) "Coping with Abundance: Subsistence on the Northwest Coast." Pp. 56–68 in R.B. Lee & I. DeVore (eds.) *Man the Hunter*. Chicago: Aldine.

—— (1974) "The Economic Life of the Coast Salish of Haro and Rosario Straits." Pp. 41–512 in D.A. Horr (ed.) *Coast Salish and Western Washington Indians 1*. New York: Garland. [Written 1951].

Testart, A. (1982) "The Significance of Food-storage among Hunter-gatherers: Residence Patterns, Population Densities and Social Inequalities." *Current Anthropology* 23:527–537.

Tolmie, W.F. (1963) *The Journals of William Fraser Tolmie: Physician and Fur Trader*. Vancouver: Mitchell Press. [Written 1830–1842].

Vancouver, G. (1798) *Voyage of Discovery to the North Pacific Ocean and Around the World, Vols. I–III*. London: Robinson & Edwards.

Vayda, A.P. (1961) "A Re-examination of Northwest Coast Economic Systems." *Transactions of the New York Academy of Sciences, Series 2* 23:618–624.

Weinberg, D. (1965) "Models of Southern Kwakiutl Social Organization." *Yearbook of the Society for General Systems Research* 10:169–181.

Wessen, G.C. (1982) *Shell Middens as Cultural Deposits: A Case Study from Ozette*. Ph.D. dissertation, Washington State University.

Wigen, R.J.S. (1980) *A Faunal Analysis of Two Middens on the East Coast of Vancouver Island*. M.A. thesis, University of Victoria.

Wolf, R., ed. (1977) *Managing Your Personal Food Supply*. Emmaus, PA: Rodale Press.

Research Annuals and Monographs in Series in SOCIOLOGY

Research Annuals

Advances in Group Processes
Edited by Edward J. Lawler, *University of Iowa.*

Advances in Health Economics and Health Services Research
Edited by Richard M. Scheffler, *University of California, Berkeley* and Louis F. Rossiter, *Virginia Commonwealth University.*

Advances in Information Processing in Organizations
Edited by Lee S. Sproull and Patrick D. Larkey, *Carnegie-Mellon University.*

Advances in Social Science Methodology
Edited by Bruce Thompson, *The University of New Orleans.*

Comparative Social Research
Edited by Richard F. Tomasson, *The University of New Mexico.*

Current Perspectives in Social Theory
Edited by John Wilson and Scott G. McNall, *University of Kansas.*

Current Perspectives on Aging and the Life Cycles
Edited by Zena Smith Blau, *University of Houston.*

Current Research on Occupations and Professions
Edited by Helena Z. Lopata, *Loyola University of Chicago.*

Knowledge and Society: Studies in the Sociology of Science, Past and Present
Edited by Robert Alun Jones, *Lowell Hargens and Andrew Pickering, University of Illinois.*

Political Power and Social Theory
Edited by Maurice Zeitlin, *University of California, Los Angeles.*

Research in Community and Mental Health
Edited by James R. Greenley, *University of Wisconsin Medical School.*

Research in Corporate Social Performance and Policy
Edited by Lee E. Preston, *University of Maryland.*

Research in Economic Anthropology
Edited by Barry Isaac, *University of Cincinnati.*

Research in Human Capital and Development
Edited by Ismail Sirageldin, *The Johns Hopkins University.*

Research in Inequality and Social Conflict
Edited by Michael Dobkowski, *Hobart and William Smith, Colleges and Isidor Walliman, School of Social Work, Basel.*

Research in Labor Economics
Edited by Ronald G. Ehrenberg, *New York State School of Industrial and Labor Relations, Cornell University.*

Research in Law and Policy Studies
Edited by Stuart S. Nagel, *University of Illinois.*

Research in Law, Deviance and Social Control
Edited by Steven Spitzer, *Suffolk University* and Andrew T. Scull, *University of California, San Diego.*

Research in Micropolitics
Edited by Samuel Long, *Pace University, Pleasantville.*

Research in Organizational Behavior
Edited by Barry M. Staw, *University of California, Berkeley* and L.L. Cummings, *Northwestern University.*

Research in Organizational Change and Development
Edited by Richard W. Woodman, *Texas A&M University* and William A. Pasmore, *Case Western Reserve University.*

Research in Personnel and Human Resources Management
Edited by Kendrith M. Rowland, *University of Illinois* and Gerald R. Ferris, *Texas A&M University.*

Research in Philosophy and Technology
Edited by Frederick Ferre, *University of Georgia.*

Research in Political Economy
Edited by Paul Zarembka, *State University of New York at Buffalo.*

Research in Political Sociology
Edited by Richard G. Braungart, *Syracuse University.*

Research in Politics and Society
Edited by Gwen Moore, *Russell Sage College.*

Research in Population Economics
Edited by T. Paul Schultz, *Yale University.*

Research in Public Policy Analysis and Management
Edited by Stuart S. Nagel, *University of Illinois.*

Research in Race and Ethnic Relations
Edited by Cora Bagley Marrett, *University of Wisconsin, Madison* and Cheryl Leggon, *University of Chicago.*

Research in Rural Sociology and Development
Edited by Harry K. Schwarzweller, *Michigan State University.*

Research in Social Movements, Conflicts and Change
Edited by Louis Kriesberg, *Syracuse University.*

Research in Social Policy, Critical Historical and Contemporary Perspectives
Edited by John H. Stanfield, *Yale University.*

Research in Social Problems and Public Policy
Edited by Michael Lewis, *University of Massachusetts* and JoAnn L. Miller, *Purdue University.*

Research in Social Stratification and Mobility
Edited by Robert V. Robinson, *Indiana University.*

Research in Sociology of Education and Socialization
Edited by Ronald G. Corwin, *The Ohio State University.*

Research in the Sociology of Health Care
Edited by Julius Roth and Sheryl Burt Ruzek, *University of California, Davis.*

Research in the Sociology of Organizations
Edited by Samuel B. Bacharach, *New York State School of Industrial and Labor Relations, Cornell University.*

Research in the Sociology of Work
Edited by Ida Harper Simpson, *Duke University* and Richard L. Simpson, University of North Carolina, Chapel Hill.

Research in Urban Economics
Edited by Robert D. Ebel, *Northwestern Bell, Minneapolis.*

Research in Urban Policy
Edited by Terry Nichols Clark, *University of Chicago.*

Research in Urban Sociology
Edited by Ray Hutchison and Ronald K. Baba, *University of Wisconsin, Green Bay.*

Research on Negotiations in Organizations
Edited by roy J. Lewicki, *Ohio State University*, Blair H. Sheppard, *Duke University* and Max H. Bazerman, *Northwestern University.*

Social Perspectives on Emotion
Edited by David D. Franks, *Virginia Commonwealth University.*

Sociological Studies of Child Development
Edited by Patricia A. and Peter Adler, *Washington University, St. Louis.*

Studies in Communication
Edited by Thelma McCormick, *York University.*

Studies in Qualitative Methodology
Edited by Robert Burgess, *University of Warwick.*

Studies in Symbolic Interaction
Edited by Norman K. Denzin, *University of Illinois.*

Monographs in Series and Treatises

Contemporary Ethnographic Studies
Edited by Jaber F. Gubrium, *Marquette University.*

Contemporary Studies in Sociology: Theoretical and Empirical Monographs
Edited by John Clark, *University of Minnesota.*

Contemporary Studies in Applied Behavioral Science
Edited by Louis A. Zurcher, *University of Texas at Austin.*

Contemporary Studies in Economic and Financial Analysis
An International Series of Monographs
Edited by Edward I. Altman and Ingo Walter, *New York University.*

Handbook of Behavioral Economics
Edited by Stanley Kaish and Benjamin Gilad, *Rutgers University.*

Monographs in Organizational Behavior and Industrial Relations
Edited by Samuel B. Bacharach, *New York State School of Industrial and Labor Relations, Cornell University.*

Political Economy and Public Policy
Edited by William Breit, *Trinity University* and Kenneth G. Elzinga, *University of Virginia.*

Public Policy Studies: A Multi-Volume Treastise
Edited by Stuart S. Nagel, *University of Illinois.*

Please inquire for detailed subject catalog

JAI PRESS INC., 55 Old Post Road No. 2, P.O. Box 1678
Greenwich, Connecticut 06836
Telephone: 203-661-7602   Cable Address: JAIPUBL